The
Working People
of Paris,
1871–1914

THE JOHNS HOPKINS UNIVERSITY
STUDIES IN HISTORICAL AND POLITICAL SCIENCE
102d Series (1984)

The
Working People
of Paris,
1871–1914

Lenard R. Berlanstein

The Johns Hopkins University Press
Baltimore and London

This book has been brought to publication with the generous assistance of the National Endowment for the Humanities.

The Johns Hopkins University Press, Baltimore, Maryland 21218
The Johns Hopkins Press Ltd., London

The paper in this book is acid-free and meets the guidelines for permanence and durability of the Committee on Production Guidelines for Book Longevity of the Council on Library Resources.

Library of Congress Cataloging in Publication Data

Berlanstein, Lenard R.
  The working people of Paris, 1871–1914

  (The Johns Hopkins University studies in historical
and political science ; 102d ser., 2)
    Bibliography: p.
    Includes index.
    1. Labor and laboring classes—France—Paris—History.
2. Paris (France)—Social conditions.   I. Title.   II. Series: Johns Hopkins
University studies in historical and political science ; 102nd ser., 2.
HD8440.P22B47   1984   305.5′62′0944361   84-47951
ISBN 0-8018-3241-1 (alk. paper)

For my parents, Belle and David Berlanstein

Contents

List of Tables and Figures

TABLES

FIGURES

Preface

The late nineteenth century is well known as a period of intensive social change, an era of visible breaks with the past, and the origin of new, sometimes strikingly contemporary, behavior. This study is concerned with the working poor (and almost poor) and with the impact of these changes upon them. Initial reservations about the value of this project would probably derive less from the subject of the study than from the chosen locale. Social historians are most familiar with the dictum "Paris is not France." One can agree with this statement and still defend the value of studying the population of the capital. The forces of industrialization, bureaucratization, and centralization, which eventually penetrated to all of France, acted in the Paris region with exceptional forcefulness. Hence, their impact registered with a special clarity there. Moreover, two developments that were quite evident in greater Paris in the late nineteenth century, the rise of large-scale industry and the expansion of a white-collar labor force, were European-wide phenomena. Even if these trends were more "Parisian" than "French," they speak to the experience of a continent passing through the Second Industrial Revolution. Thus, the study of Paris has an illustrative resonance that transcends the concerns of national historiography. Finally, one should not exaggerate the uniqueness of the Parisian masses relative to the rest of the nation. William Sewell has described French industrialization of the nineteenth century as "largely a matter of maintaining and developing France's superiority in highly skilled, high-quality handicrafts. Indeed, even factory industry in France tended to be more successful in the finer and more skill-intensive branches of the trade."[1] This description could hardly be more appropriate for the industrial situation in Paris and in its suburbs during the late nineteenth century.

If the Parisian working people were exceptional in any way, it was in their continuous exposure to economic innovations during the nineteenth century. The publications of Christopher Johnson, among others, have illuminated the social and economic impact of mass-production techniques on the handicrafts during the 1830s and 1840s.[2] Parisian wage-earners, then, were not at all in the same position as the glassworkers of Carmaux, or the peasants described by Eugen Weber and Patrice Higonnet. The Parisians did not have a "traditional" way of life that disintegrated during the course of the late nineteenth century.[3] Indeed, the necessary point of departure for investigating Parisian working people after the Commune is the realization that their culture had already been profoundly affected by the surge of capitalistic development that had occurred in the middle third of the nineteenth century. Peter Stearns has articulated, with characteristic insight, a theme of the present volume: "The turn of the century period gains much of its drama from the confrontation between workers' values, still largely turned toward the past, and a new tide of change. A culture that had been painfully established or re-established after the first shock of industrialization was now challenged. What work was for, what wives were for, what children were for all had to be rethought."[4] This study attempts to work out the contours of that confrontation, which posed most of the central problems of social change during the *belle époque*.

A book that purports to discuss several million individuals over the course of two generations is inevitably uneven in its coverage. I began my research with the intention of treating not only the traditional handicraft workers of the capital but also several social groups that have heretofore been slighted: modest white-collar workers, laborers in large-scale enterprises, especially in the suburbs (*banlieue*), and manual workers in service industries. I soon discovered that fully skilled artisans and specialized craftsmen could not be handled as a single category. Their fates became more distinct in the forty years before World War I. In the end, I found myself discussing the parallel experiences of five groups of working people—artisans, specialized hand workers, factory laborers, service workers, and humble white-collar employees. My hope is that covering these five groups side by side and comparatively will enrich our understanding of each one and of the working population as a whole.

Though comprehensiveness was not my primary goal, I am painfully aware how far this work is from achieving it. By all rights, a reader might expect to find some discussion of domestic servants in a volume on "The Working People of Paris," but I have not included this large occupational category—on pragmatic grounds. Theresa McBride has already provided the definitive work on servants in the nineteenth century, and as she has shown, they consitituted a very special case of wage-earners.[5] Similarly, the work-in-progress on female clerks and laborers by such fine scholars as McBride and Marilyn Boxer encouraged me to direct my limited time and energies to other areas. In the end, the reader will find in this volume a purview that is wide, but also selective. My selectivity at least has, I hope, the virtue of tackling some topics that particularly need investigation.

Following the lead of most recent students of lower-class culture, I have focused on the changing nature of work in the late nineteenth century, for there is excellent reason to believe that labor was the central socializing experience. The standard history of labor in the decade before the Great War entails the growth of the Confédération générale du travail, its confrontations with Aristide Briand and Georges Clemenceau, the massacre at Draveil, the ensuing arrest of labor leaders, and so on. I have eschewed this story, not because we already know all there is to know about it, but because my research uncovered a revealing series of confrontations between labor and management at the dawn of the twentieth century. Though these conflicts have failed to receive scholarly attention until now, they illuminate a great deal about the work experience in greater Paris. An understanding of them may bring us closer to the authentic attitudes of working people than does a chronicle of the tribulations of the CGT. In any case, these confrontations constituted a serious crisis of authority and deserve the historian's interest on those grounds alone.

One influential model of social change in the late nineteenth century downgrades the centrality of work and underscores the development of new off-the-job interests among the laboring population. According to this model, just as workers were losing control over their jobs, they began to adopt more privatized family lives as well as more varied and refined leisurely pursuits. Supposedly, these shifts integrated the laboring poor more fully into bourgeois society. I have attempted to test this model, but the reader should be warned that "facts" are hard to come by in these areas of investigation, and their interpretation is still more problematical. What we can discover about workers' households and sociability tends to shake confidence in a neat dichotomy of integration versus alienation, *embourgeoisement* versus class consciousness. Nonetheless, the late nineteenth century was a time of opening possibilities and new departures in spheres outside of the workplace. Exploring the subtleties of their evolution will take a good deal of time, effort, and imagination.

The historiographical and technical problems raised so far provide the context for research, but they do not evoke the emotional wellspring that attracted the author to this topic and sustained him through the inevitable problems and discouragements. Inspiration came, in my case, from the subjects themselves. I felt privileged to be able to illuminate the lives of people who were ennobled by the harshness of their situations. Henri Leyret, a nineteenth-century journalist who took the trouble to study Parisian workers first hand, was moved by their deep capacity to be fully human and to resist despair despite chronic difficulties; and I remain so moved eighty years later.[6] In our own society of mass affluence and leisure, the daily sufferings of working people of late-nineteenth-century Paris have limited relevance in any prescriptive sense. I do, however, find purpose in bearing witness to the social injustices that virtually defined their positions. To bury in oblivion their quotidian pains and their lost potential would be one more act of injustice.

I firmly hope that sympathy with the people who comprise the subject of this study has not caused me to romanticize their plight or to reach unsubstantiated conclusions. To regard them as victims of forces well beyond their control, as I do, does not seem especially controversial. The issue that generates the most passion among scholars is whether workers were becoming better integrated into the existing social order or more alienated from it. Because workers seldom made their attitudes explicit enough to judge their ultimate aspirations, this debate poses the final test of one's presuppositions. There are those historians who exaggerate the passivity and pragmatism of laborers and others who insist that working-class militancy was inevitable. My own, modest claims to impartiality derive from an initial willingness to argue for either side. I did not begin my work with an urge to "defend" nineteenth-century wage-earners against charges of shortsightedness or unrealistic expectations. I do wish to believe, however, that deep respect for the working people under investigation has resulted in greater insight and sensitivity to their predicament. The reader will have to judge.

Despite its many imperfections, this study has greatly benefited from the assistance of many people and institutions. One of the pleasures of finishing a book is having the opportunity to acknowledge these debts. I shall begin with the National Endowment for the Humanities, a grant from which allowed me to complete my research. The University of Virginia graciously covered the cost of reproducing the graphics in this volume. The secretaries of the History Department, especially Ms. Ella Wood and Ms. Lottie McCauley, prepared my manuscript with care and with efficiency. They also displayed their professionalism by making my introduction to word processing so painless. The staff of the Archives départementales de la Seine et de la ville de Paris helped me to make progress summer after summer through its prompt and efficient service. The archivists at the municipalities of Argenteuil, Ivry-sur-Seine, Puteaux, Saint-Denis, and Saint-Ouen assisted my search for useful material even when inventories were sketchy or nonexistent. The secretary-general of Bezons and his staff made my work in their hôtel-de-ville a delightful and memorable experience. As I embarked on this project, I profited from the advice and erudition of Evelyn Ackerman, Jean-Paul Brunet, and Alain Faure. Cindy Aron and Frederick Carstensen directed me to useful readings that I would not otherwise have found. Olivier Zunz was a most useful source of information and advice on a number of topics. Nicolas Papayanis graciously shared his knowledge of nine-teenth-century Parisian cabbies with me, and Marilyn Boxer was similarly generous in sharing her work with me. Jane Turner Censer took the trouble to read the section on family life and made helpful comments. Cissie Fairchilds did me the great favor of inviting me to present my work to a seminar at Syracuse University; in this way, I benefited from the insights of Professor Fairchilds, Michael Miller, and Frederick Marquardt. Linda Clark earned my lasting gratitude by reading the entire manuscript and making the kind of page-by-page comments that authors find so useful. A final and enormous debt is owed to Jack Censer, who provided much-needed encouragement, patient counsel, and unstinting service as a soundingboard for my ideas from the day this project began to take shape. One cannot hold these estimable colleagues responsible in the least for the faults of this work, but they certainly contributed to whatever value it may contain.

The
Working People
of Paris,
1871–1914

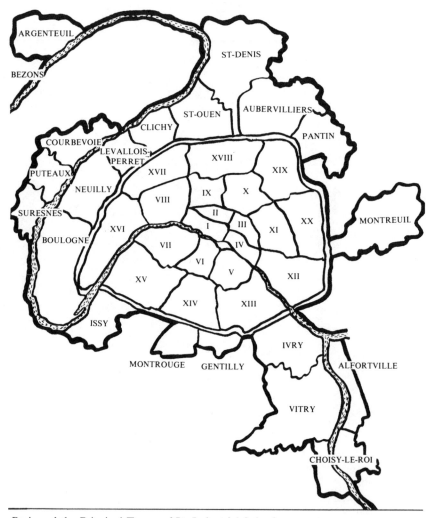

Paris and the Principal Towns of Its Industrial Suburbs

I

The Working Population

The title of this book leaves altogether too much in need of qualification. By "working people" we mean to evoke a social category that was wider than "wage-earners." Parisians who owned no property and depended on their earnings from one pay day to the next—approximately 70 percent of the population—make up the subject of this study.[1] This group was composed largely of manual laborers, to be sure, but also a sizable number of humble white-collar workers. Though one cannot be particularly comfortable with the Socialists' formula, "the proletariat of the workshop, factory, and office," minor clerks were already an important element of the working population of the capital, in our sense, on the eve of the Commune. The geographical term *Paris* is, similarly, imprecise because much of this book concerns people who did not live in the city proper. To write a social history of Paris at the end of the nineteenth century, it is necessary to treat the industrial communities on the periphery of the capital, the *banlieue*. A dynamic area in our period, it had only 15 percent of the population in the Seine Department at the end of the Second Empire but more than 30 percent (1.27 million) on the eve of the Great War. In a fundamental way, the peripheral communes were becoming the demographic and economic center of gravity of greater Paris. Not even the dates in the title express our interests aptly. They should not be taken in a literal fashion, for this study considers the grand events of Parisian history of those years, the Boulanger and Dreyfus affairs, and the like, only in passing. The *longue durée*—or what passes for such by the late nineteenth century—commands our attention.

What were the long-term social processes and structural shifts that make an examination of working people in greater Paris between the Commune and World War I a worthwhile enterprise? These decades comprised one of the few moments when the mass of French people was caught up in social change. Yet, compared with the middle third of the nineteenth century, ours was only very partially an era of fundamental innovation and departure. Under the July Monarchy and Second Empire, commercial capitalism had decisively reorganized the luxury crafts. The state had taken steps to make the urban environment more healthful and livable. The capital expanded territorially, absorbed a new population, and attained its present-day boundaries. Finally, service industries—merchandising, transportation, insurance, and banking—had begun to concentrate, centralize, and dominate the urban landscape.[2] The social history of Paris after the Commune concerns the assimilation of these developments and their intensified impact on the common people. In this study we seek to understand how those who labored in factories, offices, stores, and workshops adjusted to these changes and how they countenanced further transformations.

In at least one important manner, greater Paris of the late nineteenth century witnessed striking innovation. The environs became a center of industrial (as opposed to handicraft) production, and a sizable factory labor force settled there. Under Louis Napoleon, Parisian manufacturers had exported technological innovation to the provinces and had retained for the capital the "noble" work of finishing products with taste and refinement.[3] Parisians stayed with their traditional vocation, to fulfill the wants of an affluent consuming public. Yet, as the Third Republic progressed, making the products this public now wanted—bicycles, carriages, household amenities, and automobiles—required industrial methods and a concentration of capital.[4] The suburbs became the scene of new means to recruit, train, remunerate, and discipline its labor force. This meant that the burgeoning of Saint-Denis, Ivry-sur-Seine, or Puteaux was to be only superficially like the growth of Belleville and Montmartre some decades earlier. The populations of the suburban towns would not be integrated into the economic life of the capital in the same way. At no time before the war did the *banlieue* become the symbol of militant alienation it later would, but its distinctive development was nonetheless a reality.[5]

Thus, those moving forces of social history, capitalistic development and the penetration of the state, operated with intensity and originality in the four decades before the Great War. This situation imposes upon the historian a number of fundamental questions: How were occupations transformed? What were the demographic, cultural, and material ramifications? How was protest generated, and what forms did it take? If these questions are to receive properly nuanced answers, there must be a detailed appreciation for the contours of the working population, which were evolving during this period.

STRUCTURAL CHANGE

Visitors to Paris at the turn of the century could not help but form a casual impression of the capital's social structure as they followed the itinerary recommended by any guidebook. Partaking in the delights of the boulevards, they would have passed hundreds of stores, large and small, and numerous, imposing offices. Tourists would have been buffeted on the streets by determined shoppers and properly dressed clerks, all eager to get on with the business and pleasures of a great metropolis. The Paris of an impoverished working class and of revolutionary upheaval would have seemed distant. In paying bills, the tourist would surely have noted that the capital was expensive and would have understood that workers left the city for cheaper quarters. There was every reason for visitors to assume that Paris had become primarily a residence of the bourgeoisie and those who aspired to this status.

Scholarly opinion has largely followed this assessment. The "*embourgeoisement* of Paris" in the late nineteenth century is now a well-established theme in the history of the city.[6] It rests on more than a tourist's perception of Parisian life. The authoritative volumes of the 1911 census seem to attest to this social transformation. According to its findings, the capital was populated by a solid majority (57 percent) of employers, heads of firms, and white-collar employees (who are labeled "bourgeois" in the superficial sense of not being manual laborers).[7] This source has enabled one historian of Belleville to belie the reputation of this quarter as a stronghold of working-class Paris by claiming that 45 percent of its residents was comprised of nonworkers on the eve of the Great War.[8]

In this instance, both the casual impressions of eyewitnesses as well as the "hard" data of the census bureau have misled historians— or, rather, misstated the nature of structural change in the capital. The grouping of occupational categories for the elaboration of statistics inevitably involves problematical judgments and simplifications, but the census takers of 1911 surely overstepped the bounds of veracity at times. Two questionable practices in particular have done much to sustain the theme of *embourgeoisement*. Census officials chose to classify all the personnel of commercial establishments, no matter what their work or status, as employees. Even if one were willing to concede for the sake of argument that all office clerks and salespeople were "bourgeois," the normal understanding of that term surely does not include cooks, waiters, carters, or warehouse hands. Earlier censuses showed more sensitivity to social realities by including a category of "workers in commerce," which was a large one. Secondly, the 1911 census unfortunately included many thousands of people who did piece work at home under the rubric of the self-employed (*patrons*). Admittedly, the distinction between the two groups could sometimes be a fine one. Women in the needle trades, for example, regularly shifted between labor as wage-earners and as small subcontractors (*entrepreneuses*) of labor.[9] Among the 19,000 "*patronnes*" in the clothing industry of Belleville were many who had a neighborhood clientele, but, for the most part, the vast majority were sweated workers who rightfully earned the pity of social commentators then and since. One such observer spoke of the seamstresses of Belleville as "shirtmakers at ninety centimes a day."[10] Their categorization as bosses obviously harbors more distortion than truth. The number of female heads of manufacturing firms in Paris simply did not jump from 31,000 to 166,000 between the censuses of 1906 and 1911, as the raw data suggest.

The delicate operation of correcting census figures leads to rather basic reassessments of the *embourgeoisement* theme. In the first place, we must determine what proportion of "employees" was more aptly a part of the manual work force in the commercial sector. The census of 1886 characterized about 38 percent of the personnel in commercial firms as service workers, and it seems quite reasonable to apply this proportion to the census of 1911.[11] With this correction over a hundred thousand wage-earners return to "bourgeois" Paris at the eve of the war and a like number of white-collar positions vanish. Guidance for adjusting the isolated workers who were counted as bosses is less certain. At a minumum, we should reduce the proportion of females in the clothing trades to a level compatible with the census of 1906. These corrections produce a social structure that had not evolved very far toward property and security in the forty years before World War I (see table I-1). White-collar employment expanded impressively, but the proportion of heads of firms dropped somewhat. Moreover, the relative number of wage-earners declined a bit, but they were still the major element in the population of Paris. Over all, one must recognize a commanding stability in the gross categories of social structure between the Commune and the Great War.

A social transformation of importance was occurring in Paris in

Table I-1. Social Structure of Paris

Status	1866		1886		1911	
	N	%	N	%	N	%
Employer	169,468	22.2	269,538	19.5	316,178	19.5
White-Collar	126,006	16.5	263,468	19.1	352,744	21.4
Manual Worker[a]	468,337	61.3	849,006	61.4	977,671	59.3

Sources: Published censuses of 1866 and 1911; A.D.S., D 1 M⁸ no. 2.

[a] Domestic servants have been excluded.

the late nineteenth century, but *embourgeoisement* does not capture its essence. It would be better described as a reorientation from manufacturing to services. During the first half of the nineteenth century, the Parisian crafts had experienced a painful adjustment as entrepreneurs entered the less-than-luxury markets. In the 1840s, jewelry makers were uncertain about the status to accord the new types of domestic laborers who were just appearing in their industry; after the Commune, the existence of such workers was taken for granted.[12] The enlarged clientele which the reorganized crafts reached permitted the vast expansion and concentration of commerce. So did the railroads, as French markets became less regional and more sophisticated in their needs for credit, insurance, and such services. Paris of 1848 had only 99 stores selling ready-to-wear apparel (compared to 1,200 master tailors' shops); by 1856, there were 270 such outlets, and they numbered in the thousands by the twentieth century. Manufacturing in Paris knew no such expansion, even if the city was hardly divested of its wage-earners.[13]

One element of the *embourgeoisement* theme that retains credibility is the expansion of white-collar work. Paris on the eve of the Commune already had department store salesmen, railroad personnel, and bank clerks by the thousands, but their numbers continued to increase faster than any other group. A threefold increase in employees of the railroads, banks, and insurance companies occurred between the Commune and the war. Sales personnel contributed most to the expansion of the nonmanual sector. There were fewer than 50,000 employees of commerce in 1866, but they numbered 180,000 in 1911. Paris even developed a small army of 2,000 or so bill collectors for credit stores and utility companies.[14] The only white-collar sector that failed to display dynamism was the offices of manufacturing firms. Industry in Paris did not bureaucratize very thoroughly.[15] Contemporary observers did not fail to perceive another change in the clerical labor force, its partial feminization. At the time of the Commune, only 15 percent of all employees were women. Forty years later, females comprised about a third of office and sales personnel. Thus, the transformation of Paris into a city of services very much entailed a mobilization of women.[16]

Few changes in the manufacturing sector were so dramatic as those in services, but a certain reshuffling of this labor force did occur, too. The traditional crafts of the capital experienced a stability that translated into stagnation in the context of growth elsewhere. Furniture makers numbered about 20,000 in the 1860s and about the same in 1914. Shoemakers (17,000 in 1911), tanners (9,000), and jewelers (8,000) were similarly stable occupational groups. A decline of the building-trades workers—88,000 in 1866 and 60,000 in 1911— found compensation in the growth of printing and clothes making. In general, manufacturing and construction jobs for men grew half as fast as the active population. Had there not been a very rapid increase of females in the needle trades, the proportion of wage-earners in the labor force would have slipped substantially more than it did. The most noteworthy area of expansion for male workers was in the metal trades, surely the fitting announcement of a maturing industrial society. One in ten male manufacturing laborers on the eve of the Commune, makers of machines and metal objects accounted for one in five laborers by the war. Conventional wisdom under Louis Napoleon acknowledged that "as the construction trades go, so goes Paris."[17] At the dawn of the present century, the shaping and fitting of metal parts determined levels of prosperity in the capital. This fact serves to remind us that Paris, even the city proper, did not stand on the margins of the Second Industrial Revolution, but rather was a participant in it.

Despite the buoyancy of the metal and clothing trades, manufacturing yielded some of its importance to services. The production of commodities and construction employed 90 percent of all manual workers at the beginning of our period, but only 75 percent at the end.[18] The hypothetical tourists with which we began should have been in a position to appreciate this shift. They would have seen a proliferation of restaurants, so much so that cooks and waiters numbered nearly sixty thousand. Cabbies and transportation workers may never have been numerous enough for their clientele waiting on the streets, but their numbers doubled across our period. They rivaled the construction trades in size by the twentieth century. Other proliferating types of service workers included the maintenance personnel of stores, office "boys," carters, and warehouse workers. Such sources of employment were tangible results of markets that were larger and more sophisticated than ever.

The timing of these transformations reinforces our earlier observation that the middle third of the nineteenth century was the

Table I-2. Growth of White-Collar Sector in Paris

	1866		1886		1911
Male	108,057		196,513		240,571
% increase		81.8		22.4	
Female	17,949		66,955		112,173
% increase		272.6		67.5	
Total	126,006		245,394		352,744
% increase		94.7		43.7	

Sources: Published censuses of 1866 and 1911; A.D.S., D 1 M[8] no. 2.

period of truly original and dramatic reorientation (see table I-2). Much of the expansion of white-collar personnel and service workers was in full progress two decades before the Commune, and the rate of growth was already dissipating by the 1880s. In the twenty years after 1866, the number of employees in the capital grew by 95 percent; in the next twenty years, as the service sector matured, their numbers grew by half that rate. Well before the Boulanger Affair, department stores had ceased to be a bold experiment and were a common fact of economic life in the capital. The feminizing of clerical work corresponds particularly well to this chronology. In the first half of our period, women employees nearly tripled in number and then proceeded to grow at a rapid, but not revolutionizing, pace. The offices of banks and insurance companies were one of the few sectors in which white-collar employment continued to expand with the same vigor throughout the late nineteenth century. As for service workers, the censuses of 1886 and 1911 establish a similar pattern of growth. The impressive burst of energy that restructured the work force in Paris proper at midcentury was unparalleled. To find similar vitality under the Third Republic, one must transcend the boundaries of the city.

A sophisticated industrial economy, characterized by the heavy concentration of capital, responsiveness to technological innovation, and a large semiskilled or unskilled labor force, emerged on the edge of Paris. This factory economy did not mushroom suddenly out of cultivated fields. Most of the industrial communes grew regularly and steadily from the Second Empire onward (see figure I-1), with two general periods of acceleration, in the 1870s and at the turn of the century. Economic development reached the suburbs in several distinct waves. Firms had come to the *banlieue* since the first decades of the nineteenth century because they required cheap, extensive space or because their environmental impact was too noisome for the capital.[19] As the dynamism of the Second Industrial Revolution began to shape economic life on the periphery, new technologies and new products appeared here: rubber, cables, industrial chemi-

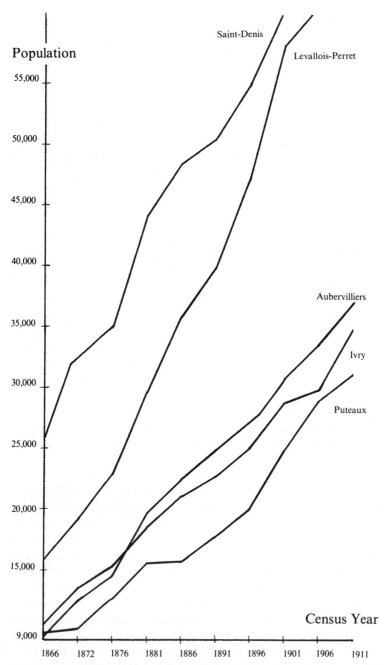

Figure I-1.   Pace of Growth of Five Suburban Towns
         Sources: Département de la Seine, *Etats des communes* (Montévrain, 1901–1905) for Aubervilliers, Ivry, Levallois-Perret, Puteaux, and Saint Denis; Statistique de la France, *Annuaire statistique de la France* for 1907 and 1912.

cals, and metallurgical construction. Finally, at the end of the century, the production of automobiles and machine parts brought the suburbs to a new plateau of prosperity and of industrial concentration. We do not follow Louis Chevalier in claiming that the *banlieue* established an independence from Paris and became an economic region in its own right; rather, the suburbs became an innovative extension of the Parisian economy.[20]

As the forces that were orientating the Parisian economy ever more toward services were losing their initial impetus at the beginning of the Third Republic, the communes of the suburbs were just entering the path to industrial maturation. "Going to Saint-Ouen" meant making a Sunday outing to the countryside well into the 1880s.[21] At this point, only six towns compared to the Parisian quarters of Belleville, Javel, or La Gare in terms of working-class concentration, as class ghettos. The largest factory in the department, the Cail Metallurgical and Machine Construction Company, was inside Paris. Twenty years later, thirteen more communes had lost their rural or residential character and had become part of the industrial belt around the capital. By this time, the *banlieue* had replaced Paris proper as the destination of most migrants to the metropolitan area.[22] The wage-earning population that encircled the city was nearly half the size of the one residing within Paris proper. What made this suburban population relatively unusual in prewar France and magnifies its historical interest was the concentration of workers who were in large-scale industry.

To place these changes in a new perspective, to perceive the economic and political realities behind our census figures and statistics, it is useful to add a spacial dimension to this analysis of social structures. Paris had long had several important barriers to class segregation: the heterogeneity of its population, the small size of enterprises, their remarkable diversity and adaptability to the urban environment, and the vigor of domestic production. Nonetheless, as figure I-2 shows, manual workers had experienced a notable degree of marginalization by the 1880s. Though wage-earners continued to comprise 59 percent of the residents in the city as a whole, thirty-five of the eighty quarters were less than 40 percent working class. Craftsmen were all but absent from certain districts of central Paris, and the working-class presence was maintained only by service personnel, who often lived on business premises. Thus, the quarter of Gaillon in the Second Arrondissement, with an active population of 6,600, had only 471 manufacturing workers. The quarter of Place Vendôme had 398 male craftsmen in an active population of 5,400. By contrast, there were twelve quarters of eastern Paris that were over 70 percent working class. One Parisian laborer in four lived in

Employees

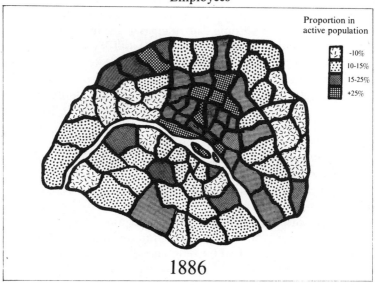

1886

Proportion in
active population

-10%
10-15%
15-25%
+25%

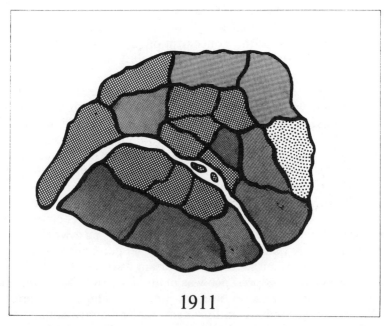

1911

Figure I-2.   Social Geography of Paris in 1886 and 1911
            Sources: A.D.S., D 1 M⁸ no. 2; Statistique générale de la France,
            Résultats statistiques du recensement général de . . . 1911 (2 vols., Paris,
            1911), II, 10–16.

12

Manual Workers

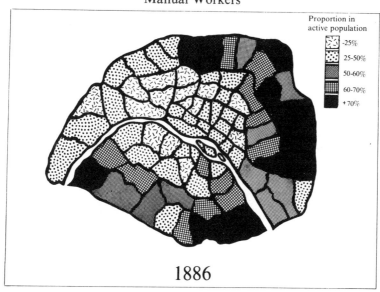

Proportion in
active population

-25%
25-50%
50-60%
60-70%
+70%

1886

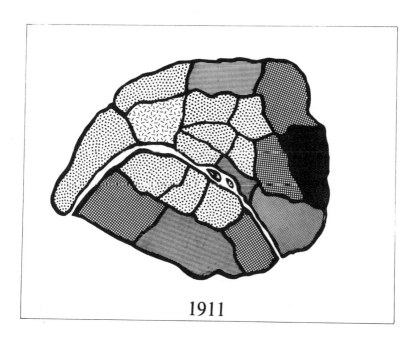

1911

13

them. The working-class concentrations in Belleville (76.4 percent), Javel (75.3 percent), Saint-Fargeau (81.2 percent) or Père-Lachaise (76.1 percent) were rarely equaled elsewhere in France, except, of course, in the industrial suburbs that bordered on these districts.

This level of segregation was all the more noteworthy in that the geography of employment in Paris proper had evolved not nearly so much in a complementary manner. Wage-earners still went to work in the central quarters of Paris and to areas immediately east of the place de la Bastille. Many of the largest Parisian crafts— jewelry, clothing, bronze objects, among them—remained anchored in the First Arrondissement, the Marais, and the streets around the canals.[23] No wonder that down to World War I and after, observers marveled at the intense animation of the rue du Faubourg du Temple and other arteries which led laborers between the eastern heights and central Paris early every morning and at dusk.[24] There were, to be sure, voluntary clusterings of workers who shared occupational or regional identities, but, for the most part, the social geography of late-nineteenth-century Paris was not arranged for the convenience of wage-earners.

Whereas the residential patterns of workers remained relatively stable down to the First World War, that of employees changed in some notable ways. First, clerks spread out to all parts of the city, and did so fairly evenly. Such patterns neatly symbolize the considerable diversity among employees: from the senior insurance clerk in the privileged Eighth Arrondissement to the railroad clerk in the popular Thirteenth. A second change was the particularly rapid growth of the white-collar population in the Fourth and in the expensive Sixth, Seventh, Eighth, and Sixteenth arrondissements. Again, unlike workers, employees were able to follow their job opportunities as these spread along the rue de Rivoli, the boulevard Haussmann and the boulevard Saint-Germain. Another intriguing aspect of the expansion of white-collar residences into the fashionable districts was that this was primarily a growth of female employees. In the Eighth Arrondissement, for example, the number of male clerks doubled between 1886 and 1911, but the number of female clerks grew sevenfold. This increase may reflect the nature of luxury commerce in this area, but something else may be involved. It is possible that the clerks who lived in the high-rent districts adopted the strategy of having their wives, salaried people, too, continue to work after marriage in order to be able to afford to live near their jobs. In any case, employees were far less marginalized than workers in terms of their lodgings. Many of them were able to shift their residences to complement their work situation and even to share the benefits of urban life in the *beaux quartiers*.

However distant the Paris of workers' sweat, misery, and revolt may have seemed to the visitor on the great boulevards, it was not. The capital changed partially and subtly during the second half of the nineteenth century. The metropolitan area reflected in its own way the economic transformations that engulfed France and Western Europe.[25] To be sure, Paris with a vigorous service sector was different from a city of handicraft workers, but only by reconstructing the experiences of the various groups of working people will we be in a position to see how that was so.

CRAFTSMEN

The declining weight of the handicrafts in the Parisian economy was relative, not absolute. Shoemakers and tailors each comprised a larger group than automobile makers, and by a wide margin, on the eve of the Great War. No city on the Continent had a larger concentration of artisans who had passed through rigorous training and had developed multiple proficiencies. They could work from blueprints or rough sketches to produce the objects of taste and refinement for which Paris was famous. Such craft workers personified *the* Parisian worker—"skilled, adroit, having several arrows to his bow," in the words of one journalist, who was expressing a common perception.[26] Yet commercial capitalism had been restructuring handicraft manufacturing for at least a half-century before the Commune, and the highly skilled craftsman was ever less the "typical" Parisian worker. Efforts to expand markets for hand-produced goods had created a new kind of worker, the specialized laborer who lacked the technical expertise and multiple proficiencies of the full artisan. One leading manufacturer of luxury furniture called these "half-workers" (*demi-ouvriers*).[27] A term more frequently used in the workshops of the capital was "small hands" (*petites mains*).[28] However derogatory their image, these semi-craftspeople comprised the largest group of workers in the capital.

Virtually every trade in Paris was differentiated into a luxury and a so-called current branch. The former produced made-to-order items and was largely the preserve of the fully trained artisans and the repository of all the traditions of the craft. In the other sector, entrepreneurs attempted to lower costs by using cheaper materials and production methods entailing specialization and a fine division of labor. These methods enabled Parisian products to compete on the basis of price and to penetrate into the local markets of distant cities by the 1840s.[29] The development of the railroads and the department store accelerated this expansion of "current" manufacturing. The history of the furniture trade nicely illustrates the dynamics that finally transformed a Parisian handicraft that had resisted change somewhat longer than others.[30] The highly talented cabinetmakers, wood sculptors, and joiners who played so prominent a role in the revolutionary history of Paris continued to exist in the thousands down to World War I and beyond. When a Russian courtier, an Argentine landowner, or an American industrialist needed a magnificent suite, where else would he turn but to the City of Lights to find the highest standards of elegance? The order would go to one of the large workshops of the Faubourg Saint-Antoine, like Krieger or Schmitt, which employed several hundred skilled furniture makers, some of whom were virtually artists.[31] These workmen, who were at the pinnacle of their crafts—and knew they were—had to share the Faubourg with semi-artisans of the current trade. Lowering the price of furniture required standardizing it and reducing the quality of the woods and the finishes. Workers in small shops repeatedly made the same piece of furniture, a night table, an unadorned dresser, or an unupholstered chair. Often, these cabinetmakers made only parts of furniture, which were assembled at another shop. Little of the aristocratic spirit of the luxury houses penetrated into the three thousand odd shops that handled this branch of woodworking by the eve of the war. They were content to produce sturdy furniture that would have a wide clientele.

Although the subdivided sector of woodworking had long existed, its expansion after the Commune, the result of "mass" marketing, was quite dramatic. The agents of its growth were wholesale purchasing contractors, department stores, and "furniture palaces." The showroom that Charles Klein built on the rue de Flandre around the turn of the century claimed to have more than two thousand varieties of dining room and bedroom sets.[32] These outlets made current production far larger than the luxury market. The figures adopted by the Ministry of Commerce at the dawn of the twentieth century placed the number of luxury craftsmen at four thousand and the number of specialized craftsmen at seven thousand (in addition to the three thousand small employers and jobbers who directed their work).[33] The most pitiable workers in the furniture trade were the thousand or so domestic laborers, called *trôliers*, who made their crude pieces in their rooms and took them to an outdoor market for sale at whatever price they would fetch.[34]

The substantial distance between the domestic laborers and the core workers at Krieger or Schmitt encompassed the diversity within the crafts in late-nineteenth-century Paris. The subdivision of the furniture trade had its counterpart in virtually every other craft in the city. Shoemaking, like tailoring, had been transformed earlier and thoroughly by the creation of ready-to-wear markets. Perhaps two thousand bootmakers (*bottiers*) still made shoes in their entirety for measure at the exclusive stores of the boulevards at the end of the nineteenth century. Roughly fifteen thousand more were specialists in the operations of cutting, bottoming, stitching, heeling, or finishing. Often, a "small hand" did only portions of such operations.[35] Likewise, there was the elite corps of two thousand jewelers who produced exquisite items of fine taste and high prices. Five thousand other jewelers, doing highly specialized and subdivided work, made trinkets for a very large, international market.[36] One manufacturer of marble decorative objects estimated that "artistic" production was only an eighth of "current" output. In harness making, only three hundred out of two thousand craftsmen worked in the luxury branch; and in the leather-goods trade, work was extremely divided except for an elite of the eighteen hundred laborers who produced for the quality shops.[37] Glove making survived remarkably long as a trade in which workers made entire objects; but by the 1870s, it, too, divided workers into the *totalistes* and the *systèmiers*, who made only glove parts.[38] The sizable carriage trade experienced an analogous transformation a few years earlier. Alongside the workshops that produced custom-made carriages, for which all parts were produced and assembled on the spot, grew firms that manufactured vehicles from ready-made components. The workers in the new firms were not capable of making the kinds of vehicles that carried the rich through the Bois de Boulogne.[39] The prestigious corporation of compositors had its own version of this evolution. Increasingly, specialized operations—paging, parceling, table setting, and others—were no longer the common skills of all printers. There was also the differentiation between those who could do varied and delicate work and the growing number of compositors who could not.[40] Ceramicists provide a final variation on the same theme. Little of the moderate-quality side of this trade remained in Paris by 1880; yet, production still involved an extreme division of labor. As one manufacturer claimed, "Not more than one worker in a hundred is a true ceramicist." Instead, there were molders, shapers, stampers, painters, and sculptors. A worker's professional competence determined how much of each operation he or she performed.[41]

The nature of vocational training inevitably reflected the specialized nature of craft production. Employers did not provide, and parents did not demand, a thorough training in the multiple proficiencies of a craft. It sufficed to learn a single operation or specialty because most shops did only that one. Hence youths learned quickly by doing, and the employer was soon able to allot a modest wage to them. Apprenticeships that were more serious, requiring a written contract and/or cash payments to the master, were increasingly rare in the late nineteenth century. In 1860, only 18.6 percent of Parisian apprenticeships had such safeguards. By the turn of the century, the proportion of such training agreements was probably not over 5 percent.[42]

The deterioration of apprenticeship in Paris was as old as the specialization of crafts. Nonetheless, figures on enrollments in design school attest to the increasing marginalization of the luxury trades, at an accelerating pace, in the last three decades of the nineteenth century. The formation of an artisan normally entailed not only a serious apprenticeship but also individual efforts to acquire the elements of design and drawing in night classes, which were sponsored by the municipality, trade groups, and charities. There was a precipitous decline in the absolute number and the proportion of working youths who took the initiative to perfect their technical skills. In the 1870s, roughly a fifth of all apprentices, about seven thousand youngsters, attended these classes.[43] This proportion neatly approximated that of all apprenticeships that were serious enough to require a written contract. By the first years of the twentieth century, however, out of a large number of working youths, only about eleven hundred students were in design classes.[44] The fully trained craftsman, once the linchpin of the Parisian economy, was a rare, if still valuable, laborer at the dawn of the new century.

A special word needs to be said about the trades that grew with industrial development, machine-building and metalworking. They did not fit entirely comfortably into the same category as the handicrafts; yet, the evolution of the metal trades bears impressive parallels with the luxury crafts, even if the pace of change was different. During the July Monarchy, copper founders or molders producing hardware, faucets, valves, engine parts, and the like had partly separated themselves from the craftsmen who made decorative objects (such as chandeliers or statuettes). The former group remained an elite, charged with making their own tools, for a short time; but soon a fairly intensive specialization overtook their work. At midcentury, master founders were already predicting the disappearance of casters who possessed multiple proficiencies, and at the beginning of the twentieth century, they pronounced this specialization "complete."[45] A similar transformation characterized machine-building. Parisian mechanics assembled, with great pride, machines that were made to order before the middle of the nineteenth century.[46] An engineer like Denis Poulot looked back nostalgically upon this time as a golden age, when his comrades knew design, geometry, turning, planing, drilling, and the other branches of metal-shaping.[47] With industrial development, machine-building ceased to be a curiosity and gained wide markets. As in the handicrafts, the social relations of production changed with this evolution. Fully trained mechanics, who claimed to have "their capital in their arms and in their brains," found work off the production process, in repair, maintenance, and toolmaking.[48] The majority of machinists were specialized in one branch of metal-working. The operations performed by turners, drillers, millers, and planers were, in their turn, subdivided even when technological in-novations did not alter them. Poulot believed that the majority of jobs for machinists in Paris of the 1880s did not require an appren-ticeship.[49] Even before the Commune, a leading builder of railroad and refinery equipment looked to his 250 machine tools to "repro-duce an infinite number of pieces that were exactly the same."[50] The dramatic scene in Emile Zola's *L'Assommoir* in which the proud mechanic Goujet foresees his replacement by a machine was over-drawn but not without a small element of veracity.

The history of the metal and machine trades, then, followed the evolution of the handicrafts, but was compressed into an abbreviated chronology. Industries were born, entered an "artisanal" stage, and rapidly subdivided and specialized—all in a matter of decades. Un-like most handicrafts, however, a few industrial crafts passed into the phase of mechanization.

Though the crafts had been experiencing changes in the social relations of production for several decades before the Commune, workers in the same trade continued to form communities. The craft helped to structure the laborer's social milieu. The Parisian furniture manufacturer, Mazaroz, was not hopelessly backward-looking in re-ferring to the craft as the worker's "second family" in the 1880s. Through apprenticeship, through informal pressures and contacts at the shop, workers from disparate backgrounds elaborated a common culture. Fewer than a third were natives to the capital, but many immigrants learned the "ways" of Parisian workers—independence, a taste for fashionableness, formality with peers, and intolerance for authority.[51] Marriage acts of 1869 attest to the enduring role of the craft in ordering social relations. Among the furniture makers of the Twelfth Arrondissement (including part of the Faubourg Saint-An-toine), half the friends and relatives who witnessed marriage acts worked in the same trade, whereas this industry employed only a fifth of the working-class residents in the district. Similarly, building workers in the Fifteenth Arrondissement had twice as many witnesses among their fellow tradesmen as their proportion in the population would warrant.[52] Data from the Tenth, Eighteenth, and Twentieth arrondissements made the general case for the meaningfulness of craft relations at the end of the Second Empire (see table I-3).

Table I-3.   Social Positions of Friends and Relatives of Parisian Craftsmen (in %)

| | 1869 | | | | | |
| | XVIIIe Arrondissement | | Xe Arrondissement | | XXe Arrondissement | |
Status	Friends	Rela- tives	Friends	Rela- tives	Friends	Rela- tives
Worker	62.1%	69.3%	57.0%	66.4%	81.0%	80.5%
(same craft)	(28.7)	(19.2)	(32.7)	(18.3)	(32.9)	(24.4)
White-Collar	12.1	15.2	16.3	20.6	3.9	10.3
Shopkeeper	19.6	12.1	19.3	10.3	10.1	8.2
(publican)	(6.6)	(0)	(6.4)	(2.4)	(5.7)	(2.1)
Bourgeois	5.9	3.3	7.4	2.7	4.8	0

| | 1903 | | | | |
| | XVIIIe Arrondissement | | | XXe Arrondissement | |
	Friends	Rela- tives		Friends	Rela- tives
Worker	66.1%	65.4%		79.6%	81.6%
(same craft)	(18.1)	(16.3)		(21.4)	(17.3)
White-Collar	16.3	17.2		6.3	8.9
Shopkeeper	14.2	14.3		8.5	7.2
Bourgeois	3.4	2.2		5.6	2.3

Sources: A.D.S., V 4E, Actes de mariage, 1869; Mairies of Eighteenth and Twentieth arrondissements, Actes de mariage, 1903.

The milieu of the craftsman at the time of the Commune was preponderantly working class. Yet class ties seem diffuse, perhaps incidental, compared to those of the trade. Workers were truly a class apart in Belleville, where the concentration of wage-earning residents was overwhelming, but in less ghettoized quarters, contacts with white-collar employees and shopkeepers were considerable. The profile of workers' relatives inflated class-wide contacts, but their friends, a more significant measure of voluntary sociability, were less class-oriented and more craft-bound.

Surviving quite well three or more decades of commercial capitalism, craft cohesiveness did not retain the same strength into the twentieth century. The marriage acts of 1903 show that occupational identity did not shape workers' sociability so much as earlier. Significantly, classwide relations were as strong or stronger than earlier despite claims of embourgeoisement and a genuine white-collar expansion (especially in the Eighteenth Arrondissement, covered by table I-3). Once again, friendships provide the most sensitive measure, and they were less craft-bound than forty years earlier. This change in the social identity of workers' contacts, trivial in itself, hints at an important reorientation of loyalties and identities among the mass of specialized craftsmen, if not among the elite of each trade. Surely, this shift in the craftsmen's sense of community had resonances in other aspects of their lives and work.

FACTORY WORKERS

To distinguish definitively between the "workshop" and the "factory" is an impossible task. After many attempts, the Ministry of Commerce renounced the effort and left it to "enlightened intuition."[53] There was no decisive gulf between the two sorts of work environments, nor was there an absolute identity between the "factory" and *grande industrie*. Not only the size of an enterprise and the level of technological sophistication but also the degree to which labor was specialized and coordinated made for the distinction. Thus, some of the carriage- and piano-construction plants with hundreds of laborers qualified only marginally as "factories" because they were more like collections of smaller shops in which handicraftsmen did much of the work. On the other hand, a rubber plant with only forty workers was a factory because the labor force was so subordinated to plantwide processes. The most novel feature of the factory, a large semiskilled labor force operating machines, certainly existed by the time of the Commune. Another distinguishing mark was that the skilled laborers needed for crucial operations tended to do more specialized work and have more supervision than their counterparts in small shops. Their sources of training and recruitment also differentiated them from artisans. Aware of these differences, the most proficient mechanics reportedly kept their distance from the automobile factories of the early twentieth century and disdainfully regarded the work done there as "boilermaking."[54] Factories of the late nineteenth century had taken meaningful steps away from the team production of handicraftsmen even if the separation was not absolute.

The Coutant Forges of Ivry, which had a labor force of seven hundred to a thousand in the 1870s, illustrates many prominent features of the pre-assembly-line factory.[55] Substantially mechanized by the last years of the Empire, it had several power hammers (*martaux pilons*) and machine tools capable of producing five hundred kilograms of bolts a day, as well as milling, planing, and threading equipment. The forging room, with its forty hand-operated furnaces, was, in some respects, a continuation of traditional forms of production; but even here there were innovations: each ironsmith had extensive equipment that was normally unavailable in small shops and that simplified the job. Before the Commune, these ironsmiths, all natives of the Nièvre Department and usually related through blood or marriage, had formed a closed caste of industrial craftsmen. By the 1880s an internal training program had broken their hold over forging.[56]

The Godillot shoe "factory," though smaller than Coutant's firm and in a trade dominated by handicraft production in the 1870s, still merited the designation.[57] Less than a third of the three hundred workers had had training as cobblers. Most operated the extensive machinery that prepared shoes for sewing or performed the finishing procedures. Godillot's factory methods were reputedly three times as productive as hand manufacturing. He also owned a heavily mechanized tanning plant employing 150 workers in Saint-Ouen. Enterprises like those of Coutant or Godillot grew in number and importance during the late nineteenth century. Paris proper contained a substantial number of large factories, both on its periphery and near its center.[58] However, it is difficult to learn about the workers in these plants because they were easily lost among the laborers in the myriad of small shops. In this section, we shall concentrate on the suburbs of the capital which became one of the more vital industrial centers in France.

Factory production in the *banlieue* never strayed far from the impetus that Parisian markets and resources gave to it. The earliest implantations of industry were cases of expulsion from the capital, in trades that literally fed on the waste of the Parisian population. One thinks of the numerous glue and fertilizer manufacturers in Aubervilliers.[59] Between the 1860s and 1880s, the suburbs appeared to be on the way to developing a distinctive economic life of their own. New industries, born of the Second Industrial Revolution, rubber, machine-building, steel construction, and the like, intruded upon the edge of the capital. Yet entrepreneurs of the *banlieue* also prospered from adapting and coopting the traditional vocation of Paris, to provide goods to the rich and powerful. The principal case in point was the production of automobiles, which became the linchpin of the suburban economy after the turn of the century. A common characteristic of the large industries of the suburbs was to produce for a moderately prosperous clientele what the rich bought from Parisian craftsmen. New methods of production, heavy capital investments, and managerial innovations were entailed in such business strategies. Christofle, "Silversmiths of Paris," presents a fine example of such initiative. Its electrochemical plating plant in Saint-Denis employed hundreds of workers and "mass" produced tableware, tea services, and ornamental houseware. Its new casting processes and alloys yielded objects of grace that did not need finely executed finishing.[60] The nearby Combes tanning factory employed over a thousand people and produced leather for the highest quality shoes made in factories and sold in department stores.[61] Likewise, the fancy soaps and perfumes of Roger Gallet in Levallois-Perret, whose plant employed six hundred workers, were intended for a large, international market, not just for society ladies.[62] Certainly, as the twentieth century opened, it was far from true that Paris produced the noble whereas the suburbs did the ignoble work. Rather, the factories of the *banlieue* exemplified the "revolution of the good," to use the term of Jacques Néré.[63] Its industries addressed the wider clientele that the forces of economic maturation favored.

The accuracy of the image of the suburbs as the home to large-scale industry varied from one commune to another and from one industry to another.[64] The production of chemicals, soaps, perfumes, and dyes was usually capital, not labor, intensive. One expert on industry reported visiting a producer of printers' ink in Puteaux and being virtually alone in a vast shop filled with much machinery.[65] The average chemical plant in Aubervilliers, Clichy, Pantin, or Saint-Denis had only about forty workers. The canning, preserving, and fabrication of foodstuffs was similarly a matter of small factories. Rubber plants, which multiplied in the western suburbs in response to demands for cables, electric lines, and tires, often attained two hundred or more workers per firm, as did tanning enterprises. Sugar refineries were large by any standard, sometimes employing a thousand or more unskilled and poorly paid laborers. It was the automobile and machine-building plants that finally made large scale industry commonplace in the suburbs. By 1910, fourteen firms engaged more than five hundred workers, and they employed a total of sixteen thousand laborers. Alongside these plants was a large number of shops and foundries that had between a hundred and five hundred workers. The number of laborers in the average metal-working plant in the cantons of Saint-Denis or Ivry was six times larger than that in the quarter of Folie Méricourt (Eleventh Arrondissement), the heart of the machine-building industry of Paris.[66]

The scale of factory development in the *banlieue* is susceptible to different assessments depending on the standards applied. Compared to the spectacular growth of large concerns in the Ruhr Valley of Germany or even in Le Creusot, factory growth on the edge of the capital appeared modest. Only three factories had more than two thousand workers on the eve of the Great War: the Renault and Dion-Bouton Automobile companies (in Boulogne and Puteaux respectively) and the French Munitions Society (in Issy-les-Moulineaux). A fourth plant, Delauny-Belleville Machine Company in Saint-Denis, was nearly as large.[67] On the other hand, the concentration of capital that had occurred in the suburbs was quite excep-

Table I-4.   Industrial Concentration in Three Suburban Towns, 1910

Size of Firm	Number of Firms	Total Workers	% Workers
	Metalworking Firms in Ivry[a]		
–20 Workers	12	87	2.3
21–99 Workers	5	254	6.9
100–499 Workers	7	1,810	48.9
500+ Workers	2	1,547	41.8
Total	26	3,698	99.9
	Metalworking Firms in Saint-Denis		
–20 Workers	42	250	2.9
21–99 Workers	15	874	10.3
100–499 Workers	7	2,015	23.7
500+ Workers	5	5,369	63.1
Total	69	8,508	100.0
	All Firms in Puteaux		
1–10 Workers	28	117	1.8
11–50 Workers	11	272	4.2
51–100 Workers	7	510	8.0
101–500 Workers	7	1,519	23.7
500+ Workers	3	3,970	62.1
Total	56	6,388	99.8

Sources: A.N., F²² 574. Industries des métaux ordinaires; Odile Meyer, "La Croissance de la commune de Puteaux entre 1880 et 1914" (Diplome de maîtrise, Université de Paris–X, 1975–1976), pp. 27–29.

[a] Figures for Ivry do not include the large Panhard-Levassor automobile plant, just across the city limits in Paris. Seventeen hundred worked in this plant, including many residents of Ivry. The inclusion of this firm would have raised the level of concentration.

tional for France and for the Paris region in particular. Table I-4 displays the size of metalworking plants in Ivry-sur-Seine and Saint-Denis, and the size of all manufacturing firms in Puteaux. Clearly, any meaningful standard would permit us to conclude that a large-factory labor force had emerged on the periphery of Paris.

The factory personnel was no less varied and complexly structured than was the artisanal labor force in Paris. Production in factories called for a great many unskilled laborers. They constituted the bulk of the work force in chemicals, rubber, and food processing, where machines dominated the production process. Machine-building, too, required day laborers to maintain the smooth flow of materials. Indeed, as automobile plants became larger and applied more sophisticated technology, the ratio of unskilled support workers to production workers increased.[68] Common hands were generally the single largest occupational category in the industrial towns of the suburbs, numbering one per seven or eight male workers. In Aubervilliers they constituted a fourth of the resident labor force.[69]

At the other extreme of the skill hierarchy were the industrial craftsmen—ironsmiths, mold makers, iron fitters, founders, well-trained mechanics, and the like. These men could often work from blueprints, perform geometrical calculations, call upon experience to set up a new job, or make crucial decisions about the speed and cut of their machines. For such application of expertise, these workers were among the best paid in the region. Yet they were reputedly not nearly the equals of the metalworkers of the Marais or of the mechanics who worked in the quarter of Folie Méricourt.[70] The skilled workers in factories served not only in the production process but increasingly in crucial support roles as toolmakers.[71]

"Semiskilled" is often the term used to describe the rest of the industrial workers in production, but we must remember that the reality was closer to a continuous hierarchy of skill levels than to a coherent, uniform group of laborers.[72] Some were tenders of machine tools that had so much built-in skill that the workers could oversee three or four at once. Others manned general machine tools (lathes, milling machines, planers, and so on) for the purpose of making large batches of the same piece.[73] They required extensive instruction from the foreman to begin a new operation. This sector of the labor force was the product of industrial maturation, but one does not even have to approach the twentieth century to find the appearance of a semiskilled factory population. The huge Cail Machine Company in Chaillot was completely retooled a few years before the Commune. With the new machines, intended to make standardized parts, six hundred workers produced what a thousand had several years earlier.[74] One knowledgeable observer of the automobile industry claimed in 1909 that no more than three in ten workers were truly skilled. The rest could be trained in a few weeks or months.[75] Wage lists from one of the largest car makers and from two smaller metallurgical construction firms for 1910 confirm this judgment (see figure I-3). Assuming that eight francs a day was the threshold of pay for skilled workers and six francs for the semiskilled, we may conclude that plants tended to be fairly evenly divided among skilled, specialized, and casual workers. Of course, such a neat summary conceals a good deal of diversity and complexity.

The female manufacturing labor force was two-thirds the size of the male labor force in the suburbs and only 44 percent of the male one in Paris proper.[76] Would it be correct to attribute the abundance of women wage-earners here to the availability of factory jobs? In fact, there was a marked similarity between the kinds of

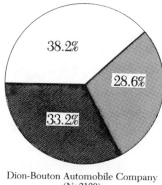

Dion-Bouton Automobile Company
(N=2130)

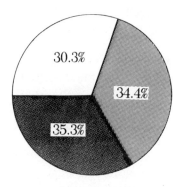

Kessler-Gaillard and Baudet-Donon
Metallurgical Construction Companies
(N=522)

KEY

Skilled
Semi-skilled
Unskilled

Figure I-3. Structure of the Factory Labor Force at Three Plants, 1910
Sources: A.M. Argenteuil, 29 F; A.M. Puteaux, I 1.128.III.

labor women did in Paris and in the suburbs. The single largest industry in the suburbs, with eighty thousand jobs, was clothes making.[77] The needle trades, not factory production, occupied most working women, even in this emerging "factory civilization."[78] The need to balance familial and work roles was likely one reason for the predominance of the traditional, usually domestic, labor for the women of the *banlieue*. Other reasons may well have involved the limited number and quality of jobs the factories offered. Unlike the textile industry of northern France, in which women workers played a notable role, the industrial mix of the Parisian suburbs did not generate an enormous number of positions for women. Food processing, perfumes, soaps, and chemicals were the fields most likely to employ females. One industry new to the twentieth century, the manufacture of light bulbs, opened jobs as *électriciennes*, since women's superior manual dexterity enabled them to assemble filaments. These industries were also among the few to offer relatively appealing work to females. A skilled perfume mixer or a chocolate maker was a prized worker who could command commensurate benefits.[79] Such positions were exceptional, however. The usual job entailed quite unattractive conditions.

For observing the limited opportunities for female factory workers, an informative exercise is to compare the industrial jobs of women in Levallois-Perret with those in Ivry. The former town had, in addition to machine-building, the kinds of industry that would have seemed to favor women, perfumes, fancy soaps, and food products. Ivry, on the other, hand had very few such firms. Nonetheless, the differences in industrial structure did not translate into markedly different employment situations for women. Out of a hundred female factory workers in Levallois-Perret in 1911, fifty-eight were nothing more than day laborers. Among the rest were a few skilled workers and many more in semiskilled positions, including numerous jobs that were not especially desirable, like those of the packers at the Roger Gallet Perfume Company or Olida Victual Company. In Ivry, 72 percent of the women in factories was also at the bottom of the industrial hierarchy.[80] Significantly, the proportion of common laborers in the work force was twice as high among females as among males, 30.5 percent compared to 15.6 percent.[81]

In summary, factories offered women limited and unattractive alternatives to the handicrafts. The work of casual laborers was painful, difficult, and often dangerous. The needle trades had, at least, the advantages of predictability and flexibility. Clearly, women in the suburbs were disproportionately occupied in the work force because their families needed money, not because of special opportunities presented by the factories.

The impetus that brought provincial craftsmen to seek employment in Paris was ancient, but what were the origins of the newer factory work force? A profile of labor recruitment in three industrial communes provide some insights. Bezons, on the outer edge of the western *banlieue,* was the locale of a large rubber and cable factory, isolated in what was otherwise still a village. Its personnel during the 1870s came from the overcrowded farmlands of Brittany and from the Hazebrouck district in the department of the Nord, a region of declining rural industry. Marriage records show that these workers had been born to propertyless and proletarianized families but not to ones that labored in factories. Thus, Bezons's rubber plant had a predominantly first-generation factory labor force in the decade after the Commune.[82] By the dawn of the twentieth century, however, the work force in Bezons had a different complexion. At that point, there was a strong element of self-recruitment in the factories of the town. Out of the working-class communities of the suburbs came about three-fourths of the workers who married in Bezons, half of them from this town, itself. The uprooted of rural life were still an important source of factory labor, but within one generation the employer of Bezons became much less dependent on this source.[83]

The town of Saint-Ouen, contiguous to Paris and near important transportation facilities, was in the part of the *banlieue* that industrialized earliest. In 1874–1876, its pattern of labor recruitment, reliance on local communities, resembled Bezons's twenty-five years later. Just under half (44.2 percent) of the workers who married in Saint-Ouen were sons of factory workers. Significantly, those who were in the first generation of factory service were children of the unskilled, both urban and rural, and occasionally of a cultivator. The sorts who were least likely to be found in the plants of Saint-Ouen were the sons of shoemakers, tailors, carpenters, and other craftsmen. Less than a tenth of the factory workers came from handicraft milieus. Three decades later, the social characteristics of recruitment had not altered. Local recruitment was still more important (70.2 percent) and the children of urban craftsmen were as aloof as ever from factory work.[84]

Ivry had significant industrial developments as early as Saint-Ouen, but it was one of the few towns in the southern portion of the *banlieue* to do so.[85] Consequently, the level of local recruitment in the 1870s was not so high as at Saint-Ouen. The heavy industry of Ivry drew, instead, upon immigrant factory labor, especially from the Department of the Nièvre. The iron mills of Fourchambault and Imphy were veritable reservoirs of talent and toil for the Coutant Forges at Ivry.[86] Slightly less than half of the factory laborers who married in Ivry were new to this work environment. Among these wage-earners was a large proportion of the sons of small cultivators and vineyard keepers from southern France. These proletarianized immigrants were following traditional channels of migration to Ivry (and to Paris). With the intensification of industrial development in the late decades of the nineteenth century, the factories of Ivry were able to draw more fully upon an indigenous work force. In the twentieth century, as in the 1870s, children of urban craftsmen were rare, and most of the workers who did not have factory backgrounds were children of common laborers.[87]

Labor recruitment in the factories of the suburbs was complex, and local factors counted for much. Yet the striking feature of the formation of factory labor forces in all three suburban towns was the marginalized recruitment patterns. Laborers came out of the lowest ranks of urban or rural society or out of established factory communities. Living on the edge of Europe's greatest concentration of craft workers, the factory population was cut off from it. Moreover, the development of a factory work force was more a matter of continuity than of disruption.[88] Employers drew upon channels of migration that were in place long before industrialization. Within a generation, factory communities became largely self-perpetuating. No wonder that the plants of the *banlieue* grew without awakening much interest or attention in the capital.

A more refined analysis of the origins of the different sorts of workers within factories does not alter these basic impressions. The day laborers were most likely to be children of propertyless rural laborers. The proletarianized peasant was also compelled to take unskilled labor in factories. Their children, however, did not usually remain in this most humble position but, rather, moved into machine-tending work. Such were the social orgins of the semiskilled laborers, who were more often than not second-generation factory workers.[89] Research on the background of the skilled laborers is confounded by the problem that occupational titles were usually not sufficient to distinguish them from the semiskilled. A "turner" could have been a worker with exceptional expertise or one of modest capacity; public records did not offer guidance on this point. By examining the marriage acts of certain tradesmen who were almost surely skilled (iron-smiths, polishers, molders, nickelers, and casters), we can overcome this obstacle, at the risk, though, of missing some practitioners of industrial crafts. Such an analysis for various communes of the suburbs reveals that industrial craftsmen did not comprise a closed caste and were becoming ever less exclusive.[90] In the 1870s, children of day laborers and cultivators comprised 22 percent of the skilled workers who married in the *banlieue*. By the dawn of the twentieth century, their proportion had risen to 31 percent. Access to industrial skills for "outsiders" was surely the result of employers' influence upon the mechanisms of training and recruitment. At the Coutant Forges in Ivry, for example, boys were put to work at threading machines, and foremen selected them for apprenticeship programs on the basis of dexterity, diligence, and docility. The status of the boys' fathers had nothing to do with admission to the exclusive train-

Table I-5. Friendship Networks of Factory Workers in Saint-Ouen

	1874–1875		1902–1903	
Status	N	%	N	%
Factory Worker	83	50.9	97	53.6
Craftsman	24	14.7	52	28.7
White-Collar	31	19.0	20	11.0
Shopkeeper	17	10.4	8	4.4
Other	8	4.9	4	2.2
Total	163	99.9	181	99.9

Source: A.M. Saint-Ouen, Actes de mariage, 1874, 1875, 1902, 1903.

ing program.[91] Relatively isolated from the rest of urban society, factory civilization had its own channels of social mobility.

The gulf between factory laborers and handicrafts workers, visible in recruitment patterns, was also mirrored in networks of friendships during the 1870s. A suburban commune like Saint-Ouen had among its residents numerous building workers, shoemakers, and printers. However, these were not the friends or relatives of the factory workers. White-collar employees, shopkeepers, and employers seem to have been closer to factory communities (see table I-5). Nonworkers comprised 28 percent of the population of Saint-Ouen just after the Commune but 34 percent of the "friends" to factory laborers. There was a certain evolution in the sociability of factory laborers by the twentieth century, though. Handicraftsmen became more closely integrated into their milieu, while the contacts with nonworkers receded considerably. Class bonds were somehow cutting into the separate spheres of "workshop" and "factory," at least in minor ways.

WHITE-COLLAR WORKERS

In the 1860s, "the employee" was the object of rather mocking public regard. He (men vastly outnumbered women at this time) was the person who carried an umbrella to work every morning no matter how nice the day, who complained about having to arrive at a gentlemanly 10:00 A.M., and who fawned before his petty tyrant of a boss in hopes of receiving a bonus. The prototype that the public had in mind was the employee of one of the ministries, actually a rather privileged member of the white-collar sector.[92] Many such employees had their baccalaureates, and even university degrees, along with some family money to supplement their salaries.[93] By the last years of the nineteenth century, public attitudes had changed: No longer the objects of sarcasm, clerks were now perceived as working people with serious problems.[94] Behind this change was not so much a deterioration of the employees' conditions as a shift in public attention from the privileged ministerial clerk to some of his more humble colleagues. Our findings about residential patterns of employees, who were dispersed over the entire city, showed considerable disparity in income and in security. The ministerial employee may well have lived in the Seventh or Eighth Arrondissement along with purchasing agents, sales representatives, insurance agents, senior office clerks, and the best-paid salespeople. The spacial distance that separated these from the humble clerks in the peripheral quarters—the group with which we are concerned in this study—symbolized a cultural and economic gulf, as well.

Far from the placid, tedious world of the ministries lived and worked the clerks of the Municipal Duties Administration (*Octroi*), who typified in many ways the modest employee. Rather than starting work at midmorning, these fellows often labored all night. They were in contact with a public that was not necessarily genteel, and a lip bloodied by an irate rate payer was a frequent occupational hazard for these clerks.[95] Sharing their position at the base of the hierarchy of authority was the mass of bookkeepers, secondary office employees, bank, railroad, and postal clerks. One bookkeeper at the gas utility called these people "the poor cousins of the ministerial employees."[96] They became a very large and distinct group as offices, stores, and public services grew during the middle third of the nineteenth century.

The essential prerequisite for becoming a modest white-collar worker was skill at numerical computations, neat penmanship, and accuracy at spelling, essentially the accomplishments of a model elementary school pupil. A primary school certificate, not to mention a baccalaureate, was often unnecessary to enter the office or store. Large administrations (banks, utility companies, railroads) gave examinations in these subjects, whereas stores were more interested in work histories. Many a humble clerk started as a stock boy with a wholesale grocer, as a notary's clerk, or as a file clerk in a local factory.[97] The occupants of these positions tried desperately to find a position in a department store or in the headquarters of a large company and to do so before the age of thirty-five, for older people were generally not hired by these organizations. Demand for these positions was far in excess of supply, and even the ambitious youth with exemplary orthography still needed a "recommendation" from someone powerful.[98]

One need not enter into the traditional debate about whether the modest employees were a new sort of bourgeoisie or a new sort

Table I-6. Social Origins of White-Collar Workers

	1869					
	C[a]		P[b]		S[c]	
Father	*N*	*%*	*N*	*%*	*N*	*%*
Retail Commerce	17	13.5	26	12.9	10	18.5
Cultivator	17	13.5	24	11.9	8	14.8
Rentier	45	35.7	57	28.3	15	27.8
Employee	21	16.7	32	15.9	5	9.2
Profession	5	4.0	5	2.5	0	0.0
Manual Worker	21	16.7	57	28.3	16	29.6
Total	126	100.0	201	99.8	54	99.9

	1903–1904			
	XVIII[e] Arrondissement		S	
	N	*%*	*N*	*%*
Retail Commerce	14	9.5	7	14.6
Cultivator	11	7.4	6	12.6
Rentier	38	25.7	9	19.6
Employee	52	35.1	14	30.4
Manual Worker	28	18.9	10	22.7
Total	148	100.2	46	99.9

Sources: A.D.S., V 4E, Actes de mariage, 1869; A.M. Saint-Denis, Etat civil, 1867–1869, 1903–1904; A.M. Saint-Ouen, Etat civil, 1867–1869, 1903–1904; *Mairie* of Eighteenth Arrondissement, Actes de mariage, 1903–1904.

[a] C = Central Paris (II[e], IX[e], X[e] arrondissements).

[b] P = Peripheral Paris (XIII[e], XVIII[e] arrondissements).

[c] S = Suburbs (Saint-Denis, Saint-Ouen); data from suburban communes concern 1867–1869.

of proletariat to recognize that they comprised an amorphous group.[99] Their family origins and the milieus from which they drew their spouses, relatives, and friends will help to place them in the society of late-nineteenth-century Paris. In order to capture the nuances, it would be well to distinguish among white-collar workers in three parts of the metropolitan area: the central Second, Ninth, and Tenth arrondissements, where high rents excluded all but the prosperous clerks; the peripheral Thirteenth and Eighteenth arrondissements, where cheaper housing attracted modest employees; finally, the industrial suburbs of Saint-Denis and Saint-Ouen, home to clerks who resigned themselves to long commutes because they could not afford to do otherwise.

Regardless of gender or the level of affluence, the majority of employees came from property-owning families (see table I-6). Typically, as contemporary opinion was quick to recognize, they were children of land-owning cultivators, active or retired shopkeepers.

Railroad employees, sales clerks, and bank clerks shared this provincial, petty-bourgeois background. At the end of the Second Empire, employees were self-recruiting only to a small degree because their milieu was still limited in size and because its rapid expansion made room for entrants from diverse backgrounds. Children of workers had to overcome numerous obstacles to enter the office or store. Even if such youths excelled in primary school, they still had to face the frequent indifference or skepticism of their parents about a white-collar future. The complaint of one laborer that his teachers always attended to the instruction of children from prosperous families and let working-class youths slide into ignorance reveals a way in which schools posed a barrier.[100] Some careers discouraged needy candidates because they began with a year or so of unpaid service. The requirements of polite manners, cash for a security bond, or a costly wardrobe were still other deterrents. The plight of one stonemason of Saint-Denis, who had to ask the municipal council to buy his son a suit so he could begin work as an attorney's clerk, was surely not unique.[101] In view of the numerous obstacles, the extent to which youths crossed the manual-labor line was substantial. Surely, the vital growth of white-collar work after the Commune aided their entry into bureaucracies. Forty years later, when expansion had slowed, recruitment from the working classes had dropped. By this time, employees had become much more of a self-recruiting "caste."

Having similar social origins, modest and well-off employees were differentiated more clearly by their choice of marriage partners (see table I-7). In 1869 sales and clerical personnel in the peripheral areas married working women, who often continued to work after marriage. Those in central Paris chose idle, young women, presumably because they could afford to or because such idleness flattered their self-image. Moreover the employees who resided in the popular quarters not only wed women who were accustomed to laboring, but they frequently took brides from specifically working-class milieus. Their ability or desire to attract the daughters of propertied families was considerably less than their colleagues in central Paris. The social orientation of the modest employees, born to families with some standing and property, was downward.

The bourgeois moral standards expected of the personnel of the ministries and forced upon salesclerks at some department stores under threat of firing marked another divide between prosperous and modest employees. Prenuptial cohabitation and concubinage, solidly a part of working-class life, were cultural forms shared with many employees. In the Thirteenth and the Eighteenth arrondissements, half (50.4 percent) of the clerks and their brides had precisely the same addresses before marriage. Although some cases may have

Table I-7. Occupations and Family Background of Wives of White-Collar Workers

	N	%	N	%	N	%
			Occupation, 1869			
	C[a]		P[b]		S[c]	
Manual Worker	58	38.9	159	69.4	45	69.2
White-Collar	14	9.4	15	6.5	3	4.6
No Occupation	77	51.7	55	24.1	17	26.2
Total	149	100.0	229	100.0	65	100.0
			Family Background, 1869			
Manual Worker	24	20.2	110	58.2	32	64.0
White-Collar	26	21.8	16	8.5	3	6.0
Propertied	69	58.0	63	33.3	15	30.0
Total	119	100.0	189	100.0	50	100.0
			Occupation, 1903–1904			
	XVIII[e] Arrondissement				S	
Manual Worker	54	34.6			26	48.1
White-Collar	59	37.8			15	27.8
No Occupation	43	27.6			13	24.1
Total	156	100.0			54	100.0

Sources: See table I-6.

[a] C = Central Paris (II[e], IX[e], X[e] arrondissements).

[b] P = Peripheral Paris (XIII[e], XVIII[e] arrondissements).

[c] S = Suburbs (Saint-Denis, Saint-Ouen); data from suburban communes concern 1867–1869.

involved the marriage of chaste neighbors, it is hard to imagine that this was usually the case. Indeed, white-collar couples of the outer arrondissements were nearly as likely to have children out of wedlock as wage-earning couples. In Belleville, the legitimization of natural children accompanied about 18 percent of the marriages.[102] Among the white-collar couples, the ratio of legitimizations to weddings was only slightly less, 13.8 percent. The clerks of the *banlieue* had similar rates of cohabitation and illegitimacy. Strikingly, their premarital habits were not at all different from those of factory laborers. The clerks of the central arrondissements, on the other hand, were more likely to uphold the dominant moral precepts. Only 28.5 percent of them shared the same addresses as their brides, and only 6 percent of these couples had children to legitimize.

While the better-off employees appeared to identify with bourgeois moral precepts, the modest employees did not display an overweening urge to do so. The analogous dichotomy was reflected in the respective identity of their friends (see table I-8). For both groups white-collar sociability was largely self-contained. When the better-

Table I-8. Friendship Networks of White-Collar Workers, 1869

	IXᵉ Arrondissement		XVIIIᵉ Arrondissement	
Status of Friend	N	%	N	%
Manual Worker	16	12.1	55	28.9
White-Collar	61	46.2	91	47.9
Shopkeeper	18	13.6	34	17.9
Merchant	20	15.1	6	3.1
Bourgeoisᵃ	17	12.9	4	2.1
Total	132	99.9	190	99.9

Sources: A.D.S., V 4E, *Actes de mariage,* 1869.

ᵃ Included in this category are professionals, office heads, and property owners.

off clerks of central Paris went beyond their own milieu, they restricted contacts with workers and befriended propertied people, including wholesale dealers (*négociants*), rentiers, and liberal professionals as well as shopkeepers. For their part, the modest clerks were not only more open to working-class contacts but had more friendships with wage-earners than with propertied people.

Perhaps, before the decisive growth in scale and bureaucratization of commercial enterprises of the middle third of the nineteenth century, employees constituted a rather unified group. Stage in the life cycle was an important determinant of status in the office. However, the development of commercial firms and of public services of all sorts established important cleavages between modest and superior clerks. The pay and the work experiences of the two groups, issues we shall soon explore, underlay differences in comportment and culture. Arno Mayer has argued that a sense of "negative commonality"—being neither bourgeois nor working class—ultimately bound all employees together.[103] In the case of Parisian employees, it would be more accurate to view this psychology as a unifying force among modest white-collar workers, and one that separated them from the superior clerks. Humble employees borrowed symbols and values from working-class and bourgeois culture, but on their own terms.

SERVICE WORKERS

Paris between the Second Empire and the Republic of Clemenceau became a much wealthier city. The value of inherited property in 1911 was six times that of 1847.[104] Typically, increasing wealth led to a greater demand for services. So did the expansion of travel and the centralization of commercial activity. All these factors and more explain the burgeoning of service work. To group together thirty thousand coachmen, cabbies, and delivery men, sixty thousand restaurant cooks and waiters, ten thousand railroad and tramway workers, nine thousand butchers' assistants, twelve thousand café waiters, and still others is to create a highly artificial category, which can only be justified on pragmatic grounds. These workers lacked traditions of solidarity and shared only a few occupational interests. We can aggregate them only because of the unusual manner in which each group was integrated into the Parisian working classes.

When the offspring of cultivators kicked the soil from their clogs and came to Paris, many did not seek employment in workshops or factories, perhaps out of an aversion to the work routine or for lack of the requisite skills. An important alternative was to enter the dynamic service sector, which was better suited to their temperament and competence. It was also likely that they would earn more total revenue (in exchange for abnormally long hours) as waiters or moving men than as casual workers in industry. Françoise Raison-Jourde has described how immigrants from the most undeveloped areas of France, Basse Auvergne, Savoy, and the southwest, transformed themselves into that "modern" type, the cab driver, with relative ease.[105] The workers who took jobs in small retail outlets, as waiters, cooks, butchers, pork-butchers (*charcutiers*) often had hopes of social mobility in mind. Some thought of their work as a stage in their lives, not a permanent situation, for they aspired to self-employment. What proportion of workers was in this category is impossible to say, just as it is futile to try to measure their success in achieving ownership. The common perception was that such mobility was exceptional. Yet the proportion of aspirants was probably as large or larger than that of craftsmen who consciously aimed to make themselves into jobbers, subcontractors, or masters.[106]

Settling in the capital on a permanent basis and establishing a family there did not necessarily help to integrate service workers into the mainstream of working-class life. We see this at once by comparing the occupations assumed by service workers' sons with the jobs that day laborers' sons took. Unskilled laborers and service workers had in common rural roots and lack of involvement with craft traditions. The difference was that day laborers worked in manufacturing, in proximity to craftsmen, and this point proved to be significant. Whereas the large majority of their sons entered the Parisian trades, the sons of service workers remained outside manufacturing (see table I-9). The divergent occupational patterns may have resulted from differential opportunities to learn a trade or may simply have been a matter of adhering to familiar territory. In

Table I-9. Occupational Choices of Sons of Service Workers and Day Laborers

| | Fathers | | | |
| | Service Worker | | Day Laborer | |
Sons	N	%	N	%
Day Laborer	18	16.2	30	22.6
Service Worker	55	49.5	16	12.0
Craftsman	23	20.7	77	57.9
White-Collar	12	10.8	10	7.5
Other	3	2.7	0	0.0
Total	111	99.9	133	100.0

Source: A.D.S., D R[1], Recrutement militaire, Ninth, Twelfth, Thirteenth, Eighteenth arrondissements, 1869.

any case, it is clear that the prestige of craft skills—"that backbone of dignity," in the words of one mechanic—was not a strong sentiment in service laborers' spheres.[107]

The milieus from which service workers drew their friends similarly reflected a position of relative isolation from the laborers of the workshops (see table I-10). The decided underrepresentation of that group and the abundance of contacts with shopkeepers and small employers (and not simply their own employers) at the end of the Second Empire is striking. This pattern of friendships remained unaltered into the twentieth century. One might, perhaps, assume that such associations were forced upon the workers in retail shops, who were isolated by endless hours of toil in an environment of clients and bosses. In fact, tramway workers, our representatives of the transportation sector, had the same sort of sociable contacts.[108]

In the end, the position of service workers in Parisian society reveals some of the significance of the evolution toward a service economy in the last third of the nineteenth century. The manual laborers in commerce and transportation did not simply take the

Table I-10. Friendship Networks of Service Workers

| | 1869 | | 1903[a] | |
Friends	N	%	N	%
Manufacturing Worker	40	25.6	27	27.0
Service Worker	41	26.3	29	29.0
White-Collar Worker	22	14.1	11	11.2
Retail Merchant	48	30.8	29	29.0
Bourgeois	5	3.2	4	4.0
Total	156	100.0	98	100.2

Sources: A.D.S., V 4E, Actes de mariage, Thirteenth and Eighteenth Arrondissements, 1869; *Mairie* of Eighteenth Arrondissement, Etat civil, 1903.

[a] Data for 1903 are based upon records from only the Eighteenth Arrondissement.

place of manufacturing workers. They constituted a different sort of population, and they gave a new texture to the social structure of the capital.

The residents of Paris who lacked property and were dependent on the earnings from their humble jobs—those whom we are labeling the working people—did not comprise a homogeneous social group. The diversity among them was great, and the cleavages were sometimes quite pronounced despite the dependence that all the working population shared. Our task now is to observe whether these groups were converging toward a common life style or becoming more pluralistic as the forces of industrial and commercial capitalism and the rationalization of business procedures intensified in the late nineteenth century.

II
Material Conditions

The kinds of work people did for a living in greater Paris shifted subtly but decisively in the late nineteenth century. Did the outlook and life style of each group change, too, in the four tumultuous decades before the First World War? Part of the answer to this question depends upon the evolution of their material well-being and on their formulation of new material expectations. Capitalistic development and the growing activism of the state surely had an impact on these concerns.

WORKERS' GETTING AND SPENDING

Just before the nineteenth century ended, two prominent health experts, Octave Du Mesnil and Charles Mangenot, undertook an informative survey of living standards among the laboring poor in one section of the city.[1] Their study deserves more note than it has received, and not only for the obvious care that went into it. The doctors' inquiry was unusual in the locale chosen and in the sorts of workers included. Most Parisians would have thought of artisanal Belleville or the Faubourg Saint-Antoine as the appropriate territory to learn about material realities of working-class life. Instead, the doctors conducted their survey in the forgotten southeastern quarter of La Gare (Thirteenth Arrondissement), a part of the city that had once belonged to the suburban commune of Ivry-sur-Seine. Du Mesnil and Mangenot could hardly have chosen better if they had consciously intended to cover the broad range of laborers—factory, artisanal, and service—in the metropolitan area. The traditional Parisian types—construction workers, shoemakers, tailors, and artificers of "Parisian articles"—resided in La Gare. Beside them, though, were the hands from the huge Say sugar refinery, brakemen for the Paris-Orléans Railroad, tramway drivers, and mechanics who made automobiles for Panhard-Levassor. The doctors' investigation did justice to a half-century of economic evolution in the capital.

The findings of this survey pose a strong challenge to the superficial image of the late nineteenth century as an era of relative prosperity for the masses. The authors' calculations of daily per capita earnings show that a majority of working-class people had not yet escaped from the chronic shortages of life's necessities. Du Mesnil and Mangenot proposed that one franc was the minimum per capita income needed by a household each day to subsist without want and without assistance. This figure may be a bit too high, but is, all things considered, quite defensible.[2] Of the 1,266 households surveyed in La Gare, 751 (59.3 percent) attained this level of earnings. However, the smallest households were the self-sufficient ones so that individuals did not fare so well. Fifty-one percent of the people in the survey lacked the requisite one franc a day.[3] It would be possible to lift a majority of the residents into marginal self-sufficiency by lowering the threshold to ninety-five centimes. Yet the point remains that insecurity and deprivation had enormous scope at the turn of the century.

The pessimistic findings from the quarter of La Gare are confirmed by a government inquiry of 1907 concerning domestic shoemakers.[4] The report covered both the well-paid makers of luxury footware, the *bottiers*, and the specialized shoe assemblers, who were among the most exploited laborers in the capital. Of the 60 households considered, 43 (71.7 percent) earned one franc or more per member a day. Once again, though, the smallest households were favored, and only a bare majority, 53.5 percent, of the 202 individuals escaped want.[5]

The continued existence of so many laborers in the abyss of material need deserves attention because economic trends of the late nineteenth century were ostensibly favorable to rising living standards. Nominal wages rose substantially if irregularly then. Most of the progress came in the 1870s and just around the turn of the century. The standard indexes of pay levels show nominal wages rising over 50 percent between the Commune and the eve of the war.[6] In turn, some prices did attain some of their peaks for the century during the 1870s and early 1880s, but they then dropped steadily until around 1905.[7] These trends were not powerful enough to transform the living standards of wage-earners in a dramatic way.

Unemployment and underemployment were among the most important reasons why the proportion of workers who could not escape the abyss of want bordered on the majority. The measurement of job regularity remains an impossibility, but it is safe to say that frequent loss of work or reduced work was a certainty for laborers of all sorts, even the highly skilled. The leading manufacturing sector in Paris, the clothing trades, suffered notoriously steep variations in labor demand. A hatter or shoemaker could expect to earn half his yearly income during four months of sixteen-hour days.[8] Weekly earnings of tailors at the beginning of the twentieth century fluctuated between 45 and 140 francs a week.[9] Workers in other industries were only marginally more fortunate. Boilermakers had to travel to the Department of the Nord each summer during seasonal layoffs to earn money by repairing steam engines.[10] The Parisian Gas Company, which needed a vast labor for its plants, but only during the fall and winter, had no trouble finding hands put out of work in chemical plants, brickyards, and glassworks.[11] Employers in all trades counted on the "fear of winter" to discipline their unruly workers.[12]

Even the narrow elite of fully accomplished artisans enjoyed only a relative freedom from insecurity. Employers kept the craftsmen who would be hard to replace in their "core" labor force, which rarely suffered loss of a job in recessions.[13] Yet, underemployment was frequent. Masters gave their core workers tasks of mediocre quality to perform and paid them less than they earned when orders were numerous. Thus, one cabinetmaker who was at the apex of his trade did 154 days of artisanal labor at eight francs a day and 152 days of ordinary piece work, for which he earned only six francs a day.[14] The fruits of consummate skill were reaped for only part of the year.

The concentration of capital in plant and equipment characteristic of factory production did little in itself to stabilize employment. The labor force at the Cail Construction Company, the largest factory in the department, could fluctuate by several hundred from one quarter to another (see figure II-1). Such shifts in hiring at individual plants reduced industrial employment in Argenteuil from 2,433 jobs in December 1881 to 1,361 a year later.[15] It was no wonder that official documents stated factory size in terms of wide ranges, between nine and twelve hundred here, three hundred and seven hundred there. The dimension of a factory labor force was purely a matter of the moment. When layoffs came, as they inevitably did, they hit hard. The closing of a chemical plant in Saint-Denis in mid-March 1896 put 69 men out of work; 43 of them had not found new jobs by May 1.[16]

Rather serious recessions struck the Parisian labor force pe-

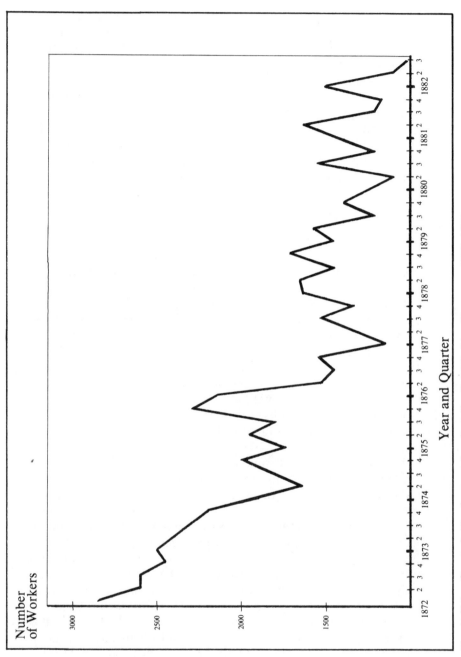

Figure II-1. Quarterly Employment Levels at the Cail Machine Company, 1872–1882
Source: A.P.P., B/a 901, Dossier: Usine Cail.

riodically: in 1878, 1883–1887, 1889, 1892, 1900, 1902, and 1908.[17] The harshest time of stress, the mid-1880s, was among the worst crises of the entire century. According to police reports, a quarter of construction workers, a third of the saddlemakers, a fourth of the bronze workers, and a majority of woodworkers were without employment at its deepest point.[18] The 1880s witnessed a genuine social crisis in the industrial suburbs. Morbidity and mortality soared; marriages were postponed, and birth rates dropped in the classic manner of demographic crises. One town council after another considered proposals to help their desperate residents redeem bedding from the pawnbrokers.[19]

Was there some mitigation of the harsh effects of work irregularity during the course of the late nineteenth century? The lack of serious employment indexes renders the response a delicate matter of guesswork. Yves Lequin found evidence of an improving situation in the silk industry of Lyons: Cyclical variations in production after 1890 were only a fourth as severe as they had been between 1850 and 1890.[20] The handicraftsmen of Paris operated in similar markets, so the possibility of extending Lequin's findings to them is tempting. Yet too many laments from both workers and employers about business conditions at the turn of the century preclude adopting the trend too firmly, if at all.[21] More convincing is the greater regularity of factory employment, as growth industries like bicycles, automobiles, and tires began to set the tempo of economic life. Significantly, the Parisian Gas Company began to experience difficulty in finding purely seasonal labor in the suburbs around 1901 and considered hiring a larger permanent work force to ensure its needs.[22] Some abatement of unemployment would have been a boon to workers, but in itself was not enough to reduce poverty on a grand scale.

Workers in many categories, even when employed, earned wages that were too small to provide security against want. The survey of the quarter of La Gare revealed the general poverty of female-headed households. Only one in three attained the levels of earnings needed for self-sufficiency. By contrast, 65 percent of the male-headed households escaped poverty. The superiority of male earnings meant only a limited well-being, however. Just over two-thirds of all households with four or more members in La Gare were needy, as were the 79.1 percent of the people in them. Such families were not at all "large" by conventional standards; but self-sufficiency was still an exceptional situation for them.[23] Moreover, even before old age, workers experienced declining wages (see table II-1). As wage-earners entered their late forties and their fifties—just as their households were reaching maximum size—their earnings were reduced.[24] The decrease was particularly dramatic for factory workers, un-

Table II-1. Daily Wages of Parisian Workers by Age Group, c. 1905–1910

	Age Groups				
	12–17	18–24	25–44	45–64	65+
Artisans					
Cabinetmakers	5.65	6.65	8.15	8.00	6.80
Joiners	1.50	7.25	8.45	8.25	6.55
Printers	4.10	6.25	8.05	8.90	8.50
Factory Workers[a]					
Turners	1.20	5.20	7.60	6.30	5.20[b]
Fitters	1.20	5.10	7.20	6.20	5.40[b]

Sources: Ministère du commerce, Office du travail, *Rapport sur l'apprentissage dans les industries de l'ameublement* (Paris, 1905), pp. 494–495; Office du travail, *Rapport sur l'apprentissage dans l'imprimerie* (Paris, 1902), p. 222; A.M. Puteaux, I 1. 128. III.

[a] This category is based on wage lists from the Dion-Bouton Automobile Company in Puteaux.

[b] There were only a handful of cases in this category.

doubtedly because piece rates readily responded to a loss of physical vigor. Even artisans found that accumulated expertise could not compensate for diminished force and dexterity, especially when their work entailed a larger share of physical exertion, as it did for woodworkers.

To reduce poverty a restructuring of the wage hierarchy was necessary, with the lowest-paid workers receiving the largest gains. The trend toward restructuring was, in principle, the inevitable result of economic maturation, but that trend was weak in greater Paris, and even negative for the largest category of workers there.[25] Highly skilled craftsmen received wage increases of about 55 percent in the forty years following the Commune. Day laborers achieved no more than this during the same period.[26] One continuous series of wage scales, covering the period 1855 to 1910, from the Joly Metallurgical Construction Company and its successor, Kessler-Gaillard, shows remarkable stabilities in wage differentials among skilled, semiskilled, and unskilled laborers.[27]

The crushing incidence of poverty among female-headed households in La Gare pointed to an evident source of hardship: the subsubsistence level of women's wages. If these earnings were catching up to men's pay at all in the second half of the nineteenth century, the pace was glacial and the progress, most incomplete. The magisterial public investigations of wages and industries in Paris of 1848, 1860, and 1893 do show that the earnings of women were rising faster than those of males—ever so slightly. In the half-century after 1848, women's average wages rose from 43 percent of men's income to 51 percent.[28] It is important to note, however, that these figures concerned the females who worked in middling and large shops. The 135,000 domestic laborers in the garment trades, for example, were underrepresented or totally omitted from these studies. There is certainly reason to believe that the earnings of such workers did not keep pace with the reported averages. Thus, even the small and slow gains toward a subsistence income that the surveys suggest may have been illusionary.[29]

The nearest approach to a general effort at wage restructuring benefited a few thousand service workers employed directly or indirectly by the Parisian municipal government. Whether the councilmen were actively seeking to make the municipality into a model employer or not, they did agree to pay living wages to their lowest grades of workers. Thus, sewermen (*égoutiers*) received 1,320 francs annually in 1880 and 2,365 francs in 1913, a 79 percent increase. In addition, these laborers gained an eight-hour day and an annual paid vacation of twelve days.[30] Such improvements were quite exceptional, however, even among workers in the public sector. The city did not use its public contracts to improve work conditions as much as laborers hoped or as much as employers feared. When it tried to do so, the provisions regarding workers were not always enforced.[31] In any case, these provisions generally concerned fringe benefits. like pay for a day of rest or overtime, rarely a matter of higher-than-market wages. It is true, as one economist argued, that the town council of Paris had some discretion over the work conditions of nearly sixty thousand laborers, but, in practice, only a very small portion of these were beneficiaries of progressive policies.[32]

The disproportionate wage gains of a few service workers were not at all the experience of the largest category of male workers, the specialized craftsmen. Learning about the earnings of this group is exceedingly difficult, and consulting the readily available documents and wage indexes will not do. These mistakenly assumed that the wage agreements of fully trained, often organized craftsmen were valid for the semi-artisans. It should be obvious that they were not.[33] Scattered figures drawn from strike records suggest a wage increase of no more than 25 or 30 percent between the 1870s and 1911 for specialized cabinetmakers, saddlers, jewelers, and tanners.[34] There is no particular reason to believe that the experience of these "small hands" was atypical. As we shall see, powerful market forces were limiting the wage gains that specialized craftsmen could expect.

Many laborers in this category clearly experienced economic maturation in the form of relative impoverishment. Their earnings dropped relative to common laborers, whose wages kept pace with those of the artisans. The skills of the specialized craftsmen did not permit them to earn more than factory operatives. The case of shoemakers allows for a rather telling comparison. Assemblers and finishers in the shoe factories at the dawn of the twentieth century performed, with machines, only a segment of the work that domestic workers did by hand. Yet, the factory laborers earned 6.5 francs a day whereas the handicraftsmen earned at most this amount, and often less. Moreover, the factory operatives were able to advance their earnings, whereas the semi-artisans had to struggle against reductions.[35] The use of personal skills at work put the traditional sorts of cobblers at a disadvantage in regard to earnings.

As the nineteenth century drew to a close, the French work force as a whole enjoyed rising incomes.[36] Parisian laborers began to lose some of their superiority in earnings over their provincial peers. Not surprisingly, migratory patterns were quick to respond to this trend. The failure of specialized craftsmen to participate as fully as other groups in wage increases was certainly an important reason for the weakening allure of the capital. The local manifestation of this national trend was the growing prosperity of the workers in suburban industry relative to craftsmen in the city. The machine-building industries brought wage increases that kept pace with those of the highly skilled workers in Paris and may possibly have created steadier employment conditions. Once again, migratory patterns quickly adjusted to the new economic realities by favoring the *banlieue* over Paris proper.[37] Provincials were sensitive to the ambiguity of material improvements within the capital during the late nineteenth century.

The incomplete victory over poverty realized in the four decades before the Great War was not conducive to altering consumer habits as far as the mass of workers was concerned. Spending was, for the most part, a matter of necessities—or choosing which necessities to purchase and which to forgo. A governmental study of eight hundred working-class budgets in 1907 found that families headed by unskilled or service workers probably spent more than 80 percent of their yearly earnings on food and rent; artisans devoted about 65 percent of their revenue to these items.[38] Contemporary observers commented on the development of new tastes among the laboring poor— for walking canes, tobacco, jewelry, fashionable clothing—but these items must have replaced, for the most part, other needed commodities.[39]

Most Parisian workers of the Third Republic were beneficiaries of the amelioration in diet that had occurred during the 1850s. Meat, wine, and dairy products became more abundant on wage-earners' tables. However, as in so many areas, the pace of change inherited from the Second Empire slowed, rather than accelerated, after 1880. In the case of meat and wine consumption, progress may have come to a standstill.[40] Any serious consideration of food consumption must separate the families with some hope for self-sufficiency from those whose efforts at coping were doomed to recurring failure. Budgetary studies of skilled workers' households reveal that the members enjoyed a varied diet and freedom from nutritional deficiencies.[41] Yet these investigations also illustrate with clarity that the tables of skilled workers were far sparser than those of even modest Parisian property-owners. Butchers brought into the city roughly 75 kilograms of meat per resident each year during the late nineteenth century; yet, artisans' families ate nothing approaching this amount.[42] A carpenter's household of five consumed only 165 kilograms in 1889; another such family of four purchased 150 kilograms. A highly proficient cabinetmaker and his four kin (three over the age of twelve) consumed 243 kilograms of meat and pork. The estimate of one prewar observer that the "average working-class adult" ate 400 grams of meat daily seems highly inflated, unless we admit that the laborer treated himself well at the expense of his offspring.[43] The cabinetmaker, for example, took his noon meal in a restaurant and ate soup, a meat dish with vegetables, salad, dessert, and wine. This case reminds us how little the working-class household was an egalitarian institution.[44] Predictably, only in expenditures on bread did craftsmen's families meet or surpass the citywide mean (about 150 kilograms a year). These households consumed strikingly less than the "average" amounts of eggs, fish, and butter.[45] Class differentials in eating had not at all disappeared, even as far as the more privileged Parisian workers were concerned.

Wage-earners with fewer skills, less regular work, and lower wages adjusted their eating habits accordingly. The different quantities of provisions brought to market in the suburban communes reflected rather important disparities between the meals of skilled workers and those of the poorly paid laborers at the dawn of the new century (see table II-2). The towns with a high percentage of industrial craftsmen and metalworkers, like Clichy and Puteaux, had

Table II-2. Annual Amount of Food (in Kilograms per Capita) Brought to Market in Suburban Communes (c. 1900)

	Meat	Fish	Fowl	Dairy	Vegetables and Potatoes
Pantin	10.3	2.5	3.5	4.2	39.3
Aubervilliers	9.4	2.0	1.9	2.1	13.8
Clichy	20.4	1.5	1.8	9.8	23.2
Puteaux	30.8	1.8	6.5	20.0	13.1
Choisy	15.4	2.8	3.9	5.1	33.8

Sources: Département de la Seine, *Etats des communes: Clichy* (Montévrain, 1903), p. 131; *Puteaux* (Montévrain, 1905), p. 117; *Aubervilliers* (Montévrain, 1900), p. 118; *Pantin* (Montévrain, 1901), p. 111; *Choisy-le-Roi* (Montévrain, 1902), p. 103.

public markets that were well supplied (relative to the eating habits of skilled workers) with meat and dairy products. Food merchants in the towns with many day laborers and with the basest industries, like Aubervilliers and Pantin, brought to market much smaller quantities of such items. On the other hand, retailers were prepared to sell large quantities of bread and potatoes in the latter towns. The family of one aged widow, a seamstress who earned two francs a day and had two children, presents a worst-case scenario. The members ate mostly carbohydrates and an occasional horsemeat steak; they never drank any wine. Free school meals saved the young son from hunger.[46] A family of ten, headed by a day laborer, provides another such scenario. These people ate soup, cheese, and bread, with an occasional meat platter on Sunday.[47] To speak of regular eating habits for the majority of workers is probably not accurate. Their meals altered with the state of seasonal (and cyclical) employment: a bit of meat during the busy season and carbohydrates at other times of the year.

The mass of workers did improve their diets in the course of the late nineteenth century, but these gains were not generally a matter of more of the quality items, like butcher's meat or wine. The laboring poor simply found it easier to purchase more calories, particularly in the form of carbohydrates. In Bezons, the residence of several hundred unskilled rubber workers, the bakers had ceased making "second-class bread" by the eve of the war.[48] The growth of cooperative consumer societies also helped workers stretch their food budgets. One government-sponsored study estimated a savings of 25 percent or more below normal retail levels for those who shopped in cooperatives—and many did.[49] They became a major element in food merchandising. Three thousand households out of about eight thousand in Puteaux in 1913 bought food at the local cooperative store, and a strike of its bakers created a serious crisis of provisioning.[50] Families with young children surely welcomed the creation and expansion of school lunch programs (*cantines scolaires*) during the 1880s and 1890s. These meals were usually more filling than nutritious—the average plate served at the schools of Clichy had no more than three ounces of meat—but they could provide a useful margin over hunger.[51] Workers struggling to stretch their budgets received their greatest help from the marketplace because the prices of bread and pastas dropped faster than food prices in general. They were, in fact, the only items for which price levels were lower in 1913 than in 1840. Rice and lentils also became more affordable, whereas potato prices fluctuated widely and dropped to relatively moderate levels only after 1880.[52] Such trends meant that filling minimal needs was somewhat easier even for the most disadvantaged workers.

As the journalist Jacques Valdour surveyed working-class neigh-borhoods, with their shops overwhelmingly devoted to serving ali-mentary needs, he concluded that "the constant preoccupation of workers is to eat and drink."[53] Valdour may ultimately have been correct about the central role of edibles in the laborers' consumer concerns, but he missed some significant and subtle changes at the margins of working-class life. The minority of wage-earners with some security and discretionary income quickly became accustomed to the emerging forms of mass consumerism, the department and the credit stores.[54] These workers applied for a line of credit at the Dufayel Department Store, so that they could acquire their "Crespin coupons" in exchange for fixed monthly payments. This new form of liquidity gave workers access to the sales counters of elegant emporia like Dufayel or Samaritaine as well as more mundane stores, like Place Clichy, Ville de Saint-Denis, Petit Saint-Thomas, Aux Classes Laborieuses, and several hundred smaller shops.[55] The list of indebted department-store consumers summoned before the *juge de paix* of the First Arrondissement in 1903 suggests an appreciable working-class participation in this form of consumerism. Printers, tailors, jewelers, and (female) hatmakers had been happy to "buy now" but were unable to "pay later." Wage-earners composed 35 percent of the residents in this district and 26 percent of the debtors.[56] Furthermore, credit buying and mixing with the bourgeois shoppers of the boulevards were not the exclusive privilege of the artisans in the luxury trades, who had traditions of stylishness and sensitivity to fashion. Merchants of bleak Saint-Denis discovered that their industrial population was all too happy to travel to Paris with its excess cash and make purchases at Dufayel or Place Clichy. In order to renew the loyalty of the consumer, local retailers had to initiate an ambitious credit plan of their own. In 1904 more than fifty stores created an "Economic Union of Saint-Denis," with its own version of the Crespin coupons, to compete with the alluring Parisian stores.[57] Insofar as the most prosperous workers developed a consumer ethic, their Socialist leaders encouraged, not reproved, them. *Humanité*, for example, praised the abundance and quality of merchandise at Dufayel, which, the journal claimed, permitted workers "to satisfy their needs without encumbering their budgets."[58]

These new shopping habits correctly suggest that workers' food purchases reflected less of what was novel and distinctive about the late nineteenth century than did their consumption of other items,

especially clothing. The market for secondhand apparel still flourished under the Second Empire, and the wage-earners who could
afford a new outfit had purchased good-quality articles destined to
last for years.[59] Gradually, though, the productive methods that were
transforming the handicrafts made relatively cheap clothes available
to workers. By the late nineteenth century, craftsmen and their families were likely to buy inexpensive articles and renew their wardrobes
frequently, while the poor would buy something new and hope it
lasted.[60] Two budgetary studies of Parisian carpenters, one from 1856
and the other from 1889, are often cited to show a stagnation in food
consumption. These same budgets, however, illustrate a striking evolution in the purchase of clothing.[61] The carpenters spent comparable portions of their incomes on apparel, but their buying habits
were different. The laborer of the late nineteenth century enhances
his work wardrobe with several articles that were not intended to
last more than a year or two. His wife bought cotton and wool dresses
each year as well as two skirts of cotton. The carpenter of the Second
Empire, on the other hand, expected apparel to be more durable.
Only the family's stockings and certain underclothing were likely to
be discarded soon. The wife's woolen and cotton dresses had to last
for five years. The carpenter of 1889 did have a holiday outfit that
was made to last, but even his Sunday pants, vest, hat, and coat were
not so expensive as the same articles owned by his counterpart of
the Second Empire, and they were not intended to endure so long.
The carpenter's family of the Third Republic did not necessarily have
a richer wardrobe, but it was more varied and undoubtedly more
sensitive to immediate fashion.

It is possible to assess the changes in working-class consumerism
by examining the profile of stores that served their needs.[62] The
social heterogeneity and lack of clear boundaries for neighborhoods
discourage this approach for Paris, but a working-class commune like
Ivry-sur-Seine offers a clear perspective on changing patterns of
spending. At the beginning of the Third Republic, Ivry had thirteen
thousand inhabitants and was still rather virgin territory for retailers.
Residents could satisfy their simplest needs in the eighty-seven retail
outlets listed in the commercial atlas but had to go to Paris for
specialized demands, to the extent they could afford any.[63] During
the ensuing forty years, the structure of retailing changed dramatically (see table II-3).

A central transformation was the vast increase in the number
of outlets, an increase that far outstripped the population growth in
Ivry. Ivry had nearly eight times as many stores in 1911 as in 1875.
The growing purchasing power behind this expansion suggests improved material conditions of the inhabitants, but more may be in-

Table II-3.   The Expansion of Retail Outlets in Ivry-sur-Seine, 1875–1911

	Outlets per 1,000 Inhabitants			Index of Growth (Number in 1875 = 100)	
	1875	1893[a]	1911	1893[a]	1911
All Outlets	5.8	—	20.6	251	322
Clothing	0.5	1.7	1.8	340	360
Unprepared Food	1.8	3.9	7.2	217	400
Home and Furniture	0.5	1.1	0.6	220	120
Butcher Shops	0.4	0.6	0.8	150	185
Drink & Prepared Food	1.7	—	7.7	—	453
Health, Leisure, and Recreation	0.3	1.4	2.1	466	700

Source: Bottin, *Annuaire du commerce Didot-Bottin*, 1875, 1893, and 1911.

[a] The number of restaurants and cafés is not available for 1893.

volved. As the population grew, so did that core of laborers with disposable incomes—the single, the highly skilled, and the fully employed. Once they formed a critical mass, stores sprang up in Ivry so that the privileged workers would not have to spend their money elsewhere. In this way, the multiplication of retail outlets exaggerated the improvements in living standards to some degree.[64] Not all kinds of stores expanded to the same extent, and the differential patterns of growth reflected the changing needs and tastes of that well-off core of wage-earners.

On the whole, the demands of consumers in Ivry were becoming more diverse in a number of ways. That clothing stores expanded more rapidly than retail outlets as a whole is not surprising. The price of apparel fell more quickly than the general cost of living, and, as we have seen, workers bought inexpensive garments that wore out quickly.[65] Over the late nineteenth century, the town attracted three hat shops, five jewelers, two corset shops, and two retailers of lingerie. Concerns about appearance also generated markets for hairdressers and barbers (25 in 1911) and for cosmetics (one). Thus, the retailers of Ivry were ever more able to help prosperous workers cut a figure for themselves on the streets. The tepid advance of commerce in household items seems to confirm the well-known thesis that workers spent their surplus cash on items not directed toward the home and family.[66] Stores for household furnishings and effects multiplied at a respectable pace up to the 1890s, but then declined in number, the only category to do so. Still, Ivry of 1911 supported a paint store, a framing shop, and an outlet for stoves. The most dynamic sector in retailing catered to recreational, health, and leisurely needs. Ivry of 1911 had two toy stores, a music shop, thirteen booksellers, and an outlet for fishing equipment. None of these specialized stores had existed at the beginning of the Third

Republic. Such additions to the commercial life of this working-class ghetto are noteworthy. They suggest that some laborers were seeking richer, more healthful lives. Yet they should not obscure the fact that the heart of the retailing boom in Ivry entailed commerce in food, both unprepared and ready-to-consume. The 16 dry-grocers' stores of 1875 had multiplied to 137 by the eve of the war, and 18 café-restaurants had become 246. Shops selling dairy products multiplied at the same pace as those catering to recreational tastes. Still rather basic were the needs of this industrial population.

Thus, the consumer habits of wage-earners in greater Paris underwent only modest innovations in the four decades before the war. Whereas the majority struggled to survive, a relatively affluent minority took advantage of the emerging instruments of mass consumerism. Their needs were still far from elaborate, but some workers were using their disposable incomes to enrich their lives and adorn themselves as their social superiors did. As workers at all economic levels aspired to higher incomes and more leisure, these concerns set the agenda for rising material standards.

WORKERS' HEALTH CONDITIONS

States of health do not readily reveal themselves to the historian—except in their most extreme form, as death rates. The bodily ailments of late-nineteenth-century workers must have been many and painful, so much so that they had to pursue their daily existence without giving heed to them. Yet there is excellent reason to believe that within the wide margin between physical well-being and mortal illness, the health of Parisians at that time was improving. Laborers of 1900 were probably stronger, freer from chronic disabilities, and better able to resist disease than their ancestors before the Commune. Correspondingly, they were able to work, reproduce, and face the harsh realities of their lives with a bit more ease.

The suburban town of Ivry was hardly noted for its comfortable conditions of life despite the expansion of its retail trade. Yet a medical survey of its schoolchildren in 1907 revealed a population that had largely escaped the chronic ravages of malnutrition and the ailments it spawned.[67] The medical and teaching personnel who participated in the survey found only 107 pupils out of 4,722 (2.3 percent) who suffered from a chronic disability. They classified only 2 students as undernourished, though they thought 6 others "debilitated, stunted, and thin." The eyes being especially sensitive to nutritional influences, 34 cases of "extreme myopia" signaled the existence of misery in Ivry.[68] In general, though, the bodies of these children seemed to have been notably free from the marks of privation and hardship. Was the traditional image of the working-class child of Paris—wan, emaciated, and disease-ridden—becoming a myth? Perhaps this survey must be taken as no more than a rough indication of improvements, but other documents leave little doubt that the amelioration was genuine.

The military recruitment records, a sensitive index of fluctuations in bodily health, demonstrate a major transformation in the physical well-being of young workers (see figure II-2). In the last years of the Second Empire, one in three working-class youths from the Eleventh or Nineteenth Arrondissement failed his medical examination. If he was a native of Paris, the likelihood of having some disqualifying debilitation was over 40 percent. Deformities, eye ailments, and "general weakness"—marks of the parents' inability to provide sufficient nutrients and a healthful environment—were the most common cause of exemptions. Declines from these levels of physical misery came quite soon after the Commune. No doubt the tightening of the conscription law in 1872 exaggerated the magnitude of the drop in exemptions, but the aftermath of the Commune was also a period of important improvements in real earnings. The declining rates of rejection also followed by almost exactly twenty years (the age of the conscripts) an appreciable amelioration in diet after the Hungry Forties. The decrease in rejection rates was continuous, so that by the eve of the Great War, those of eastern Paris were only a third of the levels they had been under the Empire. Significantly, native Parisian youths were, by then, healthier than boys of provincial origin.[69]

The industrial suburbs followed the health trends of eastern Paris, but with some unique features that reflected the special disadvantages of this population. Starting with the same high levels of exemptions, the suburban towns (represented here by Saint-Denis and Saint-Ouen) experienced improvements less rapidly and less completely than did the poorer quarters of the capital. The industrial dislocations of the 1880s hit these towns especially hard, undermining the physiques of their youths, whereas Paris experienced the economic crisis as a pause in the trend toward improvements. Only in the last decade of the century did suburban boys approach the low level of exemptions of their Parisian peers.

In order to discover just how thoroughly health improvements penetrated the working classes, we might follow the recruitment records of the most disadvantaged conscripts, those who were day laborers. Just after the Commune, the bodies of these boys were decidedly marked by the poverty of their backgrounds. After the economic disasters of the 1880s passed, however, they began to catch

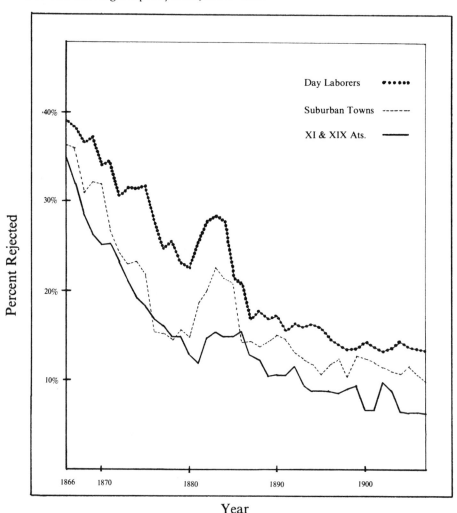

Figure II-2. Proportions of Working-Class Military Recruits Failing Their Physical
Examinations, 1866–1907
Sources: Préfecture de la Seine, *Annuaire statistique de la ville de Paris*
for the years 1880–1907; A.D.S., D R¹, Recrutement militaire: Saint
Denis and Saint-Ouen.

up to the health conditions of their peers. A differential still persisted
on the eve of the war, but the poorest segment of workers had been
largely liberated from the tragedy of chronic disablements, and this
happened at a faster pace than for better-off youths. Physical obstacles to a normal life style, once a fact of working-class life, were no
longer the common fate of even the poorest boys.

The dramatic disappearance of chronic, disabling conditions did

Table II-4. Heights of Military Recruits, 1869 and 1903

	% Less Than 1.6 Meters		% More Than 1.7 Meters	
	1869	1903	1869	1903
XIᵉ Arrondissement	17.9	3.3	12.7	18.9
XIIIᵉ Arrondissement	15.5	8.5	16.2	17.6
XIXᵉ Arrondissement	13.7	8.2	13.1	14.4
Ivry-*Canton*	22.6	14.8	17.1	28.9

Source: A.D.S., D R¹, Recrutement militaire.

not necessarily mean that workers enjoyed equally improved levels of bodily vigor and strength. A study of changing heights of conscripts warns us against excessively optimistic conclusions. As table II-4 illustrates, the average height of twenty-year-olds did increase; yet, the proportion of boys of above-average stature expanded little. The significant shift was the diminishing presence of abnormally short youths. What our two indexes of health seem to suggest is the lifting of the dreadful physical burdens under which workers had lived. Manual laborers did not achieve middle-class health standards before the war, but the most debilitating burdens of poverty had largely disappeared.

Parisian workers owed these physical improvements mainly to better nutrition. As our study of food consumption showed, wage-earners were probably not eating a richer diet, with more proteins and nutrients. Most chronic disablements, however, resulted from insufficient intake and required more calories, not more expensive food, to correct.[70] After the dietary improvements of the Second Empire, and their extension into the late nineteenth century, nutritional anemia was marginal. Workers were not eating well, but they ate enough to maintain normal bodily functions. Moreover, improving health had a cumulative effect. As mothers suffered less frequently from chronic conditions, they produced larger and stronger children.[71] Thus, relatively limited changes in diet had the salutary consequence of reducing the most debasing health conditions.

Though these alimentary changes were crucial in improving the health of workers, contributing factors were numerous. Working-class ghettos became at least marginally more conducive to healthful living. To give but one example, bakers gradually abandoned the use of water from contaminated wells to make their bread.[72] The schools of the Third Republic may have helped to raise standards of personal hygiene, too. Health depends on such a broad array of conditions that one cannot enumerate or evaluate all possible sources of improvement. What is clear is that the pathological conditions that overwhelmed workers in the first half of the nineteenth cen-

tury—deteriorating diets, overcrowding, infected neighborhoods—
were gradually reversed. Under the Second Empire, food intake
improved, and slowly, the Third Republic witnessed hard-won steps
toward a more healthful environment.[73]

Wage-earners had only a circumscribed control over the clean-
liness of their environment. Social observers found that wives kept
their homes at least moderately tidy even if they lacked the "house-
proud" concerns of their British counterparts.[74] The conscientious
housewife could do little, however, about moisture on the walls, lack
of air, or impure water. Workers' dependence on public authorities
in many essential areas of hygiene was complete. While the steps
necessary to make Paris a more healthful city were widely recognized
by the time of the Commune, meaningful activities in this direction
were minimal during the 1870s. The forces of inertia were overwhelming. Landlords insisted on their rights over private property,
and workers feared that improvements in housing and in neighborhoods might make them too costly. Spokesmen for public health
lacked effective arguments to counter this resistance and explain their
causes to the politically powerful in terms that would stir them to
action. The general indifference or fierce opposition to public health
measures that had troubled Baron Haussmann was still the rule a
decade after the Commune.[75]

Medical disasters and scientific discoveries turned the 1880s into
an era of transition in which the long-standing inertia weakened. The
fetid evening odors that became a new feature of Parisian life in 1880
reminded residents of the sanitary perils that surrounded them.[76]
Typhoid, diphtheria, scarlet fever, whooping cough, and measles,
which had been relatively insignificant for several years, suddenly
became fearsome scourges in the early years of the decade.[77] At the
very time that these diseases struck with renewed force, scientists
were inaugurating the bacteriological era of medicine by isolating
the pathogenic sources of infection. The germ theory that emerged
from laboratories provided an invaluable battery of arguments for
renewed vigor in attacking a filthy environment. The medical advances pinpointed the cause of diseases and emphasized that not
even the well-off were free from danger if a large, infected population
existed.[78] Within a few years, genuine concern about France's population levels added urgency to all life-saving endeavors. Substantial
hygienic improvements required huge sums of money, however, so
that a favorable climate of opinion brought important initiatives, but
not thoroughgoing change.

Acceptable housing for workers was an old concern, and by the
eve of the war this issue came to epitomize the workers' quest for

improved health. For most of the late nineteenth century, however, the struggle for gains generated idealism, energetic leadership, thousands of pages of empirical investigation, and few concrete results. There was no consensus on what sort of housing workers should have and no enthusiasm for the expenditures necessary to provide new lodgings on a massive scale. Even the more modest task of inspecting the existing stock of housing and enforcing set standards was not readily accomplished, for laws gave the public official little real authority.[79] In the suburbs, no town government, no matter the political persuasion, had placed restrictions on tenement development. The Radical alderman of Saint-Ouen admitted in 1905 that past administrations, including both Socialist and Radical ones, had "tolerated the construction of certain buildings that one is embarrassed to see inhabited by human beings."[80] Not until then did this town institute meaningful housing regulations. At the very same moment, the councilmen also confronted the central predicament of housing reform: Were substandard lodgings better than none at all, or than those workers could not afford? The municipal council declared its intention to license buildings that failed to meet the newly promulgated regulations.[81]

Public authorities had more control over the water supply and over the sewer systems than over the housing stock, so possibilities for improvement were greater. This was fortunate, for providing clean water was a rapid and sure way to reduce mortality.[82] Water-carried disease, like cholera and typhoid, normally caused hundreds of deaths a year in Paris. Residents of the capital had access to either spring water or to filtered river water (from the Seine or Marne rivers or from the Canal de l'Ourcq). Spring water was irreproachable from a hygienic perspective, but it was scarce and expensive. Water from springs went mainly to residents who paid for private distribution. About a third of the capital's residential buildings lacked water conduits in the 1880s, and these, no doubt, were the lodgings that most workers could afford. The public fountains were sources of water for wage-earners. Spring water was available at some fountains, but until the close of the century, most workers drank filtered river water, barely acceptable from the hygienic point of view.[83] Class divisions in Paris, thus, had a hydrological dimension.

Provisioning the home with water was one more struggle for working-class housekeepers, and the authorities did not hasten to reduce the difficulties. Rarely was there more than one fountain per fifteen hundred residents in working-class quarters, whereas the administrative standard was one per five hundred residents. The multiplication of provisioning facilities barely kept pace with population increases, and sometimes failed to do even this. The number of residents per fountain in Belleville (Twentieth Arrondissement) increased substantially between the 1880s and the twentieth century. It changed little in La Villette (Nineteenth Arrondissement), and fell a bit in the Thirteenth.[84] The scarcity of fountains meant that the plight of one resident of southeastern Paris, who had to go two hundred meters for water, was all too common.[85] The prefecture did, at least, endeavor to improve the quality of the water that the humble drank. Money was spent for more effective filtering systems, and slowly, the proportion of fountains provisioned in spring water rose. By the end of the nineteenth century, the quality of water for the masses was no longer among the capital's pressing hygienic problems.

The burgeoning towns of the industrial suburbs were woefully behind Paris in their search for pure water, and their mortality rates bore proof of this. During the 1880s, the per capita expenditure on water in Choisy-le-Roi, Saint-Denis, and Saint-Ouen was half that of Paris and a third that of a bourgeois town like Neuilly-sur-Seine.[86] Yet the industrial communes received what they paid for. No spring water flowed through the municipal pipe lines, not even to paying customers. They, and the public fountains, received water from the Seine River. To make matters worse, the private company provisioned these towns with water drawn from a point *downstream* from Paris, near Epinay. The claim of the aldermen of Argenteuil that their constitutents were practically drinking Parisian sewer water was not just shrill rhetoric, for the pumping station was downstream from one of the principal sewer collectors and at a point where the Croult River carried waste waters from the factories of Saint-Denis. Not until 1888 was this town able to negotiate a new contract with the water company and stipulate that its provisions must come from the Oise River.[87] Residents of Saint-Ouen had to wait until 1902 before they could expect to drink water drawn exclusively upstream from Paris.[88] The cost of decades of impure water in terms of high mortality must have been formidable.

The hygienists of the suburbs were quick to point out that river water, however bad, was not the most dangerous source of infection. The many residents who used well water exposed themselves to great risks.[89] Wells bore the danger of contamination from nearby cesspools, especially since landlords often allowed putrefying matter to accumulate. In 1895 the prefect claimed that the *banlieue* had 33,000 wells in close proximity to all too rarely emptied cesspools.[90] Furthermore, the industrial towns had to be concerned about effluences from chemical, fertilizer, and tanning plants entering the water supply or intoxicating the soil, which filtered the ground water. Despite these dangers, 71 percent of the residential buildings of Saint-Denis relied partly or completely on well water at the close of the nineteenth century.[91] Thus, the suburban municipal councils had to accept the dual mission of reducing dependence on well water and of improving the quality of river water even as they made it more available. Neither change occurred very swiftly.

The suburban towns, disadvantaged relative to the capital, had pronounced internal inequities deriving from the manner in which they were settled. The towns grew around urban nodes that contained and continued to attract shopkeepers, commuters, *rentiers*, and white-collar workers. Factories and wage-earners settled in the outskirts of these nuclei, in areas totally lacking in amenities. Thus, the population of Ivry-Center was 54 percent working class, while that of Ivry-Port was 86 percent in the 1890s.[92] In quarters like Ivry-Port, La Plaine in Saint-Denis, or Michelet in Saint-Ouen, wells were the sole source of water. To avoid the threats they placed upon health imposed great hardships. In one peripheral area of Saint-Ouen, housewives had to line up with their pots and buckets to collect filtered river water at 5 A.M., when street sweepers opened the faucets (*bouches d'eau*) intended to clean the pavement.[93] These working-class ghettos within working-class towns were naturally the principal stalking grounds of epidemic diseases, and they had mortality rates well above the high level of the central quarters.[94]

The best way to remove purtrefying matter was another subject of rancorous debate.[95] The goal of quick, odorless, and complete transportation of waste was not easy to realize. In the 1880s the overwhelming majority of residential buildings were served by fixed or mobile cesspools that had to be cleaned manually, a process that was odoriferous and that left streets and courtyards festering with residues. Moreover, there was no guarantee that landlords would pay to have the cesspools cleaned frequently enough; by all reports, owners of tenements usually did not. Spurred on by the epidemics of the 1880s, the state administration studied the numerous options for waste removal and decided upon using the sewers to transport both street water and night soil. The project, known as "all to the sewers" (*tout à l'égout*) promised to remove waste quickly in a closed system that did not threaten street surfaces with infection nor leave water closets in a deplorable state. The plan, highly controversial from a number of perspectives, ostensibly triumphed in 1894, with a law requiring all Parisian houses to adopt this system. Neither the legislators nor the courts granted powers to compel landlords to conform, however. Connections to the sewer did multiply—the result of demands from well-off renters for hygienic lodgings, not of administrative fiat.[96] As in the case of housing, market forces by no means ensured improvements for the laboring poor. In 1904, 40 percent of all water closets in Paris disposed of excrement directly into the sewer system; in the working-class ghetto of La Roquette (Eleventh Arrondissement) the portion was only 19.7 percent.[97]

The authorities in the industrial suburbs were not able to match even this glacial progress. A self-contained system of water disposal was not a possibility in these towns because the sewer lines were insufficiently extensive. The portion of street surface served by sewers around the turn of the century ranged from 46 percent in Saint-Denis to 10.8 percent in Alfortville.[98] The cost of extending the sewer system not only remained an obstacle to sensible improvements but also pushed aldermen into adopting, in haste, unworkable sanitary projects that had economies as their principal benefit. Induced by the hope of avoiding the expense of sewer construction, the councilmen of Levallois-Perret and Argenteuil adopted a highly controversial proposal allowing a private concern to build a pneumatic disposal system. They did so after the Parisian municipality and the prefecture had dismissed the plan as unworkable. Predictably, the private company was utterly unable to deliver on its promises, and the industrial towns were that much further behind on sewer construction.[99]

In the end, public authorities developed only a few ways to bring decisive sanitary improvements to those who could not pay for them. Humid walls, airless rooms, fetid odors, and inferior drinking water were still the conditions that workers had to endure—and, we believe, with an ever greater sense of grievance.

Efforts to improve the healthfulness of urban life were closely tied to the ideals of preventive medicine. Public health officials at the close of the nineteenth century believed that they could not only treat diseases but also show residents how to avoid illness and premature death. They undertook vigorous programs of public education designed to replace customary behavior with scientific precautions. The new medical institutions they created were accessible to needy people and active in disseminating the precepts of preventive medicine. Ultimately, this process of reeducation transformed popular prejudices about disease into an indictment of existing social arrangements.

The laborers of the Seine Department were rather privileged in having access to medical expertise. Eight hospitals gave free care or consultations to the workers who sought their aid.[100] City halls generally provided free medical attention for the indigent and weekly or monthly opportunities for consultations. The personnel of large firms might have access to care through mutual aid societies or company doctors. One middle-class social observer who investigated the living standards of a wage-earning household was surprised by the seriousness its members accorded to the advice of their doctor.[101] Nonetheless, working-class people visited doctors mainly in emergencies, and often the only advice that physicians could impart was beyond the means of wage-earners to implement.[102] Hygienists understandably aspired to improve health by preventing the contraction of disease. Two areas in particular seemed susceptible to this approach: combating infant mortality and tuberculosis.

Saving the lives of the newborn engaged much moral fervor and patriotic energy among community leaders in the last decade of the nineteenth century. The ideal of reaching working-class mothers, dispelling their customary notions about nursing, and retraining them in sound, scientific methods was an appealing one. To this end, hygienists created a network of neighborhood dispensaries to which mothers could bring their children. Here, medical personnel examined babies and counseled parents on how to care for them properly, especially how to prevent the intestinal ailments from which so many infants died. Paris received its first clinic in 1881, on the rue Jean Lanier in the Fourth Arrondissement, and after the municipal council appropriated a hundred thousand francs for the purpose, others followed.[103] Between 1887 and 1895, twenty-four dispensaries were created in the capital. They were generally well situated to reach the most disadvantaged residents. The popular Eleventh and Nineteenth arrondissements had three each; altogether, eighteen clinics served the poor, peripheral arrondissements.[104] Furthermore, charitable impulses and fear of population decline motivated social leaders to create a host of support institutions that were also dedicated to the purpose of training working-class parents in the science of puericulture. By the eve of the war, the Eleventh Arrondissement alone had three consultation centers, a day-care service with a nursing room, a soup kitchen for pregnant mothers, and at least nine agencies providing free milk, free layettes, and financial aid so that working mothers could rest before giving birth.[105]

These institutions were only part of a highly successful infant-saving campaign, however. The dispensaries could not have been effective without the active and intensive cooperation of working-class mothers, and spokesmen for preventive medicine certainly received this. Poor mothers showed an enormous receptivity to the life-saving efforts that the medical profession was willing to bring to them. One lecturer on puericulture attracted four hundred mothers at Ivry in 1892.[106] The annual number of consultations at the newly created dispensaries inevitably ran ahead of the number of newborn, indicating that a visit to the clinic had become a routine part of maternal care.[107] The proximity of medicalized nursing institutions was not necessary to reduce infant mortality, as the case of Bezons shows. Because it was a small town on the outer edge of the suburban ring, it did not receive attention from medical elites. No dispensaries or milk-distribution bureaus were here. Yet, infant mortality dropped 46 percent between 1881–1885 and 1901–1905.[108] Evidently, the working-class mothers of this manufacturing town sought medical advice, which was not made readily available to them. The example of Bezons shows that the participation of working-class mothers in reducing infant mortality was not just a matter of cooperation with scientific experts; it was the fundamental element.

The maternal concern reflected in falling infant mortality rates marked an occasion for frustrations as well as a sense of victory. Having learned to keep infants alive, mothers must have been anguished by the frequent loss of their young children. Mortality rates for children ages one to four were nearly as high, and in some periods higher, than those for nurslings.[109] One longitudinal study of 557 children born in the quarter of Gobelins (Thirteenth Arrondissement) in 1891–1893 showed that 136 of them died in infancy, and 120 perished between the ages of one and nine.[110] Unfortunately, working-class mothers could not achieve the same success in saving youngsters that they did for their newborn. The gravest threats to the health of young children were environmental; they needed clean streets and neighborhoods, and pure water, all of which were beyond the power of poor parents to provide.[111] The mortality rates of youngsters between the ages of one and four rose in the first decade of the twentieth century, and those of children ages five to nine rose notably.[112] As mothers sought to protect the lives of their youngsters, they quickly ran into frustrations from a social and political system that responded very inadequately to their needs. For this problem, the cooperative doctrines of the preventive hygienists were insufficient.

A similar, and perhaps deeper, sense of blockage and frustration arose from the other massive campaign of the preventionists, against tuberculosis. Until the last decade of the nineteenth century, this, the most common killer of adults, met with quiet resignation from the populace and silence from doctors. Belief in a hereditary disposition to tuberculosis lingered even in medical circles despite the scientific evidence that had been accumulating since midcentury in support of the contagious nature of the disease and despite Koch's isolation of the pathogen in 1882. The popular counterpart of the medical prejudices was a tradition that viewed the disease as a mark of shame, of family taint, and of social inferiority. After 1890, however, many physicians were ready to crusade against tuberculosis, which they now recognized as preventable through simple steps.

Their campaign, formalized by the formation of the Society for Preservation against Tuberculosis in 1899, was fundamentally educational. Hygienists taught that more nutritious foods, warmer clothing, abundant fresh air, sunshine, and above all, better housing, could save workers from the scourge.[113] Doctors lacked, however, a response to the obvious objection that workers could not afford these preemptive measures. They were able to avoid the conclusion that workers suffered from tuberculosis because they were poor rather than because they were immoral by stressing the supposed links between consumption and alcoholism. Yet, it seems clear that the preventive approach to tuberculosis raised the social question in a new and pressing form, and socialists were quick to insist on the matter.

One way in which the new understanding of tuberculosis penetrated into working-class culture was, as with puericulture, through dispensaries. Following infant clinics by a decade and multiplying at a slower rate, the antitubercular dispensaries provided free consultations, lectures, and preemptive care. Workers' receptivity to these institutions was immediate and cordial. The Jouye-Tanies dispensary in Belleville gave nearly 4,000 consultations a year.[114] The industrial suburbs had only one antitubercular clinic in 1906 (in Saint-Ouen), but all public authorities endeavored to found them, so there were at least five by the war. The newly created unit in Saint-Denis cared for 2,300 people in 1913.[115] These clinics indirectly propagated the message that the way of life workers could afford was at the root of tubercular infection.

Laboring people also gained insights into the nature of the disease and its relation to their poverty through means that were meant to be therapeutic, not instructional. As the disinfection of the lodgings and the effects of the tuberculosis victims became routine in the 1890s, the appearance of the sanitary operators excited the concern and imagination of workers.[116] In Saint-Ouen, disinfection teams complained of being hampered by large crowds of neighbors who badgered them with questions, spread rumors of epidemics, and even clamored against landlords.[117] A letter from one widow who had lost her husband, a tailor, to consumption illustrates the shift in the popular comprehension of the disease. The widow wrote to the mayor of Saint-Ouen in 1899 that she and her three children needed temporary lodgings until their home could be disinfected; otherwise, she noted, "we will surely catch the deadly disease, which is said to be very contagious." Significantly, her neighbors were pressing her to carry out the disinfection at once for fear of catching the illness.[118] By the commencement of the twentieth century disinfection was no longer a frightening operation; workers routinely expected it after the funerals of their departed.[119] Evidently, resignation before this scourge had given way to a quest for protection from it.

Medical elites were traditionally quick to denounce the benightedness of the masses, but at the end of the nineteenth century they reported success in communicating with laboring people. Doctor Dubousquet of Saint-Ouen was convinced that the municipal efforts to instruct residents about contagious diseases had been fruitful. Working-class parents boiled water in times of cholera epidemics and redoubled efforts to keep their homes clean.[120] Doctor Courgey of Ivry observed that workers, especially of Ivry-Port, were ever more sensitive to the squalor of their housing and lack of pure water and aspired to better conditions.[121] The judgments of these physicians were confirmed by the surfacing of health improvements and preventive medicine as a major political issue. "Questions of social hygiene are the top priority of all public powers," proclaimed the Radical aldermen of Saint-Ouen in 1908.[122] They, themselves, had introduced the first housing code and tried to ameliorate the water supply, but their opposition to the Left, the Socialists, successfully capitalized on the electors' rising health concerns. In 1912 Socialists captured most city halls in the industrial sectors of the *banlieue*, and their campaigns were devoted in large degree to matters of hygiene and housing.[123] Posters from one commune implied that a vote for the Radicals was a ballot in favor of the propagation of tuberculosis.[124] Once in power, the Socialists addressed public health concerns on a variety of fronts. They pressured the water company to provide as many public fountains as their contracts stipulated. Councilmen set aside funds for the construction of bath houses and laundries. Intent on offering children the opportunity to leave their blighted neighborhoods for the countryside, they expanded vacation camps. The centerpieces of their programs were ambitious housing projects because these epitomized working-class sanitary needs and because rising rents were an emotional concern of the period. In one of the emerging centers of the automobile industry, Puteaux, the newly elected aldermen had made a solemn commitment to improve housing. They were prepared to devote half a million francs to a substantial project.[125] The Socialist councilors of Saint-Ouen broke ground on a development that was to have 110 subsidized "hygienic dwellings," a large bath house, and a recreational center.[126] For all their rhetoric and good intentions, the officials of the extreme Left were unable to offer more than symbolic gestures and marginal improvements in public health. The very agenda they helped to create was far beyond the financial means of any public power.

Ultimately, medical preventionists may have succeeded more than they ever intended in educating the laboring poor about the social aspects of disease. Working people were receptive to their message and developed a sense of the right to enjoy good health.[127] What workers learned from hygienists inevitably led them to demand more from the social system than it could provide. Health concerns became one more argument among others for social reorganization.

EMPLOYEES' STANDARDS OF LIVING

The earnings and the living standards of manual workers were public issues in a way that those for white-collar employees were not. Consequently we know considerably less about the material conditions of the salaried personnel. Moreover, a clerk's "pay" was a complex package of salary, fringe benefits, commissions, and intangibles, like status and security. Capturing a sense of the salary hierarchy is exceedingly difficult but, fortunately, is not necessary for our purposes. We need only seek an understanding of what the modest employee, who could aspire to only a mediocre position, was likely to earn. For a first approach to this issue, it would be well to examine the job openings announced in a prominent occupational journal, *L'Employé*. Even though this was the organ of a conservative, Christian union with deep roots in the prosperous sectors of the clerical labor force, the 2,700 openings in 1907–1909 paid quite modest salaries (see table II-5). Three-fourths offered less than 1,800 francs a year, less than the wages a skilled laborer might have expected if he worked regularly. Some were so low because room and board (a sleeping place on the store floor or counter?) were provided. Yet, even jobs requiring experience and special expertise did not entail particularly large pay. A bookkeeper who knew both English and German "perfectly" was offered only 150 to 200 francs a month, and employers regularly sought "fully trained accountants" for 200 francs a month.[128]

The records of the Workers' Arbitration Council (*Conseil de prud'hommes*), to which employees brought 2,300 complaints in 1910,

Table II-5. Monthly Salaries (in Francs) for Clerical Positions Reported in *L'Employé*, 1907–1909

Salary	Number of Jobs	% Jobs
25–99	1,236	45.9
101–149	759	28.2
150–199	602	22.4
200–249	56	2.1
250+	39	1.4
Total	2,692	100.0

Source: L'Employé, no. 167 (5 mars 1908), p. 48; no. 190 (5 février 1910), p. 24.

Table II-6.   Salaries (in Francs) of White-Collar Workers from the Records of the Workers' Arbitration Council, 1910

Category		Number of cases	Average Annual Income
Bookkeepers and Office Clerks	Male	112	2180
	Female	79	1260
Accountants		136	2520
Stenographers-Typists (female)		76	1550
Purchasing Agents and Commercial Representatives		64	4200
Insurance Agents		21	3100
Salesclerks	Male	41	870[a]
	Female	30	580[a]

Source: A.D.S., D 2 U^{10} nos. 4–6.

[a] These figures do not include commissions on sales.

allows us to place these modest salaries into a larger perspective. A clear bifurcation of revenues emerges from this source (see table II-6).On the one hand, senior employees at insurance companies, commercial representatives, and purchasing agents had incomes that clearly surpassed those even the elite of manual workers could have hoped to earn. Also in this category, but not included in the records of the council, were undoubtedly senior bank employees and the salesmen at the quality department stores. On the other hand, a great many positions paid much less. Routine office workers, bookkeepers in small offices, and salespeople in stores with a popular clientele earned what skilled workers might, or less. The description *L'Employé* gave of bookkeepers "vegetating, cursing their fate, in positions at 150, 175, or 200 francs a month" accurately portrays many thousands of modest white-collar workers.[129] The humble employee was not strongly differentiated from the better-off manual workers in terms of potential earnings.

The remuneration of female employees was somewhat different in this regard. Their income was consistently above that earned by female manual laborers. A typist-stenographer of ordinary ability had every chance of commanding the same salary as that of even the finest seamstresses who worked in the fashion houses of the rue de la Paix.[130] The saleswomen at Printemps who took home more than two thousand francs in salary and commission per year were surely among the best-paid females in Paris.[131] Moreover, the differential in potential earnings between men and women was not so great in sales as in manufacturing. This was because comparable training and work experience in sales were possible in ways that were not in industry. The office stood somewhere between the workshop and the department store in terms of the earnings' differential. In this environment, women began with salaries close to those of their male peers, but experience worked to the disadvantage of females. In one major bank, entering women earned 75 percent of the starting pay for men; by the time both groups were in their thirties, women earned only 57 percent of the average salary for males.[132]

Did employees fall behind manual laborers as the earnings of the latter group rose? Some historians cite the impoverishment of clerks relative to laborers as a reason for the radicalization of employees at the end of the nineteenth century.[133] Many more studies will be needed and many more documents must be uncovered before it will be possible to construct the general salary indexes needed to test this claim. At best, we can present the pay scales in a few bureaucracies and depend on them to suggest a common trend (see table II-7). The advances in salaries and wages made by the personnel of the Northern Railroad Company, the Parisian Gas Company, and the municipality of Puteaux cause us to question the claims of relative

Table II-7. Indexes of Wage and Salary Gains in Three Administrations

	100 = pay level circa 1900		
	Northern Railroad Company		
Year	Station Clerks	Mechanics	Shop Workers
1894	100.4	98.2	107.9
1898	100.9	98.1	101.3
1903	109.0	98.1	97.5
1908	116.3	98.0	107.5
1910	118.3	101.4	117.0
1912	129.0	108.5	125.0
	Parisian Gas Company		
	Manual Labor	Employees	Office Heads
1872	72	72	—
1875	—	—	59.5
1886	87	90.2	88.0
1892	94	92.2	94.4
1896	95	94.6	96.0
1900	—	100.0	100.0
1901	100	—	—
	Commune of Puteaux		
	Road Menders	Employees	Head Clerk
1873	62.4	63.2	46.2
1879	70.1	68.4	57.7
1885	80.5	73.7	84.6
1897	100.0	100.0	100.0
1912	137.1	135.8	130.8

Source: François Caron, *Histoire de l'exploitation d'un grand réseau. La Compagnie du chemin de fer du Nord* (Paris, 1973), p. 322; A.M. Puteaux, D, I. 10; A.D.S., V 8 O¹ nos. 149, 153.

immiserization for clerks. Furthermore, though management seemed to reward their employees with the same size pay increases that laborers received, clerks also benefited from some important gains in fringe benefits, like vacations or free provision of coal. These gains did not necessarily mean that white-collar workers had to view their financial position with equanimity. There is no reason to believe that wage-earners were the sole or the primary group with whom clerks compared their well-being. It would have been surprising if modest employees did not use supervisors and managers as a reference group; and, in this regard, the clerks had more cause for chagrin. Their gains seemed to have been outdistanced by those of their supervisors, if the case of the Parisian Gas Company is typical.[134] Since social status was increasingly a purchasable commodity, this situation could not have been comfortable for employees whatever their position relative to laborers.[135]

In any case, direct comparisons between manual and clerical workers ring false until the issue of security is considered. Mature employees did not usually suffer a loss of earnings as a result of sickness or seasonal recession. Far from experiencing a diminution of earnings with age, many clerks could expect promotions, if modest ones, and the comforts of a pension. There were, however, numerous employees who did not enjoy a full share of this security. Young salespeople had to expect a change of jobs several times before finding a lasting situation. At Bon Marché, a substantial majority of the employees were not with the company five years later. These salesclerks and their colleagues experienced much anxiety as they approached their thirtieth year. The large retail outlets did not usually hire clerks over that age, with the result that if an employee had not succeeded in finding permanent position by then, he or she was condemned to the low earnings and insecurity characteristic of employment in neighborhood stores.[136]

Clerical work in small offices and in manufacturing firms had many insecurities, too. *L'Employé* proclaimed that bookkeepers or accountants worked hard without recognition from the boss and frequently lost their jobs just as old age rendered them unable to find a new post.[137] The journal's melodramatic lamentations, "he finishes by dying in misery," does, in fact receive some confirmation from the records of the Workers' Arbitration Council. This body received five times as many complaints of unjust firings from office workers as from salesclerks (and more from saleswomen than from salesmen). Nor did bosses appear to have been especially respectful of age or seniority. Half of the accountant-bookkeepers (*comptables*) fired were over thirty years of age, and a third had been in their jobs for at least eight years.[138] Security was not an unreasonable expectation for humble white-collar workers, but it was far from universal.

Employees never measured their salaries in terms of the requirements for subsistence, and they did not wish others to do so. The clustering of their residences on particular streets in working-class quarters betokens a standard of housing that was higher than that of most workers. So, too, were the employees' expectations in regard to their food and, especially, their clothing.[139] In an effort to capture the employees' subjective appreciation of their revenue, we shall do well to consider the situation at the Parisian Gas Company. In 1892 the director stated that 2,700 francs was a minimum living salary for his clerks and that he hoped to promote his personnel as quickly as possible to that level.[140] Not only did the unionized employees accept this target figure without protest, but a decade later, *L'Employé* placed the minimum salary necessary for an employee with a family at a comparable figure, 3,000 francs.[141] The general expectation, then, for employees was an income on which a bit more than a third had to be devoted to food. Employees apparently hoped to live in lodgings that might have cost about the "average" Parisian yearly rent of 500 francs and to spend at least modestly on wardrobe and leisure. Were such expectations likely to be met?

Though the director of the gas company was correct about the income clerks felt they needed, he was surprisingly out of touch with the salary scales of his firm. Clerks did not rise to salaries of 2,700 francs, not quickly, and not at all in most cases (see figure II-3). Over three-fourths (77.7 percent) of the 2,300 white-collar workers earned less than this figure. In fact, this "living income" was the very level at which the hierarchy of earnings narrowed decisively, so that most employees could not expect to attain 2,700 francs even after a lifetime of service. The indications are that the salaries paid by the gas company were in line with those of other administrations. The station chiefs who worked for tramway companies earned no more than 2,400 francs, and only one in six was at this level.[142] At a large Parisian bank, it was possible to earn more than the living salary level in 1914, but the average pay (for employees over the age of twenty-two) was only just above it, 2,764 francs.[143] Similarly, the clerks who attained the highest grades of the Municipal Duties Administration (*Octroi*) earned up to 3,400 francs in 1910, but just one in five had an income over 3,000 francs.[144] Some serious voices even raised doubts about the earnings of the employees who were reputedly the best paid, the department-store clerks. The *Journal des employés* argued that the average salesclerk earned nothing like the 3,500 or 4,000 francs often attributed to them. Salaries (com-

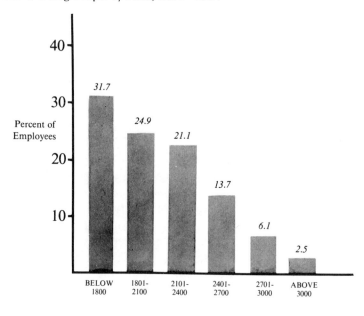

Annual Salaries *(francs)*

Figure II-3.   Profile of Salaries Paid by the Parisian Gas Company, 1891
Source: A.D.S., V 8 0¹ no. 153.

mission included) of 2,000 francs were far more common. *L'Employé*, a much more conservative newspaper, claimed that incomes above 3,000 francs were seen at only the few, most prestigious emporia and were not nearly so high elsewhere.[145] Clearly, there was frequently an important disparity between an employee's likely earnings and the income level he or she thought necessary to maintain an adequate life style. Many thousands of clerks—perhaps the majority—spent their lives with a sense of squeezing by, if that.

The modest employee who found a steady job attained no more than sparse comforts. Food purchases occupied at least half of his or her budget. A spacious, light, and airy lodging was probably beyond the income of most. The material situation of one railroad employee of the Twelfth Arrondissement suggests just how exiguous conditions could be for clerks who earned approximately 2,200 francs. His apartment, in an insalubrious location over stables, had two small, humid rooms. The furnishings of his kitchen-dining room consisted of little more than a plain wooden table, six chairs covered with soiled upholstery, and a stove. The bedroom, shared by five people, had three beds and three armoires. The family enjoyed meals that were only marginally better than those of artisans, with a little more meat, dairy products, and some sweets.[146] Perhaps, the bareness evident in this white-collar household was partly the result of having three young children, an exceptional situation, but it is not likely that this employee's comrades lived dramatically better.

If wage-earners struggled to avoid deprivation, humble employees struggled to achieve even small comforts. Their regular income was often not enough for this, so they sought additional revenue. The supply of clerks willing to take home paperwork from wholesale dealers and agencies always exceeded demand. The office workers at the Cail Machine Company sold chickens to bring in extra cash. The bookkeepers at many workshops doubled as salesclerks and earned commissions.[147] Employees did not shrink, for considerations of status, from having their wives bring home an income. In the Thirteenth Arrondissement, just under half (48.8 percent) of white-collar couples did so.[148] This proportion was lower than among wage-earning couples (66 percent), but, then, some employees' wives were from propertied families and had never been prepared to work for a living. Purchasing apparel and furniture on credit was a necessity, as well as a temptation, and all the more so because stores were eager to open accounts for employees with stable positions. G. Zehftmann, "purveyor of all merchandise on credit without a down payment, to employees and civil servants" on the rue Parmentier (Eleventh Arrondissement), was one of dozens of such outlets by 1900, and the inevitable consequence of this temptation was widespread indebtedness.[149] A sampling of fifty dossiers relating to employees of the prefecture—who stood a step above the humble clerks in terms of family backgrounds, education, and earnings—reveals that eleven had liens on their salaries.[150] The director of one large public utility complained that "most" of his clerks did, too, and they took days off from work since they were not going to collect their full salaries.[151] It is no wonder, then, that employees attached great importance to bonuses, campaigned rancorously for seemingly minor extras (like free coal), and manifested minimal gratitude for their extensive fringe benefits. The clerks' frequent claims to be living in "misery" were no less deeply felt for not being literally true.

White-collar employees entered the post-Commune era with decidedly better health than wage-earners. Young clerks were 50 percent more likely to pass their recruitment examinations than were young manual laborers. The heights of conscripts, a measure of bodily vigor, record a decisive advantage for white-collar workers at the end of the Second Empire (see table II-8). None of this can be surprising. The children of property-owning families for the most part, clerks rarely experienced the nutritional shortages that under-

Table II-8. Heights (in %) of White-Collar and Working-Class Conscripts, 1869 and 1903 (Twelfth and Eighteenth Arrondissements)

	Less Than 1.6 Meters		More Than 1.7 Meters	
	1869	1903	1869	1903
Manual Workers	22.2%	15.1%	17.4%	25.2%
Clerks	9.3	11.2	32.8	31.0

Source: A.D.S., D R¹, registers of Twelfth and Eighteenth arrondissements, 1869, 1903.

mined the physiques of laborers. Their housing, water supply, and access to healthful environments were probably more conducive to a robust constitution, too.

If workers ultimately benefited greatly from the sanitary and dietary improvements of the second half of the nineteenth century, employees experienced fewer advances. Their physical advantages over wage-earners diminished, indeed, nearly disappeared. By the twentieth century, young manual laborers were no more likely to have chronic conditions that inhibited their normal activities than were young white-collar employees, as shown by the identical rejection rates of military conscripts.[152] The proportions of short and tall youths were similar for both occupational groups by the new century. There was even a slight drop in average height of clerical youths in the Twelfth and Eighteenth arrondissements, but the change was small, and one should not make too much of it. Evidently, employees were not able to benefit from improving diets and sanitary conditions to the extent that workers were. Ameliorations at the end of the nineteenth century invigorated the most wretched portion of the population, but they had little effect on the groups that did not have a history of severe material want.

White-collar employees would not have been surprised to learn of their diminishing advantages in health. During the course of the late nineteenth century, they became far more informed about threats to their bodily strength. The campaign waged by preventive hygienists reached them at least as much as workers. Trade journals spread dismal news about the dangers to clerks' health. They learned, for example, that the mortality rate for adult (ages twenty to thirty-nine) salesclerks was among the highest of all occupational groups in Paris. Even the gentlemanly bookkeeper reportedly had a death rate that was well above construction, metallurgical, and chemical workers.[153] The effort to alter popular fatalism about tuberculosis had its effects on humble employees as well as workers. The death toll among postal employees was widely publicized, and as these clerks organized, they politicized the issue. One study of occupational groups treated in the antitubercular dispensaries in 1911 showed that employees were at least proportionately represented among the invalids, so the concern in this milieu was not at all displaced.[154]

Though the growing lamentations among white-collar groups about their health conditions paralleled those of workers, there was an important difference. Workers bemoaned their limited access to clean water, their filthy neighborhoods, and, above all, their disease-ridden housing. White-collar employees, for their part, were principally concerned with sanitary conditions at the workplace. Perhaps because they had more commodious housing—or assumed they did, at any rate—clerks explained high mortality rates in terms of the stuffy, humid, dusty, and confining environments in which they worked. Their occupational press frequently lamented the "martyrs of the basement," department store clerks who held subsidiary positions off the sales floor and whose incidence of untimely death was presumed catastrophic.[155] One provincial clerk who spent some time working at Bon Marché affirmed that contracting tuberculosis was an anxiety that weighed upon him and his colleagues almost as much as did making mathematical errors on their sales slips. The back spaces of large stores bore in his mind that "murderous" image that trade journals applied to them.[156] The clerks of the Parisian Gas Company attributed their frailty to insalubrious contacts with the public at the bill-paying window—a complaint frequently heard from postal workers, too—and to their office situation. According to the union newspaper, the office chiefs sat comfortably near the furnace during the winter while the mass of clerks froze in unheated parts of the room. The claim that "not even those beasts of burden, the coal shovelers, put up with such attacks on their health," was absurdly exaggerated, but was, nonetheless, stated with conviction.[157]

Clerks customarily noted the disparity between the respectable dress expected of them and the paucity of their resources. Though genuine material want was exceptional, clerks were pressed by the insufficiency of their income. The living defined as minimally acceptable for clerks with families was only an aspiration for many thousands of them. The growth of credit stores may only have raised those standards and provided risky temptations that were difficult for modest employees to resist. Thus, even if employees did not suffer a diminution of earnings relative to manual workers, they did have economic grievances against a social system in which they were far from being the most disfavored.

III

The Work Experience

The subdivision of the crafts, mechanization, mass-marketing, intensified competition, cost-cutting, finally, scientific management—these forces in the decades before World War I promised unsettling changes at the workplace. Yet successful resistance to innovation and accommodations between employers and workers were sources of much continuity through these years. By the time the new century began, however, the old rules were no longer fully applicable. The work cultures of laboring people, those collective expectations and practices that they brought to their jobs independently of managerial authority, were threatened anew, and, in many cases, more seriously than at any other time in the nineteenth century. Manual workers and clerks had either to mount meaningful responses or suffer from their inability to resist.

HANDICRAFT WORKERS

Historians usually attribute to the preindustrial work of craftsmen "life-organizing" qualities, to use Peter Stearns's evocative phrase.[1] Their long hours and irregular schedules precluded most off-the-job activities except for socializing informally with the comrades of the shop. If artisans worked at home, their wives were likely to help them perform their trade, and their children were likely to inherit the parents' occupation. Such patterns of work lingered long into the nineteenth century, as Yves Lequin has shown for the Lyons region.[2] By the time of the Commune, work was only marginally

74

Table III-1. Patterns of Occupational Inheritance, 1869 and 1902–1903

| | Son's Occupation | | | |
| | Same Industry | | Nonmanual Work | |
Father	N	%	N	%
	1869 (Xᵉ, XIᵉ, XIIᵉ, XIIIᵉ Arrondissements)			
Building	84	77.5	4	3.6
Furniture	153	78.3	13	6.6
Leather	56	74.2	3	3.9
Metalworking	148	79.1	13	6.8
Tailoring	56	40.0	40	28.7
Shoemaking	61	45.2	21	15.6
	1902–1903 (XIᵉ, XVIIIᵉ Arrondissements)			
Building	31	56.7	5	9.1
Furniture	41	48.3	9	10.6
Leather	20	52.5	3	7.9
Metalworking	62	69.0	10	11.1
Tailoring	30	38.0	19	24.0
Shoemaking	33	41.2	17	21.2

Source: A.D.S., D R¹, Recrutement militaire; D 2 M, Listes électorales.

life-organizing for the thousands of craftsmen in Paris and its suburbs. Most of them did not labor at home; but even those who did, like basket weavers or shoemakers, did not usually marry an economic partner. Wives could contribute to the family purse through labor of their own. Yet one way in which the life-organizing nature of a trade persisted was the likelihood that the son of a Parisian handicraft worker would enter his father's line of work (see table III-1). Despite the multiplicity of occupational alternatives and the varied sources of vocational or academic training that Paris offered, youths could hardly have been more inclined to assume the family trade if they had been raised in the midst of household production. More than the route of least resistance, occupational inheritance represented a strategy to maximize the potential for professional growth and earnings.

The key to interpreting the patterns of occupational selection on the eve of the Commune is the disparity between certain industries, like furniture making and construction, on the one hand, and shoemaking or tailoring, on the other. For all the specialization that had occurred in the former areas, there was still a clear hierarchy of skills. Above the broad base of specialists stood a substantial pinnacle of artisans. The many routine craftsmen at the base could hope to place their children in an advantageous position to acquire skills. Wood, metal, and leather workers of the Second Empire perceived that training within their respective industries was the best strategy for providing their offspring with a chance for a decent life. Shoemaking and tailoring, however, were trades that had become thoroughly debased, and this had happened relatively early. Tailors faced threats from increasingly sophisticated sewing-machine operations, from females in the ready-to-wear trade, and from foreign male workers.[3] A cobbler expressed his despair about his craft in the 1880s by proclaiming that "with five hundred francs [of equipment] ten years of experience is for nothing."[4] Under these circumstances, the craft did not provide the kind of future that parents modestly aspired to give their sons. One bronze assembler, the son of a tailor, recalled that his father had forbidden him to work with the needle because the remuneration was always so poor. His mother found him another apprenticeship.[5] Such a change in careers was not at all an isolated example. Tailors and cobblers were active in finding places for their offspring in some of the better-off trades, like printing.[6] Significantly, their sons entered white-collar positions more frequently than did those of better-paid craftsmen. Evidently, there were trade-specific as well as class barriers to the clerical sector. Some tradesmen were more prepared than were others to have their offspring desert the handicrafts.

In the industries characterized by a meaningful hierarchy of skills at the end of the Second Empire, the hope was not so much to keep the children in specific trades, narrowly defined, so much as to permit them to enter the more favored branches of the industry. Thus, cabinetmakers aspired to make their sons into wood sculptors, the workers in the furniture industry who had the strongest pretensions to artistry. Likewise, a core maker (*noyauteur*) in a foundry probably hoped that his son would become a molder, or, better still, a founder.[7] Roofers and masons were in the rudest trades among construction workers, so it is not surprising that their sons strove to be carpenters or even stonecutters. If boys did not remain in the father's precise craft, the trend was to move into a more skilled line of work in the same industry. Just this hope for some occupational advancement was lacking in the more thoroughly proletarianized trades.

Why occupational inheritance in the Parisian crafts declined during the late nineteenth century is an intriguing and far-reaching question. A change in recruitment records makes the gathering of the more recent data a laborious task, so our sample is small and confined to the Eleventh and Twentieth arrondissements.[8] Despite this reservation, the decrease in family continuity is clear—if the reasons for it are not. Apparently, Parisian handicraftsmen in a wide range of trades adopted habits that had characterized shoemakers forty years earlier. Furniture and jewelry making had ceased to serve the modest aspirations of their practitioners. Even construction workers, whose traditions encompassed a disregard for formal schooling, came to rely upon it more than ever for the career orientation of their children.

The logic of our previous analysis points to the leveling of trades as the key to the decline of endogenous recruitment patterns. Such reasoning dovetails neatly with a familiar theme in the history of labor: that technological and managerial innovations successfully debased the traditional crafts by the end of the century.[9] One prominent student of American labor views the struggle on the part of craftsmen to defend their mastery and their autonomy at the workplace as the central issue of labor history in the decades before the Great War.[10] Do the figures on occupational inheritance announce a lost struggle and the intensified proletarianization of the Parisian craftsmen? In order to place the decline of endogamy in its proper perspective, we must explore the work experience of craft workers, both the fully competent and the specialized ones, in this age of material and technological advancement.

Fully competent craftsmen were well aware of a malaise in their industries by the dawn of the twentieth century, and they frequently grumbled about mechanization as one cause of this stagnation.[11] Yet it seems unlikely that they failed to place their children in their own industries for fear of displacement by machinery. Very few artisans could echo the despairing comments of the shoemaker cited earlier. Technological conservatism was the rule in nearly all crafts. The manner in which the high standards of production in a luxury trade and the craftsman's traditions combined to ensure successful resistance to even the modernization of simple hand tools is nicely illustrated by the case of jewelry makers in the first decade of the twentieth century. Workers in the current and imitation branches of the industry used fixed blowtorches (*chalumeaux*), which fed the flame with compressed air and gas from a centralized source. Such equipment was rather expensive and was owned by the employer. Makers of fine jewelry, however, insisted on using their personal, portable blowpipes, which depended on their lungs to keep the flame burning. This kind of instrument entailed some dangers to the craftsman, since one tube was attached to a gas tank, and incidents of asphyxiation occasionally occurred. Yet quality jewelry makers refused to adopt the safer and more modern equipment. After the important firm of Savary installed the compressed-gas apparatus, it stood unused at the workbenches. The jewelers claimed that only their personal pipes allowed them to regulate the size and temperature of the flames carefully enough to add exquisite details to their pieces.[12] Such a defense of ancient methods barely disguised efforts to perpetuate the "secrets" of the trade in face of a certain degree of standardization imposed by the equipment. Perhaps, it also reflected the fear that bosses were willing to forgo some "exquisite details" in search of a less costly product. The jewelers accepted the risks to their health in order to practice their trade as they saw fit.

The need to resist changes in the production process was rather infrequent in the world of the luxury handicrafts. Machine processing of inexpensive furniture was a reality by World War I in the eastern *banlieue*, but high-quality effects were almost entirely handmade. At most, frustrated employers who faced unruly workers could threaten to install machinery to perform preliminary operations, but even this remained an idle threat, for the most part.[13] A visitor to the woodworking shops of the Faubourg Saint-Antoine after the war noted how rare it was to find anything but the simple tools of handicraftsmen.[14] The workers who produced the carriages for Europe's aristocracy found their prejudices against machines and standardized parts reinforced by clients and bosses. Firms in this branch of the industry made all parts themselves down to the automobile age. A number of important bicycle manufacturers did no differently into the 1890s.[15] Similarly, quality pianos were produced in their entirety in one workshop, sometimes a very large one, like that of Alexandre in Ivry or Pleyel in Saint-Denis. The stockrooms of these firms even had tree trunks from which encasements were made. The workmen treated each piano and all its parts as a unique entity.[16]

All this is not to say that the workshops of the capital stood in grand isolation from the engineering advances of the late nineteenth century. The quickening pace of technological innovation after 1890 touched a few trades—but without truly entering the mainstream of production. With the aid of equipment from the United Shoe Machine Company, manufacturers had the ability to make a product that had all the appearances of hand-sewn shoes by the 1890s; yet the number of *bottiers*, the elite of the shoemaking trade, actually rose between then and the war, from twelve hundred to about two thousand.[17] The machine production of quality felt hats was possible at about the same time, and, again, the Parisian trade escaped decisive transformation. The hatters of the capital worked in the made-to-order sector, and clients continued to seek the smartness they gave to hats constructed to measure. The sizable silk-hat industry, concentrated in the capital, was not touched by mechanization.[18] The case of printing has still more significance because it was not tied to a local clientele that demanded objects made for them personally. After numerous false starts, composing machines of genuine practical value, like the Lanston monotype casting and setting machine, became available around the turn of the century. However, such equipment was suitable only for rather basic jobs, like newspaper or catalogue printing.[19] In higher grades of printing, the trained eye of a compositor made sure all type was perfectly even. The new technology quickly diffused to the shops that had the appropriate work, and then resort to the linotype decelerated. Between 1900 and 1902, the number of linotypes in the Department of the Seine grew from 50 to 182.[20] By 1911, far from having spread to most shops, the machinery was used by only 416 printers, 12 percent of them. Most of those who did use the linotype in production were in the suburbs.[21] Once again, Parisian craftsmen were protected from technological displacement by the quality of the work they performed and by the refinement they imparted to their product.

Relatively secure from direct competition from machinery, Parisian artisans did not fear intrusions upon their work procedures until the last decade of the nineteenth century. For the most part, luxury workshops lacked an authority who purposefully initiated and pursued rationalizing policies. Employers and their skilled craftsmen had worked out an elaborate framework of accommodations that left workers a great deal of autonomy. However, masters became more asssertive under the strained economic circumstances of the closing years of the century. Though bosses failed to reshape work experiences in a profound manner, they did succeed in transforming their shops into battlegrounds over small innovations. The troubles in the crafts probably played a part in convincing handworkers to look elsewhere for their sons' jobs.

Parisian craftsmen tolerated authority at the workplace with difficulty. When a master silversmith reprimanded one of his polishers for taking the day off, the worker replied that he "had no need for a lecture" and quit. He invited his comrades to join him for a drink, and they all left the shop at 8:30 in the morning.[22] Such confrontations, though not the substance of everyday life, had their place in the workshops of the capital. Artisans expected a good deal of autonomy at the workplace and had a highly developed sense of acquired rights. Parisian hatters in the made-to-measure branches of the trade provided a model of organization in protection of their work culture. Upon arriving in Paris, a hatter first visited the union hall to procure a card and a list of approved employers. When he went to a shop to seek work, he asked to see, not the boss or the foreman, but rather the oldest worker, whose approval he needed to secure a job. Once at work the hatter did not have to fear interference from the foreman either, for the latter took his cronies from one job to the next and was unlikely to be an abusive supervisor.[23] Such customs were unusually formalized and institutionalized. Most craftsmen were like stonecutters or carriage makers, who did not found their autonomy on the closed shop or on union regulations.

They looked to collective wage agreements (*tarifs*), to their monopoly on technical competence, and to informal power relations at the workplace to preserve their mastery, which was genuine enough.[24]

The tradewide agreement on wages was the focal point of employer-worker accommodations in the handicrafts, and its significance transcended the issue of pay.[25] By specifying both time and piece rates, the agreement limited the employer's scope for manipulating the pace of work and the artisan's need to overtax himself to attain an acceptable income. These stipulations mattered a good deal, for many skilled workers were on piece rates.[26] Moreover, the *tarif* reduced the uncertainty entailed in leaving one boss for another. Above all, it had a noticeable effect on the worker's relations with his comrades in the shop by preventing the individualization of wages. Laborers protected by a *tarif* were far less likely to make efforts to distinguish themselves before the boss and compete with their comrades; solidarity came much easier to such craftsmen.[27] For these reasons, bosses never conceded the principle of a collective contract. They continued to demand the right to reward each worker as he or she merited. In practice, though, the *tarif* was an established reality.

Craftsmen feared their employer as the person who could fire them or reduce their hours during the slow season, but, generally, the boss's presence in the workshop was not a forceful one in terms of regulating work procedures or tampering with the pace of work. Having made the business decision to operate in the luxury side of the market, the employer had an interest in maintaining the highest standards of artistry and traditions of excellence. Among employers were many former practitioners of the trade, and they were often captured by its lore. Such was the case for many carpentry contractors who were former members of the legendary journeymen's associations (*compagnonnages*).[28] The furniture maker Mazaroz, the employer of six hundred cabinetmakers, would have one believe that a return to the corporative structures of the *ancien régime* was eminently practical and immediately realizable.[29] Such employers were not likely to revise work practices with an eye to innovation. Contemporaries feared, however, that the employers who knew the trade thoroughly were being replaced by those who understood only the commercial aspects of the business. During the industrial crisis of the mid-1880s, upholsterers complained that "almost half" of their bosses had no appreciation for their ways of work; a master cabinetmaker claimed that most of his colleagues were ignorant of production methods.[30] Such employers presumably left matters of work procedure to the foreman. The scope of this shift away from owner-artisans is difficult to measure, but it may not have made much difference in any case. Even technically competent bosses rarely took an active part in the details of work. In shops with more than a few laborers, it was normal for the owner to spend most of his time in the office and leave the details of work to his foreman.[31] He was the effective authority in the workshop under most circumstances.

Was the foreman the first among workers or the last of the managers? There was a visible and noteworthy transformation in his role during the last decade of the nineteenth century, but in general terms he was well integrated into the artisan's work culture. Background, training, and recruitment destined foremen to be so. Given the widespread distrust of vocational schools among employers, they had little alternative but to choose them from the pool of the most proficient workers.[32] Class-conscious union members could, as easily as not, become foremen.[33] Many who became supervisors in workshops had unquestionably shared the hardships and uncertainties of working-class life with their underlings. Even the foreman at Barbedienne, the premier bronze firm in Paris, who was surely a craftsman at the pinnacle of his trade, had received no special favors during his apprenticeship and owed nothing to the generosity of employers.[34] Likewise, "master journeymen," the supervisors of construction sites, shared the provincial identities of the masons from the Limousin or the stonecutters from Normandy. Their distrust of the insurance firms which covered work accidents and their hatred of the contract system of labor (*marchandage*) signaled a closeness to the wage-earner's outlook.[35] They were not the sort of foremen who could wholeheartedly become the allies of their employer.

The practice in several large trades and hundreds of individual workshops was to appoint a foreman whom the craftsmen were willing to accept. Thus, the owner of one small foundry fired two foremen because they did not suit his workers and balked only when the founders rejected still another nominee.[36] The frustrations of a precision-instrument maker were similar when he pleaded with his workers to select a foreman among themselves since he wished to deal with a single authority on the shop floor. The problem for this manufacturer was that his craftsmen wanted no supervisor whatsoever; and appointing a foreman caused them to quit.[37] The supervisor who lacked the esteem of his subordinates suffered open scorn and eventual harassment.[38] Clearly, overseeing Parisian craftsmen was a delicate matter for which employers had no easy solution.

Until the Great War, the large majority of foremen respected the work culture of their craftsmen. Yet unquestionably a changing tone to power relations in the workshop marked the last decade of the nineteenth century. Foremen in greater numbers than earlier were making demands that artisans found excessive, and craftsmen found themselves defending established patterns of work at individual shops. Confrontations and resistance replaced accommodation at times. The contours of strike activity attest to the rising conflict over work roles. During the 1870s and 1880s, the comportment of the foreman was simply not an issue in work stoppages. Given the superior skills and organizational capacities of the workers we are considering, it is easier to assume an absence of grievances than a lack of ability to protest about their discontents.[39] Starting in the mid-1890s, however, to have a foreman cashiered became an appreciable goal of artisans' strike activity. Between 1893 and the opening of the new century at least a dozen strikes against the foreman occurred. Antagonisms multiplied thereafter, with three or four such protests each year. The year 1910 brought a crescendo of hostility with thirteen confrontations involving craftsmen and their supervisors.[40] These clashes touched a wide variety of industries, but they were especially frequent in the jewelry, furniture, decorative bronze, and ceramics trades—in short, the heart of the artistic crafts.

The strike at the Osselin jewelry firm in 1903 was characteristic of the issues behind these strikes, if not of the passions they evoked.[41] Annoyed by the persistent problem of tardiness, the foreman of this shop compelled all the workers to remain at their benches after closing hours because one jeweler had come to work late that day. A delegation of workers demanded that Osselin fire the foreman immediately, and when the boss refused, the workers struck. The conflict lasted for two months. During its course, Osselin's country home was bombed, and nine of his workers were arrested for this crime. Incidents never arose from frontal attacks on craftsmen's work procedures. They entailed revisions of details which amounted to an undermining of the artisan's autonomy. Foremen tried to make their workers be punctual, take fewer breaks, or maintain expected productivity levels. For their part, the artisans lashed out at their supervisors' "severity," and especially at their "arrogance." The workers' sense of dignity was clearly wounded by the new constraints. They resented as well the loss of foremen who sympathized with their work culture.

The accelerating decay of apprenticeship contributed in an indirect manner to the heightened tension between craftsmen and their foremen. Unable to find very proficient laborers among the workers trained in Paris, bosses selected their shop supervisors among recent immigrants. Such foremen were not necessarily familiar or sympathetic with the customs of craftsmen in the capital. The locksmith Gaston Lucas, a son of Poitiers who became a foreman not long after his arrival in the capital, discovered a work culture that he could hardly approve. The Parisian locksmiths' habit of moving from shop to shop and their suspicion of the boss dismayed him. Lucas even regarded the collective wage agreement as a temporary inconvenience that he hoped workers would learn to disavow.[42] Obviously, there could not be much fellowship between such a foreman and his workers.

Behind the newly displayed "arrogance" of the foremen were employers under economic pressure. They wished to impose more demanding and controlled routines on their craftsmen. The luxury trades were engulfed in an atmosphere of "crisis" at the turn of the century.[43] Like all Parisian industries, they had entered a deep recession in the mid-1880s, but unlike others, they never managed to recover their full vigor. A few trades (wood sculpturing, carpentry) declined in absolute terms, but for the most part, it was a matter of stagnation, increasing competition, and markets that were less receptive to their products. Journalists cited ominous trade figures that showed that the French were now buying from Germans, English, and Americans what the world had once sought in Paris. Furniture imports grew more than threefold between 1892 and 1908; the value of imported fancy-leather goods (*maroquinerie*) doubled.[44] Though public commentators were apt to blame the malaise on the debased apprenticeship system and on exorbitant wage demands, its roots were in structural economic changes: a growing acceptance of ready-made products, their improving quality, and a certain democratization of wealth. In the face of these changes, Parisian crafts retreated to the styles and models that had made their reputations but no longer enjoyed much favor.[45]

While many employers were beset with a sense of helplessness, others sought to squeeze more profit out of their shops by attacking their workers' autonomy. They hired foremen who were not favorably disposed toward craft customs and encouraged them to be firm. One new owner of a chandelier workshop was determined to gain control of the work regime and did not even expect help from his foreman, who was a union militant. The new boss threatened to put on piece rates those workers who failed to produce enough by the hour and formally warned his personnel to accept his comments on their work with good grace.[46] In the building trades, contractors met competition from preformed materials and metal scaffolding by making greater use of the hated subcontractor.[47] Other employers had their foremen install punch clocks, cut time spent on breaks, or fired workers who did not produce enough. One foreman at a shop making statuettes enraged workers by attempting to hire workers who were not union members.[48] In short, some employers thought that the Parisian trades could no longer afford the artisan's work culture and set about to attack its details, if not its substance.

Craftsmen reacted bitterly to this challenge, partly to prevent a genuine deterioration of work conditions, but also to defend their dignity. This managerial offensive agitated the workshops of the capital and contributed to an occupational dilemma for artisans' offspring. To discern still more powerful reasons for the decline in the endogenous recruitment of tradesmen, we must explore the work experiences of the specialized craftsmen.

Craftsmen who were specialized in the work they performed and usually limited in their capacities were the "forgotten majority" of nineteenth-century Paris. Relatively weak in organizing potential, they were unable to articulate their concerns with the same clarity as their more accomplished comrades. These "small hands" allowed workers in the luxury sectors to speak for them even when their interests were not entirely being served. Archival sources and monographs naturally reflect this bias. Yet, their very numbers demand that specialized craftsmen be drawn out of their obscurity.

Had all specialized handicraft workers labored beside fully accomplished artisans, in the same shops, the histories of the two groups might have been very similar; but they did not. The elite of craftsmen were generally concentrated in the shops of leading manufacturers, often quite large ones, while the small hands usually worked under the supervision of the multitude of jobbers (*façonniers*), who did a narrow range of work with the help of a few laborers. There may have been as many as three thousand such small bosses in the furniture trades and four thousand in bronze making.[49] Home labor was also common for semi-artisans, especially in the various clothing trades. Entrepreneurs found it profitable to put out an article as many as two or three times for each operation. The dispersion of specialized craftsmen in thousands of small shops made them easy to overlook. When the Ministry of Commerce conducted an inquiry on wages and work hours, it arrived at the conclusion that only 30 percent of Parisian laborers were on piece rates. The findings were fallacious because the researchers took their data from the large and important workshops, which had relatively few small hands in them.[50]

Limited in their vocational proficiencies, semi-artisans were obviously more susceptible to the threats of technological displacement than were the fully competent workers. Shoemakers provide the classic example of handicraftsmen who found themselves competing with machinery because theirs was one of the first trades in which equipment was able to produce high-quality goods.[51] In hand production, three specialized workers, a stitcher, an assembler, and a finisher, generally worked on each shoe. At Dressoir and Prémartin, the largest shoe factory in Paris and in France at the dawn of the twentieth century (with a labor force of twelve hundred), ninety-two different laborers worked on each shoe. Mechanized procedures doubled output per worker.[52] Similarly, compositors whose level of expertise permitted work only on catalogues, newspapers, and handbills had something to fear from the linotype. The large printing plants in the suburbs, which produced material of low quality, adopted type-setting equipment with alacrity. Such machinery decisively accelerated the entry of women into the printing trade.[53]

If replacement by machinery was the long-term outlook for specialized shoemakers and printers on the eve of World War I, the immediate situation was more nuanced. Large-scale shoe manufacturers continued to employ domestic craftsmen, and in impressive numbers: Plé, an employer of 325 cobblers, was not at all unusual in having nearly a third of his labor force working at home as late as 1905. Despite the much vaunted advances made in shoemaking machinery, manufacturers claimed that products requiring lightness and elegance were still best made by hand.[54] Cobblers' most violent resistance was not to the introduction of equipment but rather to efforts to transform workshop laborers into domestic producers. Shoe assemblers physically attacked the foreman at one large shop because they thought he was contriving to have them work at home.[55] These craftsmen correctly feared that a lowering of wages might follow such a change. In printing, of course, the powerful Typographical Society tried to control the use of the linotype. Quite aside from these efforts, many master printers reduced the disruptive potential of the machinery on their own initiative by assigning to the operators the task of repairing the new equipment.[56]

Competition between machinery and specialized handicraft workers was, in fact, a secondary theme in their intertwined histories. For the most part, technological advances had created and continued to create industries in which "small hands" could find work. Decades before the Commune, stamping equipment produced pieces of jewelry that specialized craftsmen could assemble.[57] New alloys and new molding procedures created thousands of jobs for chiselers of routine talents in the decorative trades. One manufacturer of ornamental bronzes proclaimed that Barbedienne, the foremost company in his field, was the only firm to employ highly skilled chiselers.[58] As we have seen, carriage making grew rapidly during the Second Empire because entrepreneurs began to construct commercial and ready-made vehicles with standardized parts that workers had only to fit and assemble.[59] In truth, up to the twentieth century, machinery created more semiskilled positions than it suppressed. Perhaps technological advances at the dawn of this century had the potential to reverse this situation, but such potential was only realized in the decades beyond the First World War.

A more generalized and serious threat to specialized craftsmen in the four decades after the Commune was the spread of sweated conditions—declining piece rates and demand for quantity over quality—in their crafts. The organization of specialized trades established pressures and opportunities for entrepreneurs to move in that direction. Already, the division of labor, the predominance of piece rates, and the growth of price-elastic markets had brought such conditions to thousands of men and women in the garment trades before the Commune.[60] Specialized craft workers had to worry about how thoroughly and rapidly these conditions would spread.

Vulnerable though semi-artisans were, a deteriorating work situation was not their inevitable fate. Since the intensified subdivision of the crafts earlier in the nineteenth century, employers had bought labor peace by accepting restraints on sweating. Moreover, the still-incomplete penetration of mass-marketing techniques permitted some escape from downward pressure on piece wages, at least until the last decades of the century. The thousands of toolmakers constituted a special case, if a large one. They were isolated from the rationalizing forces that often led to sweating because the market for their products was not so price-elastic. Thus, screw threaders earned wages that would have thrilled a shoe assembler even though they were "common laborers for whom the machine does practically all the work," in the opinion of one machine manufacturer.[61] The collective wage agreement was the first line of defense against sweating for specialized craftsmen in the consumer-goods industries. The *tarif* was as important to "small hands" as it was to artisans. It was preferably an agreement written by workers in the luxury sector and defended by them, for if semi-artisans had to devise their own collective contract, the rates were likely to be lower and the enforcement more timid. Fully trained craftsmen had an interest in supporting decent piece rates, not only for reasons of trade (and class) solidarity, but also because they, too, were subject to its provisions during the slow season or hard times, when they undertook "current" work.[62]

Whether or not specialized craftsmen worked securely under the provisions of a collective agreement depended very much upon the nature of their employer. The most fortunate of semi-artisans worked directly or indirectly for leading manufacturers in the luxury sector, for these employers were inclined to accept the *tarif*. Producers of luxury goods were often polymorphous enterprises that had a place for some "small hands." The metal firm of Gaget, Gauthier, for example, made a line of zinc products ranging from public monuments—the Statue of Liberty among them—to drainage pipes.[63] All their workers were paid in accordance with the *tarif*. More commonly, semi-artisans worked for luxury manufacturers indirectly, under the direction of jobbers who subcontracted work from the important firms. Again, the industry-wide agreements were usually operative in these situations, too. Uncertainty mounted if specialized craftsmen took work with jobbers whose connections to the luxury sector were remote. Yet, even then, there was hope for protection from sweated conditions. These small employers were often full participants in the culture of craftsmen. To become a jobber was the aspiration of many artisans, even those who were Socialist militants.[64] Thus, when passementerie makers struck for higher wages in 1882, about a third of the jobbers who employed them belonged to the union, and they accepted the demands at once.[65] The distinction between small employers and workers among specialized joiners (*menuisiers à façon*) was muted. The six hundred joiners who employed some three thousand workers were organized into a union that upheld the collective contract of the industry. The union's delegates to a parliamentary commission spoke of their constituents as "workers" and even supported the controversial pay scale of 1882, which contractors in the building industry had firmly rejected.[66] Such employers as these would have shared in the resistance to sweated conditions.

Union solidarity played a meaningful but quite uneven role in protecting specialized craftsmen against ever lower rates and a faster pace of work. Here and there were closed shops even in such demeaned trades as basket weaving, tawing (the preparation of sheep, goat, lamb, and kid skins), and shoemaking.[67] More common was another sort of situation: Semi-artisans worked under the supervision of a foreman who was a fully skilled craftsman and a union militant. One producer of copper ornaments fired his foreman, a union secretary, for fomenting a strike for higher wages and for refusing to discipline his workers.[68] At a tawing shop in the southern suburbs, the unionized foreman was also the strike leader in a wage dispute.[69] Given the importance of such protection, one can easily imagine the consternation of case makers (*gainiers*) when a foreman broke with the union and became an exploitative jobber.[70]

The unfortunate reality that specialized craftsmen faced was that the barriers and accommodations that had saved them from sweated conditions operated in an ever more hostile economic environment, especially after the mid-1880s. The foreign competition that worried manufacturers of luxury goods was still more fierce for commodities of lesser quality. Imports rose most sharply in such "Parisian" trades as imitation jewelry and imitation leather items.[71] Moreover, the opportunity for a job with a manufacturer in the luxury sector, or with one of his jobbers, under industry-wide wage scales, was diminishing. Department stores and other large-scale distributors bypassed established workshops and placed orders directly with subcontractors for goods at a saving. The declining wealth of Parisian jobbers in the second half of the nineteenth century, noted by Adeline Daumard, was surely related to such developments.[72] The consequences of these changes for thousands of "small hands" in woodworking illustrated the fate of specialized handicraft workers in most trades during the late nineteenth century.

The distance between the versatile cabinetmaker and the semi-artisans was widening—all to the detriment of the latter group—in the three decades before the First World War. Up to about 1880, the wage agreement of the trade seemed to apply to both sorts of craftsmen, and leading manufacturers employed both, either directly or through their jobbers. Though the highly competent workers formed the great bulk of union members, some "small hands" belonged as well, and most others rallied to the defense of their *tarif*.[73] A labor dispute that erupted in July 1880 demonstrated that these barriers to sweated conditions were still very much intact. Cabinetmakers initiated a strike for higher wages and met resistance from the two leading manufacturers of the Faubourg Saint-Antoine, Krieger and Schmidt, as well as from many jobbers and small employers who did work in their homes. When efforts to hire enough nonunion workers failed, the employers turned to a lockout. This tactic began to drag on too long for the jobbers, who were ready to accept the revisions in the *tarif*, but Kreiger and Schmidt were able to compel their continued cooperation by threatening to withdraw subcontracting business.[74] This conflict illustrated the essential solidarities that still existed in the furniture industry: Specialized employers had close ties to luxury manufacturers, and craftsmen of diverse levels of proficiency joined in defense of collective agreements.

The decade of the 1880s, with its strikes and recessions, was very hard on this unity. In the crisis of 1883–1884, between a third and a half of the cabinetmakers were out of work, and the general cry was that foreign competition would destroy the less-than-luxury production in Paris.[75] Under pressure to cut costs, manufacturers transferred some preparatory and routine work to shops outside the capital. Krieger, for example, had a plant with three hundred workers in Belgium.[76] In addition to these difficulties, which proved to be more than momentary, the furniture industry had to sustain the reshaping influences of "mass" marketing techniques from department and credit stores. The laments that arose over their deleterious effects on taste shows that the large retail outlets were expanding the "current" sector at the expense of the luxury trade.[77] The purchasing agents of these retailers severed the ties between luxury and current sectors of the industry by placing orders directly with jobbers and bypassing the manufacturers of high-quality goods. To keep its huge showrooms filled with moderately priced items, Klein's Furniture Palace did not need to do its buying through a Schmidt or a Mazaroz, and it did not. Such pressures weakened the occupational unity that protected specialized cabinetmakers from deteriorating work conditions.

A series of strikes by specialized furniture workers after 1890 illustrates how much more insecure their situation had become in a little more than a decade. Woodworkers who made night tables, chests of drawers (*commodes*), and English dressing tables profited little from having their own sections within the Union of Cabinetmakers and Workers in Sculptured Furniture. The collective wage agreement was unable to protect them from falling piece rates. The workers who produced commodes were receiving only 31 francs for each piece, which brought them no more than 5.5 francs for a twelve-hour day. The *tarif* of 1880 had promised them 41 francs, and their strike of 1893 was able to raise the rate to only 36 francs.[78] The downward pressure on piece rates that resulted from mass-marketing was evident from the fact that the huge Dufayel Department Store sold "quality" dressers at only 58 francs.[79] The craftsmen who produced English dressing tables saw their piece rates fall from 5 to 4.5 francs, and they responded by working longer hours. In 1906 specialists in night tables were able to raise daily wages from 6 to 6.5 francs, but cabinetmakers in the luxury shops earned 9 francs by then.[80] These job actions by "small hands" show that the industry-wide agreement was not able to protect them against declining or stagnating piece rates, longer hours, and a faster pace of work. Furthermore, by the turn of the century, mechanized furniture shops in the eastern *banlieue* were beginning to pose a new threat to hand producers of moderate-quality effects.[81]

The market pressures that weighed on specialized cabinetmakers did not spare other Parisian crafts. In the costume jewelry industry, which employed about thirty-five hundred workers, sweating was an established fact by the 1880s. One manufacturer of cameos claimed that his workers could earn up to 9 francs in a day (in 1884) by producing eighteen cameos; this pace he considered compatible with taste and craftsmanship. Yet, he admitted that workers in many other shops had to produce two or three dozen trinkets to earn a living wage, so that speed was all that counted.[82] At the same time that purchasing agents in furniture retailing were placing orders directly with furniture jobbers, their counterparts in saddlery and leather goods were reducing the costs of production in a similar manner.[83] Finally, mechanization was an impetus toward sweating in a few trades. It was not only the shoemaker who could proclaim, "If I desire revolution, it is not to harm anyone but to destroy all these machines."[84] Tawers and workers in certain branches of tanning had to compete with factories like that of Combes, in Saint-Denis, with its fifteen hundred workers. The result was a series of piece rate reductions in their trades after 1890.[85]

The fate of an ever increasing number of specialized male craft workers was already the lot of most working women. Indeed, writers on the sweating system sometimes assumed that all its victims were female because women wage-earners were concentrated in the garment trades, which responded earliest and most thoroughly to mass-production methods.[86] The production of artificial flowers, undergarments, and ready-to-wear apparel achieved, during the Second Empire, a subdivision and specialization finer than any that furniture or carriage making developed thereafter. More so than the trades of the Faubourg Saint-Antoine, the garment industries were organized on the basis of subcontracting, with each layer dependent upon low wages for a profit.[87] The female jobbers (*entrepreneuses*) were often well integrated into the work culture of their personnel.[88] Yet they probably did not, and could not, offer effective resistance to sweated conditions on behalf of their workers. Unlike class-conscious tawers or case makers, subcontractors in the clothing trades made business decisions on the commonplace assumption that women's earnings were simply supplementary and that a living wage was not necessary. The price for behaving otherwise in this intensely competitive industry was immediate failure.

Just as women wage-earners were on that unenviable cutting edge of sweated conditions, so certain sorts of home workers were among the first to experience competition from factory methods. Because men's apparel, underwear (especially men's), and work clothing were not subject to pronounced seasonal fluctuations, the concentration of production was viable. The opening, in 1893, of a clothing plant employing seven hundred workers (two-thirds of them female) in the suburb of Montrouge was noteworthy in itself. What especially excited public opinion about this new enterprise—and announced new difficulties for domestic seamstresses—was that all the operations were performed internally. No resort to home work was necessary.[89] Specialized sewing and buttonholing machinery raised workers' productivity beyond levels that subdivision, no matter how fine, could achieve. Similarly, several thousand domestic shoe stitchers (*piqueuses*) were among the first in this industry to have their earnings squeezed by technological innovation.[90] When the male assemblers at one shoe factory rebelled against the supervisor who tried to impose domestic labor upon them, it is possible that their anger was inspired at least in part by the misery of female domestic workers in their trade.[91]

Specialized craft workers, male and female, increasingly found that their skills could bring them an expected living if they worked at a frenzied pace for long hours. No wonder that their productivity compared reasonably well to that of more "modern" sorts of laborers.[92] After the Commune, their employers abandoned their accommodative practices and adapted to mass-marketing conditions handily. In doing so, they made their workers victims of economic maturation.

We are now in a position to resolve the problem of declining endogenous patterns of occupational recruitment. A fundamental transformation of work experiences was not at the roots of this decline. Neither technological wonders, nor employers' efforts to rationalize, nor cost-cutting measures burst into the world of craftsmen without considerable warning. It was nonetheless true that Parisian artisans had been better integrated into the national economy at the end of the Second Empire than they were on the eve of World War I. Their malaise was as much psychological as it was economic. Foreign competition troubled them, but more problematical was the failure of the luxury crafts to remain arbiters of taste. The malaise manifested itself in a number of ways: the stagnation of employment in the crafts while other sectors of the Parisian economy grew; a decrepit apprenticeship system in which neither parents nor employers were willing to invest; the need to battle foremen and bosses to preserve work traditions; even the abandonment of trades by youths who had received a thorough grounding in them.[93] Numerous were the channels by which the elite craft workers could communicate their loss of confidence to the mass of small hands.

From a statistical perspective, the occupational choices of the specialized craftsmen were the crucial ones. An ever greater portion of them faced a predicament similar to the one that shoemakers knew several decades earlier: Opportunities for attaining decent conditions within the trade were narrowing, while the probability of genuine and permanent hardship was growing. Under these circumstances, handicraft workers discovered that new and possibly advantageous career options were easy to arrange for their offspring. It is noteworthy that machine-building, a dynamic industry in which workers escaped the threat of sweated labor, did not experience the same decline in endogenous recruitment. The more general case, though, was that the crafts were no longer providing the same promise for their practitioners that they had under the Second Empire.

FACTORY WORKERS

If the handicrafts granted only measured responses to the problems posed by economic changes, factories were, in principle at least, the scenes of tumultuous transformations. Only in a relative sense was this actually the case, though, as far as greater Paris was concerned. Managers did not permit technological innovations to establish the pace at which the work regime was altered. Their responses, too, were measured.

It would have been difficult, indeed, to bring massive changes to the work of the third of factory personnel composed of common laborers. Despite their rural roots, they fitted poorly into E. P. Thompson's classic scheme of irregular, task-oriented work yielding to repetitive, regular exertion.[94] Day laborers did the carrying, stocking, and piling, by nature irregular and task-oriented work. These activities were rude, debilitating, often dangerous (as we shall see), and supervised in a cursory manner. Casual laborers took orders from team heads, workers, foremen, and managers. They did play off one superior against another and, as supervisors at gas factories observed, were able to take a nap or two each day in the courtyard of their plants.[95]

We must distinguish three sorts of workers in the production process itself: the operators of specialized machines into which most of the skill and judgment were built; the operators of general machines, who did repetitive operations on large batches of pieces; and, finally, the skilled workers who adapted the machine to a particular job. The transformation of these groups in face of new technology is difficult to follow because information on the use of new machinery (as opposed to its invention) is lamentably thin. The little we can learn about the introduction of technological innovations suggests two periods, in particular, in which specialized machine tools replaced general ones, the end of the Second Empire and the turn of the century. The turret lathe, automatic screw machine, universal milling machine, and automatic gear cutter made some mechanics into machine tenders in the literal sense of the term. The Potter-Johnson automatic chucking and turning machine, which could produce complete engine pistons from rough castings in twenty-five minutes, required only one operator for three machines. On a conventional lathe, the same operation required three hours. As "brain wheels" were added to manual cutting tools, the motion of the machine could readily be adjusted to suit different jobs. Women were able to take over some metal-cutting operations; Dion-Bouton employed them to tend Brown and Sharpe millers, and a few handled gear cutters after the new century began. Such machines responded to the demand for interchangeable parts in the bicycle, metal construction, engineering, and automobile industries. With their use, the number of semiskilled laborers expanded.[96]

Such machines also exposed skilled workers to the prospect of technological displacement. Yet the threat was realized neither thoroughly nor quickly. In the cases of mold making, a crucial operation in industrial production, basic inventions came too late to have made much of an impact before the First World War.[97] Several features of Parisian factories retarded the adoption of the technology that was available. Production was hardly ever organized in a linear manner, with a sequential flow of parts from one workroom to the next. Rather, each shop within a factory performed a distinct operation and sent its output to the storeroom. The pressures to remove bottlenecks in production were, thus, weak.[98] Moreover, factories with central planning departments were virtually unknown in greater Paris down to World War I. Instead, individual workrooms had considerable independence, and methods of production were determined by foremen, whose training and empirical know-how were usually not conducive to innovation. Progressive engineers were troubled by the foremen's hesitation before mechanical advances.[99] Moreover, factories in greater Paris (and probably all of France) tended to produce a very diverse product line, and specialized machinery brought returns only by producing large batches of the same pieces. This explains why manufacturing retained many aspects of handicraft methods at the Glass and Crystal Company of Saint-Denis, even in the twentieth century. This plant of 860 workers made a variety of items: test tubes, laboratory beakers, stemware, and decorative objects. Each was made by a team headed by a skilled glassworker, and the traditional hierarchy of the craft was still very much in evidence.[100]

The burgeoning machine-building industries provide an excellent test case for the impact of technological innovation on the skilled factory workers in greater Paris. As engineering firms, particularly in the United States, turned out labor-saving machine tools, the potential for de-skilling expanded. Yet, Parisian managers were not quick to order the machines or to build their own. A representative of the United States Department of Labor noted that important entreprises began to take serious advantage of machinery with built-in skills at the turn of the century. This informed observer also noted that automatic machines, when finally purchased, were not utilized as fully as possible.[101] Still another witness to industrial practices at the advent of the new century berated Parisian foremen for overlooking the precision built into these machines and for having parts worked by hand even though that operation was not necessary.[102] In part, such under-utilization was the result of the scarcity of well-informed supervisors and of the pragmatic conservatism of those foremen who themselves had learned on the job. It was also significant that Parisian machine manufacturers were not very specialized and did not produce one type of machine in quantities large enough to push new equipment to their technological limit. Huré, for example, one of the largest engineering firms in Paris, made no less than 150 different kinds of machines at the turn of the century. Bariquand and Marre, one of the most imposing companies in the Eleventh Arrondissement, included metal hair clippers in its product line because machine tools did not provide sufficient volume of business.[103]

In 1908 the Hotchkiss armament firm in Saint-Denis installed Jones and Lanson turret lathes and had to fire six turners before its laborers would agree to use the new machines. This incident, sometimes cited as a clear "sign of the times," in fact, expresses the ambiguity of technological displacement in Parisian industry.[104] On the one hand, that the introduction of the turret lathe at this date should have caused such a commotion demonstrates how belatedly Parisian manufacturers continued to rely on general machine tools even though specialized ones were available. The turret lathe was not, by the twentieth century, the newest miracle of engineering genius.[105] From another perspective, the dispute at Hotchkiss poses questions about the kinds of skilled workers who were displaced. The highly trained machinist who could work up pieces from blueprints was not being threatened; rather, the intimidated ones were the narrowly skilled men who had acquired proficiency at one operation but lacked the ability to transfer their skills to other jobs without extensive instruction. The specialized machine, in fact, replaced turners who had earned 77 centimes an hour, just barely the wages of skilled men, with semiskilled operators at 65 centimes.[106]

The dynamic engineering industries at the turn of the century had an insatiable demand for workers who could adapt machine tools to new jobs by selecting proper speeds and cutting procedures. Large plants needed them for tool and repair workrooms; jobbers needed them to make small batches of a piece with precision.[107] The newest products of Yankee ingenuity were not a threat to them. Indeed, skilled mechanics usually admired complex machinery. Some union members even mocked a large Parisian plant for having equipment that, they claimed, belonged in the Cluny Museum of medieval art.[108]

Often, the skilled workers' discontents with new production methods were based not upon threats to their status but, rather, upon the escalation of work intensity at the same pay. Workers found themselves protesting the monopoly that employers sought over returns from their investment in technology. At the Forges of La Villette, for example, new furnaces allowed rollers (*lamineurs*) to produce twelve to fourteen thousand kilograms of metal a day rather than ten thousand. These metallurgists had to agitate for more pay to compensate for their greater efforts.[109] Likewise, the well-paid stokers at the Parisian Gas Company found that new equipment, installed in 1889, raised productivity about 20 percent at the cost of greater exertion on their part. Their status was never challenged in a technical sense, but the stokers wanted more money.[110] This sort of dispute may well have been just as common, or more so, than the one that disrupted the Hotchkiss plant for a few days.

No industry did more to reshape factory life in greater Paris than automobile manufacturing, and none has done more to inform the historian's vision of the work experience in factories at the dawn of the twentieth century. For these reasons, as well as for its size (about fifteen thousand by 1906), the automobile labor force merits special attention. The impact and pace of technological change in this industry have, in fact, been the subject of contradictory assessments. Historians tend to stress the persistence of craftmanship in French automobile making. One team of scholars notes that "the shift from skilled labor using artisanal methods to mass production employing semiskilled and unskilled labor [was] slow" and not characteristic of this industry before the Great War.[111] To a contemporary expert, however, the striking feature of automobile production was how much it was able to dispense with the fine skills of accomplished mechanics and rely on rather commonplace workers.[112] This disagreement arises not so much from contrasting evidence as from the different standards applied to the same facts. Historians, impressed by the accomplishments of Henry Ford, have been inclined to minimize changes in the French automobile industry. Yet contemporaries were quite correct to stress the dynamism of this industry in comparison to most others. At the turn of the century, the production of cars was experiencing extensive and noteworthy reorganization. The industry shifted from a pioneering stage and quickly expanded into large-scale production in a number of plants. The startling growth of the earliest car manufacturers, Dion, Clément, and Panhard-Levassor, the opening of large, new plants by them, and the founding of more firms (Renault, Darracq, Lorraine-Dietrich) announced innovations in production. If only to handle labor constraints, work in the growing industry had to take new forms. Indeed, one can profitably speak of a pre-assembly-line rationalization during the first decade of the twentieth century.[113] In the earliest days of car manufacturing, work was performed without system or set procedure; each car was a product unto itself. By 1900, assembling cars was a matter of specialized tasks; men paid at semiskilled rates replaced "master assemblers." The fabrication of parts also experienced much progress, as employers purchased grinding machines, gear cutters, and other automatic machines suitable for producing large quantities of parts. Yankee ingenuity bolstered the productivity of the plants that bordered on the Seine River: 700 of the 1,025 machine tools at Panhard were made in America. Darracq, far from the largest car maker by 1908, had 82 automatic machine tools.[114] Managers were groping their way toward a sequential arrangement of machines, as, for example, in the new Lorraine-Dietrich plant constructed in Argenteuil in 1905.[115] The important automobile plants were, thus, leaders in making work more specialized and repetitive than ever before.

Nonetheless, the role of skilled labor was only partly transformed. De-skilling did occur, but the industry needed workers' judgment and dexterity in tool rooms and repair shops, and on the production line as well. Wage lists from the body, gear, and motor workrooms of the Dion-Bouton plant in 1910 show that a quarter of the fitters (23.1 percent) and a third of the turners (31.1 percent) were skilled mechanics.[116] To have reduced the range of tasks over which workers had discretion below this level would have required an enormous investment, a wholesale scrapping of machines, and the inventing of new ones on a large scale. Only Henry Ford had the will to accomplish such a task.[117] Yet skilled workers in the Parisian industry were already but a part, not the core, of the production process.

In most handicrafts, traditions set standards for work conditions. Indeed, artisans and employers rarely engaged in a dispute that did not entail a recounting of the old ways. Factory work, on the other hand, had fewer such traditions, and the marginalized recruitment of its labor force would seem to promise a certain pliancy on the part of workers. Yet as David Montgomery has argued for North America: "The veterans . . . of industrial life had internalized the industrial sense of time, and they regarded both an extensive division of labor and machine production as their natural environment. However, they had often fashioned from these attitudes neither the docile obedience of automatons, nor the individualism of the 'upwardly mobile.' "[118] Factory workers in greater Paris, and not only the most highly competent of them, were quick to create their own "customs" of the workplace and erect collective forms of control over their jobs.

A single type of factory discipline under which all workers in a particular plant labored was not characteristic of Parisian industry before World War I. Managers would not even have thought that desirable. Most large factories had three sorts of work regimes.[119] Certain laborers were paid by time and received as much oversight from the foreman as he had time to give. At the Cail Machine Company or the Coutant Forges in Ivry, only the casual hands were in this situation. Then, there were laborers under the charge of an internal subcontractor (*marchandeur*), who made his profit by getting work done as quickly as possible. This intermediary, usually a highly skilled worker, either hired craftsmen to do what he could not handle or engaged unskilled laborers, whom he reportedly drove unmercifully.[120] By the twentieth century, management (especially in the machine-building industry) resorted less frequently to subcontracting.[121] The regime that covered the majority of workers entailed payment by piece rates, which implied a certain laxity of supervision and a reliance on the voluntary efforts from wage-earners.

It is correct to speak of piece rates as a form of factory discipline because they set the pace of work and the intensity of supervision more than any other factor. Generally, work at piece rates presupposed a relaxed vigilance on the part of management. Rather than heavy fines to curb lateness, factories had multiple entry hours and a grace period for latecomers. Workers could sometimes come and go with a certain amount of freedom even through the gates of large and sophisticated plants.[122] When management had doubts about the effectiveness of its supervision over workers paid by the day, it might, as the Mors Automobile Company did in 1902, introduce piece rates into as many shops as possible.[123] The freedom to leave a plant momentarily for a break or a drink, a right often assumed by skilled workers at the forge, was not unknown among casual hands in factories, too.[124] The piece-rate mode of payment proved acceptable to all sides because it gave employers the individualized wage they desired and workers, a margin of freedom. The resulting accommodation was necessarily an uneasy one.

A visitor to the factories of the *banlieue* just after World War I noted: "There reigns everywhere in the workroom productive activity, and all the workers, leaning over their machines, seem careful not to waste a moment: they are paid on piece rates."[125] This visitor may have happened upon an exceptionally orderly plant, or—more likely—his observation was the product of wishful thinking and naiveté. Such constancy on the job was not the rule. Numerous were the complaints that laborers dawdled or talked to comrades and then rushed through their work to make up for lost time. The management of Bariquand and Marre created a new layer of supervision, the team heads, to control the problem, which was widespread.[126] Some workers took pride in their ability to waste time and then quickly produce pieces that passed inspection. Indeed, this tempo could easily evolve into a diversion for combating monotony.[127] Such comportment was symptomatic of the universal bane of management, "soldiering" by their piece-rate workers. Laborers feared that diligence would lead only to lower rates, and they learned from experience that rapid production resulted in layoffs. Collective understandings about limiting output seemed a necessity from their point of view. Managers bemoaned the situation, sometimes read tracts on "scientific management," but were slow to take action.[128]

The work regime in most factories was a product of tacit and intricate compromises for both labor and management, with piece rates serving as the *modus operandi*. The director did not have the unquestioned control over work procedures that the masters of the early mechanized textile mills reputedly had. On the other hand, laborers, even highly skilled ones, had to fashion a work culture that fell short of providing the mastery that artisans in smaller shops enjoyed. The industrial craftsmen, laborers who had much discretion over the way they performed their tasks, could not usually transfer their "culture of control" intact from shop to factory. Mold makers, casters, polishers, ironsmiths, sheet-metal workers, and iron-fitters agreed to work at piece rates—but for a price. They often earned more than comrades paid by the day in small firms.[129] The collective wage agreement, the closed shop, the fraternal foremen were absent, or only partially effective, in many factories. Far from relying on a *tarif* to regulate their earnings, the molders, locomotive assemblers, and wheelwrights at Cail in 1881 had to take what the foreman gave them, and he did not always deign to set the rate before the job began.[130] Molders maintained a closed shop at Dion-Bouton but not at the Gouin Metallurgical Construction Company, where few were unionized.[131] Furthermore, factory managers rarely had to defer to the will of their industrial craftsmen in selecting a foreman. The owners of smaller shops may have fired several supervisors at the behest of their metal polishers, but at Bariquand and Marre, polishers worked under a foreman who did not share their work culture and whom they despised. Likewise, mold makers, surely among the proudest of industrial craftsmen, put up with a severe foreman at the Cothias Alloy Company.[132] As we have seen, management also had some ability to control the training and recruitment of their most skilled laborers.

Even the relative freedom from interference that technical proficiency gave to skilled workers was pregnable in factories. The jewelry makers' consummate refusal to consider even minor changes in work routines contrasted markedly with the industrial craftsmen, who faced continual, minor innovations in tools and equipment. Some welcomed such changes as "progress." The trained workers in factories shared their expertise not only with foremen, who were sometimes hostile to their culture, but also with engineers. In 1887 molders and casters at a large plant struck when the engineer interfered one time too many with their work. They demanded that he address his observations to the plant director, who would politely communicate them to the craftsmen.[133] Such an arrangement, which the workers failed to win in any case, might have preserved their dignity, but did not solve the problem of unwelcome supervision. Indeed, this sort of strike was too frequent to suppose that there was a solution within a factory setting. In all these ways, then, industrial craftsmen were disadvantaged relative to their peers who produced one-of-a-kind items in the smaller shops.

Below the level of the superior craftsmen, management did not find all the docility and pliancy for which they might have hoped. Machine operators who performed more routine operations had formulated certain collective arrangements to confront supervisors by the twentieth century, if not earlier. Their "culture of control" was far less elaborate than that of the industrial craftsmen, but it did at least insist on the right to limit output and work discipline. Supervisors who tried to interfere with the habit of soldiering were labeled "brutal slave-drivers" and resisted for being "too severe."[134] If a foreman applied too much pressure, he often became embroiled in shouting matches or even physical confrontations. Then, the issue was quickly transformed into a violation of the laborers' "dignity," a charge that mobilized a great deal of support in defense of the right to work with a minimum of interference. The 280 fitters, turners, and millers at the Cohendet Machine Company initiated a strike in 1899 with just such considerations in mind. They could not accept the former worker whom management had just promoted to talley-clerk because he "knew all the tricks" and could make it difficult to limit output or take surreptitious breaks. Only when the clerk quit voluntarily did the workmen return to their jobs.[135] The laborers in question were not the elite machinists, but rather modestly skilled and semiskilled machine-tool operators who earned up to 7.5 francs a day. Their provocative behavior was by no means an isolated case.

Individualistic efforts to maximize earnings on piece rates were subordinated to collective understandings about limiting production. There is no evidence that employers found the means to crush this sort of workers' control before the First World War—though they were increasingly ready to try.

In the struggle to establish a pliant labor force, paternalism has been an expensive but seemingly worthwhile instrument of managerial policy. Employers in most industrial regions of the world have been eager to provide an extensive range of benefits in return for workers' obedience.[136] In greater Paris, however, paternalism was not especially pervasive or successful. To be sure, conditions for its effective implementation were not ideal here. The isolation and moralization of the labor force, achievable in a mill town, were impossible in the capital. Employers could not attain the proprietary sense and domination over local politics that were possible in other settings. Moreover, the desperation to attract and retain workers, which inspired many a paternalistic gesture, was less necessary in this metropolitan area, the premier magnet of immigration in France. Nonetheless, the printer Paul Dupont demonstrated how much a thoroughgoing policy of paternalism could accomplish even in his volatile trade. The 550 workers in his plant at Clichy enjoyed subsidized housing, profit-sharing provisions, complete medical care, and pensions. In return for the benefits, his laborers kept their distance from the Typographical Society and even allowed Dupont to introduce female compositors, whereas the unionized workers in the smaller shops vigorously resisted this measure.[137] Parisian employers rarely emulated Dupont's successful example, however. Most remained curiously indifferent to paternalist means for moving the balance of forces on the factory floor in their favor.

In the face of rising public concern about working-class housing, the nonchalance of factory owners regarding their laborers' lodgings is noteworthy. Time and again, they built large plants without a thought to housing in suburban communities that were unprepared to receive the influx of workers.[138] When Pierre Rattier built a rubber plant in the still-rural commune of Bezons, he saw the lodging problem solely in terms of public transportation. He bullied the municipal council into improving tramway service—incidentally opening new areas of recruitment for his factory, but at the expense of the town, not to him.[139]

Employers who conceived of paternalism as an important element of industrial relations were usually careful to hire families rather than individuals. Factory directors in greater Paris had spotty records, at best, in their concern about the relatives of workers. The Marquis de Dion, whose right-wing philosophy imparted a proclivity for such concerns, made family hiring a conscious policy at his automobile plant. Just under four-fifths of the fourteen- and fifteen-year-old boys in Puteaux whose fathers worked at Dion-Bouton also found jobs in this plant.[140] Many other owners did not share the policies of the marquis just as they rejected his politics. Only 22 percent of the youths in Ivry and Argenteuil worked in the same factories as their fathers in 1911.[141] Articles in the working-class press of Argenteuil suggest that workers resented the absence of openings for their offspring.[142]

It is true that Parisian factory owners had rather admirable records in founding and funding such self-help institutions as mutual aid societies. Factory laborers did have a great deal more protection from financial losses resulting from illness than did craftsmen.[143] There were also employers, like the tanner Combes of Saint-Denis, who could be moved by the hardship of his workers to make gestures of laudable generosity. During the industrial crisis of 1889, Combes gave ten francs a week to two hundred of his workers and donated eight thousand francs to their cooperative grocery.[144] On the whole, however, the paternalistic actions of employers in greater Paris were narrowly conceived and incomplete. Company directors answered requests for aid and charity from workers with an eye to checking resentment rather than rewarding loyalty. Thus, laborers with records of faithful service received the same pittance as those with tenuous claims on corporate largesse.[145] The tragic flooding of the Seine River in 1910, which closed most plants in the suburbs and put many thousands out of work, provided a test of paternalism—and neighborly charity—for employers. Here was a genuine community crisis that should have elicited the benevolent concern of all factory owners, but it did not. In Puteaux, the Unic Automobile Company did give its 300 workers six francs a day, but Charron (573 workers), Vinot-Deguingant (183 workers), and even Dion-Bouton (2,639 workers) were closefisted in the face of the emergency.[146] Workers and employers rarely shared a community of interests.

Neither laborers nor managers were satisfied with industrial relations in the decade or so before the Great War. Though rarely prepared to go as far as the time-motion studies that Renault instituted in his automobile plant in 1907-1908, employers did want to raise output and productivity.[147] Workers were firm in defending their work culture and may even have become more sensitive than ever to minor challenges to it. As factory directors and workers faced the new century, compromises on operational procedures gave way to confrontation.

In October 1880, the managers of the distinguished Pivert Perfume Company in Aubervilliers instituted a series of crushing fines on female workers: five hours' pay for not finishing their assigned task and two days' pay for each day missed. Seventy-five women struck in protest despite the hopelessness of their plight.[148] Their desperation was a reflection of managerial heavy-handedness. Thirty years after this incident was forgotten, a mechanic named Marcel Pailloux crushed his left hand by catching it in the transmission belts of the spring factory in which he worked.[149] These cases, trivial in themselves, hint at the anarchical, if not savage, qualities of factory life. The image of factory labor has long been shaped by visions of harsh actions perpetrated on an uprooted population in an environment to which they could not easily adjust. Having examined the everyday and the constant in industrial relations, we now turn to the exceptional event to penetrate into the largely hidden world of factory work. Exploring instances of managerial abuse and of work accidents confirms the thrust of our previous discussion—that factory labor was far more a matter of adaptation than of surrender to an irretrievably alienating environment.

Factory workers were inured to a physically wearying and monotonous routine. Occasionally, though, their resigned calm was broken by outrage in the working-class community over some insupportable situation in a factory. Two Socialist journals, *L'Emancipation* of Saint-Denis and *Le Travail* of Argenteuil, provide a sounding of this episodic anger. During the first decade of the twentieth century, both published a series of exposés on factory abuses under the rubric "Our Prisons." An analysis of sixty-nine articles provides insight into the tensions that factory workers experienced at the dawn of the present century. To be sure, the coverage of the abuses was not systematic, nor did the editors seem conscious of any specific patterns of conflict. Their reporting was not even inspired by the current strike activity about them. Despite these gaps (and, in some ways, because of them), "Our Prisons" comments usefully on the texture of factory life, and having two, independent series enhances the reliability of the analysis.

The exposés of both newspapers were strikingly similar in their content. The kinds of industries in which there were outrages, the nature of abuses, and the victims were alike in Argenteuil and Saint-Denis. The profile of abusive situations was quite predictable in some ways. Most were concentrated in the rudest industries: fertilizers, quarrying, chemical products, rubber, and leather-working (see table III-2). They occurred most often in small and middling factories, which outnumbered large ones by a wide margin in the suburbs. The majority of cases entailed female and youthful victims, but this might

Table III-2. Factory Abuses, as Reported by Two Socialist Newspapers, 1902–1912

	N	%
Industries with Incidents		
Chemical	10	14.5
Leather	11	15.9
Fertilizer	12	17.4
Food Processing	9	13.0
Rubber	12	17.4
Quarrying	5	7.2
Metalworking	10	14.5
Total	69	99.9
Nature of Abuses		
Insulting Worker	12	17.4
Inflicting Discomfort	14	20.3
Unhealthful Conditions	15	21.7
Demanding Overwork	13	18.8
Unjust Firing	10	14.5
Other	5	7.2
Total	69	99.9
Victims		
Adult Females	36	52.2
Children	5	7.2
Adult Males	28	40.6
Total	69	100.0

Sources: L'Emancipation and *Le Travail*, 1902–1912.

simply have been a reflection of the editors' efforts to arouse ire by showing the dangers to which the helpless were exposed. One noteworthy feature of the profile was the disproportionately low incidence of abuses in the machine-building industry, the largest in the two towns.

Typical of the abuses was the case of the foreman in a sugar refinery who compelled the female packers to work without heat in the winter. In another incident, the supervisor of a food-processing plant made sexual demands on his underlings. The arbitrary actions of individuals were the source of outrages more often than were the deliberate policies of management. For male laborers, it was less a matter of causing physical discomfort than of attempting to annul an acquired right or of demeaning them through provocative behavior. The Socialist journals reported on foremen who suppressed a break or a customary free drink and, in doing so, enraged workers. The most common source of men's anger was the supervisors' use of foul or violent language to address them. For both male and female laborers, the foreman was usually the perpetrator of abuses. The newspapers implied that these supervisors were acting without the approval of the higher authorities in the plant. In fact, the Socialist press generally appealed to the director to right the situation.

The intolerable managerial policies focused on one issue in particular: efforts to raise workers' productivity. The press castigated employers for firing older workers who were less productive or for reducing piece rates. Above all, the series noted the attempt to accelerate the pace of work through "excessive" pressure. These efforts were normally a good deal less heavy-handed than those imposed by the perfumer Pivert, but they were still quite irksome.

Given the original purpose of the exposés, to make workers conscious of their suffering at the hands of capitalists, it is ironic that they point in the direction of a certain normalization of industrial relations. Abuses rarely arose from conscious policy, and draconian measures to impose control over the work force were, by and large, absent. The series "Our Prisons" delineates quite clearly the principal fault-lines of tension: the discretionary power of a callous foreman and the limited designs of management to counter workers' efforts at limiting output. Although the editors seemed unaware of doing so, they drew a portrait of the strains that were generating much protest at the turn of the century.

Deep feelings were stirred in working-class communities not only by the abuses perpetrated by supervisors but also by severe industrial accidents.[150] These exposed, as nothing else could, the precariousness of the worker's existence. Emotions ran high when employers or insurance companies tried to dodge their responsibilities. Legal questions raised by accidents were the principal concern of workers who sought the free juridical consultations sponsored by the municipality of Saint-Denis. When the Socialist candidate for deputy, Veber, a physician, was accused of having worked for an insurance company, he took special pains to refute the charge.[151] Industrial accidents were hardly a rare event, and their incidence, far from being random, was tied to the structure of factory work.[152]

The declarations of work accidents occurring in the Nineteenth Arrondissement, a district with a substantial number of large plants, reveal the dangers of factory labor as well as the adaptations that workers made to them.[153] During 1911, some 3,900 accidents in the factories of the district were reported in accordance with the law of April 9, 1898 (see table III-3). The injuries recorded were not necessarily serious, but they did at least entail some "incapacity to work."[154] Though it is impossible to calculate accident rates for want of information on the number of factory workers, injuries were clearly a common phenomenon. Not all factory labor was equally threatening, however. The case of the mechanic Pailloux, presented earlier, is a

Table III-3.   Work Accidents in Factories and Artisanal Shops, 1911–1913[a]

	Factory		Workshop	
	N	%	N	%
Victims				
Machine Operator	106	33.7	73	30.9
Other Production Workers	19	6.1	68	29.8
Maintenance or Support Workers	181	57.6	51	21.6
Apprentice	8	2.5	44	18.6
Total	314	99.9	236	100.9
Timing of Accidents				
Midnight–5:59 A.M.	21	6.6	3	1.3
6–9:59 A.M.	81	25.5	68	28.9
10–Noon	37	11.7	43	18.3
Noon–3:59 P.M.	25	7.9	66	28.1
4–5:59 P.M.	84	26.4	38	16.2
6–Midnight	69	21.8	17	7.2
Total	317	99.9	235	100.0
Nature of Accidents				
Fall or Hit by Object	113	36.6	42	18.3
Hurt by Tool or Machine	68	22.0	123	53.5
Injured While Moving Object	77	24.9	29	12.6
Burned	12	3.9	6	2.6
Cut by Material	29	9.4	22	9.6
Other	10	3.2	8	3.5
Total	309	100.0	230	100.1

Sources: A.D.S., V bis 19 Q[6], nos. 10–28; V bis 3 Q[6] nos. 9–13.

[a] This table is based on a one-in-ten sample of accidents in factories of the Nineteenth Arrondissement and a one-in-fifteen sample of those in workshops of the Third Arrondissement.

"classic" one in that it fitted the common image of the factory as a nightmare of dangerous equipment and tangles of transmission belts. Yet it is not a representative case. Laborers who did not work in the production process were more likely to receive injuries than were machine operators. Falling, being hit by a heavy object, hurting oneself while loading—these were the physical tolls of factory labor; less so mangling a finger in a machine tool. Day laborers, the most common victims, were shuffled from one job to another, given little supervision, and stationed in awkward places. Significantly, it was these factors more than the monotony of the job or a pace of work that set the stage for most accidents.[155] The timing of the injuries reinforces these observations. They were events of the early morning, late afternoon, and, especially, the night. The work was not inherently so dangerous, but drowsiness and exhaustion made it so.

Accident declarations from the artisanal Third Arrondissement, home to jewelers, bronze workshops, and the needle trades, provide a useful contrast. Comparing accident rates is not possible because we cannot know the number of workers in this section of Paris. Still, the 3,800 declarations suggest a rate not much lower than the one for the Nineteenth. The significant point is that the work process in the handicrafts was relatively more dangerous than was production in factories. Typical of the injured in this district was Julien Perin, a lens grinder who mangled his finger in his lathe.[156] Accidents were a constant danger, too, not simply in the late hours, after an exhausting day, but also at midmorning. Perhaps the craft workers' varied work routines led them into dangers that machine operators in factories could avoid.

Inferences from a profile of industrial accidents need to be drawn with caution; by themselves they prove little. The data do reinforce the impression, however, that factory employers were unsuccessful in raising the pace of work to levels that made laborers unable to cope. Moreover, the accident records reveal a labor force that had largely mastered its machinery and one that was able to live with the monotony of factory work.

A final assessment of the quality of integration entailed in factory labor derives from an examination of job mobility. There seemed to be little to discourage a peripatetic existence. Rewards for loyal service were small; conditions and pay varied widely from one plant to another. Above all, employment in any one factory was highly irregular. Despite these discouragements to persistency, the scattered evidence on the subject shows that an appreciable segment of the factory work force remained with the same employer for a few years, at least. A nomadic existence was not the goal of factory workers nor their inevitable fate.

Neither the Hotchkiss Armament Company of Saint-Denis nor the engineering firm of Farcot in Saint-Ouen was an especially benevolent employer. Yet an important part of their labor forces remained from year to year. In 1908, 17 percent of the 550 workers at Hotchkiss had been present for at least five years, and 12 percent had seniority of ten years.[157] The figures from Farcot for 1884 were even more impressive. Of its 550 laborers, 120 had worked at this factory for twenty years.[158] The case of the Rattier Rubber Company in Bezons shows that persistency was characteristic of the unskilled workers outside the machine-building industry, too. The wage-earners in this village with a factory had mobile antecedents, but once they took jobs in Rattier's plant, they tended to remain. The rate of residential stability between 1876 and 1881 was 65.4 percent, and over 50 percent for the decade after 1876. We can assume that continued residence in Bezons meant continued work in the rubber plant since there were no other alternatives.[159] The workers at the coal-

distilling plants of the Parisian Gas Company offer a final and revealing test case of job mobility. Seasonality of employment was a
clear-cut feature of these factories; the summer work force was only
half the size of the winter one. Yet, year after year, carters, coal
shovelers, and day laborers returned for their jobs. Of the 3,537
manual workers present in 1904, 73 percent (2,585) had been with
the company in 1896. More than half (51.6 percent) of the stokers,
rather well-paid workers, had ten consecutive years of seniority.[160]
Such workers obviously struggled to retain their jobs with the gas
company because the circumstances of their employment did not
permit it as a matter of course. Apparently, an appreciable proportion of the factory labor force sought rootedness and a relative predictability of employment. Workers' collective pressures and their
accommodations with management meant that they did not have to
pay an unacceptably high price on the job for these modest benefits.

SERVICE WORKERS

The rural immigrants who took jobs in the service sector put up with
some of the rudest conditions that Parisians were asked to endure.
Some were on their feet, literally, from dawn till dusk; at night, they
were locked into stores only to make a bed for themselves on the
floor or a counter.[161] Whereas contractors put roofs over the construction sites to protect workers from the elements, cabbies or carters habitually endured inclemency.[162] It is little wonder that cooks,
hairdressers, and the like suffered from abnormally high adult mortality rates.[163] Making a living by serving the needs and whims of
Parisian consumers imposed a marathon of toil upon them. Butchers'
assistants were at work by 4:30 in the morning and did not leave
their shops until after 8:00 in the evening. Barbers and hairdressers
worked for fourteen or fifteen hours a day with one afternoon of
liberty a week. Teamsters stayed on the job fifteen to seventeen
hours. By comparison, tramway workers, who generally alternated
ten- and fourteen-hour days, had moderate work schedules.[164]

Of the two branches in the service sector, transportation and
commerce, the former had more potential for changes in the contours
of work. Labor in retailing and in personal services was difficult to
rationalize or reorganize. The employers, working beside their aides,
would have had to alter their own routines appreciably. To observe
the limits of rationalization in this sort of labor, we have only to
consider the case of the Duval Restaurants, the familiar mass-eating
establishments in central Paris in the late nineteenth century. The
quest for efficiency led Duval, whose staff of twelve hundred served

over three million meals per year, to reorganize in two ways. He decided to pay his waiters rather than have diners tip them. Whether this measure increased his control over the staff is unclear since the habit of tipping persisted. Second, Duval aspired to lower wage expectations and fashion a pliant personnel by hiring women to wait on tables.[165] Such moves did not change work or power relations substantially, and this innovative restaurateur even found that his waitresses were far from docile.[166] Still less did Duval's changes present a model for the mass of family businesses and tiny concerns.

The abuses about which commercial workers complained in the late nineteenth century were hardly novel. Waiters resented the portion of tips they had to give to the boss or the penalties they paid for broken dishes. Hairdressers grudgingly contributed toward the cost of washing the shop windows.[167] Above all, there was the emotional issue of paying fees for job placement. Most workers in retail trades had to surrender their first week's earnings or a portion of their monthly income to a placement service, which controlled all job openings. The high cost of procuring a job was especially vexing to workers who changed positions frequently, for they lost a considerable sum with each move. Of course, these fees made the cost of leaving an unhappy situation high.[168]

The potential for hearing novel complaints from workers in the transportation sector was greater because these laborers faced managerial innovations more fully. Indeed, capital concentration and the rationalization of work procedures advanced more thoroughly in certain branches of transportation than in most manufacturing industries. Nicholas Papayanis has described the sudden restructuring of the cab industry with the creation of the Imperial Coach Company in 1855.[169] This development, which resulted in the replacement of small entrepreneurs and independent drivers by a huge enterprise, had parallels in carting, though the change was not so dramatic. Originally, the teamster industry was organized as cabbing was. Many carters, possessing their own wagons and horses, contracted individually with wholesalers or manufacturers to perform a specific task. From the 1850s, though, transportation entrepreneurs began to develop a greater hold over this sort of work; according to the police, they dominated the carting industry by the 1880s and had converted most carters into wage-earners.[170] In a sense, then, the "classic" transformation from independent trade to proletarianized labor in a concentrated industry was more applicable to these service workers than to nearly all craftsmen.

Concentration, however, was not sufficient to set the conditions for a disciplined work force. The small employers in retail trades were better positioned to fashion one because their personnel were under their direct supervision. The transportation workers were inevitably beyond the employer's sight, a situation that made surveillance not impossible but heavy-handed. Like the Imperial Coach Company, employers in transportation were reduced to hiring secret agents to spy on their personnel. Reported incidents led to firings or weighty fines. Carters paid five to twenty francs—one to four days' pay—for each accident, whether they were at fault or not. The penalties for tramway workers were, at the minimum, a fifth of daily earnings. Ticket-takers had to sustain these fines and reimburse the company for any losses they caused.[171] The burden of these sanctions, however, did not at all ensure that these disciplining procedures had the desired result. Transportation workers had strong traditions of independence and probably did not permit company inspectors to alter their work patterns very much.[172]

The case of the lamplighters who worked for the Parisian Gas Company illustrates the limited responses of "outdoor" service workers to the surveillance policies of their employers.[173] In effect, the lamplighters ignored as best they could both the secret inspectors and the heavy fines. They continued to interrupt their labor with a trip to the café or with a nap; they fell far behind schedule or failed to complete their routes. Virtually every lamplighter the company employed accumulated a number of fines, not just over the course of their careers, but each year. Having to pay a penalty every few months apparently did not curb the faults that produced those sanctions. Presumably, the gas company did not fire these workers because new ones would have behaved similarly. The wearying workday that service laborers were expected to endure made it inevitable that they would impose, as fully as possible, their own pace and conditions.

Thus, service workers were both on the margin of structural change and directly in the maelstrom, but this, in itself, did not matter very much as far as work experiences were concerned. Their work regimes, among the rudest of any group, were not much affected by attempts to rationalize and discipline. Service workers accepted harsh fines and firings as they did the hard counters on which they slept or the cold winds that bit them as they drove.

WHITE-COLLAR WORKERS

If work culture in the handicrafts was strongly colored by nostalgic visions of a happier past, so was the situation of white-collar employees in the late nineteenth century. Tailors extolled the taste and artistry that supposedly reigned in their trade only fifty years before the Commune; clerks, for their part, recalled the personal relations with an employer, the duties that exposed them to all aspects of a business, and the prospects they themselves had for becoming bosses.[174] Collective traditions emanating from the preindustrial era were often as relevant to clerks as to artisans. Just as in the handicrafts, business forms that predominated in an earlier age were still very much alive on the eve of the war. About half the modest white-collar workers of greater Paris were employed in small- or moderate-size firms, even in the twentieth century. It was still rather common for a book-keeper who had labored many years in the office of a small workshop to borrow money from the boss when the latter retired and purchase the business.[175] In the stores of the Parisian boulevards, numerous were the offspring of provincial shopkeepers who eventually returned home to run the family business. Contemporary social observers generally thought about white-collar workers in terms of great bu-reaucracies, but the solidarities of small enterprise were very much alive.

The belatedly won right of clerks to take grievances to the Work-ers' Arbitration Council (*Conseil de Prud'hommes*) permits us to explore the realities of work in small firms. Large commercial or-ganizations were decidedly underrepresented, probably because they used private means to deal with work-related disputes. Clerks from small and middling entreprises brought nearly 2,300 cases to the council in 1910, indicating many tensions in their milieu.[176] The of-fices of manufacturing firms, wholesale houses, and agencies of all sorts seemed to have been especially contentious settings compared to retail shops. As we have noted earlier, plaintiffs from offices outnumbered salespeople five to one. The retail employees who did appear before the council were nearly twice as likely to be women as men. The fact that the great preponderance of cases (79 percent) concerned demands for compensations following sudden firings means that insecurity was the chief problem on the minds of these plaintiffs. The contexts of the terminations were not always described in detail, but one can discern three sorts of tensions in offices as the most common. About a third of the cases resulted from the employer's decision to reduce the size of his staff. The predicament of one accountant who had worked for a plaster manufacturer for fifteen years and suddenly found himself without a job was not an isolated one. The cases that came before the council do little to support the proposition that seniority provided much protection from these sit-uations. Another fourth of the lawsuits grew out of altercations and disagreements. The bookkeeper of an artificial-flower manufacturer was fired when he refused to change his vacation plans to fit the needs of his boss. A saleswoman received notice when the employer overheard her mocking him. It is significant that disputes were always with the employer, not with an office manager or a superior. Personalized relations with the boss apparently prevailed in this milieu—though they were not always harmonious. Alleged incompetence was the most frequent cause for firings (39 percent of the known cases). In these instances, too, employees with several years' seniority were plaintiffs as often as were beginners. Apparently, mistakes could override a record of loyal service. The small office was not only an insecure environment, but a demanding one as well. Employers prosecuted their clerks for losses incurred through their errors. One manufacturer sued his accountant for the 350 francs lost when the receipts were not prepared on time. A stenographer found herself owing 325 francs for the loss of business resulting from her negligence. There were scores of such cases before the Workers' Council in 1910. The employees' occupational press was surely correct to stress the insecurities and anxieties that clerks suffered.[177]

Opportunities for personalized relations with the boss, varied duties, and advancement were not merely memories from an earlier age but were tied to rough-and-tumble conditions that idealized visions of the past did not include. Duties were carefully allocated, and sanctions for falling short of them were severe. If the ideal of paternalism survived in the small offices, it was tempered with sternness. On the other hand, the diligent, capable clerk, working under the attendant eye of his boss, could probably rise to a superior position after many years' service. The view expressed by a union newspaper that "one was not an office worker or an accountant by vocation or taste, but only by need" may well have expressed the frustrations of the many clerks whom the system did not reward.[178] Employers might have responded that these clerks had not measured up to the job when given a chance in a competitive and overcrowded line of work. Nostalgic visions usually overlooked these harsher realities.

"Secure," "enervating," "tyrannical," "satisfying," "petty," "nerve-wracking"—all these terms appeared in contemporary descriptions of work in the large store or office. Contradictory though the terms are, each touches on a bit of truth. The contradictory aspects of white-collar work in large bureaucracies derived ultimately from the managerial goals that regulated such labor: running the organization efficiently and encouraging employees to identify with the enterprise. If these goals were complementary from the manager's point of view, the policies they dictated did not seem so to many employees. In effect, directors of large bureaucracies were attempting to break with the personalized relations and unspecialized work in the small shop and office. At the same time, they wished to preserve the presumed solidarity between boss and clerk in that environment.

Clerical and sales employees had to identify with their employer and perceive their organization as more than a source of income. The office personnel, in daily contact with the company's financial records and internal documents, knew the "secrets" of the organization. Not only did security dictate the need for a loyal and discrete personnel, but businessmen were culturally resistant to the notion of opening their books to strangers. The personnel inevitably represented the organization to its clientele and to the public. Office directors who read in the newspaper about a scandal caused by one of their employees knew they faced a delicate problem of "image repair."[179] The need for loyalty and identity made managers conceive of white-collar work as a *commission*: After a probationary period, the company offered the clerk a permanent position that brought lifetime benefits; in accepting, the clerks committed themselves to the company. At the Parisian Gas Company, the letter of commission, written on costly stationery, contained paternalistic language designed to convey a sense of belonging and was signed by the director himself.[180]

Fine gestures, however, could not obscure the serious problems entailed in transferring the solidarities of small commerce to large, bureaucratic settings. The work employees did and the supervision to which they were subjected seriously encumbered efforts to elicit the desired commitments from employees. Office workers in this setting did minutely divided work that failed to instill a sense of responsibility for an operation. One handbook of office work from the dawn of this century listed nineteen distinct job titles.[181] The work of copying documents or shipping orders, once the early steps in training for higher positions, had become separate occupations. A series of job descriptions from one corporation with over two thousand clerks repeated *ad nauseum* the same tasks: copy, enter, fill out a slip, file.[182] Office managers aimed at unvaried routine, for such work promised order and security.

Sales work was not quite so routine and could grant more room for individual initiative. Department stores with a prosperous clientele wanted "skilled selling" from their clerks, who had to know the product line, to sense the customer's tastes, to present merchandise properly, and to promote it discretely.[183] Commissions rewarded sellers for doing this well. There were, however, thousands of salespeople who worked for dime-stores (*bazars*) or emporia with a humble clientele.[184] In these outlets, skilled selling was not the rule.

Employees merely kept an eye on the merchandise and totaled the bills.

This kind of routine work gave a narrow meaning to the sort of "careers" that white-collar work promised. Office head was the highest position for which clerks could realistically hope, and this post usually entailed the same work underlings performed with the addition of supervisory duties. Managerial roles were normally out of the question, and the average clerk was not likely to become chief of his office, even after a lifetime of service. The ratio of clerks to bureau heads in the major railroad companies was about a hundred to one.[185] The Accounts Receivable Department at the Parisian Gas Company had 318 employees and 4 chiefs in 1901; the Collection Department had 173 employees and 3 heads.[186] In the postal service, the ratio of clerks to supervisors was five to one in the 1870s, and eleven to one by the last decade of the nineteenth century.[187] Administrations like that of the Bon Marché Department Store, which recruited management from within the ranks, were exceptional.[188] Most organizations required special training or education for their superior posts. Even a position that was unencumbered with technical requirements, like principal clerk at the municipal pawn shops (*Mont-de-Piété*), could be reached only through a competitive examination to which outsiders were admitted, so that ordinary clerks were unlikely to be promoted through the ranks.[189]

In lieu of genuine opportunities for advancement to managerial positions, bureaucracies made "careers" out of specialized work. A single job was generally divided into several "classes" through which an employee moved in the course of a lifetime. Thus, a receipt clerk passed through seven grades during his career with the Municipal Duties Administration (*Octroi*). Rising through these ranks involved an increase in income but no new responsibilities.[190] Such were the usual rewards for devotion and industry that large enterprises had to offer their clerks.

The ethos of the small office or shop, with emphasis on personal accountability and rewards, may have survived for a time in the bureaucratic milieus.[191] Very soon, though, administrators came to rely on means other than promotions to build solidarity with their personnel. The effort to mold clerks to the organization consisted fundamentally of providing extensive fringe benefits and paternalistic gestures. Protection from the insecurities of illness and old age were nearly universal in large organizations. Often employees could expect half-pay after twenty-five or thirty years of service, and they did not even have to make contributions to the pension fund. Unlike manual laborers, for whom incapacity brought immediate hardship, the em-

Table III-4.   Employees' Annual Vacations (c. 1900)

Company/Status	Duration (days)
Bank of France	
Employees	7–14
Principal Clerks	21
Bureau Chief	30
Omnibus Company	
Office Boys	10
Employees	14
Principal Clerks	14
Subchiefs	21
Water Company	
Employees	14
Subchiefs	21
Crédit Lyonnais	
Employees	10
Section Head	15
Société Générale	
Employees	8–11
Principal Clerks	15
Subchief	21

Source: A.D.S., V 8 O¹ no. 149, Dossier: "Revendications du personnel, Etat des congés annuels . . . (9 novembre 1900)."

ployee could expect a month or more of full pay when ill. The Société Générale bank reportedly spent a hundred thousand francs a year on medical services for its two thousand employees.[192] A benefit that was not common before the Commune but became an accepted part of white-collar life was the annual, paid vacation. Table III-4 shows the length of holidays enjoyed by clerks at several enterprises by the turn of the century. Managers were willing to foster some variety in the lives of their agents, at least off the job.

Employers found many opportunities to grant privileges to their personnel. Giving time off (sometimes compensated) for honeymoons was one gesture that symbolized the solicitude of the company for its employees' contentment. Paying funeral costs and permitting co-workers to attend the rites emphasized the sense of community employers wished to encourage. There were also liberal leave policies for "family affairs," with time rarely deducted from vacations. The railroads were even quick to take up the campaign of populationists by offering child support to large families.[193]

Large organizations clearly wanted employees to find within the company the security traditionally guaranteed by family property. The cost of providing this was increasingly burdensome, as table III-5 shows in the case of two typical companies. Yet, for all the solid advantages of these benefits, white-collar workers could not define their relations to the employer primarily in terms of them. The em-

Table III-5. Rising Cost (in Francs) of Employees' Fringe Benefits at Two Companies

Year	Value of Benefits	Year	Value of Benefits
	Parisian Omnibus Company		
1856	4,704	1875	153,708
1860	41,693	1880	287,834
1865	110,838	1885	290,625
1870	137,827	1890	378,337
	Parisian Gas Company		
1860	171,137	1880	924,658
1865	378,264	1885	1,274,281
1870	426,537	1890	1,661,638
1875	628,890		

Source: A.D.S., V 8 O¹ no. 153, Procès-verbal de l'audience donnée le 2 novembre 1892.

ployee's work regime dispelled the pretense of partnership with management.

The workday of employees, if not physically exhausting, was usually prolonged. The gentlemanly hours of the bank clerk, nine to noon and two to six, were the privilege of a minority of employees. The twelve- or thirteen-hour days of department store clerks were notorious and nearer to the average situation. One clerk at the Bazar Grande Montrouge worked until 3:00 A.M. for several days in a row and was then fired for refusing to work another night. Clerks at the Félix Potin Groceries worked twelve-hour days as did the office staffs of wholesale houses during the spring and fall.[194] Even bank clerks were not totally free from such burdens: Employees at the branch offices of the Bank of France (and presumably others) worked eleven hours or more for six days a month and had to sleep at the bank one night in three to guard the strong boxes.[195] Employees profoundly resented such long hours.

Skilled craftsmen may have had more discretion over their work pace than did employees. White-collar work was, in effect, task oriented but clerks did not determine the task. Salespeople had to follow the flow of customers and the pressures of commission pay. The intensity of their work was greatest at the end of their long day.[196] In the large offices managers generally established work quotas that had to be met before a clerk could finish the day. At the Parisian Gas Company, employees had to issue 250 receipts a day or enter 300 debits into the general ledger. Even the office heads claimed that this was impossible to accomplish in seven hours, so that overtime (uncompensated) was a daily reality.[197] Having to add up bills or register columns swiftly but accurately under the threat of fines held employees in terror.[198]

In the face of the rising costs of benefits companies seemed to have set deliberate policies of understaffing and counted on speed-ups to compensate at the turn of the century, if not earlier.[199] The volume handled by the postal service grew 30 percent between 1901 and 1905 but its personnel grew only 16 percent.[200] The number of gas concessions grew 6 percent a year in Paris during the 1890s, but the gas company expanded its staff only 1 percent a year in that period. Office managers calculated that their staffs were 10 percent below what they should have been even when the work quotas set by management were used as the basis of calculation.[201] The railroad companies were surely not alone in declining to hire more agents when granting vacations to their clerks, thereby pushing some of the costs of this benefit upon the personnel.[202] Organized employees complained through their press of having to take home work at night "to the detriment of their health and family life."[203] Most artisans would not have tolerated the sorts of sanctions managers used to achieve compliance with their rules. Fines and threats of fining forcefully shaped the work environment of salespeople. Department store clerks feared making errors as they totaled bills not only because they were fined but also because the mistakes were noted in their dossiers. If the company lost money, clerks had to make up the difference out of their own pockets. The 3,500 employees at the Louvre Department Store paid enough in fines to cover the cost of the inspection service, which had a budget of 55,000 francs.[204] The possibility of being fired was a more serious threat that hung over salespeople without much seniority. Michael Miller found a dismissal rate of 39 percent at Bon Marché.[205] Managers insisted on adherence to the house rules and procedures, often for their own sake. The case of one clerk at the Galeries Lafayette, fired for drinking coffee during the pre-opening routine, was typical of the few grievances that came before the Workers' Arbitration Council from department stores.[206] Irregularities in one's private life could also result in termination. Surely, the most common reason for dismissal, though, was the failure to generate sufficient sales.

Bill collectors, meter readers, and other "active" (or "outside") agents were similarly burdened with threats of sanctions. Working beyond the sight of managers, handling cash without direct supervision, and dealing directly with customers, these employees were the targets of much managerial suspicion. They were fined more than other employees and fired quite readily. Those of the Parisian Gas Company preferred to pay out of their own pockets the money they lost through error rather than report it to the company. The Place Clichy Department Store had the policy of suspending an agent at the moment a customer's complaint was filed and of firing him if there was a second complaint, even an unsubstantiated one.[207] These clerks might have justifiably defended themselves on the grounds that there was sometimes no perfectly decorous way to collect a bill.

The surveillance of office workers was less oppressive. Every bureaucracy had its regulations for fining, but they were sparingly applied, at least before warnings had been issued. Two of the largest railroad companies abolished their fining policies altogether before the new century opened.[208] Tippling or wearing threadbare clothes did not result in dismissal, as would certainly have occurred in department stores.[209] When managers were dealing with clerks who were not in the presence of clients, they tended to be more lenient.

A concern that all employees shared equally was whether they would receive a bonus or promotion that year. Even the privileged ministerial employee braced himself for the announcement on January 1.[210] Corporations firmly insisted on the right to reward employees solely on the basis of individual effort. Clerks, on the other hand, would have preferred the policy of the Prefecture of Paris, which based two-thirds of all promotions on seniority. Indeed, many employees claimed that it was not even feasible to assess their worth as individuals because work was so minutely divided and routinized that no personal initiative was possible.[211] Clerks suspected that favoritism and nepotism were important channels to rewards. Emotions ran high on this issue. It caused the first public protests among postal and railroad employees, in the 1880s.[212] That so few clerks received bonuses or promotions each year—only 11 percent of them at the gas company—was a matter of recurring disappointment and anguish.

Even the fringe benefits designed to bolster loyalty to the company became sources of discontent. White-collar workers rarely viewed the medical care they received from their employers as more than perfunctory.[213] Complaints about the skimpy but free meals from the company canteen were universal. Clerks disliked having to purchase extra dishes in order to receive a substantial and varied meal, and they claimed that the company took a profit on such sales.[214] They frequently questioned the generosity of their retirement plans. Employees were well informed about the improved benefits offered by other bureaucracies—the prefecture and the railroad companies were pace-setters in these matters—and impatient when their administration was slow to meet the new standard. So little gratitude did bonuses generate that members of one large employees' union proposed striking immediately after the boss handed them their gratuities.[215]

In the end, managers and employees diverged significantly in their outlooks on fringe benefits. A significant segment of clerks regarded them not as rewards for devoted service but rather as part of their just compensation for demanding work and limited futures. Hence, they pressured for even fuller packages of benefits, more regularly bestowed, and considered discretionary bonuses as earned supplements to their income. Employers could not accept such assumptions.

Like craftsmen and factory workers, white-collar clerks sought to stake out some mastery over their work regime, or at least to set limits to the demands that their superiors might make upon them. Explicit "soldiering" was commonplace. When employees entered an office, fellow clerks told them to look busy all the time so as to discourage management from increasing the work load.[216] The search for shortcuts in performing assigned tasks was universal. Cashiers at the Parisian Gas Company were supposed to receive payments until 4:45 in the afternoon, and only then were they to sort their cash and have their receipts verified, activities that kept them an hour or so after closing. Habitually, though, cashiers began to count and sort their cash in the midafternoon so that they were prepared for verification from the moment their counters closed. Customers who came a bit before closing and needed change were out of luck. Similarly, the clerks in the Accounts Receivable Department were continually devising new and abbreviated ways to complete their pay-in slips. They claimed that more thorough reporting was a waste of time, but managers fought the innovations on the grounds that they made the check for accuracy more difficult.[217] (This outcome may also have been on the clerks' minds when they proposed the changes.) Bureaucratic rules usually required employees to remain at their posts under all but exceptional circumstances. In practice, they found reasons to absent themselves from their places fairly regularly. Two salesclerks were able to carry on a courtship in a tightly supervised department store.[218]

The coming and going of clients supposedly regulated the pace of work for many white-collar workers who served them directly, but clerks found ways to impose their pace on clients to some degree. Employees at bill-paying counters made customers wait and did the paperwork that was supposed to occupy them after closing hours.[219] Salesclerks probably handled customers in the same manner, especially after developing a "feel" about which ones would or would not make a purchase. A final safety valve on the strains at work entailed absenting oneself, a practice made painless by having paid sick days. The number of absences due to illness among agents of the Northern Railroad Company was two and a half times higher than that of laborers, who lost pay for their days off.[220]

To counter managerial pressure against these practices, employees developed informal means to test authority and discourage its application. The office seems to have been the scene not of genteel demeanor but rather of a good deal of bickering, rudeness, scowling, and back talk. Reports on the gas company employees commonly contained the criticism that they "took observations poorly." That this effort to discourage supervision had its intended effect upon timid or uncertain superiors is clear; a frequent comment in their dossiers was that they "lacked the forcefulness to make themselves obeyed."[221] The reputed tendency of humble clerks to cower before authority was, apparently, highly exaggerated.

The culture of white-collar workers seems to have been non-competitive as well as antagonistic to the aggressive colleague. A union delegate who visited Britain contrasted the individualistic ethic of salespeople in London with the cooperativeness taken for granted at Parisian department stores.[222] On the other hand, persons judged to have been promoted unfairly could expect informal sanctions from their underlings: personal snubs, the withholding of useful information, the dissemination of past secrets, and the like.[223] Anonymous "poison pen" letters to company directors contained, above all else, unfavorable comments on recently promoted clerks.[224] An adversarial relationship, not an identity of interests, existed between management and many humble employees. Clerks had little confidence that the administration would reward them justly, and they looked to co-workers for support against superiors.

The marriage acts of modest employees hinted at rather strong habits of off-the-job sociability among co-workers in offices and stores. Such associations would only have reinforced the solidarity of employees at the workplace. Whether these collective understandings were as strong as those among craftsmen is not clear, but they did represent a force with which managers had to contend.

What undoubtedly helped to reinforce solidarity among employees was a sense of closing opportunities and unfulfilled expectations, which exacerbated the normal tensions at work. The last years of the Second Empire and the first decade after the Commune had been a rather encouraging time for clerks who lacked useful contacts and had only basic computational skills. Office and sales staffs were then expanding as rapidly as they ever would. The cost of fringe benefits was not yet escalating so rapidly as to promote managerial efforts to limit growth. This privileged era did not survive the depression of the mid-1880s. A trend toward cutting costs and making do with the staffs at hand paralleled in some ways the rationalizing efforts of manufacturers. A common step taken by organizations as diverse as the Postal Service and the Parisian Gas Company was to substitute inexpensive "auxiliary" clerks for commissioned ones. The former were paid about five francs a day, qualified for none of the fringe benefits, and could be dismissed at will. Managers also noted that auxiliaries, hoping to attain regular positions, were often more pliant than were commissioned clerks. Auxiliaries formed 6 percent of the personnel at the gas company in 1881 and just under 12 percent in 1893.[225] Variations on this cost-cutting strategy included increasing the probationary period clerks spent before being considered for commission and firing employees just before they could qualify for commission.[226] Not surprisingly, tenured clerks equated the auxiliaries with the foreign laborers who threatened Parisian craft workers with lower wages and standards.

The managerial quest for inexpensive, efficient, and pliant agents favored the influx of women into offices, but other factors as well influenced the employment of women. Cultural stereotypes were often sufficiently strong to restrict opportunities for females. The Postal Service operated on the principle that contact with the public was unsuitable for women; only in the 1890s did budgetary pressures and a number of other considerations finally open the Parisian bureaus to female clerks.[227] Elsewhere, cultural imperatives prevailed over economic ones. Railroad companies were certainly active in cost-cutting measures; yet, only 2.5 percent of employees in this industry were female in 1911.[228] The gas company had no more than 24 women among its 2,300 clerks at the turn of the century, all stenographers. The decision to fill other positions with females was raised at a board meeting in 1899 and dismissed without discussion.[229] Barriers were lower in sales work, perhaps because the clientele was often female and because women were especially skilled at relating to customers and promoting stock. Only department store magnates who were particularly sensitive to bourgeois proprieties, like the Boucicauts of Bon Marché, sought to avoid the employment of females. At the Galeries Lafayette and the Louvre Department Store, however, women constituted, respectively, a half and a third of the sales personnel.[230] The salesmen who suspected that department stores experiencing financial trouble staffed their counters with females might have had an explanation for the timing of women's entry into the stores but not for the expansion of their presence, which was a consequence of their success on the job.[231]

New office machinery had the potential to disrupt established clerical routines but drew fewer comments than did the entry of women. The impact of typewriters was to alter traditional channels of training and promotion, especially in small offices. Letter-copying had been the usual, entry-level post for a young clerk, and through it he was expected to learn about the business and advance to more important positions. With machine copying, this task became a permanent job, usually for women. Young men had to start in posts of greater responsibility, requiring more extensive preparation.[232] Clerks who had little but good penmanship to recommend them had a new career barrier but failed to make their complaints heard. The keyboard adding machine had a still more ambiguous impact.[233] Given the annoying pressures on clerks to compute rapidly and accurately, the invention might have improved their work situation—at the expense, of course, of the few virtuosos of addition who advanced on their unusual talents. It might also have raised the level of training required at entry since mere skill in arithmetic was less valuable. Yet this technology entered offices slowly and belatedly, if at all. Just before the war, employees and managers still assumed that human computational skills were all important, and they hardly acknowledged the existence of the adding machine.[234] The problem of male employees was not competition from women or machines but decelerating growth in clerical employment and an increased hardheadedness among employers.

White-collar workers approached their work much more in terms of instrumentality than in terms of solidarity with their organizations. Employees did not expect much stimulation or fulfillment from their jobs. Hopes for careers entailing responsibility or power did not motivate most clerks. They transmuted paternalistic benefits into earned compensations so systematically that they often had little gratitude for managerial bounty. All this is not to say that employees were above being "bought off" with regular pay and extensive benefits; the large majority probably were. Yet managerial goals were nonetheless undermined.

Modest employees were bureaucrats without being careerists. It is not at all clear that many accepted the cultural and psychic imperatives of careers open to talent; yet they were most comfortable in bureaucratic settings. Indeed, employees desired more routine and more regularity in their work conditions, not more responsibility or opportunities to prove themselves. They evinced skill at bending rules to their own purposes. Few would have thrived in the small-firm environment upon which they reflected so nostalgically.

IV

Off-the-Job Life

Work remained the principal socializing experience for the common people throughout the nineteenth century. It was central in establishing their self-image, their ambitions, and their patterns of sociability. Yet the late nineteenth century was a period of innovation in life off the job. Wage-earners' forms of recreation and of familial organization were more like those of the propertied classes by 1914 than they had been on the eve of the Commune. Such transformations raise intriguing and potentially far-reaching questions about working-class culture: Was it becoming more privatized and domesticated? To what extent was work becoming more instrumental in the laborer's constellation of values? Do these changes mark an evolution toward *embourgeoisement*? This chapter documents the palpable but highly uneven changes in private life. Our findings suggest that off-the-job comportment of manual workers, though altering in detail, remained an arena of tension and unfulfilled expectations, not one around which people could build their lives. Modest white-collar employees, on the other hand, were all too eager to build their lives around their leisurely pastimes.

THE LEISURE OF WAGE-EARNERS

Among the reassuring images of the *belle époque* are the lively boulevards, crowded theaters, and noisy concert halls. But were these forms of commercialized entertainment not reserved for the "new" middle classes, young, unattached men from solidly bourgeois households, and the more daring members of the propertied classes? Historians have frequently portrayed the decades before World War I as a period of cultural impoverishment for workers. They argue that artisanal traditions, collective festivities, and local celebrations declined in vitality by the late nineteenth century, whereas the newer forms of commercialized leisure did not become part of working-class life until the interwar years. "What seems to be characteristic of the period before the First World War," writes Michael Marrus, "is the impoverishment of leisure, the sheer lack of things for ordinary people to do with the time they were not working." He ties this loss to the increased volume of drinking. Peter Stearns finds that wage-earners were slow to formulate new tastes in leisure even as they derived less meaning from their work.[1] We shall see that trends in working-class recreation were less bleak, at least in greater Paris. Indeed, for certain sorts of laborers, recreational activities assumed considerable intensity. For all workers, they were a revealing indication of outlook and aspirations.

Before the quality of off-the-job life can be discussed, we need to know more about the amount and distribution of free time. There was, of course, an unprecedented reduction in the official workday between the Commune and the First World War. Until the 1890s most industries or crafts had days of eleven or twelve hours. By the turn of the century the ten-hour day became by far the most common schedule.[2] Certain privileged craftsmen, like typographers, attained a nine-hour day by the war.[3] Curtailed workdays, did not, however, translate directly into increased leisure time. For one thing, the trajectory between home and work had been lengthening since the mid-nineteenth century in Paris. Any factory could expect to draw workers from several communes by the twentieth century, and it is far from clear that workers were able to benefit from innovations in urban transportation. More significantly, only a minority of laborers worked the "regular" day of official statistics. Fully trained craftsmen were the ones most likely to do so—though not in the dead season. The specialized craft and domestic workers were unlikely to have standard days and weeks of labor. Makers of billfolds told a parliamentary commission that only in the luxury workshops were there regular workdays; being employed by jobbers, as most were, meant "a constant state of layoffs and overwork." Engravers and makers of metal ornaments worked their help with intensity from Thursday to Saturday and gave them little to do for the rest of the week.[4] Handicraftsmen contributed to this irregularity by intermingling labor with socializing. Thus, porcelain painters vaunted their freedom: "We may return to work at half past one, two o'clock, or three o'clock; we sing; take a smoke." Metal polishers did not begin work before eight o'clock and passed a part of the day at the café.[5] Domestic labor in the garment trades was notorious for its seasonal instability. Charles Benoist found that in 1890–1891 one seamstress worked three days of four hours, two days of five hours, eight days of six hours, five days of eight hours, seven days of nine hours, twenty-four days of nine and a half hours, ninety-six days of ten hours, three days of ten and a half hours, ten days of eleven hours, thirty days of twelve hours, fifty-nine days of thirteen hours, seven days of fourteen hours, and two days of nineteen hours.[6] Women in this trade did housework or found other remunerative chores during the slow season. At least these wage-earners could determine from experience what their work schedules would be and set their own pace accordingly. This cannot be said for factory workers. Until the end of the nineteenth century, they had the most unpredictable patterns of work and free time.

Historians are quite familiar with the distinction between "preindustrial" and "industrial" work patterns, but the models are difficult to apply to the realities of factory life in greater Paris in the 1870s and 1880s.[7] The tempo of labor imposed by the *industrial* system was characterized by the same successive bouts of overwork and idleness as in cottage industry. This was true for workers at Cail, Farcot, and Gouin, which were among the largest and best-organized plants in the region, all in the most technologically advanced industry, machine-building.[8] Such factories worked from one order to the next, so that the terms of employment were necessarily irregular. Exacerbating the irregularity was the common managerial practice of prolonging the workday and canceling rest days to fill an order. Once the work was completed at all due speed, massive layoffs and curtailed hours soon followed. Companies apparently competed for contracts on the basis of the ability to fill orders quickly. They entered challenging (and sometimes unrealistic) bids and worked under the threat of heavy fines for lateness.[9] The police noted the consequence of such practices at the Farcot Machine Company: "In nearly all workrooms, laborers are fired, and the ones who remained are worked day and night."[10] Cail furloughed 200 wage-earners in May 1874 but worked the remaining 1,800 overtime and half-day on Sunday. A large order from the Egyptian government in 1873 animated that plant all Saturday night and all day Sunday with no new hands hired. In December 1876, laborers at Cail complained of having had to work four days without sleep.[11] Ironically, not only a pressing order, but also the absence of new orders impelled managers to work their personnel overtime, so that pending jobs could be finished and shops closed. Thus, in November 1877, Farcot laid off eighty workers and had the rest of his mechanics labor "a part of the night."[12] Directors did try to distribute work more evenly for the most skilled and valuable portion of their personnel, but similar efforts were lacking as far as the mass of laborers were concerned. In all probability, some factory workers accepted such work patterns as natural and inevitable without actively desiring any other. The Parisian police did note, however, that some (perhaps many) workers were troubled by the strains of this tempo but dared not protest or refuse overtime. The need to earn while there was a chance to do so made laborers upset about a temporary reduction of their day from fourteen to twelve hours in the 1870s.[13] By the twentieth century, though, factory workers clearly manifested a desire for a more predictable schedule.

Irregularity of work was not at all unique to the machine-building industry. This situation obtained, as well, in the factories that bleached, dyed, and printed fabrics in Puteaux. When orders arrived, laborers worked until late at night and soon found themselves out of jobs.[14] This practice explains the seemingly contradictory concerns of the newly formed finishers' union. It wanted to negociate longer workdays during the slow season and, at the same time, limit their daily toil to thirteen hours (6:00 A.M. to 7:00 P.M.) with only half-days on Sundays and holidays.[15] Dyers had no more expectation of a routine work week than did mechanics.

A closely related issue was the day of rest. Work on Sunday, often for a full day, was commonplace. The only reservation that the mayor of Puteaux, a factory owner, had with Sunday labor was that his workers might not be able to vote for him.[16] In many industries, especially metalworking, Sunday labor was readily accepted because workers took Monday off when they could. "Saint Monday" was a deeply ingrained habit among mechanics, preferred to Sunday rest because it required fewer ceremonies and bourgeois pretenses.[17] Machine builders often married on Monday, and efforts by employers to bring workers to the factory by making it a pay day could provoke a strike.[18] Saint-Monday was not a tradition for all workers, though, and many labored without a rest all week when there was work or took days off out of sheer exhaustion. Employers made Sunday a pay day, too, to compel attendance.[19] In short, breaks in the work week were irregular and often nonexistent.

Monday through Saturday, 6 A.M. to 6 P.M.—this was supposedly the deadening routine of factory life. Some workers would have welcomed such a routine in the 1870s and 1880s. Yet a regime of overwork succeeded by unemployment was more the rule than was an unvarying schedule. There are, however, a few indications—fragmentary, it is true—of a significant reorientation of work routines by the dawn of the twentieth century. Doctor Dubousquet of Saint-Ouen noted in 1889 that working forty-eight or seventy-two

Table IV-1. Patterns of Requests to Hold Weekend Entertainment in Saint-Denis, 1884–1914

| | 1884–1898 | | 1900–1914 | |
	N	% of Sunday Evening	N	% of Sunday Evening
Saturday Evening	90	69.8	92	80.7
Sunday Afternoon	83	64.3	100	87.7
Sunday Evening	129	—	114	—
Monday Afternoon	68	52.7	38	33.3
Monday Evening	107	82.9	71	62.3

Source: A.M. Saint-Denis, J, 3/8/5/2; J, 3/5/5/4.

hours without stop, common only a while ago, was no longer so prevalent.[20] The agitation for a ten-hour day on the eve of the Exposition of 1900, and the still more massive display of enthusiasm for eight hours in 1906, would have made no sense if the work tempo of the 1870s persisted into the twentieth century. Moreover, the prominence of Monday as a holiday declined. The requests for authorization to hold dances, soirées, and concerts in Saint-Denis show that Monday was still a significant day of lesiure in the twentieth century, but not so much as it had been (see table IV-1). Similarly, the programs of the music hall in Puteaux by 1906 were scheduled largely for Saturday and Sunday, with only occasional performances for Monday.[21]

Several forces seem responsible for the regularization and normalization of work time. New industries, especially automobile and bicycle manufacturing, did not work from one order to the next, but depended on steady consumer demand. A significant number of laborers pressed for a new tempo of work in order to increase earnings and reduce physical strains. Moreover, management became more mindful of productivity and the pace of work. One consequence of this growing concern was a tendency to push workers harder, but a more benign strategy was to moderate fluctuations in work schedule. Employers at a number of plants were happy to capitalize on their workers' desire for an "English week," with a half day on Saturday, as an inducement for them to be present all day Monday.[22] Thus, an "industrial" pattern of factory labor took root in greater Paris and won a wide acceptance from workers at the end of the nineteenth century.

Ultimately, statements about the amount of free time in the late nineteenth century need to be highly qualified. The labor patterns of specialized craft workers were not susceptible to reductions in a uniform manner; moreover, the spread of sweated conditions probably lengthened (or at least intensified) their toil. Changes were more dramatic in the industrial suburbs, where shorter days had a greater impact on leisurely patterns because time off the job became more predictable. In any case, laborers were quite capable of "finding" free time: by engaging in a pleasurable activity most of the night, even after a grueling day at work.

By all accounts, the industrial suburbs comprised the ideal environment to confirm the claims of cultural impoverishment. "When in the evening, working-class trams disgorge their flood of laborers from Paris," proclaimed a priest in the interwar years, "these men have only one resort: the bistro. Neither theater nor cinema."[23] This observer echoed what many others had to say. Few Parisians would have thought of going to Saint-Ouen, Pantin, or Saint-Denis for a good time. The last was a notorious eyesore by the 1880s.[24] The *banlieue* had the largest families, the poorest ones, the immigrants who were least prepared for urban life. For all this, the poverty of leisure activities in the industrial suburbs before the Great War has been greatly exaggerated. By the dawn of the twentieth century, the residents of the *banlieue* were as fully accustomed to mass, commercialized recreational activities as people chronically short of cash could be.

Working-class life in the suburbs was drab and often enervating, but it did not exclude an enthusiasm for dancing and opportunities to do so. Numerous were the balls that lasted well into the morning; when musicians put down their instruments at 2 A.M., the revelers often raised the cash for a few more hours' entertainment.[25] In the 1880s the twenty thousand or so adults of Saint-Denis, 70 percent of them wage-earners, did not have to go to Paris to satisfy this passion. Their somber town had twenty dance halls and four cabarets. At least five of the halls catered to single workers. They were dank, narrow rooms; their proximity to boardinghouses or brothels suggest ties to prostitution. The police had suspicions about their owners, who were often foreigners. Most other dance halls, however, were large and perfectly suitable for family attendance, as was the practice among Parisian craftsmen. A sign of the vitality of this recreation was that a former director of the famed Moulin de la Galette in Montmartre opened an elaborate hall on the rue Saint-Rémy in 1886.[26] During the last decade of the century, café owners added Sunday afternoon concerts in order to attract families. A domestication of the dance hall was in progress, for the morally dubious ones disappeared, and open-air dance halls in bucolic settings appeared.[27] With the normalization of Sunday holidays in factory work, they served more than ever as a setting for family recreation.

Though factory laborers lacked the reputation for taste and flair that luxury craftsmen had, they were by no means ignorant of the theater. From the 1890s, municipal councils strove to save residents the trouble and expense of traveling to Paris to satisfy their need for diversion by bringing theater to their towns.[28] The alderman of Boulogne-sur-Seine began constructing a 925-seat theater in 1894.[29] The municipal council of Puteaux bought a 427-seat theater in 1896 and leased it to an impresario for neary 2,700 francs a year at the turn of the century.[30] The government of Levallois-Perret built a commodious meeting hall intended for mass meetings and commercial spectacles.[31] The most ambitious public project of this nature was the Theater of Saint-Denis. Ready for use in 1900, it had 1,284 seats and a stage of 266 meters. Following the vicissitudes of this facility is an instructive endeavor. It demonstrates not only the undeniable enthusiasm of the industrial population for commercial spectacle, but also its changing tastes.

The councilmen who voted funds for the theater were accused of being out of touch with the electors and unrealistically intent on moral uplift. In fact, these officials did not have to worry about building a theater for an audience that did not exist. Their project began as a success. In 1900 they leased their building to an impresario who contracted to bring the riches of the Parisian stage to this suburb. He intended to present not only the current successes like *Le Voyage de Suzette*, *L'Arlésienne*, and *Cyrano de Bergerac*, but also comic opera, and even grand opera. Upon the classical repertory the director decided to draw with restraint, given the unschooled tastes of his potential audience. The final contract (signed in April 1901) called for a full, seven-month season. There were to be performances on Saturday and Sunday of every week, one on holidays, and occasional Thursday matinees, to which schoolchildren would be admitted free. The price of tickets was roughly between a fifth and an eighth of daily wages: 2 francs and 1.5 francs for reserved seats, and less desirable places for 75 and 50 centimes.[32]

The councilors' claims that there was a demand for theater proved justified. For nearly three years, it ran much to their satisfaction and that of the impresario. Audiences were large enough to cover the cost of the lease and ensure a profit. However, in 1904, a "Casino-Music Hall" opened on the rue de Paris, and soon the municipal theater was in financial trouble. The aldermen saw that "the more the vogue of the Casino-Music Hall takes shape, the more our theater declines." One director after another took a chance on reviving dramatic productions in Saint-Denis only to beg to be released from the contract. The problem was not that demand was insufficient for two commercial operations; it was, rather, that the workers preferred lively music hall programs.[33]

The Casino quickly became a dynamic success. Tickets sold at the same price as those of the theater, and the auditorium, which had at least seven hundred seats, was often filled. In favoring Casino over theater the populace of Saint-Denis was satisfying a desire for excitement, variety, and fast-paced distraction. A play had appeal, but following the plot took much concentration, and workers may have found it hard to relate to the story line or to the dominant sentimentality. The typical performance at the Casino—a succession of singers, performing animals, acrobats, and dancers—had the variety and glamour they preferred.[34] Historians have often associated music halls with the middle classes of great metropolises; the entertainment supposedly mirrored the pace of life in a great city.[35] Yet it is no less the case that the Casino struck a responsive chord amid an industrial population in a somber factory town. The kinds of spectacle that the Casino presented, in fact, had roots in traditions of street entertainment.[36] The acts were not new, but the setting and presentation were.

Ultimately, one music hall did not satisfy the demand for this sort of pastime. The municipal theater returned to solvency only after it adopted a variety program accompanied by cinematic presentations. Moreover, a new "Cinema-Casino" opened in 1910. Thus, the population of Saint-Denis and neighboring communes came to support enough variety entertainment for workers to have a genuine choice.[37]

The audience streamed to the showcases in their holiday outfits. Though their clothes may frequently have borne marks of wear and mending, the spectators still sought stately surroundings that transported them into a fictive world of excitement. The Casino used some of its profits to refurbish in a more elegant manner. The new Cinema-Casino pleased its clientele with its glowing electrical marquee.[38] Customers came to shows with families, so if performances touched on the risqué, there were loud complaints. The director of the Casino had to adopt a policy of making programs suitable for mothers and children.[39]

The populace of Saint-Denis (Dionysiens) obviously expected to see singers, acrobats, and dancers in order to escape the dreariness of everyday life in a setting that removed them momentarily from their factory world. Perhaps, in this sense, the flourishing of commercial leisure did represent a step toward what Joffre Dumazedier calls the "leisure-centered society," in which people identify themselves more in terms of their leisure than of their work.[40] However, it was a small and ambiguous step. Their money and applause did not only go for a pure and mindless escapism. Performances that included doses of "realism" and specifically working-class commentary enjoyed considerable success—enough to make profit-oriented theater owners cater to this interest.

A taste for the artistic presentation of social issues roughly followed the ebb and flow of class confrontation in greater Paris. In 1903, in the midst of an important strike wave in the machine-building industries, the municipal theater at Saint-Denis interrupted its routine of fashionable melodramas with a play based on Zola's *Germinal*.[41] The apogee of popularity for social commentary also accompanied the culmination of industrial protest, 1906–1908. During the massive general strike for the eight-hour day in May 1906 the theater once again presented *Germinal*, and the Casino offered its series of "artistic propagandists." Appearing in November was Maurice Lecoeur, whose program proclaimed that "misery, prostitution, crime, alcoholism, madness, and tuberculosis were nothing but the consequences of faulty social organization."[42] His performance attracted enough attention to justify an extended run. Sensing the public's support for such material, the directors of the Casino saw fit to include "realistic" songs and monologues along with the usual jugglers and dog acts. The effort to give audiences what they wanted was making the Casino into what the Socialist press called "a school for propaganda for the development of generous and humane ideas."[43]

The Socialist singer Gaston Montéhus was the headliner for this sort of performance. His highly sentimental pieces were based on the dichotomy between the wealthy few and the miserable masses. Though they lacked a specific call to insurrection, "all belongs to the worker" was a frequent refrain.[44] Montéhus interrupted his act with a collection for strikers or a drawing to raise money for victims of work accidents. The Socialist press continually reported on the warm receptions Montéhus received from the audiences. What lends veracity to these reports is his numerous return engagements at the Casino. He appeared in March 1906 for the first time; again, in January and April 1907, and in January the next year. Then, not again until 1910, a year of considerable labor unrest, did Montéhus grace the Casino.[45] Clearly, workers of Saint-Denis were prepared to be moved, thrilled, and entertained in a number of ways, and this included poignant presentations of a world with which they were all too familiar. At moments of heightened antagonism, such spectacle was a useful emotional release.

Even three theaters for live performance did not fully satisfy the Dionysiens' passion for commercial spectacle. Cinema became popular, though not quite so much as vaudeville. The first request to hold a cinematic presentation in Saint-Denis came in 1896, and within four years, such showings were commonplace.[46] The municipal theater began to present films to fill its large hall in 1907, and the Casino-Cinema increased the richness of choice. Despite lower prices for films than for music hall—the most expensive ticket was 1.25 francs, and children paid only 20 centimes for a matinee—cinema remained secondary to variety. Cinema did not have its own showcase in Saint-Denis until 1910, and films were presented less often (usually Thursday afternoon and evening). It may have been that adults preferred the live entertainment, and youths craved films. One working-class boy recorded that, when he finished school, took a job, and first had pocket money, his greatest pleasure was to attend the cinema.[47] Whereas the novelty and glitter of singers and acrobats may have delighted parents, the film attracted youths through its semblance of reality and through action.

A noteworthy comment on the breadth of enthusiasm for commercialized leisure was that the first facility devoted exclusively to film opened in the quarter of La Plaine, one of the poorest sections of Saint-Denis.[48] This district was a refuge for large families and for laborers with few skills. Its acutely high rate of communicable diseased revealed the hygienic inadequacies and squalor. Yet an entrepreneur thought it worthwhile to open a "stylish" hall and show films Saturday through Monday. Thus La Plaine, not yet endowed with a proper supply of safe water, now had a worldly night life.

The music halls and cinemas did not exhaust the recreational choices available to the residents of Saint-Denis in the first decade of the new century. Outdoor concerts were a regular Sunday afternoon feature by 1900. A circus put on several performances every year, and there were some boxing matches.[49] A particularly successful addition to the recreational options was a nearby amusement park, the Butte Pinson, which opened in 1908. Containing "all sort of distractions and games," it became a diverting variation on the traditional Sunday outing.[50] Thus even this activity was being transformed into commercialized recreation.

Explaining the laborers' tastes for these diversions is easier than accounting for the money they were able to devote to support theaters, music halls, cinemas, and amusement parks. Of course, it is no accident that these leisure institutions appeared as the suburbs began to grow more rapidly than the capital; a large mass of potential consumers was a prerequisite for such entrepreneurial activity. Nor was it coincidental that commercial leisure expanded with the high-paying machine-building industry, especially automobiles. This trade brought to suburban towns a substantial number of laborers who earned craftsmen's wages, eighty centimes an hour and even a franc. Mechanics who were single or had small families undoubtedly comprised the core of audiences. The aged or unskilled laborers with large families may never have been inside the Casino. As for the bulk of the population between these two extremes, we must imagine that their budgets rarely permitted expenditures on diversion. Nonetheless, it is wholly likely that these workers and their families "found" discretionary income in the same way that they "made" leisure time—through sacrifice. The turner who made seven francs a day ate if he earned only five; a working mother added still more hours of stitching to her impossible schedule. The richness of recreational life in an industrial town like Saint-Denis demonstrates that workers gave such diversion some priority.

When workers spent their limited funds on spectacle, they did not neglect youngsters. The commercial leisure was meant to be a family activity.[51] As such, cinema, variety, and even the dance hall helped to mold the family into a unit of recreation and leisure. No wonder, then, that charity administrators in Ivry found that children were using the new clothes they were given for wear at school as their Sunday outfits.[52] Youngsters took advantage of the new recreational institutions to elaborate their play-world. The Thursday school break quickly became a time for movie matinees. So much of an acquired right had it become that youngsters in Saint-Denis reportedly staged a sizable protest against parents who refused to give their children the twenty centimes for the film. The protesters' cries of "Film! Film! Film!" marked a new obligation that parents were to assume—perhaps even if they could not truly afford it.[53] The recreational luxuries of one generation quickly became necessities for the next.

Physical activity and competitive gamesmanship took their places beside show-business spectacles as leisurely forms that the working population sought. The taste for sport was quite clear in Puteaux, the "nursery of the automobile industry." Up to the 1890s, the annual communal festivals were celebrated with fireworks, musical concerts, and games of chance. By the new century, planned activities centered around physical competition: footracing, cycling, marksmanship, and gymnastics.[54] The town council of Ivry subsidized at least seven athletic clubs by 1903. Some youths in this working-class ghetto sought to capture the sports-minded glamour of the English aristocracy by joining the "Athletic Club."[55] Despite the prohibitive cost of acquiring a bicycle, the practice of cycling had somehow reached the mass of working people. The proportion of twenty-year-old recruits who could ride attained 25 percent in Pantin and 58 percent in Puteaux.[56] Ball games were, perhaps, less popular because playing fields were few, and parents, fearing injuries, discouraged participation. A local championship match in soccer attracted only two hundred people in 1910, a poor crowd by the standards of the Casino.[57] Still, factory youths had sports as recreational alternatives to film and stage presentations.

The new commercialized and physical pastimes were not only exceedingly popular; they also had the approval of the leading social critics of the industrial towns, the militant Socialists. These public figures did not call for an autonomous working-class culture. Far from regarding these leisure activities as possible opiates of the masses, Socialist spokesmen vociferously championed them, even the profit-making ventures. They praised the recreational choices as useful and richly deserved rewards for the laboring people. Thus, the editors of *Emancipation*, in Saint-Denis, did not see the Butte Pinson amusement park as a wasteful way to separate a worker from his earnings; rather, they regarded it as a delightful opportunity for the poor to find some of the pleasures that their exploiters derived from holidays by the sea. They publicized the Casino as if it were a Socialist institution, and not only when performers like Lecoeur or Montéhus appeared.[58] The Socialist journalists greeted the normal fare of jugglers, acrobats, and animal acts warmly too.

Sports shared in the Socialists' wholehearted approval of mass leisure. By 1910, all the larger communes of the industrial suburbs had soccer associations, which were intertwined with the political youth groups. *L'Emancipation* instructed mothers on how to make uniforms for the communal team: black jerseys with red stars.[59] During the first decade of the twentieth century, the editors of the *Courrier socialiste* of Saint-Ouen tacitly (and probably unconsciously) modified their conception of appropriate pastimes for Socialists. When the journal first appeared in 1903, study groups and lectures received much attention and support in its columns. Six years later, "Sports" became a regular feature, and the educational endeavors went all but unmentioned.[60]

The militants would have been naive in their support of the new recreation if sports and spectacle were serving as effective channels for integrating the laboring population in the bourgeois social order. However, class distinctions quickly penetrated into leisure institutions. Merchants and employers minimized interclass contacts by attending the Casino on Friday night, whereas workers attended on Saturdays, Sundays, and Mondays.[61] Youths generally developed sporting groups based on class.[62] Moreover, the Socialists seemed to have understood that workers could be just as sensitive to inequities in leisure as to those at work or in the home. The subtle ways in which commercialized leisure validated the social order seemed minor in comparison.

The rise of the new institutions of leisure would simply have been a matter of enhanced local color if they did not reflect deeply rooted social and cultural trends.[63] Music halls, cinemas, and theaters appeared because the population of the industrial suburbs was growing rapidly, industries that paid relatively well flourished, and because the free time of factory workers was more regular and predictable. Workers could organize their leisure and, to some extent, mold it to their needs. The gymnasts, animal trainers, and singers who filled some of this free time had long been familiar spectacles, but in informal settings. Entertainment was being privatized: marketplaces and fairs were replaced by glamorous showcases; crowds became audiences. With this shift, the family, not the community, was the principal unit comprising the audience. Finally, it is evident that the expansion of leisure activities compares favorably with the growth of other consumer markets in the suburban towns. Spending on recreation obviously had some priority among workers. Their visits to the Casino, the Cino-Pathé, or the Butte Pinson surely expressed powerful aspirations for a fuller life.

The history of Carnival celebration in nineteenth-century Paris gives some credence to the argument of cultural impoverishment for the craft workers of the capital. The exuberance and bawdiness of the popular festivities disappeared in the second half of the nineteenth century, replaced by a carefully regulated event, orchestrated from above.[64] Is this change symbolic of a more general collapse of artisanal and communal recreation? The limited evidence available cautions against exaggerating the decline of trade sociability. Parisian craftsmen proved to be remarkably successful in preserving traditional forms of diversion, even as they were slow to adopt new ones.

Craft sociability and collective play were possibly more resistant to change than were production processes and occupational inheritance patterns. The drinking ceremonials whereby workers received newly hired comrades, the "quand-est-ce," long remained an important source of solidarity. The new worker had to buy a round of drinks for his comrades and thereby won the right to be called "Mon Vieux." This rite survived quite well, at least up to the war, and claims for its deterioration may have been based largely on nostalgia.[65] Some observers thought that the poorest-paid wage-earners, like nail makers, could not afford the custom, but the "quand-est-ce" managed to survive in seemingly unlikely circumstances.[66] When one Parisian youth entered the assembly shop of a shoe factory in the Thirteenth Arrondissement during World War I, he found that the specialized cobbler "retained the spirit and playfulness of yesterday."[67] The "quand-est-ce" was very much alive and so, unfortunately for the youth, were other ordeals to which craftsmen subjected newcomers. One such ceremony was the "passage of the glue," in which workers wrestled the initiate to the ground, opened his pants, and poured glue into his rectum. The youth in question was several times the victim of this prank. Another amusement entailed pulling the stool out from under a worker who was about to be seated. All this transpired within a factory, among workers who rarely inherited crafts, and in a trade supposedly under the immediate threat of mechanization. These rituals nonetheless preserved the bawdiness and vulgarity of traditional Carnival.[68]

The most cherished of family recreations, the outing to the countryside for a drink, a picnic, or a meal, remained a source of relaxation and renewal. It has been suggested that the growth and annexation of the villages surrounding the capital and the industrialization of the *banlieue* severely curtailed such excursions, but this contention is exaggerated.[69] The carpenter who found enough greenery in Ivry, amid the machine-building and chemical plants, to enjoy a Sunday picnic with his family was surely typical.[70] Even the most developed industrial town of the suburbs, Saint-Denis, still had stretches of verdure in the twentieth century.[71] To many residents of Belleville before the war, Sunday continued to have only one meaning, to take their families to the *banlieue*.[72]

The leisure of working-class women was, likewise, more a matter of stability than of deterioration; and arguably, even a matter of enrichment. Most wives integrated socializing with daily chores. As such, the market and the laundry were privileged centers of feminine gregariousness.[73] Women who may have left their neighborhood shops and ventured into the commercial districts of the central city would have found their pleasure enhanced by the unaccustomed variety and quality of goods. Window-shopping was an activity that was accessible. It is, likewise, difficult to see why the traditional recreation of working women should have deteriorated more than that of shoemakers. Jeanne Bouvier, a seamstress, described the talk that took place in workshops about sensational events and about serial novels.[74] The dissemination and cheapening of the mass press would only have complemented such interests.

Theater had deep roots in popular entertainment, and many Parisian workers had special affection for this activity. In 1872 the police commissioner of Belleville noted that "the taste for theater could not be more widespread among the workers, who do not deprive themselves of it at any time, not even in difficult moments."[75] Another police agent made a more qualified assessment, attributing a passion for the stage to the craftsmen in the artistic trades, whose work demanded refinement and a display of elegance.[76] Both were correct; it was a matter of degree. Crafts seemed to have been decisive channels for communicating an interest in the theater, and artisans oftened explained its appeal as a matter of corporate heritage. The laborers in luxury trades which had high levels of literacy as well as artistic pretensions made theater a frequent activity. Porcelain painters, for example, pointed to their love for stage performances as a sign of their respectability. Mechanics considered their partiality for theater as an accompaniment to their technical learning. Tailors had a reputation for voracious reading and for attending performances frequently.[77] Luckily for them, cheap and even free tickets were widely available.[78] At the same time, less refined workers would attend the theater on special occasions. When the seamstress Jeanne Bouvier was hired by a leading fashion house and earned five francs a day, she treated herself to an occasional visit to the Opéra-Comique. That was thought to be a special pleasure for wives and daughters.[79]

Perhaps no aspect of workers' traditional off-the-job life was the subject of so much public discussion and hand-wringing at the end of the nineteenth century as drinking. The source of anxiety was the increased consumption of distilled liquor, especially absinthe. On a per capita basis, the use of such liquors nearly tripled between 1860 and 1900.[80] Apprehension was not simply a matter of class antipathy; militant Socialists were concerned about the level of intoxication among fellow wage-earners. The New Year's wishes for one Socialist editor in 1905 were for workers to unionize, join the Free-Thinkers' Circle, and keep away from *apéritifs*.[81] Employers were joined by friends of working people in claiming that the best-paid laborers were most inclined toward overindulgence.[82] On the surface, links might seem to exist between drinking and a deteriorating artisanal culture, but other interpretations are more plausible.[83] Henri Leyret, a journalist who posed as a publican to study working-class culture in Belleville during the 1890s, reported that the vast majority of wage-earners drank because they came to the pub, and they came more for sociability than for drink. It was the one place they felt comfortable; indeed, workers chose their cafés with care so that they were at their ease.[84] Moreover, the workshop economy of the capital and the culture of craftsmen endowed cafés with a multiplicity of functions beside drinking. They were places for being paid and seeking work, among other activities. Pub culture, which remained rich by all reports, was an enhancement of workers' leisure life, not a sign of its deterioration.

What characterized the free time of Parisian craftsmen in the late nineteenth century was not so much its impoverishment as its stability in the face of widening options. Crafts remained an important conduit of sociable traditions even though they weakened as communities and fewer people inherited their occupations from their parents. Artisans held tenaciously to their recreational forms and seemed hesitant to adopt new leisurely activities. Our impression—and in view of the paucity of testimony, it must be a speculative one—is that the Parisan hand workers did not display the same intensity of enthusiasm for commercialized entertainment as did their peers in the factories.[85] Their budgets showed little more than derisory sums spent on commercial spectacle.[86] One worker who installed shutters, a well-paying job, devoted his free time to visiting friends, reading newspapers, and taking walks. Even a foreman locksmith never seemed to have the money for film or music hall.[87] Nor were the elite craftsmen notably active in reshaping patterns of work and free time. It was the laborers in the automobile and large machine-assembly plants who wished for an English week, with a half-day on Saturday, whereas the mechanics in the smaller shops remained faithful to their craft tradition of Saint-Monday. The secretary of the Mechanics' Union on the eve of the war contrasted the attitudes of machinists in the smaller shops, who were only moderately enthusiastic about the issue of expanded leisure, with the aspirations of workers in the large plants, who went so far as to accept lower earnings in exchange for more free time.[88] The handicrafts workers of Paris remained intent upon building their lives around their work and its associated pleasures.

WAGE-EARNERS' FAMILY LIFE

When a Parisian shawl weaver and his wife were in painful financial straits, they sent their young son to live with his maternal grandfather. Soon the parents ceased to have more than superficial contacts with the boy, and the grandfather became the permanent guardian.[89] Such shifting of working-class children from one household to another was a common phenomenon and raises important questions about the quality of domestic relations. The Prefecture of the Seine found just how common the practice was by creating a Service for Morally Abandoned Children in 1880. The original purpose of this new welfare institution was to assume the guardianship of young vagrants and delinquents if parents proved too corrupt or ineffectual to serve in that capacity. The service soon came to fulfill an entirely different purpose, however; poor parents began to turn their children over to the service, tainted though it was by an aura of criminality. By 1886, nearly half of the youngsters under the care of the service had been given up by their parents. With seven to nine hundred arriving in this manner each year, the service was virtually a sort of foundling home for legitimate children beyond infancy.[90] These examples seem to support Lawrence Stone's contention that the working-class family was "often indifferent, cruel, erratic, and unpredictable."[91] Yet the examples do have an ambiguous quality that prevents us from distinguishing measures of callousness from reactions to hardship. The history of the service also provides a useful illustration of that ambiguity. In 1887 a scandal over the mistreatment of some youngsters in one of the homes received wide press coverage. The number of children remitted to the service immediately plummeted by half and parents reclaimed about a fifth of the youngsters.[92] This incident not only places parents' intentions in a more benevolent light but points to a central problem of all such evidence: It stops short of clarifying how family members understood their domestic relations.[93]

Guidance through the ambiguous history of the nineteenth-century working-class family—a field in which finding evidence, interpreting it, and generalizing from it all pose particularly delicate problems—comes from two influential models. According to one perspective, the working-class household "familialized" at the end of the century. Proponents of this view believe that there was a growth and deepening of affective relationships and that dependents' needs and individuality received more recognition. Thus relationships that had triumphed among the propertied classes by the end of the eighteenth century presumably reached the urban masses a century or so later.[94] For Alain Corbin, the growing apathy of Parisian workers for mercenary sex at the bordello signified a new taste for domesticity.[95] In the opinion of Peter Stearns, a greater home-centeredness was the consequence of a work life that was becoming ever less meaningful.[96] Whether consciously or not, some historians apply this model in a banal form, asserting that rising living standards and more security removed the sharp edges from family life. The general thrust of the "familialization" argument is to suggest that workers were becoming more integrated into the existing social order. Easily as influential as this perspective is the functional viewpoint, which insists on more continuity than change down to the Great War. This alternative vision emphasizes the strict family discipline, rooted in tight material conditions, which generally overruled affective behavior.[97] Ultimately, this latter model bears the weight of evidence better, but "familialization" proves more suitable for posing questions about family life and points toward potential areas of structural change.

The necessary starting point for all studies of the working-class family in the nineteenth century, and an aspect that both models slight, is the emotional vitality that characterized most households.

Octave Gréard, the superintendent of education in the 1870s, observed among his pupils a powerful "love of family," and abundant evidence shows that members thought of the family primarily as a unit of affection.[98] René Michaud, the son of an impoverished widow of the Thirteenth Arrondissement at the turn of the century, easily perceived behind his mother's gruff gestures the deep wellspring of concern for him.[99] Amédée Domat's mother, a charwoman with eight children (surviving from fifteen births), imparted to her offspring the certainty of being loved and even found time to supervise their homework.[100] The parental obligation to sacrifice for children was accepted and went beyond providing the bare necessities. When doctors asked one poor couple why they did not have more children, since charities would supply food and clothing, the parents objected that it would not be possible to provide five or six children with basics and with "a few pleasures" beyond them.[101] These doctors discovered in one needy household that parents and older children slept on the floor while the youngest members had use of the single bed in their dwelling.[102]

Advocates of the "familialization" model see such emotional vitality as appearing or solidifying at the end of the nineteenth century, but there is excellent evidence that it existed decades earlier. Exceptionally rich documents on Parisian working-class domestic life from the middle of the century, the records of the Orphanage of the Prince Imperial, assure us that powerful affection was central to the wage-earning family before the Commune. The orphanage placed young sons of deceased workers in foster homes headed by close relatives and periodically investigated how they were treated.[103] Emerging from the notes and reports of the inspectors were households with deep emotional bases, in which children were far more than resources for the family purse. Foster mothers worked furiously to maintain an aura of respectability in the household and usually succeeded despite the stench of poverty. The children's schooling and medical care provided numerous occasions for parents to sacrifice their own meager resources, and this was done. Parents were sensitive to youngsters' favorite foods and games and were happy to offer them these simple pleasures. The child's sense of well-being at home was such that employers had to complain about apprentices returning home at the slightest application of discipline.

If we seek to understand how this emotional vitality manifested itself, all the evidence draws us to the focal role of the mother in the working-class household. She guaranteed a critical minimum of nurturing and often a good deal more.[104] As the center of a tightly bonded group, she inspired closeness among siblings so that the family had a chance to survive in the case of her death.[105] The mother's ascendency was based not on the father's degradation, but rather on his distance from the everyday concerns of the household. The son of one day laborer did not think his father cruel or aloof, but his long hours of work and a pub-centered sociability kept him out of touch.[106] The bronze assembler who left home at 5:30 each morning and finished work at 8 P.M. was in similar circumstances.[107] The work schedule of males and the culturally ascribed roles for women resulted in sharp specialization in activities, and mothers assumed most responsibilities for managing the family. The records concerning the Municipal Apprentices, adolescents who won cash awards from the city to support vocational training, testify to the shallow involvement of father in family concerns. Even when boys had problems at work, it was the mother who addressed the difficulty. Only when mothers suffered physical and verbal abuse from the son's boss did the husband intervene, and sometimes not even then.[108] There is evidence that children were hurt or disappointed by their fathers' distance even if they understood it as inevitable.[109]

For none of these features of working-class domesticity is it necessary to draw major distinctions among skilled and unskilled laborers, craftsmen, service laborers, and factory workers. The sources point to a fairly uniform culture of the family that transcended these divisions in greater Paris. The general features of family relations in the household of Amédée Domat, son of a day laborer, differed little from that of Gaston Lucas, a foreman locksmith.[110] About a third of the stepparents of Imperial Orphans was unskilled laborers, and it is impossible to find significant differences between these parents and the skilled ones.[111] The industrial suburbs were home to many refugees from regions with strong traditions of child labor.[112] Yet their acceptance of new modes of childrearing and adjustment to them must have been quite rapid. As unskilled laborers spilled into the suburbs before the Ferry laws on education, the result was not a surge of laboring youngsters but rather a drastic shortage of places in public school; nearly 3,500 fewer places than children requesting enrollment in the Arrondissement of Sceaux (southern *banlieue*) by 1877.[113] Saint-Denis had 4,062 pupils in 1876 but only 91 school-age children (69 boys and 22 girls) working in the industries of the town. Moreover, parents and children took school attendance seriously. During the first year of compulsory education (1882), the scholastic commission of Saint-Denis had to investigate only 11 cases of prolonged absence at one primary school which had an enrollment of 460.[114] Whether or not the immigrant workers came to the *banlieue* with a commitment to keeping children in school, they soon conformed to prevailing practices in the capital.

Given the longstanding role of the mother as the emotional focus of working-class households, the "familialization" thesis means nothing if it does not bear on the domestication of husbands. In this regard, it is desirable to examine the observation of Henri Leyret, a student of working-class life in Belleville of the 1890s. Leyret believed that "the workingman's love for his children borders on being an obsession," for which he was willing to make endless sacrifices.[115] Was this simply a matter of the father being a distant but faithful provider, or was Leyret commenting on men who had become more engrossed than ever before in the daily functioning of their families? Literary sources fail to shed sufficient light on the question, but demographic analysis offers the possibility of gauging the changing emotional foundations of the working-class family. Patterns of births and deaths altered dramatically during the four decades before the war—because parents took deliberate action. The mechanics of this change provide insights into the dynamics of family life.

For twenty-five years after the Commune, infant mortality in greater Paris was among the highest in France, especially if the children sent out to nurse are counted.[116] On the other hand, births were only marginally controlled once stable households were formed. During the 1870s and 1880s, crude birth rates were in the range of 35 to 40 per thousand in the working-class quarters and for the industrial suburbs. These were similar to rates in the textile towns of the Nord at the same time or of France on the eve of the Great Revolution.[117] If the average household was, nonetheless, small, the size was the result of the large number of young couples, the sterility induced by medical problems, the transfer of children to smaller families, and, of course, mortality. In 1906, well after infant mortality had begun its dramatic decline, a third of all married couples had buried at least one child.[118] This is not to say that parents lacked a material incentive to control births. The majority of married men aged forty-five to forty-nine had at least three children at home (see table IV-2). Need was the inevitable price of high fertility.

Table IV-2.   Size of Households in Saint-Denis, 1896

Children	Cumulative Percentage	
	A[a]	B[b]
0	17.7	7.1
1	41.7	24.9
2	64.0	49.0
3	81.1	71.2
4	91.5	86.7
5	96.6	95.5
6	99.0	98.1
7 +	100.0	100.0

Source: A.M. Saint-Denis, F, 3/5/2/1.

[a] All married couples.

[b] Married couples with husband 45–49 years old.

Working-Class Quarters:

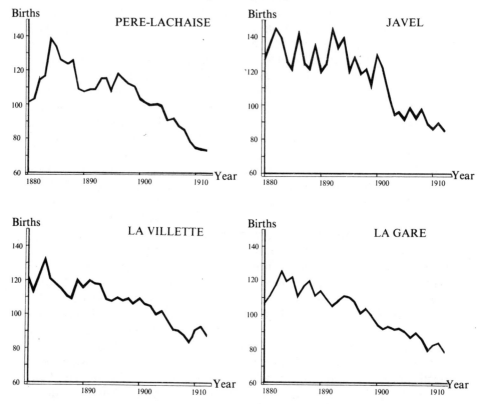

Figure IV-1. Fertility Levels (Births per 1,000 Females ages 15–44) in Various
Quarters of Paris and Suburban Towns, 1880–1912
Sources: Préfecture de la Seine, *Annuaire statistique de la ville de
Paris* for 1880–1912; A.D.S., D 1 M⁸ no. 2.

If "familialization" were more than just a theory, one would
expect a gradually declining fertility rate as parents increasingly recognized the individuality of each child and sought to devote resources
to their offspring—or at least to keep them alive. In fact, the demographic transition in greater Paris occurred in a quite different
manner among wage-earning families (see figure IV-1). Irreversible
declines in the fertility rate in the overwhelmingly working-class quarters like Père-Lachaise (Twentieth Arrondissement), La Villette
(Nineteenth), Javel (Fifteenth), and industrial towns like Saint-Ouen
occurred suddenly and only just before the turn of the century. The
contrast is clear with quarters that experienced an influx of white-
collar and petty-bourgeois couples, like Sainte-Marguerite (Elev-

Suburban Towns:

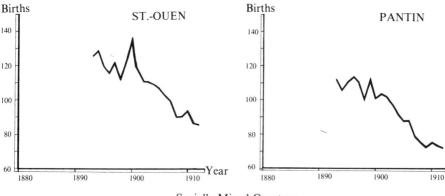

Socially Mixed Quarters:

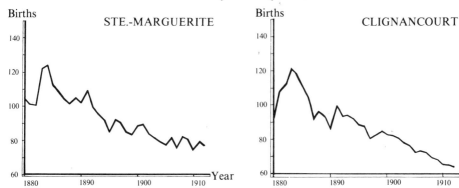

enth) and Clignancourt (Eighteenth). There, fertility dropped with the building of commodious housing in prime locations.[119] Once the descent began in the working-class ghettos, it proceeded rapidly: 30 percent between 1901 and 1912 in the quintessential residence of craftsmen, Père-Lachaise; 33 percent in Javel, a quarter with many construction workers and metalworkers; 25 percent in Pantin, the home of many day laborers. The result of this family limitation was a distinct narrowing of the reproductive differences among white-collar, petty-bourgeois, and working-class families by the time of the Great War. There was not a gradual infusion of the will to plan families with care; control of births among workers arrived with the suddenness of a command.

The timing of the decline of working-class fertility leaves little doubt about its cause or about the parent most responsible for it. Workers had significantly fewer children after infant mortality commenced its dramatic fall. Control of births constituted an adjustment to a new family situation, which was the accomplishment of the working-class mother. Medical elites may have provided the institutional support for the women's lifesaving concerns; but ultimately mothers had to seek out and act upon scientific advances—and they did.[120] Infant mortality rates dropped about 20 percent between 1896 and 1900 in ghettos like Père-Lachaise and Saint-Ouen. It seems highly probable that before the drop in infant deaths husbands had been more resistant than wives to contraceptive practices. As a result of their spouses' efforts to save their children, fathers had to adapt. Ultimately, they may have done more than adapt; once planning was employed in earnest, parents may possibly have revised and lowered their target family size.[121]

The dynamics of the working-class family were substantially transformed at the dawn of the twentieth century. Parents came to expect individual children to live, had fewer of them, and conserved their emotional and financial resources for these few. It is not the classic case of working-class parents gradually coming to assume new obligations toward their offspring as middle-class models of domesticity filtered downward. Instead, mothers were finally able to act upon traditional attachments to their children, and, in doing so, they imposed new modes of behavior on their husbands. The fall in fertility did not necessarily signify an entirely new emotional basis for the father in the working-class household. Arguably, though, it prepared the way for a new closeness that had not characterized the father's position before the end of the century.

Just as the new demographic realities were altering the situation of young children, parents had to countenance the changing social position of their adolescents. The traditional role of youth, participating in the family economy, was becoming more problematical. This situation offers another test of the familialization perspective, which postulates a growing acceptance of youth's individuality within the family. Once again, the model fails to convince, for rising tensions, even despair, seemed to characterize relations between parents and their maturing children in the decade or two before the Great War.[122]

Parisian mothers traditionally used their emotional ascendency over children to socialize them to dependence and submissiveness. These working-class mothers of Paris did not instill patterns of highly self-reliant and aggressive behavior which poor parents in other parts of the world sought to impart.[123] Parisian parents wished their children to form their identities as entirely as possible within the family. Thus, when a cobbler and his wife learned that ruffians at public school were taking their son's lunch, they did not encourage confrontation, but rather placed the child in a parochial school.[124] Mothers catered to a child's delicate health or temperamental weakness. They viewed the city of Paris not as an arena with which their children would have to learn to cope but rather as a harsh and threatening environment that might easily overwhelm them. Gone entirely by the mid-nineteenth century was the familiarity with street life that had been so much a part of popular culture in the eighteenth century.[125] A child's inevitable play on the street was a source of anxiety for parents; to raise them outside Paris was considered an action of incalculable moral benefit. The mothers of the Imperial Orphans were fearful even of night schools, which they blamed for generating all sorts of dangerous contacts.[126] Such anxieties explain the favor that Catholic children's clubs (*patronages*) held for nonpracticing parents.[127] Fending for oneself was not a way of life these working-class parents wished to inculcate.

In a similar manner, working-class parents were reluctant to envision their children as independent individuals with an existence outside the family. Parents of the Municipal Apprentices, working-class youths who won several hundred francs for their exemplary behavior in school and for their vocational promise, found that their notions of family obligations put them in conflict with public officials. The administrators of the award regarded the prize money as the personal possession of the youths; it was to be saved for their majorities. The parents of the apprentices, however, could not help thinking of the sum as a safety net for family emergencies. Almost inevitably, administrators received requests for advances on the prize money. Such requests were not made for trivial reasons; they followed periods of unemployment or illness of family members. Yet these emergencies did not concern the interests of the young apprentices directly. As one administrator complained, "These parents refuse to acknowledge that the money is meant for the prize winners."[128]

If maintaining their adolescents' identity within the family was a moral good and a financial necessity to working-class parents, doing so became more problematical in the decade before the Great War. There are compelling signs—indirect, it is true, but an abundance of them—of a crisis of sorts surrounding the raising of adolescents. Though there was not a generalized revolt against parental authority and against family obligations, parents did exhibit anxiety over the relations between generations. A simultaneous increase in youths' financial dependence and their demands for more personal autonomy were at the roots of parental discomfort. As a result of compulsory schooling, laws intended to discourage child labor, the dearth of apprenticeships, and machine production, youths spent a longer time outside of the labor force. In Ivry in 1911, 57.5 percent of the four-teen- and fifteen-year-old boys and 32.8 percent of the girls were without jobs. Thirty-five years earlier, the corresponding figure had been 30.7 percent and 20.4 percent.[129] The vision of an adolescent on the streets, without a job and without supervision, must have been particularly upsetting to laboring parents. Moreover, working-class children were at least as susceptible as were their parents—and probably a good deal more so—to the quest for a richer life through enticing leisure activities and mass consumerism. After acquiring his first job, René Michaud was eager to live *"la belle vie,"* which meant cinema, above all. Michaud later claimed to have limited his expenses to the pocket money his mother allotted, cheating only occasionally; but other adolescents may have been more rebellious.[130] Similarly, the production of inexpensive gloves, perfumes, cosmetics, and other adornments provided a strong temptation to working daughters. Ob-servers noted the eagerness of young seamstresses to find room in their narrow budgets for such items, so that daughters missed the money handed over to their parents all the more.[131] The traditional role of urban youths, to participate in the family wage economy, was becoming less realizable and less appropriate, yet another role was, as yet, out of the question.

Family conflict between generations began to trouble public opinion and to inform public discourse on the "youth problem" at the turn of the century. The suicide of a twenty-year-old worker after a confrontation with his father caused the Socialist press in Argenteuil to lament the frequency of generational conflicts and declare that "obedience should be based on love, not authority." The editors returned to this theme in several issues.[132] Working-class spokesmen also began to project parental concerns upon the issue of juvenile delinquency in a new manner. Before the end of the century, youthful violence and criminality had not yet produced a sense of family breakdown. Saint-Denis in 1885, for example, experienced a rash of muggings by a gang of youths, but no generalized sense of crisis resulted from these incidents.[133] Large groups of youngsters battled on the fortifications of Saint-Ouen in the 1880s, but officials worried about the damage to property, not the permanent threats of uncon-trolled youths.[134] After 1900, such delinquency was taken as evidence of an underlying youth problem that threatened family life.

Parisian and working-class opinion was very much stirred by concern over the "Apaches" in the first decade of the twentieth century. These were supposedly gangs of young thugs who exhibited a conscious defiance of the law, a cult of toughness, and absolute scorn for established authority. Such gangs may well have had some basis in fact, but they certainly did not have the overwhelming prominence that the working-class press attributed to them.[135] A mugging that occurred in Ivry, a murder of a youngster in Belleville, or public disorder by adolescents in Saint-Denis were proclaimed the work of the Apaches.[136] Working-class opinion projected upon the Apaches the problems of family life. The Socialist newspapers assumed that Apaches were recruited among wage-earning households. A series of articles in *L'Humanité* described how youngsters were dutiful sons one day and Apaches the next. The implications were clear: Any child could rebel against convention—or fall victim to the Apaches.[137] Explanations for the genesis of such gang delinquency comprised a litany of the changes, real or imagined, that were modifying the place of youths in the family and in society: the progress of machine production, restrictive labor legislation, compulsory schooling, the deterioration of apprenticeship, and, especially, the absence of the working mother from the home.[138] The link between private problems and social problems could not have been more direct. Moreover, the press portrayed the gangs enacting what must have been the fantasies of working-class adolescents: liberation from adult control, freedom from the obligation to work, and easy access to sensual pleasures and brassy entertainment. A Socialist editor warned parents that their children had to choose between being workers or Apaches.[139]

The concern about youths impelled public officials in the working-class communes to do more than express discouragement and wring their hands. The newly elected Socialist councilors of Puteaux feared that youngsters were too exposed to the temptations of alcohol and ordered the closing of all pubs within 350 meters of school buildings.[140] Several years earlier, the aldermen of Saint-Ouen had lamented that youths were no longer getting jobs until the age of fifteen or sixteen, "to the endless anxiety of their parents." They passed a resolution in favor of creating pre-apprenticeship programs in public schools.[141] To discuss working-class youths after 1900 was to confront a social problem, and there can be little doubt that an aspect of this problem was tension within the family. Parents had yet to come to terms with the new work conditions of their children and with their expectations for fuller lives.[142]

Thus, the working-class family of greater Paris in 1914 was, as in 1871, a haven from the cruel world and a focus for the ultimate loyalties of its members. With contraception, shorter work hours (for some), and privatized leisure, the potential existed for subtle but basic changes in family roles. However, this promise could not be realized in the absence of dramatic improvements in material conditions. It is little wonder that youths bore the pressures of this incomplete change.

FAMILY LIFE AND LEISURE OF WHITE-COLLAR WORKERS

The limited source material on working-class families appears copious beside the documentation on white-collar domesticity. Employers did not produce memoirs of their youths, nor did social commentators direct much attention to this milieu, undoubtedly because white-collar employees were traditionally better integrated into the social order.[143] Challenging this assumption does not seem necessary, but how were they integrated: as imitators of the Parisian bourgeoisie, or did they have their distinctive modes of family life? The paucity of evidence is unfortunate because, beyond compiling a few statistical profiles, we must resort to speculation.

Modest employees clearly took a more calculated approach to family life than did manual workers. They married about a year and a half later than did wage earners (29.4 in the Eighteenth Arrondissement); their brides were on the average about a year and a half older (25.7 years) than were those of wage-earners.[144] They also had smaller families, presumably through more careful planning. The census of 1891 showed that 873 railroad employees living in the quarter of La Villette had 430 dependents under the age of twenty; 799 such clerks in the quarter of Goutte d'Or had 584 dependents.[145] According to a survey of nearly 600 households in 1906, wage-earners were nearly twice as likely as clerks to have four or more members in the households they headed.[146] Evidently, the one-child ideal already had a hold on white-collar workers.

Were these families small because parents chose to invest heavily in the futures of their offspring? Even if employees had no aspirations to send their children to the university, expenses entailed in preparing for a superior clerical position could be significant. Youths might spend an additional year in public school and then enroll in a commercial course for training in accounting and foreign languages. Such a background could prove advantageous, especially in an era of narrowing opportunities for clerical workers. A daughter's marriage to a purchasing agent, and still more to an engineer, required a dowry.

These potential expenditures did not seem to worry the majority of white-collar employees. A study of the career paths of their sons suggests little investment in the children's futures. Out of 168 sons of employees living in the Thirteenth and Eighteenth arrondissements at the end of the Second Empire, only three were in a liberal profession or preparing for one. Furthermore, 31 percent of the sons had not even remained in clerical work but had taken jobs as manual laborers.[147] Generally, these young men were in the more skilled and lucrative trades, like printing and jewelry making, but there were also cobblers, tailors, and waiters among them.

Clerks may well have been as eager for their children to participate in the "family-salary economy" as workers were for their adolescents to contribute to the common purse.[148] At the request of hundreds of their clerks, the Western Railroad Company agreed to hire their fourteen-year-old sons as office boys at six hundred francs a year in 1884.[149] Thereafter, the youths would be competitively selected for promotion into the ranks of employees. The Christofle Silversmith Company graciously accepted the sons of its clerks as office boys as soon as they finished primary school.[150] Indeed, whenever employees made assertive demands for better pay, management could remind them of their dependence upon the company for jobs their children needed.

Though employees did not make extraordinary sacrifices for their children, they still went into debt, and they were no more likely to leave property to their heirs than were craftsmen.[151] Was this because employees were quicker and far more thoroughgoing in their formulation of new material needs than were wage-earners? There is evidence that employees made leisure and consumerism central to their family lives. The hypothetical family budget presented by the largest union of department-store clerks in 1880 offers guidance to the kind of expenditures that they recognized as being most satisfying and desirable. Outlays on clothing covered 17.5 percent (375 of 2,200 francs), and spending on recreation attained 26.4 percent (580 francs).[152] Clerks would surely have had a difficult time realizing such a spending pattern, but the budget does, at least, point to the psychological prominence of these items.

White-collar workers were eager patrons of commercialized leisure. They sometimes dabbled in higher forms of culture too. A fifth (21.1 percent) of the young clerks called to military service from the Thirteenth and Eighteenth arrondissements claimed some accomplishment on musical instruments, especially the violin and flute.[153] The newspaper of a sizable Catholic union stressed the employees' enjoyment of polite parlor games.[154] There may have been some truth to this claim, and some element of image-building as well. White-collar employees were also to be found in pubs. Twelve percent of their marriage contracts had publicans as witnesses.[155] The dossiers of employees who worked for the Prefecture of Paris showed that inebriation was not an insignificant problem.[156] The most distinctive expenses of clerks were those for the annual vacation. The budget proposed by the salesclerks' union allocated 18 percent of yearly income to this activity. The lengthy workdays of department-store clerks compelled them to concentrate much of their leisure into this brief period. They undoubtedly took advantage of the special excursions to their *pays* which railroad companies were offering at the end of the century.[157] The great psychological impact of an annual retreat is suggested by the demands for vacations made by wage-earners who worked beside the employees enjoying this benefit.[158]

White-collar families were also eager consumers. As we have seen, some credit stores attempted to appeal specifically to this group.[159] It seems likely that they succumbed a bit too often to this temptation. Clerks composed 29 percent of the population of the First Arrondissement and 42 percent of the debtors brought before the *juge de paix* for defaulting on their consumer debts.[160] Clothing was an especially enticing purchase and sometimes led to dangerous levels of indebtedness. More than one in ten employees of the prefecture had a lien on his salary, to the benefit of haberdashers in most instances.[161]

The impression that modest white-collar clerks were open to the emerging imperatives of urban life—to dress well, have a rich life off the job, relax, and enjoy themselves—is reinforced by the requests for salary advances made by the clerks of the Parisian Gas Company. In 1896 alone, 73 of 465 employees of the Accounts Receivable Department took steps to acquire some extra cash from their employer. Their letters of request collectively portray the employees' milieu as one in which both stark necessity and self-indulgence had prominent places.[162] Just over a third (25) of the requests were motivated by basic needs for shelter or medical care. On the other hand, clerks were quite candid about the importance of expenditures on nonessentials. Employees claimed a need for "distinguished" clothing for themselves or "comely" wardrobes for their wives and children. (One employee assured his boss that he would take advantage of the sale prices.) They purchased new suites of furniture for an attractive household. Vacations motivated a sizable number of requests for advances. A typical letter began, "Knowing the great importance of a pleasant vacation to the employee, Monsieur Director. . . ." Leisure and consumer expenditures were already an assured part of white-collar culture.

The few glimpses we can catch of the white-collar employees' family life suggest that they were the segment of the laboring population most willing—even eager—to substitute off-the-job compensations for rewards at work.[163] Factory laborers may have shared their enthusiasm for a rich, commercialized leisure but had much less access to it. One ought not be surprised that employees' protests were shaped very much by the desire for more leisure and by fears of losing the compensations they had already acquired. Laborers, by contrast, had to struggle to enhance both their work lives and their time off the job.

V

Politics and Protest

The triumph of a socially conservative republic after 1877 helped to translate the discontents of propertyless Parisians over the harsh realities of their lives into mass support for revolutionary workers' parties. The intensity of their anger and of their class consciousness was undoubtedly raised by some of the trends we have noted earlier: the spread of sweated work, the deterioration of office work, and the quest for a richer, fuller life on the part of many laboring people. Yet, the "working class" of Paris remained rather fragmented and compartmentalized down to the Great War. Its protests took diverse forms. Related only indirectly to the success of socialism was a series of uncoordinated confrontations between workers and employers at the dawn of the twentieth century. These conflicts marked the most serious crisis of authority at the workplace since 1848.

WAGE-EARNERS AND SOCIALISM

The political evolution of working people in a few areas of France during the last third of the nineteenth century was sometimes quite dramatic. Indifference or right-wing affiliation gave way to proletarian consciousness and a marked preference for Socialist candidates.[1] The political transformation of wage-earners in greater Paris was not so marked. The workers' movements in the capital had helped to define the extreme left during the entire century. Laborers of Paris were the repository of traditions and active memories from two revolutions that ostensibly aimed at the reorganization of class relations. The workers of the capital, and the industrial suburbs as well, did not have to discover a voice for protest in the late nineteenth century. They had to clarify their aspirations and the means they would employ to achieve them.

A class-conscious and potentially insurrectionary movement of wage-earners developed in Paris between the Revolution of 1830 and 1848.[2] From its inception, this movement had two mutually reinforcing goals: the creation of a democratic republic and the reorganization of economic relations for the well-being of workers. Subdivision of the trades, falling wages, and deteriorating material conditions characterized the decades of the 1830s and the 1840s. Such hardships caused workers to search for ways to modify or abolish capitalistic production, which had free wage labor as its central feature. The elite organized craftsmen aspired to replace private ownership with producers' cooperative associations through peaceful means. Still very much in control of the production process, these artisans regarded the role of the boss as superfluous. Others hoped to achieve greater prosperity by modifying free enterprise through massive public works projects or by guaranteeing the right to work. Laborers, even the many who were largely confused about the proper way to alter the economic system, assumed that permanent advances were not possible without a republic in which the voice of "the people" overrode the selfish interests of the clergy, aristocracy, and bourgeoisie. Such a democratic regime would supply the impetus to defeat the egotistical forces of capitalism. Advocates of cooperative association believed that credit and preferential contracts from the state would ensure the triumph of this form of ownership over individual enterprise. The republic was not only a means to economic improvements; it was a good in itself which generated passionate devotion among the wage-earners of the capital. Their republican socialism was as much a quest for the just political order as for a favorable economic system.

This movement of ideas and vague aspirations achieved the status of a blueprint for a new social order with the mass mobilization entailed in the Revolution of 1848.[3] The workers of Paris turned this revolution into the first (and, arguably, the only) one in which labor was the central issue. Through huge demonstrations, participation in clubs, newspapers, and organization under the aegis of the Luxembourg Commission, workers extorted from a reluctant Provisional Government many promises, both familiar and original. The proclamation of the "right to work" was an ambiguous formula that, in its most extreme interpretation, gave assurances of employment in the trade of one's choice. Democratically elected representatives of

Parisian trades stuck to more familiar grounds. They forced upon employers, too disoriented to resist, strict regulations over hours, hiring, and especially over wages, in the form of collective agreements. William Sewell is correct to see these regulations as "the organization of work in the style of Parisian workers."[4] This action broadened the privileges that most skilled workers in luxury trades already enjoyed. Whether such regulations were seen as ends in themselves or the first step in the destruction of private enterprise depended on the level of workers' consciousness. In any case, Parisian laborers had to defend their social republic in futile and bloody class warfare, followed by brutal repression.

The Commune of 1871 was, without question, the formative political experience for Parisian workers of the late nineteenth century. Demands for amnesty for Communards, a veneration of its heroes, and reflection upon its dramatic moments were sources of solidarity. Looking back on the events of 1871, working-class spokesmen applauded the intention of the Communards to end capitalistic exploitation, but the status of the Commune as a social revolution was far from clear.[5] It was not a repetition of 1848, in which the position of labor in the social order emerged as the focal issue. Instead, the significance of the Commune lay in the attempt to create a radically democratic government that, unlike the conservative republic of 1848, welcomed its working-class constituency. The bourgeois character of the state was to be eliminated through direct election of all officials, recall, and the reduction of civil servants' salaries to the level of wage-earners' pay. The Communards also encouraged the hopes of cooperative Socialists by decreeing preferential contracts for producers' associations and consigning abandoned factories and shops to their use—without truly calling into question respect for private property.[6] Working-class militants of the post-Commune era aspired to combine the achievements of 1848 and 1871: a state apparatus mobilized for the protection of workers' interests, with those interests as its central concern.

Parisian workers emerged from the furious repression of the Commune with a profound attachment to the Radicals, the party of advanced republicans, and without a sense of needing a party of their own. That most Parisians, whether wage-earners or not, could agree on the support of Radical representatives was evident in the election of 1876, when they captured fifteen of twenty Parisian seats.[7] Workers were preoccupied with the defense of the republican regime until that election, and for at least another decade, the mass of Parisian craftsmen entrusted Radicals to express their hopes and grievances. Many leaders of trade unions, on the other hand, quickly became dissatisfied with the republican Left once the monarchist crisis of

May 16, 1877, passed. The militants doubted that workers could emancipate themselves from capitalism without seizing the state, and they eventually abandoned cooperative socialism in favor of revolutionary collectivism. In 1878, for example, the heads of the tailors' union expressed their utter scorn for the Radicals and declared themselves "Socialists"—though precisely what they intended by this term is unclear. The motivation behind their excoriation of the Radicals appears to have been the alleged foot-dragging by the deputies of the extreme Left on the issue of amnesty for the Communards.[8] The proud leaders of the mechanics' union were, likewise, alienated from the Radicals by 1879 for their failure to "champion workers' causes."[9] Once a republican form of government was solidly founded, tensions between Radicals and their working-class supporters were inevitable. Radicals were unwilling or unable to act on the economic issues that now became paramount.[10]

Militants were ready to found a workers' party, and they did so in 1880.[11] Conflicts of personality and doctrine soon brought to working-class politics its notorious divisiveness. Of the several formations that developed, two had some following in Paris. The Blanquists enjoyed the prestige of association with the Commune. Their approach was to scorn doctrine and stress the need for workers to seize the state. The Parti ouvrier socialiste révolutionnaire, or Possibilists, formed by fission in 1882, quickly emerged as the strongest working-class party in the capital. It had roots in the labor movement and an orientation that emphasized trade organization, municipal independence, and even the worthiness of immediate reforms. In contrast to these parties, the Guesdists, with their insistence on revolutionary theory and centralized organization, found little reception in greater Paris. At first, these political options mattered hardly at all to most wage-earners of Paris.

The mass of working-class voters hesitated before following the lead of organized militants. In the municipal election of 1881, the new workers' party received only 5 percent of the vote. The election three years later yielded a total of about 35,000 votes for the three Socialist formations (Possibilist, Guesdist, and Blanquist). Again, in the legislative election of 1885, Socialists captured less than 8 percent of the vote on the first round.[12] By this time, however, the economic troubles that were to drive a fatal wedge between the Radical party and working-class voters had already begun. During the crisis of the mid-1880s, Radicals were unsuccessful in communicating their concerns for and devotion to the well-being of their wage-earning constituents. Militants intensified their disaffection with capitalism during this crisis and hoped for an insurrectionary response, but they also had elaborate programs of immediate action for the emergency situation. Ceramicists, invited to address a parliamentary commission in 1884, proposed giving twenty million francs to unions for distribution to unemployed workers, opening public food stores to sell bread and meat at cost, and instituting the eight-hour day with no reduction in pay.[13] Carriage makers demanded the suppression of all indirect taxes, the eight-hour day, and twenty-five million for the unemployed. In addition, they called for legislation that anticipated the social reform agenda of the early twentieth century: laws against insalubrious housing and workshops, compensation for work accidents, workers' pensions, and other measures.[14] The severe recession compelled workers, militant and otherwise, to test the value of that republican solidarity upon which Radicals had claimed working-class votes.

By the spring of 1886, a year impassioned by the continued economic difficulties and by the Decazeville miners' strike, workers' disaffection from the Radicals finally became a mass affair. In the by-election of May, the Radical candidate Alfred Gaulier faced Ernest Roche, a militant who made a reputation as a friend of workers during the Decazeville strike. Roche was vehemently supported by the Socialist press, which up to that point had none of the influence of the Radical dailies, like *Le Rappel*. Gaulier was still able to poll 145,000 votes in Paris, but Roche received nearly 100,000.[15] Belleville, in rapid transition now from the fortress of insurrectionary republicanism to the bastion of socialism, gave Roche a clear victory over the Radical candidate with 46.5 percent of the vote (8,347 to 7,195). Roche also captured 40 percent of the vote in the Eleventh Arrondissement and 38 percent of the vote in the Eighteenth Arrondissement.[16] Desertion of the Radicals, however, was not yet an established pattern among the mass of Parisian working-class voters. In the municipal election of 1887, the Socialist vote was only half that which Roche had received, while the Radicals retained the same strength they had had three years earlier.[17] Clearly, the majority of Parisian workers was not yet prepared to entrust the parties of their class with their support. The voters of La Gare, of Javel, or of the Faubourg Saint-Antoine regarded these new parties as too weak, divided, or doctrinaire for effective representation.

The political and economic crisis of 1888 completed the alienation of Parisian wage-earners from radicalism, but, once again, a mass following for socialism was not the automatic consequence. Bread prices shot up in the summer of that year; there were even food riots in the suburbs. The Floquet ministry, commonly regarded as Radical, angered workers by refusing to remove duties from grain and by confronting strikers. The Radical municipal council of Paris similarly discredited itself by failing to satisfy navvies (*terrassiers*), hairdressers, and waiters (*limonadiers*), who staged violent strikes that aroused the public.[18] At the moment, the flight from radicalism was all the more effective in that Parisian workers had a political alternative that excited them, General Georges Boulanger. The general had the prestige, momentum, and glamor that Socialist parties apparently lacked. Workers seem to have been attracted by the promise of a strong leader whose election would end parliamentary immobilism and address their hardship. Patriotism and the hope of ending, once and for all, monarchical threats to the republic added to his allure.[19] Workers were ready to question the possibility of realizing their aims within a liberal republic, but the parties of working-class revolution still did not entice them.

The collapse of Boulangism finally gave Socialist parties their claim on wage-earning voters in Paris. Permanently alienated from the Radicals, workers were won over to socialism partly by the influence of the Panama scandal, which convinced many voters that politicians of the Right and Center were venal, and the massacre of Fourmies (May Day 1891), in which troops fired on strikers and killed nine of them.[20] In the legislative balloting of 1893, Socialists elected seventeen deputies, compared to fourteen for the Radicals.[21] Their bastions of support, the Eleventh, Twelfth, Thirteenth, Eighteenth, Nineteenth, and Twentieth arrondissements, in addition to quarters in the Tenth and Fifteenth, were already clearly established and would not change before World War I. For some students of Parisian politics, this election marked the sudden transcendence of a revolutionary tradition based on seizing power for "the people" in favor of a new quest for deputies who came out of workers' ranks and offered an alternative vision of the economic order.[22] The change was, perhaps, not so marked. There was little about the manner in which working-class voters finally transferred their support to Socialist parties that affirmed a commitment to their ideologies or a familiarity with their programs. The Socialists' circuitous route to electoral victory in Paris suggests that their task of educating laborers had just begun.[23]

The political evolution of factory workers on the periphery of the capital is far less familiar than that of Parisian craftsmen. In some ways, it was more thoroughgoing. Yet historians have rested a bit too comfortably on the assumption that artisans were the source of all political enlightenment up to the war.[24] Parisian militants need not have despaired about the retrograde views of their comrades in the factories of the suburbs, even in the earliest years of the Third Republic. Their opinions and voting strength were solidly orientated toward the same advanced republicanism as the Parisian artisans.

The political culture of the factory workers in Paris and in the *banlieue* was rich and frequently passionate. The police spies who kept an eye on laborers at Cail, at Farcot in Saint-Ouen, at the Claparède Machine Company in Saint-Denis, and at the various dyeing plants in Puteaux knew that the repression of the Commune had not dampened their republican ardor. These spies found a politicized population which read Radical newspapers, carried on political discussions in cafés, attended rallies in Paris, and even spread propaganda on the shop floor.[25] The police reported in 1873 that "the working class is more preoccupied with politics in Saint-Denis than in Paris."[26] The sheet-music peddlers who passed by the Cail plant during lunch breaks did their best business on ditties that mocked Marshal Patrice de MacMahon and Adolphe Thiers, or faithfully followed the ups and downs of Léon Gambetta's popularity.[27] Individual factory workers rose to positions of influence not only over their comrades but also over middle-class Radicals. Grossetête, a tanning worker, became councilman for the Arrondissement of Saint-Denis in the 1870s, and the planer Leger was a municipal councilor of Saint-Ouen.[28] The police reporters emphasized that factory workers had the most advanced opinions. They supplied electoral backing for Radical municipalities which outraged the Government of Moral Order and which were occasionally dissolved by it.[29] Working-class opinion in the *banlieue* reacted strongly to the fortunes of republican candidates; when setbacks occurred, there were murmurings in favor of upheavals, even if these workers did not pose an immediate danger of insurrection.[30]

The same myths and slogans that animated political life in the *faubourgs* did so in the industrial suburbs. The legacy of the Commune was fundamental. Workers gained prestige by bragging about their participation, which they did at the risk of prosecution. Delegations of workers from Claparède, Farcot, or Cail visited tombs of fallen insurrectionaries. Municipal resolutions in favor of the "arming of the nation" and the dissolution of the army won workers' warm approval.[31] Certainly, one of the most emotional issues was the question of amnesty for the Communards. In the end, though, anticlericalism was the concern that generated the most passion.[32] Civil burials were on the ascendancy; they already constituted one in five rites in Puteaux in 1875. The mayor of this town, the owner of a large dyeing plant, won workers' favor through his outspoken hatred of priests. Whether or not his own laborers appreciated his decision to keep his plant open on All Saints' Day is unclear, but the symbolic act certainly pleased the rest of the working-class electorate.[33]

Sharing the advanced republican sentiments of Parisian craftsmen, factory workers, nonetheless, had a lower level of class consciousness. Their republicanism did not envision a means to end the capitalist system or to alter in any fundamental way relations among classes. Even the economic improvements that workers expected from a republican regime received vague articulation at best. Radical solidarities tended to smooth over some of the antagonisms against authorities at work which, in Paris, were strong.[34] Even though relations between foremen and workers in factories were not at all so intimate as in the workshops of Paris, supervisors in the large plants often had much influence over the political views of their underlings. Three foremen were leaders of the Radical party in Puteaux.[35] The foreman at Farcot permitted Radical propaganda to circulate in the workrooms, and his firing, probably for political reasons, engendered much bitterness.[36] Factory workers firmly resisted political overtures from important employers, like Farcot or Francillon (in Puteaux), whose republicanism was moderate at best. Yet they readily voted for employers whose Masonic and free-thinking associations were well known.[37] Such elected officials were not very sensitive to the special identity of their working-class electors, but neither were the leaders who arose directly from this milieu. Grossetête, for example, the tanning worker of Saint-Denis, angrily berated the laborers from the Claparède factory who attended a talk by a Radical deputy in their work clothes. Though the meeting was held just after the factory closing, and it is hard to see how the workers could have done otherwise, Grossetête claimed that their clothes manifested disrespect for the political leader.[38]

Certainly, factory laborers expected economic benefits from a Radical republic, but precisely what sort was not clear; in times of hardship "true" republicans would "do something" for workers.[39] If the voters had in mind the programs for massive aid and the regulation of work conditions proposed by the Parisian ceramicists or carriage makers, their leaders failed to articulate such demands. The agenda of the Republican-Radical-Socialists of Saint-Denis in 1877 was drafted with the participation of Grossetête and at least five other working-class Radicals; yet it contained only two specifically economic provisions among its twenty-one articles: a call for the progressive income tax and for the "placement of credit in the hands of those who can employ it directly." Beyond this, social justice was to be achieved through the separation of church and state, universal education, and autonomy for communes, among other political and humanitarian measures.[40] There can be no doubt that recessions tested the loyalty of workers to radicalism and revealed the inadequacies of the program for them. Then, the occasional speech calling for the "overthrow of the bourgeoisie" and "war on capitalism" found resonance in factory communities even as it shocked middle-class Radicals.[41]

The definitive establishment of the Republic and the economic crises of the 1880s set the stage for the decisive weakening of radicalism in the industrial towns of the *banlieue* as in Paris. Indeed, cells of Blanquists and Possibilists arrived quietly and attracted support even with little help from newspapers and with few public rallies. Guesdism, supposedly the persuasion most suited to the factory proletarians, had only a minor presence in the Parisian suburbs.[42] Generally, the Socialists brought new working-class leaders to the communities, since few Radicals deserted their ties with the republican Left. The success of the Socialist challenge to radicalism in the midst of the crisis of 1886 was impressive. Four industrial communes— Pantin, Puteaux, Saint-Denis, and Saint-Ouen—voted for Roche over Gaulier in the by-election. In the last two towns, the victory of the Socialist candidate was crushing.[43] The tallies in Clichy and Levallois-Perret were so close that the Socialist groups could surely claim a moral victory.[44] They were not, however, the only ones to profit from the discomfiture of radicalism. Boulangists were able to attract voters who had already supported the revolutionary parties over radicalism. The electors of Saint-Ouen had put a Socialist majority into their city hall in 1886, but much of its popularity dissolved in face of General Boulanger. Indeed, nearly a month after Boulanger's flight from France, he was still able to win a municipal by-election in Saint-Ouen. He and his party garnered almost as many votes as the Radicals and Socialist groups combined in the balloting of April 28, 1889.[45] Like their comrades in Paris, the wage-earners of the suburbs had only begun to commit themselves to workers' parties as the nineteenth century entered its last decade.

The demise of Boulangism left the way for socialism to supplant radicalism as the leading political force in the peripheral factory towns. Saint-Denis, Saint-Ouen, Aubervilliers, Puteaux, Suresnes, Ivry, Villejuif, Choisy-le-Roi, and Gentilly all sent Socialists to the Chamber of Deputies in the election of 1893. Socialists maintained their hold on most of these seats down to the Great War and extended their victories to other districts in the suburbs. For all this success, though, Socialist parties did not achieve the same degree of domination over political life that Radicals had enjoyed during the decade following the Commune. Their victories were often fragile, and significant setbacks occurred.[46] The Socialists' most evident failing was the inability to win municipal elections or to maintain their control over local administrations after scoring temporary victories. The new parties of the extreme Left could not duplicate the unfailing loyalty that workers had previously displayed for advanced republicanism.

The vicissitudes of the Socialists in the municipal elections of the *banlieue* do not make a clear statement about the voters' class consciousness because too many local factors becloud the issue.

Nonetheless, one pattern emerges from a comparative analysis: Working-class electors rewarded moderation and practicality; they did not consistently reward revolutionary zeal. The councilmen of Saint-Ouen eventually learned this lesson after the town elected one of the first Socialist municipalities in the suburbs (and in France). A coalition of Blanquists and Possibilists triumphed in 1886. The new councilors, the majority of whom were in the machine-building trades, soon claimed that Saint-Ouen was the premier Socialist commune in France in terms of ardor and daring.[47] Taking office meant more to them than the right to direct local affairs. Saint-Ouen was to be a platform on which they could display their revolutionary resolve and their solidarity with all the workers of France. The councilmen's sense of limits was expanded by the belief that a proletarian insurrection in the near future was a distinct possibility. With these larger concerns in mind, the Socialists sought to make the city hall into a guardian of social welfare. They created a home for the victims of industrial accidents, a municipal pharmacy, and, when the price of bread rose, a public bakery. Offering their town as a model to employers, the councilors granted municipal workers an eight-hour day and the right to elect supervisors.[48] Finally, the Socialists of Saint-Ouen endeavored to be a source of support and moral leadership to revolutionaries everywhere. They voted important sums of money for strikers at Decazeville, Vierzon, Paris, Carmaux, and elsewhere.[49] Confrontations with the central government seemed to have been situations they welcomed. The minister of the interior dissolved the municipality at least two times, once for preaching revolution and veneration for the Commune and once for flying the red flag at a ceremony. Mayor Basset brought Saint-Ouen national notoriety in 1887 when he was removed from office for having given a revolutionary address to schoolchildren and awarded Socialist books to prize-winning pupils.[50] Such audacity and energy presupposed a revolutionary electorate united behind its councilors, which proved not to exist.

After 1892, the revolutionaries' control over city hall weakened as a result of unsuccessful partial elections. Fighting between a revolutionary "majority" and a Radical "minority" dominated the council sessions through the mid 1890s. With the election of 1898, Socialists fell to minority status. Radicals, and not even very advanced ones, reemerged as the principal power on the municipal level and soon did not have to share their authority with the Socialists. During the first decade of the twentieth century, working-class Saint-Ouen was run by councils that hardly included workers.[51] While affirming its lay spirit, the new majority backed away from closing religious schools. They passed in silence over the massive strikes of 1906 and failed to protest the "massacre" of Villeneuve-Saint-Georges in 1908. These republican councilmen even refused to honor the Socialists' request to name a street after Emile Zola.[52] Working-class voters tolerated such moderation. Though electors of Saint-Ouen continued to send the Socialist Doctor Meslier to the Chamber of Deputies, municipal lists headed by him lost to Radical lists. Since the days of the Commune, Saint-Ouen had not had a town council so reluctant to challenge the status quo.

The Socialists' failure to maintain unity was surely one reason for the loss of their mandate. Soon after achieving control over the municipality, questions of ideology, strategy, and personality fragmented the revolutionary movement. Blanquists and Possibilists attacked each other more than their common opponents and refused to cooperate in elections. The former mayor, Basset, factionalized revolutionaries still further by leading a "Socialist-Revisionist" group, an outgrowth of Boulangism.[53] Such bickering undoubtedly left voters confused and directionless. Yet lack of unity was not the only reason for the Socialists' defeat. Their eventual unification as the Workers' International (SFIO) did not bring victory. The Radical triumph over the Meslier list in 1908 was not especially close.[54] The workers of Saint-Ouen did not insist that members of their own class run their commune, nor even that symbolic revolutionary positions be honored. Radicals effectively used the claim that they could administer the schools and local finances more effectively than could their opponents to the left. The tax increases that Socialists' welfare programs required might have engendered hostility too. The insurrectionary ardor of the late 1880s seemed foreign to Saint-Ouen a decade later. Working-class voters may have expressed revolutionary aspirations by sending Socialist deputies to the National Assembly, but the promises of piecemeal improvements from Radicals won support in local elections.

The Socialist municipality of Saint-Denis, the largest industrial town of the suburbs, had a parallel, if briefer, history.[55] Here a coalition of Socialists won the municipal election of 1892 quite unexpectedly. The victors inaugurated their administration with spectacular struggles against two pillars of bourgeois authority, the clergy and the police. To challenge the former, the council prohibited all religious ceremonies on the public thoroughfares and engaged in a series of demonstrations that led to the arrest of some councilmen. The stormy relations between the council and the police derived from efforts to remove the commissioners' offices from edifices owned by the municipality. The symbolic activities of the councilmen of Saint-Denis were no less inflammatory than those of their comrades and neighbors in Saint-Ouen. In contrast to their vigor in challenging established authority, however, the Socialists did not articulate a program of social action. Jean-Pierre Brunet attributes their failure to rally the electorate to the absence of such a program. Socialists lost the very next election (1898) and remained out of power for fourteen years.

The electors of Ivry-sur-Seine did not turn their city hall over to Socialists until 1896, three years after they had selected a deputy from the extreme Left. When they finally did, it was a surprisingly pragmatic administration. The councilors avoided unnecessary wrangling with the central authorities. Thus, when the prefect ordered them to illuminate buildings in celebration of the president's return from Russia, they protested that there were better uses for public funds, but they followed his orders.[56] The councilors had nothing but praise for a proposal to give the municipal workers an eight-hour day, but prudently declined to do so on fiscal grounds. Similarly, Socialist officials encouraged their workers to state their grievances on May Day but responded with excuses for their inability to alter the situation.[57] Clearly, the aldermen of Ivry lacked the bravado of their comrades in the northern suburbs. They would never have been able to proclaim that their town was the premier Socialist commune of France. Yet these councilmen and their party maintained their hold over the city hall continuously to the war.

Not until 1912 did the SFIO fully replace radicalism as the commanding political force in the *banlieue*. Helped by anger over rising prices, the Socialists captured the long-coveted municipalities of Saint-Denis, Saint-Ouen, and Puteaux and came ever closer to completing the "red belt" around Paris. These new Socialist councils of the second decade of the twentieth century were infused with a spirit of sober responsibility and with an eagerness to improve the lives of their constituents. The first Socialist mayor of Puteaux, Lucien Voilin, set the tone by stating that the goal of his administration was to "demonstrate that the proletariat is capable of managing public affairs."[58] Here and in other industrial towns Socialist councilmen addressed the pressing problem of workers' housing with ambitious but financially viable projects. Beyond this, they strove to offer the possibility of more healthful lives to their electors by building public bath houses, sending poor children on vacations in the country, funding antitubercular dispensaries, and other such measures. Acts of symbolic defiance were limited to naming streets after Socialist heroes. Thus, socialism consummated its success in the suburbs as an energetic but tame force.

By the eve of the Great War, socialism had the physiognomy of a mature movement in the industrial suburbs. One customarily conceives of the typical Socialist militant as the autodidactic crafts-

Table V-1. Number of SFIO Members per 1,000 Eligible Voters, 1910

	Paris		
Arrondissement	*N*	Arrondissement	*N*
I	2.3	XI	7.8
II	4.9	XII	13.1
III	6.8	XIII	10.2
IV	5.9	XIV	6.1
V	10.9	XV	7.9
VI	3.6	XVI	3.5
VII	2.6	XVII	7.5
VIII	1.1	XVIII	10.8
IX	4.7	XIX	9.2
X	5.9	XX	12.2
	Suburban Communes		
Commune	*N*	Commune	*N*
Alfortville	29.1	Montreuil	14.1
Aubervilliers	11.7	Levallois-Perret	11.2
Boulogne	6.1	Pantin	5.3
Choisy-le-Roi	10.8	Puteaux	13.2
Clichy	4.1	Saint-Denis	8.8
Gentilly	19.0	Saint-Ouen	12.0
Ivry	17.9	Suresnes	12.6
Issy-les-Moulineaux	16.5		

Source: Humanité, no. 2230 (26 mai 1910).

man or the Paris-born artisan, proud of his vocational proficiencies and impatient with his employer.[59] Yet, by the eve of the war, the SFIO was able to recruit its members just as easily among the essentially factory population of the *banlieue*. The "density" of party members (card-holding members per thousand electors) in nearly all industrial towns was of the same order as that in the working-class districts of the capital (see table V-1). Seven communes had higher rates than the classic stronghold of the Left, Belleville. Moreover, the local leaders who represented the party and served on administrative bodies were neither outsiders nor the handicraftsmen who had been displaced from Paris. The laborers in machine-building, chemical, and leather factories were responsible for the strong Socialist presence.

One historian of Belleville recently described its socialism as "faithful to the old traditions, capable and prepared to integrate itself further into the existing social order; and at the same time, ready to dream of the revolution that remained its essential objective, but was so distant that one did not really know if it would be realized."[60] Much the same could be said of socialism in the industrial suburbs by the eve of the war. It met with greater obstacles and more resistance here than in Belleville, but it came to represent, better than all other options, the reforms and the dreams that animated workers.

The watershed for political life in greater Paris in the late nineteenth century may have been the triumph of socialism over radicalism. Yet at no time before the war did Socialists win more than close victories, and they could never truly claim exclusive spokesmanship for wage-earners. The laborers' milieu was pluralistic; the harsh realities of working-class life did not elicit uniform responses. To consider only the Socialist voters is to ignore the mass of workers who approached, and sometimes surpassed, a majority.

In Belleville (Twentieth Arrondissement), Socialist militants found conditions for the propagation of their message as favorable as they might have realistically expected. Uniformity, social and demographic, was the key to the electoral power of the extreme Left in this district. Belleville was quintessentially the home to craftsmen, whose traditions and associations nourished several strands of Parisian socialism. The Twentieth Arrondissement had few workers of other sorts to dilute these traditions. Moreover, no other district had such a high proportion of native Parisians; the political outlook of the craftsmen who resided here had the weight of family inheritance.[61] The Bellevillois lived on intimate terms with the memories and myths of valiant working-class insurrections. These characteristics explain the exceptional commitment to Socialist candidates. We can estimate, in a rough manner at least, the maximum proportion of wage-earners who might have voted Socialist by assuming that all votes for the SFIO came from workers. In the election of 1910 (the first round), as many as 58.5 percent of all workers eligible to vote in the Twentieth Arrondissement might have cast ballots for the Socialist candidate. If one further assumes that working-class abstention was at the same level as general abstention, then it is conceivable that three-fourths of all wage-earners who voted chose the Socialist for deputy. Adherence to one line, however, did not generally characterize the working-class suffrage (see table V-2). In other districts of Socialist strength, under half of all registered workers, and only a bare majority of all voting workers, could have supported the SFIO. In a predominantly working-class residential area like the Thirteenth Arrondissement, the level of support fell dramatically lower. The industrial towns of the suburbs were more like the Tenth or Eleventh arrondissements than Belleville. Outside of its fiefdom in northeastern Paris, the extreme Left faced less than optimal conditions of diversity and mobility.

Workers failed to support Socialist candidates for a variety of

Table V-2. Maximum Percentage of Wage-Earners Who Might Have Voted Socialist in 1910 Election (First Round)[a]

District	% of All Registered Workers	% of All Voting Workers
IIIᵉ Arrondissement	22.9	29.3
IVᵉ Arrondissement	30.0	37.8
Xᵉ Arrondissement	42.3	52.7
XIᵉ Arrondissement	42.9	53.6
XIIIᵉ Arrondissement	30.0	37.0
XVᵉ Arrondissement	51.5	63.8
XVIIIᵉ Arrondissement	49.4	75.3
XIXᵉ Arrondissement	51.1	76.3
XXᵉ Arrondissement	58.5	75.0
Saint-Denis	35.5	56.3
Aubervilliers	33.2	48.8
Saint-Ouen	40.1	57.2

Sources: Humanité, no. 2199 (25 avril 1910); *Emancipation*, no. 434 (30 avril 1910); A.M. Saint-Ouen, "Elections."

[a] This table is based on the following assumptions: (1) that all Socialist votes came from wage-earners; (2) that the workers' rate of abstention was the general one.

reasons, and this failure complicates the interpretation of their political goals. Some laborers decidedly lacked class consciousness, but others were committed to alternative forms of protest. Paris, the European capital of revolutionary movements, had many traditions of class conflict, not all of them subsumed in Socialist politics. A scorn for parliamentarianism, for middle-class party leaders, or a craving for direct action channeled some revolutionary energy in other directions, to anarchism and to syndicalism.[62] Syndicalism was not avowedly hostile to socialism but was simply aloof from the pursuit of electoral victories. Socialist politics was weakened to some degree by the existence of other leftist orientations, and a mediocre Socialist vote was not necessarily tantamount to an absence of revolutionary aspirations. In the aggregate, though, Socialist voting remains a meaningful measure of class consciousness. In northeastern Paris, syndicalism was, without doubt, as strong as in any other part of the metropolitan area, but the Socialist showing at the polls in this district was nonpareil. Our regrettably imprecise sounding of working-class allegiances reveals a very significant minority of wage-earners who lacked class consciousness, supported other parties, or were not concerned about workers' movements of any kind.

The obstacles to a more thorough development of class consciousness were numerous. There can be no mystery about the failure of militants to convince many thousands of workers that they had an interest in participating in a movement; grinding poverty and work without respite hardly bolstered confidence that their actions could make a difference. One day laborer in the Nineteenth Arrondissement, whose son upbraided him for his political indifference, might have agreed with the adage that revolution was for those with full bellies.[63] Political cultures imported to the capital from areas of emigration also limited class consciousness in some cases. The Bretons provided contemporaries with the clearest example of workers who resisted assimilation into Parisian ways, at least for a generation. They constituted one of the few bulwarks against working-class anticlericalism.[64] One Socialist journalist found reason to hope for the rapid political evolution of the Bretons around the turn of the century, but his very observations demonstrated that they still formed a distinct community.[65] To a lesser extent, Savoyards, Auvergnats, and certain groups of Flemings presented similar resistance to assimilation.[66] The degree to which workers' voting patterns had more to do with their origins than with their conditions in Paris was substantial. Finally, some wage-earners did not feel a sense of grievance against the social order. They had improved their situation, or conceived that they had. A secretary of the mechanics' union just prior to the Great War thought that there were many such workers among the semiskilled in the automobile industry.[67]

That coachmen, mechanics, and tailors each had a distinctive political culture seems likely, but documenting the nuances from aggregate data is not possible. Factory workers aside, no category of wage-earners was so geographically concentrated as to have clearly revealed its voting pattern. It is significant that in districts with a high proportion of service workers, like the Third, Thirteenth, or Tenth arrondissements, the levels of working-class support for Socialist candidates were moderate at best (see table V-2). Such observations prove little in themselves, but they do help to place in perspective the fears of unionized workers for the Metropolitan Railroad at the turn of the century that their organization was not growing because the secretary was a well-known Socialist.[68] Union leaders readily admitted that their comrades did not have much sense of solidarity with other sorts of workers and joined the company union in far greater numbers than they did the independent one.[69] Moreover, workers in the butchering shops and slaughterhouses of La Villette were notorious recruits for anti-Semitic gangs in the 1890s. They probably contributed to the victories of Nationalist candidates in the Nineteenth Arrondissement at the dawn of the twentieth century.[70] To be sure, not all service workers offered challenges to revolutionary movements of the Left, but it would not be surprising if their limited integration into working-class milieus was reflected in their politics.

Did the workers who suffered most from economic maturation, the specialized craftsmen, have a distinctive political stance? Since they were the most numerous among wage-earners in Paris proper, their votes could not have been dramatically different from the averages presented in table V-2. Chronic poverty may have grounded many into a fatalistic acceptance of their situation. Furthermore, it is possible that "small hands" did not protest the deterioration of their conditions because they lacked the familial roots in their trades that the artisans had. They came from still more disadvantaged situations.[71] Once won over to socialism, however, specialized craftsmen may well have been strongly inclined to assume a militant role. The strength of socialism in the suburban town of Alfortville may be an example of such political comportment. This commune had little factory development—one forge with two hundred workers was the only enterprise of note. Yet the density of SFIO membership was far and away the highest in the metropolitan area, more than twice the level of Belleville (see table V-1). This anomalous situation is explained by the presence of many craftsmen who had been driven out of Paris by high rents and by flooding. The inhabitants of the town described themselves as "people of the *faubourg*." Domestic tailors, carton markers, chiselers, and jewelers were numerous in Alfortville. Characteristically, the first Socialist mayor of the town was a cabinetmaker from the Faubourg Saint-Antoine.[72] The proportion of militants in Alfortville suggests that the difficult situation of "small hands" did enrage some and stir them to uncommon political activity.

In the end, the failure of Socialist voting habits to penetrate to a vaster proportion of workers was a manifestation of the still-limited impact of revolutionary ideology upon working-class culture. Numerous were the observers who noted that wage-earners' outlooks and systems of belief were transformed only superficially by socialism. When the journalist Henri Leyret set about to understand the workers' way of life in Belleville during the 1890s, he was surprised by their empirical approach to life's problems. They seemed guided "more by common sense than by scientific and egalitarian rhetoric." The Bellevillois were also ambivalent on the issue of class solidarity; they blamed themselves for their inability to unite against the boss.[73] René Michaud, who studied the revolutionaries of the Thirteenth Arrondissement at first hand, affirmed that even they had confused dreams, directed "less toward the inauguration of a new world than toward a return to a form of life they had known." The former life, often a rural one, seemed more idyllic with the passing years. When they protested, they often had immediate reforms in mind.[74]

Workers' contacts with the dominant culture were many and

openly embraced. The prestige of the "good employer" and his moral ascendancy over workers did not disappear with the electoral triumphs of socialism after 1893, as the municipal elections in the suburbs demonstrate. Factory workers honored the managers who dealt generously and respectfully with them, and readily placed them in public office. Vitte, the director of the cable plant in Bezons, Berthoud, the owner of a wax factory in Saint-Ouen, the founder Thivat-Hanctin in Saint-Denis all garnered the workers' favor and votes even after the turn of the century.[75] Socialist leaders in Argenteuil claimed that the Radical employer Morel was able to capture all but 150 workers' votes in their town in 1904.[76] The evolution of workers' habits in newspaper reading did not point to greater class consciousness. In the 1870s *Le Rappel*, the advanced republican journal, was the most influential newspaper among workers in the industrial suburbs. By the turn of the century, wage-earners consulted not the Socialist press but rather *Le Petit Parisien*, the mass-circulation daily that made no effort to appeal specifically to labor.[77] The editors of *Le Travail*, always struggling to keep their journal afloat, denounced the workers of Argenteuil for neglecting their class press in favor of "petty-bourgeois" sheets. Only a few schoolteachers, union members, and municipal employees supported the revolutionary newspapers, the editors claimed.[78] The manual laborers of greater Paris were too diverse and too engulfed in the struggle for survival to be more than superficially touched by an abstract ideology. Leyret noted that the workers he observed, though frequently pressed by hardship, resisted despair and demoralization.[79] They struggled to make a viable life for themselves, but they did not draw uniform lessons from this struggle.

To a considerable extent, then, socialism as a mass movement represented a linear development that did not entail a sharp break from the forms of protest and aspirations embodied in radicalism. The underlying alterations in outlook were subtle and slow to take root. Ignorance of ideologies, or confusion about them, surely characterized the masses, whether they voted Socialist or not.[80] Class consciousness ebbed and flowed like the taste for "social realism" at the Casino of Saint-Denis. Still, deep-rooted changes were in progress. With the declining solidarities along trade lines and the decisive drop in occupational inheritance, craftsmen were less closely tied to corporate conceptions of economic emancipation.[81] Factory workers sharpened their sense of social grievance and pressed extensive economic changes on their leaders. Socialism was becoming an institutionalized response to problems for many workers, probably a majority. But just as this was occurring, new concerns at the workplace became ever more pressing.

STRIKES AND A CRISIS OF INDUSTRIAL DISCIPLINE

One leading student of strikes makes the interesting distinction between those of pressure and those of expression.[82] The former were founded on carefully defined goals, whereas the goals of the latter had a symbolic resonance. In the second instance the workers were trying to communicate a message that employers did not wish to hear. This analytical dichotomy breaks down under careful scrutiny; yet, in a global sense, it has its uses. The character of Parisian strikes evolved from pressure to expression between the Commune and the First World War. Such a shift marks the emergence of new sorts of combativeness among wage-earners of the capital, and especially of its suburbs.

The repression of the Commune and the prosecution of the leaders who were not killed stifled the labor movement only momentarily. By 1872, the police found that Parisian workers were sullen and by no means chastened. The commissioner of Saint-Denis proclaimed (with obvious exaggeration) that "the ideas of the International on capital and labor have penetrated to all levels [of the working classes]."[83] Within another four years, labor organizations, as they had existed at the end of the Empire, were essentially reconstituted.[84] This recovery soon found expression in a rather puissant outburst of strike activity. The conquest of power by republicans, the support for higher wages offered by the Parisian municipal council, and especially the continuous prosperity of the period 1878–1882 produced in these years one of the most important strike waves prior to the twentieth century.[85] The frequency of work stoppages in 1881 (42 strikes) or 1882 (37 strikes) was only occasionally surpassed in the years preceding the Great War.[86] During this strike wave, workers rarely struggled in vain for organizational support and mastery over offensive techniques. The strikes in this period were quintessential "pressuring" ones and displayed sophistication in their coordination and carefully articulated goals.

Fully two-thirds (65.7 percent) of the strikes in this Parisian wave were industry-wide; the union made a specific set of demands and called workers out of shops whose owners refused to accept them. As many as a third of these strikes used the technique of focusing on one or several employers while the rest of the tradesmen worked and contributed to the war chest. Some provisions for the support of strikers generally existed even if they were not generous. Clog makers could not afford to distribute aid to their comrades, so the union provided the addresses of provincial employers with whom strikers could seek work.[87] All this coordination had one overwhelming goal at its roots: higher pay. Over 80 percent of the strikes focused

Table V-3. Profile of Strikes in the Department of the Seine, 1878–1882

	N	%
Strike Demands		
Wage		
Offensive	87	79.8
Defensive	7	6.4
Hours		
Offensive	10	9.1
Defensive	0	0.0
Work Organization and Authority		
Fire Foreman	1	0.9
Rehire Worker	0	0.0
Miscellaneous	4	3.7
Total	109	99.9
Industries		
Furniture	24	18.6
Construction	17	13.2
Metalworking	20	15.5
Glass and Ceramics	8	6.2
Clothing	11	8.5
Textiles	11	8.5
Printing	3	2.3
Food Processing	5	3.8
Leather Goods	4	3.1
Chemicals	3	2.3
Carriages	1	0.8
Maintenance and Transport	11	8.5
Miscellaneous	11	8.5
Total	129	99.8
Outcome[a]		
Success	32	41.0
Compromise	9	11.5
Failure	37	47.4
Total	78	99.9

Sources: A.P.P., B/a 168–182; A.N., F[12] 4663.

[a] The records did not indicate the outcome of many strikes.

on wage demands. Given the relative prosperity and the inflation of the period, it is not surprising that the vast majority were offensive (see table V-3).

If the protests had a good deal of uniformity, it was not because a narrow range of industries absolutely dominated the labor actions. Wood and construction workers were able to stamp their mark on the strikes, but their methods and goals were shared by laborers in many other trades. Especially visible were the metalworkers, who launched a "general" strike in 1881 in Saint-Denis.[88] The work stoppages in the Department of the Seine already stood out from the mass of strikes in France as a whole in the late nineteenth century. Following Michelle Perrot's analysis, we can see that the provincial strikes were far less organized (72 percent without unions) and less premeditated (51 percent) than the labor protests of the capital.[89]

Workers of the Parisian metropolitan area at this time did not have the sorts of strikes that engendered a festive atmosphere of liberation or degenerated into riots. Some did produce outbursts of anger, but these were directed almost exclusively against strikebreakers, not against employers. The violence that occurred was not at all spontaneous and had the weight of tradition behind it. August Meniel, a twenty-six-year-old joiner in sculptured furniture, learned the sanctions which his trade imposed on scabs through family tradition—only too well; when he found his father working, he openly called him a "coward" and threatened to beat him.[90] The manner in which saddlers handled their scabs after the strike of 1878 amounted virtually to ritualized violence. They carried the strikebreakers out of the workshop and threw them in a pool of dirty water and then stood around the pool insulting them. These actions, highly controlled, were surely not intended to do bodily harm; they were meant to reaffirm the fraternity of the "righteous" and to exorcise the faithless. The insults did not cease until the scabs left the shop.[91]

Little was distinctive about the twenty-three strikes by factory workers at the birth of the Third Republic. They occurred predominantly in the machine-building industry, largely because most other factory industries used women and the unskilled, who had a low strike potential. Like craftsmen, factory laborers struck overwhelmingly in favor of higher wages. Violence erupted in these strikes still more rarely than those at the workshops, but always with the same purpose of punishing scabs. The threats of reprisals at the huge Say Sugar Refinery (1,700 workers) in 1882 had more coherence than the strike itself. The day after strikers had renounced efforts to raise their wages to forty-five centimes an hour, 1,500 of them, along with their family members, surrounded the plant after work and yelled, "Death to the Italians," strikebreakers who prudently remained inside the factory.[92]

During the five-year period centered upon the turn of the century, the anatomy of strikes in greater Paris was markedly different.[93] Industry-wide strikes nearly disappeared and were replaced by struggles within individual firms (89 percent). The construction and woodworking trades played a less important role in strike activity, whereas service industries and clothing (broadly defined) became more disruptive (see table V-4). Most dramatic was the restructuring of strike demands. Wage issues became substantially more defensive. Still more significant, strikes were no longer exclusively about pay. Questions of work organization and authority were now major sources of confrontation. Behind the new shape of labor agitation was an altered

Table V-4. Profile of Strikes in the Department of the Seine, 1898–1902

	N	%
Strike Demands		
Wage		
Offensive	103	42.2
Defensive	49	20.1
Hours		
Offensive	16	6.6
Defensive	1	0.4
Work Organization and Authority	75	30.7
Fire Foreman	(21)	(8.6)
Rehire Worker	(13)	(5.3)
Pay Mode	(14)	(3.7)
Work Rules	(12)	(4.9)
Union Matters	(9)	(3.7)
Other	(6)	(2.5)
Total	244	100.0
Industries[a]		
Furniture	20	12.3
Construction	18	11.1
Metalworking	17	10.5
Glass & Ceramics	8	4.9
Clothing	29	17.9
Textiles	2	1.2
Printing	6	3.7
Food Processing	5	3.1
Leather Goods	7	4.3
Chemicals	5	3.1
Carriages	2	1.2
Maintenance & Transport	31	19.1
Miscellaneous	12	7.4
Total	162	99.8
Outcome		
Success	38	18.4
Compromise	52	25.2
Failure	117	56.2
Total	207	99.8

Sources: Ministère du commerce, Office du travail, *Statistique des grèves* for the years 1898–1902.

[a] The strikes of 1899 are not included in these figures.

economic climate and new pressures from management. There was, as well, a transformation in attitudes toward work procedures and authority on the part of labor and management.

To explain the expanded proportion (and absolute number) of strikes against pay reductions, one must consider the changing economic climate, which was decidedly less prosperous than at the beginning of the Third Republic. In particular, 1900 and 1902 were years of recession, and 60 percent of the defensive strikes took place in those years.[94] The chief victims of efforts to pare down wages

were the specialized craft workers in the industries that were operating increasingly under sweated conditions, shoemakers, jewelers,
tawers, and cabinetmakers. Quite aside from recession-related protest, the strikes of 1898–1902 bear witness to a meaningful shift in
the relations between laborers and their work. At the founding of
the Third Republic, conditions of work had not been an issue; wage-
earners sought monetary compensations for their labor, performed
under rules they accepted. By the end of the nineteenth century,
this was no longer the case. The labor force of Paris and its suburbs
found the work experience unacceptable in an absolute sense; even
though some workers were benefiting from rising earnings, no wage
increase could compensate for the new conditions. Thus, there were
strikes to alter the mode of pay (14), to change work rules (12), to
rehire comrades fired for insufficient production (13) or union matters (9), and especially, to banish a hated foreman (21). Whether
the employers or their workers bore principal responsibility for the
new contentiousness over work procedures is a focal issue to which
we must return. For now, we have at least located the roots of the
increasingly "expressive" contours of Parisian strikes at the turn of
the century.

The controversies over work experience emerged, not necessarily first, but certainly most dramatically, as a crisis of factory
discipline—the term "crisis" is not too strong.[95] Simply put, factory
laborers confronted their superiors in a new manner and refused to
work under the prevailing conditions. There had long been instances
of raw, even brutal, industrial relations in the plants of Paris, and
especially of its suburbs. Owners closed factories suddenly without
paying their workers; employers publicly accused their laborers of
being drunkards who would use any pay increase to consume more
alcohol.[96] Yet, if our previous analysis of factory abuses has any
validity, industrial relations had become fairly "correct," if not cordial, in most instances.[97] Foremen, the linchpin of the power structure in factories, rarely evoked deep animosities before the turn of
the century. At the repair shops of the Paris-Orléans Railroad, which
employed over a thousand workers, only four laborers were fired
for insubordination during 1872.[98] Moreover, the foreman often enjoyed the respect of his workers and, as we have seen, influenced
the political views of the rank-and-file during the 1870s and 1880s.
It was, nonetheless, true that when workers were faced with an
unwelcomed innovation, they blamed him. Several incidents dating
from the late 1880s mark an escalation of the tension between laborers and their supervisors. In 1887 the personnel of the Chemical
Products Company in Saint-Denis sustained a pay reduction of twenty-

five centimes a day. The order clearly came from the plant director but the workers attributed it to the foreman. Threats to kill him circulated, and not just idle ones. A thirty-two-year-old Breton worker brought a gun to the factory, shot the foreman in the courtyard, and continued to hold off the police for the rest of the night.[99] This crime, the individual act of a poor, troubled laborer, was prophetic; guns and attacks on foremen became notable themes in industrial relations thereafter.

Less than a year after the violence at Saint-Denis, a foreman again suffered for the unpopular decisions of his employers, this time, at the Forges of Alfortville. When all the stokers (*chauffeurs*) were put on piece rates, they angrily assembled at lunch and sent a death threat to the foreman. Despite the fact that he was newly hired and not responsible for the changes in pay, rage continued to build during the afternoon. A crowd of women and children gathered at the closing; when the foreman passed through the gates, they chased, bit, and struck him with such vehemence that he had to take refuge in the plant.[100] In 1888 collective protest against the foreman was still an isolated event; not so in 1899. In that year there was an explosion of anger—but controlled anger—against foremen in the machine-building industries. Workers engaged in firm and coordinated efforts to compel their employer to fire the foreman who troubled them on the job. In view of the symbolic importance of the foreman, such strikes betokened nothing less than a challenge to managerial authority, a breakdown of the compromises and accommodations that had prevented work routines from becoming a matter of conflict up to this point.

It is frequently asserted that automobile workers entered decisively upon the strike scene during the protest for the eight-hour day in 1906.[101] Actually, during the crisis of factory discipline at the very end of the nineteenth century, automobile workers placed themselves on the cutting edge of strike activity. In 1899, four dramatic work stoppages had as their goal the firing of foremen whom workers could no longer tolerate. The machine-tool operators of the Anglo-French Automobile Company exploded in anger at the end of January and demanded the dismissal of the supervisor because he had fired a worker who had protested the suspension of the five-minute grace period for lateness. The machinists persevered in their demand for over a month.[102] In June protest moved to the largest vehicle producer in the region, Dion-Bouton, and to the fief of the haughty spokesman for car manufacturers, the Marquis de Dion. Workers formed a delegation that insisted upon the cashiering of the foreman Gosselin, whom they accused of treating them brutally. The marquis, faced with a weakening of his authority as a result of complicity in the recent antirepublican outburst at the Auteuil Race Track, assented.[103] A month later Clément, a leading car and bicycle manufacturer in Levallois-Perret, hired Gosselin as a foreman. Upon hearing of this appointment, all 350 of the automobile laborers at the plant refused to continue working. When Gosselin actually came to the work, the bicycle workers laid down their tools, insulted him, and one attacked him. The affair ended tragically, for Gosselin returned with a gun and shot a laborer.[104] While resistance to the foreman was inspiring protest at Clément, workers also opposed the foreman at the Gardner-Serpollet Automobile Company in Paris. With the news that their foreman had fired three workers, the 250 laborers at this company demanded his dismissal.[105] These incidents, far from dissipating discontent, only intensified it. In September the workers at Dion once again rose in anger over their new foreman, the "slave driver" Pivot, successor to Gosselin. Rather bitter recriminations went on for twelve days, during which Pivot needed police protection. The strike ended only when the foreman agreed to quit. During their resistance, the personnel of Dion engaged the solidarity of comrades at Clément and at the Darracq Automobile Company, who refused to accept subcontracting work from Dion.[106] Truly, this was not a series of discrete events but rather a veritable rebellion in the automobile industry.

The challenge to the authority of the foreman in the car-making industry continued, occasionally with much fury, throughout the first decade of the twentieth century. Darracq, in Suresnes, exploded with anger in July 1902. As in the case of Clément, its 350 workers struck before the new foreman had arrived because his reputation for harshness had preceded him.[107] At the beginning of the next year, the Mors plant in Paris was struck by its 550 workers, who refused to work under a "gross and insulting foreman."[108] Inspired by this example, the personnel at the Richard Car Company in Ivry sent a delegation to see the director about a foreman who had fired a worker, and when the manager would not rescind the decision, 420 workers left their jobs in protest.[109] The events of the next year at La Minerve, a small car maker in Billancourt, demonstrated that the disciplined strike was not enough to contain the emotion now generated by the issue of authority at the workplace.

The surfacing of long-held indignation took the form of frenzied revolt at La Minerve in March 1904.[110] Workers in the assembly workroom had resented for some time the "arrogance, injustice, and harshness" of their foreman, according to police reports. Their discontent turned to riot when he fired a laborer for a minor reason. During the lunch break that followed the firing, the workers spread their indignation to comrades in the lathe shop and the tool room.

All the wage-earners went to the director and demanded the immediate firing of the foreman. The latter, frightened by the agitation, took out his revolver from his vest pocket, an act that threw laborers into a frenzy of rebellion. They spread out through the plant and destroyed work material and equipment while singing "La Carmagnole" and "L'Internationale." This festival of liberation ended only when the police cleared the factory.[111]

Rather than ending their protests in this outburst of passion, automobile workers intensified their aggression against foremen. There were at least five more incidents of some importance before the general strike of 1906. Two of the affected plants, Gardner-Serpollet and Mors, entered their second round of protests, but not with any diminution of venom. Workers at Mors followed the foreman home and watched his residence, so that he needed police protection. The factory director responded by closing the shop in which the agitation was most intense.[112]

Confrontation over foremen and the authority they represented marked a massive display of discontent. Over 3,000 automobile workers, roughly one in five, participated in such strikes between 1899 and 1906. Challenges to managerial prerogatives were by no means confined to this new industry, however. Builders of telephone equipment exploded in anger against their foreman's "excessive severity" before the automobile workers did, in 1898.[113] Thereafter, the machine-construction industry was as beset with strikes as the car plants were. Workers at the General Cycle Company struck because the "arrogance" of their foreman was "absolutely intolerable." When the director of this plant investigated the charges, he admitted that his workers had a just grievance and offered to transfer the supervisor to another post; but this was not enough for the laborers. They stood firmly for his firing and struck for twenty-eight days to enforce this stipulation.[114] Disturbances disrupted operations at the Charles Company, a manufacturer of steam engines, when boilermakers defied a foreman who had fired an older worker. The laborers accused the supervisor of being "brutal and carried away," and they returned to work only after the director sent them personal letters admitting that his supervisor had been "abrupt" and promising more cordial relations.[115] A third of the nine hundred workers at the Gouin Machine Company struck in support of three workers fired for fighting with a supervisor. Again, in 1899, machinists refused to work under the direction of a supervisor who was "too demanding"; this time at the Bariquand and Marre Machine Company on the rue Oberkampf (Eleventh Arrondisment).[116]

As the new century began, the metalworkers were joined by wage-earners from a diverse array of industries in opposing the foreman. In 1901 four hundred women who worked in the state-owned match factories at Pantin and Aubervilliers left work for five days to rid themselves of a supervisor who had fired a comrade for what they took as a trivial reason.[117] Similarly, the huge Dupont Printing Shop in Clichy, long a model of managerial authority in an industry that had few models, succumbed to the crisis of discipline in 1903. Until then, Dupont had successfully excluded the Typographical Society, renounced collective wage agreements, installed labor-saving machinery, and introduced female compositors with impunity. His careful selection of workers and generous paternalism made his plant immune to protest.[118] Five hundred printers did strike, however, for the removal of a foreman who was "too severe" and who made them wait too long after the day was over to receive their pay.[119] In 1901 half the personnel at the Hattat Shoe Company (350 workers) refused to tolerate their supervisors's "revolting vulgarity" any longer. The Coruble Shoe Company was the scene of a strike-riot that presaged the one among automobile workers in Billancourt in 1904. Exasperated by the demands that the foreman placed upon them, mechanized shoe assemblers grabbed him, and in a ritualistic effort once reserved for humiliating scabs, tried to remove all his clothes. When the foreman escaped, the laborers began to upset machinery and chanted "L'Internationale."[120]

Unskilled workers generally struck out of desperation; yet they, too, occasionally participated in the anti-authoritarian strike wave at the dawn of the twentieth century. The gravitation of the miserable laborers at the large Hirsch Distillery in Argenteuil toward participation is especially illuminating. In 1902 the brutalizing conditions of work and low pay (four francs a day) at this company, owned by a Jew, had engendered anti-Semitism among the laborers and rendered them susceptible to right-wing propaganda. By 1905, however, the workers were protesting their subjugation at the workplace in a new manner, for they struck for the dismissal of the foreman.[121] Even the largely foreign and itinerant quarry workers struck against their foreman. Laborers at the Morel Quarries did so in 1909, on the eve of an industry-wide walkout, to improve work conditions.[122] Apparently, the limits of the insupportable had expanded to include the vexing actions of supervisors.

Disruptions arose out of specific confrontations though the ultimate issue, how much more intensive the work regime would become, was at the heart of the dispute. Two separate but closely related themes emerged from the grievance statements of the strikers. On the one hand, workers complained that foremen were "too severe" or "too demanding." This claim signaled an altercation over workers' efforts to limit their output on piece rates. Wage-earners also asserted their will to be free of pressure to be more efficient by protesting the firing of slow workers. At the Corre Automobile Company, at Neuilly, the personnel affirmed their opposition to tightly regulated hours. The workers demanded the dismissal of a foreman who had fired a worker "for no good cause"; the unfortunate laborer had arrived on the job a half-hour late.[123]

Equally as inflammatory as the foreman's "severity" was his reported crudeness, vulgarity, or brutality. The laborers at the Roch Company, a maker of automobile parts, returned to work after the employer promised that the supervisor would be "more conciliatory."[124] At Gardner-Serpollet, the foreman provoked a strike through his "arrogance" and "crudeness."[125] No doubt, the foreman displayed "arrogance" by pressuring the laborers to work faster or unleashed his vulgar tongue in a shouting match arising from such interference with work procedures. At the Mors Automobile Company, 626 workers struck to defend their dignity against a "gesture made in anger"; but the foreman was incited by the workers' resistance to his interference with their work routines and hiring procedures.[126] The foreman's insults became a focal issue in the strikes either because they replaced work-pace demands as the emotional issue or because strike leaders saw some advantage to casting the grievances in those terms.

In most cases outbursts over the foreman had roots in specific altercations over work routines; a smaller number of strikes reflected pent-up resentments of the supervisor's demeanor or of his inconsiderateness. The second strike at the Mors Automobile Company was of this nature. Workers expressed their repugnance at having to watch the foreman strut about the floor with a large cigar in his mouth and with "a provocative and derisive air."[127] It was a strike in quest of dignity as much as anything else. So was the protest at Clément, for the personnel could only refuse to work under the direction of a man whom their comrades in Puteaux had labeled a "slave driver." In a more practical vein, the print workers at Dupont resented being kept late to receive their pay, and shoe-machine operators at Hattat experienced the "revolting crudeness" of their foreman when he opposed their precautionary habit of stockpiling work materials.[128]

There are good reasons why automobile and machine builders lashed out at their superiors suddenly in the very last year of the century. The electoral power of working-class parties had grown markedly in Paris and its suburbs since 1893, and the workers gained confidence that a friendly government was in power when the Socialist Alexandre Millerand entered the Waldeck-Rousseau cabinet in June 1899. At the same time, workers' emotionally-charged republicanism was much offended during the course of the Dreyfus Affair. Such tensions played a visible role in the inception of the strike wave at the Dion-Bouton plant. Workers were angry at their employer's role in the notorious attempt to insult the president of the Republic at the Auteuil Race Track. One of the reasons for their hatred of the foreman Pivot was his heavy-handed efforts to recruit workers for a demonstration in favor of the Marquis de Dion, who had been arrested.[129] These political forces coincided with a push from the mechanics' union to organize automobile workers. In truth, unions were not important to the strike wave as a whole, but it is possible that militants had some role in crystallizing grievances.[130] The single most important trigger of the crisis was the approaching Exposition of 1900.[131] The prospective festivities ensured that vehicle makers would be quite busy and under pressure to settle disputes quickly. The issues of the moment unleashed a spiraling series of confrontations between labor and management over work routines.

Management attempted to counter the limitations on output that workers on piece rates sought to impose. It was not surprising, then, that outbursts against foremen coincided with efforts at pre-assembly-line rationalization in the automobile industry and with rising imports of American machine tools.[132] The irate laborers at Dion-Bouton walked off their jobs in the shadow of a new plant being constructed on the route Nationale (Puteaux) for specialized machines. In general, the means foremen used to boost productivity were not very innovative: badgering workers, correcting their ways of working, rebuking them for wasted time. These measures were supplemented by attacks on the flexibility of work hours entailed in piece rate production. Furthermore, managers and foremen found ways to make workers feel more insecure. They dismissed the ones who were slow or insubordinate. Compelling laborers to waive their rights to compensation in case of abrupt firing provided an undercurrent of antagonism in several strikes.[133]

Though these measures of rationalization were far from thoroughgoing in themselves, they provoked a heightened reaction among workers. Indeed, a central feature of the workers' outbursts was their intensity. Directors of the Hattat and Dupont plants had to wonder why workers struck without even presenting a prior set of demands. Apparently, the laborers wanted a protest as much as they wished a redress of their grievances. It was not only at the Minerve Automobile Company, with its frenzied revolt in 1904, that employers had the occasion to be quite intimidated by the anger of the workers. When a foreman fired a worker at the Richard Motor Company in Ivry for speaking in favor of the Mors strike, management could calm its incensed personnel only by creating a permanent grievance commission, and it did so most reluctantly.[134] The director of the Panhard-Levassor plant was alarmed by the physical response that a foreman's simple reprimand brought from one worker and shocked by the eagerness of the labor force to support this act of insubordination.[135] Such restlessness on the part of factory workers bears note because most of the measures provoking it could not have been absolutely unprecedented. Laborers at the Cail, Gouin, and Farcot plants had complained about tight surveillance, pressure to work harder, and rigid enforcement of hours even before the establishment of the Third Republic; yet such issues did not foment strikes at that time.[136] The workers at the Dupont Printing Company and the Hirsch Distillery first broke with their customary pliancy in the first years of the twentieth century. Managers were clearly caught off guard and unprepared to deal with the anger that they provoked by tightening work routines.

Though frequently compelled to make momentary concessions, some managers soon endeavored to reassert control over their work force through rather draconian measures. At Panhard-Levassor, the troubles that flared up in 1903 determined the director to rid the plant of its trouble-makers. He used the strike to fire 150 of the workers suspected of being "hostile to their employer."[137] Similarly, Clément suddenly locked out its 1,200 workers in September 1905 and did not rehire a tenth of them in an effort to "relieve itself of its bad workers and militants."[138] The general strike over the eight-hour day in 1906 intensified managerial attempts to discipline the labor force. It is doubtful that employers would have taken such severe steps if workers' resistance to authority had been more measured.

Examining the spiral of counteroffensives, each escalating in intensity, one should not lose sight of the roots of confrontation: a work culture that had impeded employers from achieving their production goals. As the twentieth century began, managers of greater Paris had yet to settle questions about work pace, work schedules, and dismissal policies. Their first efforts to tighten these regulations had often provoked more resistance than they were ready to handle.

Management could not help noticing, and being most disturbed by, the sorts of workers who were responsible for the antiforeman protests, for these outbursts came from below the elite factory workers. Industrial craftsmen, laborers who had wide discretion over their jobs, who headed teams, and who retained control over training and recruitment, could insist on freedom from supervision. Thus, the unionized iron molders at Dion-Bouton, the metal polishers at Clément, or the iron fitters at the Vadrine Chassis Company might obtain nearly the same mastery at the workplace that artisans in shops producing luxury goods enjoyed. The workers who were most involved in the crisis of factory discipline at the turn of the century, however, were not drawn from this group. Rather, they were the skilled and semiskilled machine operators who performed fairly routine or subdivided work, who could not claim independence solely on the basis of their technical proficiencies, who worked relatively isolated from one another, and who had little if any tradition of organization. The workers who challenged management at the Charles Machine Company and won humiliating concessions from their employer were boilermakers and day laborers earning only 50 to 80 centimes an hour, whereas highly skilled mechanics received a franc or more.[139] At the Gouin Machine Company, the strikers were operators of specialized machine tools earning only 7 francs a day on piece rates.[140] The machine-tool rooms at both Dion-Bouton and Gardner-Serpollet were the focal points of strike activity. The seven hundred turners, fitters, filers, and planers who took action against Pivot earned between 6 and 7.5 francs a day.[141] Similarly, the compositors who initiated the strike at the Dupont printing plant were paid only 5 to 7 francs on piece rates.[142] They had little in common with the organized printers in the Parisian shops who handily dominated their employers. The routine laborers were usually not more militant than industrial craftsmen and were certainly not more organized; but the former group may well have been the targets of most attempts to raise output. From management's point of view, industrial craftsmen justified their autonomy through their skills, and routine workers did not. Moreover, the increasing amount of capital put at the disposal of commonplace laborers encouraged employers to insist on its full utilization. In any case, this crisis of factory discipline was not principally a matter of resistance to deskilling on the part of industrial craftsmen.

Far from precipitating or leading these challenges to authority, industrial craftsmen frequently assumed a detached posture. The conflict at the General Cycle Company started with the turners, probably routine machine operators, since this was a technologically advanced plant. The organized and well-paid metal polishers joined later, and they used the work stoppage to make their own demands for an end to piece rates. About 100 of 240 fitters and turners at the Hurtu bicycle factory soon engaged in a display of sympathy, but mold makers and metal polishers did not walk out with them.[143] The metal polishers at Dion-Bouton, all union men, joined the murmurings against Gosselin in 1899, but they struck over their own wage grievances. Similarly, at Clément, the metal polishers used the strike against the foreman for their particular ends, to repeal a recent reduction in their wage agreement.[144]

Though the elite factory workers tended to remain aloof, the srikes to oust the foreman for severity or arrogance had the emotional power to mobilize all other sectors of the factory labor force. A cardinal feature of these protests was their large size and high level of participation. The workroom in which an intolerable supervisor was in charge rarely marked the limits to the outbursts. The laborers of that shop were usually able to explain their grievances to other workers and to engage their support. At the Hattat Shoe Company, workers in all specialities participated in the strike against a foreman who vexed the assemblers and finishers. The compositors at Dupont initiated a protest that quickly spread to 400 workers, including 100 women. At the Mors Electric and Automobile Company, all 560 workers walked off their jobs over the introduction of piece rates in one shop at the end of 1902. Just a month later, workers were ready to duplicate this total strike over a "gross and insulting" foreman. Not surprisingly, three years later, tinsmiths who were inflamed by a foreman's threatening gesture were able to convince all 626 wage-earners in the plant to leave their jobs and to remain out for two weeks. Sympathy actions by mechanics in other plants were not uncommon either. Such solidarity recalls the observation of one journalist who studied the factory workers of the *banlieue* after the Great War and discerned, among workers who were not otherwise militant, a powerful sense of obligation to unite against managerial authority.[145] This anti-management impulse mobilized thousands of workers in protest at the turn of the century.

The workers' impressive show of solidarity in protecting their work practices and defending their "dignity" had rather ill-defined implications for their political outlook. In greater Paris, as elsewhere, vociferous demonstrations against work authority did not carry over to other arenas of class struggle.[146] So little did the strikes at Dion-Bouton galvanize working-class voters in Puteaux that Socialists lost their majority in the first legislative election following the protests over Gosselin and Pivot. The candidate of the extreme Left garnered less than a third of the vote in the first round of the 1902 election. Socialists had to throw their weight behind the Radical candidate in order to prevent the victory of a nationalist military officer (undoubtedly the favorite of the Marquis de Dion).[147] Union membership probably grew in this era of escalating conflicts over work routines; but, in the automobile industry, the proportion of organized workers hovered around only 1 to 3 percent.[148] The crisis of factory discipline arose from the immediate, ad hoc experiences of workers, and they were slow to draw wider lessons from it.

On the other hand, the laborers' vigor in defending their work culture was impressive, not only to students of the subject in retrospect, but to the managers against whom it was directed. French employers had a reputation for their ferocious resistance to encroachments upon their authority; yet two-thirds of these strikes resulted in cashiering the foreman or in compromises that addressed the workers' concerns. As we have seen, managers often found themselves in humiliating positions of having to admit culpability. At Mors and elsewhere, the labor force refused to permit even the face-saving device of allowing the supervisor to remain at the plant in a different capacity. Such demonstrations certainly put the employer on notice against more thoroughgoing incursions upon workers' ways of performing their jobs.

The attempt to introduce time-motion studies at the Renault plant, the failed strikes of 1912–1913 at that firm, and the national debate over the rationalizing precepts of Frederick Taylor that ensued have unfortunately monopolized the historian's vision of industrial relations before the Great War.[149] The crisis was older and broader than this perspective suggests. The crisis of factory discipline was not confined to the automobile industry; it was not merely an outgrowth of "scientific management" precepts; nor was it the affair of an exceptionally bold entrepeneur like Louis Renault. Work routines that had solidified by the end of the Second Empire were seriously challenged in the last decade of the nineteenth century. These challenges entailed limited and unimaginative efforts to raise output and were quite widespread. Moreover, workers were much more successful in resisting these challenges than they were in resisting Renault. Finally, the crisis extended well beyond the factories of greater Paris.

The furor over factory work routines at the end of the nineteenth century was part of a larger crisis of industrial discipline, for craft workers in small shops, too, were rebelling against the authority to which they were subjected. Employers in the artistic trades customarily expected to yield much of the mastery over the production process to their labor force. Some of the artisans' supremacy began to erode, however, in the last decade of the nineteenth century. Faced with greater competition and the "revolution of the good," some bosses decided that workers' control over production required modification. From the early 1890s, craftsmen found their bosses meddling with their work procedures on an unprecedented (if still modest) scale and their foreman rejecting the validity of their work culture. No less than factories, workshops became scenes of labor strife over the question of authority.

Craftsmen regarded the hardening of management's position as threats to their dignity as well as to their job autonomy. As such, small changes in procedure could provoke angry responses. In 1902 ceramicists were stung by the "insolence" of a new foreman who rejected poorly made objects and had them rectify the work at the end of the day with no supplementary pay.[150] Meanwhile, at the Nelson Furniture Company, a new foreman installed a punch clock, much to the chagrin of the cabinetmakers. The craftsmen refused even to enter the shop until the apparatus was removed and considered their willingness to allow the installation of a time piece of any sort as a major concession.[151] Copper-plate engravers deserted their shop when a new foreman was more demanding than his predecessor and attempted to end the custom of bringing wine into the workplace.[152] The strike of wood gilders in 1910 was provoked more by a sense of betrayal than by a re-ordering of work procedures. The new supervisor was only "a bit more demanding," but the fact that he had been a former union secretary made his challenge to the gilders' work culture all the more insupportable.[153] Craftsmen, thus, contributed to a sense of crisis over work by rejecting even small changes in the workshop.

Crafts like construction, which entailed much internal subcontracting, waged vigorous defensive action against the extension of the subcontracting practice in the decade before the war. The Federation of Building Trades led an angry struggle in 1908–1909.[154] When the Chamber of Deputies manifested an interest in ending this hated labor practice through legislation, other craftsmen launched strikes to encourage such reform. Piano makers, whose employers had turned ever more commonly to subcontracting in order to cut costs, were especially active in this regard.[155]

By no means all craftsmen's strikes over work organization were defensive. Workers in prosperous trades were quite concerned with enhancing their autonomy at work, perhaps because the mastery traditionally enjoyed by other workers was slipping. Metal polishers, for example, were fortunate enough to work in an expanding craft; demand for their skills in making bicycles and automobile parts created shortages of labor, of which they were happy to take advantage. In 1893 and 1894 their union launched a major offensive to eliminate piece rates.[156] Similarly, the assemblers of metal scaffolding (*charpentiers en fer*) were the beneficiaries of construction methods that hurt the traditional woodworking members of the building trades. In 1910 they used their advantageous position to enforce closed shops where they did not already exist. There were at least ten strikes over the issue in that year.[157]

Significantly, even craftsmen in favorable situations were relatively more interested in protecting their job autonomy than in raising their earnings. Such had not been the case after the Commune.

Indeed, the unions of copper molders and metal polishers asked members to accept slightly lower wages earned by the hour rather than to work on piece rates.[158] The artisans in stagnant crafts had no choice in the matter; the need to defend their mastery over work was imposed upon them. Clearly, in the decade or two before the Great War, matters of work routine were of greater conscious concern than they had been earlier. When laborers took to the streets in massive numbers to demand a shortened work day in 1906, they had this very much in mind.

The culmination of the crisis in industrial discipline was the vast demonstration focusing on the eight-hour day in the spring of 1906. It occurred at a moment of heightened class consciousness and intensified questioning by workers about how they intended to relate to the established order. The success of "realistic" artists at the Casino of Saint-Denis illustrated wage-earners' self-absorption at the time.[159] The general strike became one of the most massive acts of noninsurrectionary protest ever staged in Paris. As many as 200,000 workers in the department participated, and the movement touched a wide spectrum of Parisian trades.[160] Automobile workers and mechanics in general continued to express frustrations by taking to the streets on May Day. The police estimated that 12,000 of 70,000 mechanics in the Department of the Seine struck. Nearly every sizable automobile, chassis, and machine-building plant was closed by the movement.[161] At one large cable company in the Fifteenth Arrondissement, workers attempted to storm the factory and battled police.[162] As many as 50,000 construction workers may have joined the movement.[163] The walkout was virtually complete among the skilled jewelers, cabinetmakers, wood sculptors, and joiners.[164] The demand for eight hours could not have been meaningful to the specialized craftsmen who had irregular work schedules; yet, some sacrificed for the movement. No less than 1,300 of 5,000 imitation-jewelry makers struck. At one particular address in the Faubourg Saint-Antoine, the police found thirty furniture jobbers' shops that were struck by their 150 workers for about a week.[165] Such participation signified that the solidarity between skilled and specialized craftsmen was still a living force in some regards. Especially noteworthy was the cooperation between handicraft workers and factory workers; for once these groups had a sense of partnership. Cabinetmakers suddenly discovered an interest in establishing contacts with laborers in the mechanized furniture shops that had just begun to appear in the eastern suburbs. Until the general strike the artisans had not even thought of their lowly comrades, except perhaps to lament their existence. Now the craftsmen resolved to supervise the revolutionary education of factory workers and convince them that eight hours was not a "utopian" demand.[166] Only an extraordinary crisis could have brought the proud *faubourg* to reach out to the suburbs.

The demand for shorter hours had the power to mobilize such protest in part because it posed solutions to the problems that engendered the crisis of industrial discipline. Workers were quick to see in the curtailment of the work schedule a means for curbing overproduction and absorbing the excess labor supply that allowed employers to tread on established work procedures. Moreover, the shorter workday meant to many wage-earners the sort of freedoms from discipline that they sought when they battled the foreman. Behind the united front of artisans and factory workers were slight differences in anticipated goals. Time off seemed more important to workers of large-scale industry, whereas handicraftsmen saw leisure as a means to an end at the workplace. Speakers at the automobile workers' rallies did not overlook the labor question, but they stressed the value of leisure and the "dignity" it would impart to their lives. Craftsmen, on the other hand, touted the short day as a way to repair the damage from competition and new technology.[167]

These nuances in the meaning of an eight-hour day translated into divergent strike strategies. Workers in the large machine-building plants and in the automobile industry were rarely faithful to the original purpose of the general strike. They opted, instead, for the "English week," with a half day on Saturday. The granting of this demand by the management of important factories like Delauny-Belleville (2,200 workers), Panhard-Levassor (1,700 workers), Westinghouse (600 workers), and Carbonnes (400 workers) encouraged laborers elsewhere to fight for it.[168] On the other hand, mechanics in the older machine shops and handicraftsmen thought of the shorter day more in terms of the quality of their work than of their leisure. Jewelers, masons, and woodworkers of all sorts held out for eight hours. Only printers settled for a nine-hour day. Cabinetmakers struggled for twenty-nine days before admitting defeat.[169]

One of the most meaningful features of the general strike of 1906 was its inconclusive denouement. Workers left their jobs in a massive display of solidarity and, for the most part, returned to work defeated. Yet the strike did not purge them of rebelliousness. The protest simply set off another round of confrontation between labor and management. As workers straggled back to their shops, employers resolved to master their personnel. Machine builders renewed efforts to exclude militants from their plants. They took firmer control over hiring practices and issued harsher shop rules. Some factory managers even removed the stools that workers had installed for their comfort near their machine tools and had the seats burned in the courtyards of the plants.[170] Master craftsmen were no less vengeful. Woodworkers, for example, insisted that their artisans accept piece rates. Masters cooperated in blacklisting hundreds of militants.[171] Neither the defeats most workers suffered nor the managerial reprisals crushed workers' will to struggle against authority. The very next year witnessed at least four outbursts by mechanics to rid themselves of a detested foreman.[172] The recession of 1907–1908 quieted them more than fears of managerial repression, but the challenges resumed thereafter. A wave of protests that encompassed the automobile industry in 1910 included attempts to drive out foremen from Darracq and from Charron.[173] Likewise, craftsmen did not end their resistance to the incursions upon their autonomy, not even in the trades most exhausted by the general strike. The events of 1906 were symptomatic of the confrontational stances of labor and management in the first decade of the twentieth century but did little to diffuse the hostility. Manufacturing in the Parisian metropolitan area, from the most traditional to the most advanced, approached the Great War with old compromises dissolved and new settlements uncertain.

Service workers decisively expanded their visibility on the strike scene during the last years of the nineteenth century. In the period 1878–1882 less than a tenth of all strikes in greater Paris involved service workers. At the turn of the century they were behind about one strike in five. The large majority of these stoppages (59 percent) concerned transportation workers, a sign that Paris was ever less a "walking city." Workers in retail foods sales also also went off the job more often. Did this heightened combativeness signify that manual laborers of the service trades participated in the revolt against work authority that animated the manufacturing labor force? They did so in their characteristically ambiguous manner, or not at all.

Service workers walked off jobs primarily over pay-related issues around the turn of the century; 84 percent of their strikes were about money. There were exceptions, coming especially from the transportation workers. Those of the Vanves Company struck in 1901 over the severity of an inspector and compelled the management to curb his rigidity.[174] The massive railroad strike of 1910 is much more difficult to classify. Its formal goals were higher wages, improved benefits, and better amenities, but this protest had features that marked it as part of the crisis of work discipline. An important precipitant was managerial pressure to derive more work from the personnel. Faced with escalating costs after 1900 and the inability to raise ticket prices for political reasons, the railroad companies (especially the Northern) pushed their workers to greater exertion. The laborers did not challenge the authority of their employer when the strike broke out, but many politicians contended that it was a veritable revolt against the authority of the state. Sustaining three thousand firings after the collapse of the strike, the railroad laborers paid more dearly than did automobile workers who challenged their foremen.[175]

In the retail trades, anger over work authority did not proceed beyond periodic demands by waiters for the right to wear mustaches.[176] The narrow range of strike issues in this sector is partly explained by workers' success in achieving a resolution to their outstanding grievance: their forced recourse to fee-charging placement agencies. Over sixty thousand service laborers had had their income and mobility restricted by the obligation to pay for procuring a job. They staged angry protests, such as those by waiters (*limonadiers*) in 1888 or by butchers' aides in 1891.[177] In 1904, just as antiforeman agitation reached its heights of frenzy in the automobile industry, the state suppressed fee-charging agencies for butchers, hairdressers, cooks, bellboys, soda-jerks, waiters, bartenders, among other groups.[178] In any case, this issue was only tangentially about work conditions. By permitting workers to change jobs without financial loss, the legislation expanded individualistic solutions to discontents at work. The central thrust of protests against placement agencies had always concerned earnings.

Another obvious source of potential protest for service laborers entailed the length of the workday. There was some contention over this matter, but it was sporadic and fragmented. These job actions never attained the coherence and resolve that salesclerks displayed over the question of hours in the early twentieth century. With the exception of hairdressers, service workers did not have a presence in the general strike of 1906.[179] All in all, the militancy of service workers developed apart from that of other wage-earners.

THE PROTESTS OF EMPLOYEES

"In spite of their social origins and their petty-bourgeois prejudices, employees are recognizing more and more that they are a part of the proletariat," proclaimed the Socialist journal *Emancipation* in 1902.[180] Only a few months earlier, it had concluded that most clerks were "reactionaries; they consider themselves bourgeois."[181] This contradiction was excusable, for white-collar employees were a complicated group that resisted being situated into simplistically conceived class categories. As we have argued earlier, it makes more sense to treat them as an interstitial group. In any case, clerks who thought of themselves as proletarians of the office were few in number and without influence. Indeed, a latent tension existed between employees and manual workers. Unionized accountants acknowledged this tension in the mid-1880s, and employees' journals lamented that it was still very much the case in the twentieth century.[182] Marriage records suggest that workers and clerks were able to form friendships fairly frequently, but at the workplace, such harmony did not prevail. Police spies found much aversion between workmen and office personnel at the Cail Machine Company, even as the latter group formed a union in the 1870s.[183] Strikes sometimes turned latent tension into visible hostility. The firing of a cabinetmaker for being late and attempting to sneak into his shop did not provoke a strike; but when a bookkeeper demanded that the worker leave at once, the other craftsmen became angry and insisted on the dismissal of the clerk before they would return to work.[184] A strike at one automobile plant brought violence between the two groups. Laborers tried to storm the factory in the hope of attacking scabs, and the office workers held them off with stones and revolvers.[185] It would be hard to find examples of strikes in which clerks came to the aid of manual workers, except when their own interests were deeply implicated in the outcome of the protest.

Even the employees who conceived of themselves as participants in the struggle against capitalism and were committed to cooperation with manual workers did not truly "recognize that they were part of the proletariat." Members of the Union of Accountants sent representatives to various Socialist congresses in the 1880s; yet they disagreed on whether to campaign for the right of employees to bring abuses before the Workers' Arbitration Council. One leader argued against it on the grounds that "employees are superior to workers from all points of view."[186] Twenty years later, the self-image of the clerks had not been degraded. The leaders of the employees' union at the Parisian Gas Company publicly affirmed their affiliation with the Labor Exchange (*Bourse du Travail*), were proud to head a "red" union, and openly championed Socialist candidates. Yet they still refrained from asking the company to create a dining hall for clerks on the grounds that it "would not be consistent with the dignity of employees."[187] These Socialist employees found a grievance in the fact that a few laborers in one department earned more than certain clerks did. The long years of service that some laborers had accumulated did not prevent young clerks from making claims for superiority.[188]

Such "petty-bourgeois prejudices" derived from the knowledge that employees had a more integral relation to management than did laborers. The respective manners in which white-collar workers and manual workers made requests for charitable aid from their companies illustrate the thoroughly different assumptions each group made about its place in the organization.[189] When the wage-earner needed assistance, he asked his wife to make the plea, just as she would apply to the municipal charity board. Ancient traditions of subordination were, thus, respected. The clerk, on the other hand, penned the request himself, asked for assistance in his own name, and often stopped short of attempting to evoke genuine pity. For clerks, it was not so much a matter of asking for charity as of calling upon the company, which had extensive obligations to them, to provide a proper level of support. In the end, sympathy for manual workers and aspirations of cooperation with them did not make for a genuine identity with them. The employees' self-definition had not succumbed to proletarianization.

However constant the psychological distance between the personnel of the office and that of the workroom, at least an important segment of white-collar employees eventually followed the political evolution of laborers. Analyzing the voting comportment of clerks must remain a matter of some uncertainty because they were not deeply rooted in the class system, the touchstone of Parisian political life, and did not have sufficiently concentrated residences to make their electoral choices evident. Nonetheless, it is scarcely subject to doubt that they were part of the Radical consensus, along with workers and small employers, from the Commune to the mid-1880s.[190] They seemed to accept, or were resigned to, the rough-and-ready economic realities that they had found in the small offices and stores, perhaps because their traditions were rooted there.[191] Employees did not have a developed sense of being part of "the social problem" at this time. The largest and most rapidly growing union of department-store clerks, the *Chambre syndicale des employés de commerce*, forcefully rejected a "collectivist" stance in the early 1880s. Occupational organizations that avowed their Socialist connections remained minute, a preserve of ideologues.[192] The debate among accountants concerning the Workers' Arbitration Council expressed the ambivalence of clerks about reform legislation on their behalf. Observers correctly charged that employees did not make their grievances known to the public, and the result was that the state did not intervene in the clerks' favor with their employers.[193]

With the social crisis of the mid-1880s and the demise of the Radical consensus, white-collar employees seem to have been more willing to retain their party affiliations than were laborers, who moved to the left, and shopkeepers, who eventually moved to the right. Clerks formed about a sixth of the electorate of the Eleventh Arrondissement in 1910, but they constituted a quarter (23.8 percent) of the members of the Radical-Republican-Socialist electoral committee.[194] In the Fourteenth Arrondissement, about one in five voters was a white-collar worker, but a third of the Radical electoral committee was drawn from this group.[195] Surely this loyalty was the reason why Socialist politicians appeared at employees' rallies to denounce Radicals as the false friends of the clerks.[196] Many employees apparently accepted the "solidarist" outlook of advanced Radicals, who sought social peace through piecemeal reforms. The political comportment of white-collar workers, however, also entailed much polarization and a readiness to reject either parliamentary democracy or free enterprise.

Resentment of workers, chauvinism, and respect for the Church recruited some—probably the better off—clerks for the Right. One of the districts of Paris that Nationalist candidates found most hospitable was the Second Arrondissement, home to many department-store clerks and employees of the numberous wholesale houses along the rue Sentier. It appears that the extreme Right won elections here with the cooperation of many of these employees. In 1902 they were overrepresented on the electoral committee of the Republican-Nationalist candidate Gabriel Syveton, secretary of the League of the Fatherland, who railed against "international Jewry" and "the Masonic sect." Composing a fourth of the electorate, employees were 35 percent of Syveton's sponsors. Far from being an anchor of the Radical party here, as in the peripheral arrondissements, employees were disengaged in the Second. They composed only 17 percent of the Radical electoral committee.[197] In this district, where rents were high and clerks paid dearly to reside near their jobs, many had entered a new alliance with disaffected shopkeepers and large employers.[198]

The Right may have profited from the resentments of the better-off employees, but many of the humble clerks eventually found in socialism a proper defense of their interests, a means of protesting their subordination, and an expression of their aspirations by the turn of the century. The Socialist orientation of the department-store clerks' union was no longer a matter of controversy or contention, as it had been twenty-five years earlier. Adhering to the *Parti socialiste français* in 1900 and using funds to support candidates of the extreme Left no longer prevented the union from enrolling six or seven thousand dues-paying members.[199] Another sign of support for socialism was the leadership that white-collar workers gave to it on the local level. In no commune of the Seine Department was their role negligible. They comprised 20 percent of the Socialist candidates for the municipal council in Saint-Denis in 1904, 15 percent of those in Saint-Ouen, and 24 percent of those in Ivry.[200] In these industrial towns, workers shared power with and gave votes to white-collar employees.

Voting patterns in the commune of Ivry provide information about the timing of employees' acceptance of socialism. In particular, we must compare suffrage in two wards having crushing majorities of working-class residents (Ivry-Port and Petit-Ivry) with that in the central ward, which had a more diversified population and in which employees composed 22 percent of electors. The Socialist tidal wave of 1893 apparently left clerks relatively untouched, for the Socialist candidate, Jules Coutant, lost to the Radical candidate on both the first and second ballotings in the central ward.[201] In the next election, 1898, however, Coutant carried this district with a margin that was comparable to those in working-class wards.[202] Political historians agree that the Dreyfus Affair did not affect this election.[203] The significant development was probably that socialism had lost some of its ferocity after its earliest victories and after prosperity returned to France in the 1890s. Whatever their ultimate hopes, Socialists seemed ready to serve the disadvantaged within the existing social order, and clerks were now eager for such help.

A significant segment of white-collar workers shifted to the Socialist parties at the same time that they abandoned their reticence about asking for the state to aid them in correcting abuses at work. They now actively demanded legislation to shorten hours of work, guarantee a day of rest per week, facilitate the suing of employers, eliminate contracts that compelled them to waive their rights, make work conditions more comfortable, make work conditions more healthful, limit the weight of liens on their salaries, and abolish fines. Whereas leaders of the Railroad Employees' Union had not favored the nationalization of the lines in the 1880s, it became part of the union's platform at their congress in 1893.[204] Employees at most utilities also wished for a take-over by the state in hopes of better pay, more regular promotions, and a richer package of benefits. Clerks sought legislation to deal with unsanitary work conditions, too.[205] In short, by the twentieth century, many employees had come to conceive of themselves as victims of a social order that required, if not a revolution, then at least extensive reform. As clerks cast about for politicians to support these reforms, they found in the Socialists their firmest allies, whereas the record of the Radicals was mixed and often disappointing. Salespeople had occasion to learn this lesson in 1899, when the Parisian municipal council failed to limit the use of outdoor display counters, as the clerks had demanded. Socialist councilmen were alone in resisting pressure from shopkeepers and store owners.[206] Efforts to win legislation in favor of white-collar workers cemented alliances between clerks and parties of the extreme Left.

The editor of one occupational journal proclaimed that his fellow employees were "reformist, not revolutionaries."[207] There is no reason to challenge his basic claim, but it does merit elaboration. Clerks' desires for social intervention to improve their lot became firmer and more focused during the last two decades of the nineteenth century. Their interests could easily lead them to the support of parties that were still avowedly revolutionary on the grounds that the reformist Left was unable to deliver on its promises. Indeed, there were employees who did not dread a working-class revolution because their vision of the collectivist society was a comfortable, bureaucratic one. As one bookkeeper at the Parisian Gas Company argued: "Why should I fear the Revolution? I would prefer to be a civil servant (*fonctionnaire*) in the Social State to being a slave for the monstrous company for which I now work."[208]

One of the peaks of clerical militancy had already passed by the time of the Commune. In the spring of 1869 department-store clerks agitated for a Sunday of rest and a twelve-hour day. A union was formed in March, and in May a modest strike took place. Salesclerks launched a much more massive walkout several months later. For the first and last time in the nineteenth century, an industry-wide strike occurred. About eight thousand of twelve thousand employees of department stores participated for about a week, but they did not prevail. Employers stood firm and punished strikers. The owners used the failure to consolidate their control over their personnel.[209] The legacy of this strike and its repression weighed upon employees throughout the rest of the century. This scale of protest was not replicated in the four decades before the Great War.

The rarity of massive demonstrations was not a matter of apathy or complacency. In truth, the crisis of industrial discipline that troubled the manufacturing sector was very much a crisis of *work* discipline; employees were restless and unhappy about work conditions and increasingly prepared to take collective action to change them. The problem for clerks was to find the proper form of action. There were a few outbursts of violence. Shopclerks in Saint-Denis, for example, used force to chase customers from stores that did not close by 8 P.M. as part of their pressure for shorter hours in 1902 and 1903.[210] Such protest could not be a model for the vast majority of white-collar workers. They were, for the most part, unprepared to resort even to peaceful strikes—and for good reason. Employees realized that the degree of solidarity among them was not very high. The obligation to present a united front against an employer, which was a strong moral imperative among wage-earners, was nòt so among clerks, though perhaps it was spreading. With fragmentation likely, employees were frightened by the high cost of strikes. Less willing than workers to tolerate the immediate privations that walkouts inflicted, clerks found the long-term cost totally unacceptable. Dismissals might entail the painful loss of fringe benefits, pensions, and security, all of which were often irreplaceable. Employees' special role as part of management—albeit a subordinate one—made strikes too costly. Unions, even those with angry members, generally renounced their use.

Their position as part of management also gave clerks hope that there were less painful means to achieve some of their ends. They wished to believe that managers would make concessions when faced with a united personnel that politely, but firmly, demanded change. The principle on which clerks founded their union activity was not confrontation but negotiation. The police described the policy of the largest union of department-store clerks, representing 6,000 or more members in 1907 as "a politics of conciliation and reform, largely tempered. . . ."[211] The leader of the Parisian Gas Company Employees' Union, which had over half the 2,300 clerks as members, attributed its success in providing improvements to "the good behavior (*sagesse*) and moderation which the unionized have always shown."[212] Labor leaders did nothing to encourage some of the largest strikes, like the one at Dufayel Department Store at the end of 1905.[213] Even when negotiations failed and strikes ensued, employees were hesitant to assume an avowedly hostile stance toward management. The bookkeepers of the Nozel Metal Company in Saint-Denis and Passy were one of the few such employees of small offices to strike. They did so only after several weeks of fruitless negotiations over shorter hours (nine instead of eleven) and annual raises. Their formal statement of strike goals was laced with conciliatory terms: "Your personnel, which is devoted to you, would be forever grateful if you met these demands."[214] The strikers strove to preserve the pretense of being part of management.

Mindful of their superiors' power over them and eager for a dialogue with them, employees seemed likely candidates for company unions. Management did, in fact, attempt to impose these organizations on its personnel when clerks seemed ready to form their own unions.[215] It is a measure of employees' seriousness of purpose, however, that these "yellow" unions were rarely successful. The dynamic and growing organizations were the independent ones. Employees resisted pressures to join company organizations more vigorously than did transportation workers with the Metropolitan Railroad.[216] Clerks may have been disinclined to make large sacrifices in their protests, but they were earnest about being firm and demanding in their negotiations. Even the largest Catholic union of clerks adopted a favorable, if passive, stance toward workers' movements.[217] The right to independence and to a serious dialogue with management was one employees were ready to protect energetically.

The important strikes among white-collar workers before the Great War were direct consequences of the breakdown of the negotiated path to reforms. They derived some of their fervor from the employees' sense of betrayal that such a breakdown provoked. One of the most significant protests of salesclerks occurred at the Bazar de l'Hôtel de Ville (BHV) in the fall of 1909 over the question of closing hours.[218] Several months before the protest, the director had acceded to the employees' demands to close at 7 P.M. rather than 7:30 on weekdays and 8 P.M. rather than 10 P.M. on Saturday, but then announced the cancellation of this "experiment." The loss of what seemed a duly-won right enraged clerks, not only at the BHV but at other stores (Louvre, Pygmalion) as well. There were angry demonstrations at 7:00 on the day that managers vowed to remain open; clerks (not always from the store itself) intimidated customers and sang "L'Internationale." Over a hundred employees at the BHV were dismissed during the course of the strike that followed.[219]

The most significant strike of office workers occurred among the postal employees just as the salespeople at the BHV were beginning the "experiment" of shorter hours.[220] Frustrated negotiations were an important background factor. There had been a deterioration of promotion opportunities and increased work loads for some time before the strike. What crystallized discontent was the arrival at the head of the Postal Service of an official, Simyan, who displayed no intention whatsoever of bending or holding out hopes of change. He antagonized clerks by issuing harsh rules on promotion procedures and by canceling residence subsidies (which especially hurt Parisian clerks). The strike that ensued was about removing Simyan and opening new channels of negotiations as much as about the accumulated work grievances.

The largest and most dramatic strike of white-collar employees occurred at the Dufayel Credit Department Store at the end of 1905.[221] Again, the principle of negotiation was central to it. Earlier in the year, about 1,400 of the 1,850 employees had joined a union in the hope of improving work conditions through a dialogue with the owner. The effort began propitiously, with Dufayel agreeing to meet monthly with union delegates. Suddenly, three union leaders were demoted, and the meetings with the director ceased. The clerks blamed two supervisors for the troubles and, in a manner that mirrored workers' challenges to authority, demanded their "displacement." Eventually, over 1,500 employees stopped working for ten days, and they received the support of clerks from several of the other credit emporia (Bon Génie, A Jean Bart, Aux Classes Laborieuses, Ville de Saint-Denis, and Samaritaine). The strike was unique in the post-Commune era in mobilizing the solid majority of salesclerks. They rallied because their hope for improved conditions had been dashed. The means through which they had hoped to gain some control over the workplace had been nullified.

There were several other department-store strikes, especially during that high tide of class tension, 1905–1907, but they were rather limited affairs. The bill collectors at three firms (Place Clichy, A Jean Bart, and Aux Classes Laborieuses) demanded better pay.[222] At the Galeries Lafayette in 1907, a strike over work schedules (the time of opening and duration of lunch) raised the sorts of concerns that all employees shared. Yet only a tenth of the labor force of 2,700, mainly package deliverers and bookkeepers, struck.[223] The failure of salesclerks to participate prompted the Socialist journal *Humanité* to attribute their reticence to the commission system of pay, "which prevents the development of any sentiment of solidarity."[224] It would have been more to the point to note that employees were aroused to strike, not by the abuses themselves, but by the breakdown of conciliatory efforts to reduce these abuses.

Organized employees were aware that their means for influencing company policy were limited even if they understandably chose not to stress this fact. Several of the issues that concerned them the most, especially starting pay, promotions, and bonuses, were not points on which management was usually willing to make significant concessions. Having ruled out strikes, employees were not able to accomplish much directly, but they did endeavor to engage powerful allies on their behalf. Since so many organizations were dependent on the good will of the public or held concessions from a governmental body, clerks were sensitive to the benefits of shaping public opinion. Attempts to embarrass an intransigent management were common. The same union leaders who preached moderation in tactics vilified company directors through the press.[225] Much more frequently than wage-earners, employees called upon public officials to pressure management for generous treatment. An extension of this strategy was to urge the public assumption of a concession. No group campaigned more fervently for the "municipalization" of the gas utility than the clerks of the Parisian Gas Company. They contributed to election campaigns of councilmen who supported the effort and kept the issue before the public.[226] Similarly, railroad clerks were eager to become civil servants and not simply remain the personnel of private companies. These tactics certainly did not place the fate of employees in their own hands, but they often represented their best hope for significant ameliorations.

The modest white-collar workers of greater Paris seemed to present a classic case of proletarianization. Their work conditions deteriorated in the last decades of the nineteenth century, and they came to recognize that a laissez-faire approach to social problems was not appropriate for them. Hence, clerks organized in impressively large numbers and made their grievances known. Above all, they defined themselves as victims of the social order, people who needed the sorts of social legislation that had heretofore concerned only wage-earners, and usually the most dependent of them. This change occurred at least partly in the context of a wider crisis of authority at the workplace, whether employees were conscious of this or not.

Proletarianization was not, however, the final determinant of their situation. Their self-image did not suffer from it, and their impulse was to assume more continuities with management than with labor. Equally important, white-collar employees based their protests on principles that did not assume proletarianization. Reasoned and firm protest from within, not walking off the job, won their approval. Employees correctly perceived that declaring their independence from management might cause far greater losses than benefits.

VI
Conclusion

The Apaches, Klein's Furniture Palace, the Casino of Saint-Denis, and the insurrection at the Minerve Automobile Company—these colorful symbols define the cutting edge of structural change in the Parisian agglomeration. The four decades between the repression of the Commune and the First World War were as rich in social change as almost any equivalent time span in modern French history. Among the outstanding achievements of these years was the growth of an important industrial region on the periphery of the capital, where vineyards had been cultivated under Napoleon I. This area was soon dominated by the principal growth industry of the twentieth century, automobiles. At the same time, Parisians' demands for services decisively reoriented the economy. The channels by which consumerism reached the masses, already visible at the end of the Second Empire, were commonplace by 1900. Science and maternal sentiment revolutionized the life chances of infants and made the rational planning of families the prevalent practice. Was the late nineteenth century, then, that crucial period of transition when traditional modes of behavior disintegrated and when "modernity reached the masses"?[1] The experience of the propertyless working population of Paris permits no such sweeping claims. Manual and clerical workers here had a gradual and continuous exposure to capitalistic and industrial innovations, to new forms of production, distribution, and state intervention. By the time of the Commune, their work cultures and expectations were already different from those of their predecessors in the first third of the nineteenth century. The distinctive feature of the prewar era for these humble people

198

was the partial breakdown of the accommodations that had carried them through the earlier periods of economic transformation. The result was intensified frustration at work and deepening conflicts over authority. Thus, a venerable theme of labor history, that economic changes at the end of the nineteenth century repaired the destructive features of early industrialization and integrated the workers more firmly into the existing social order, rings false in the light of the experience of Parisian workers.

Paris was not only a political and cultural capital, but also an old manufacturing city with a grand tradition of preindustrial production. Before the first half of the nineteenth century was over, decisive departures from this tradition had become evident. The hand manufacturing of one-of-a-kind commodities ceased to be the focus of Parisian industry before 1848. By the Second Empire, large-scale enterprises distributed items made by subdivided, specialized trades. Such reorganization rendered working people of Paris ever more diverse. Within the half-century before the Commune, well-trained craftsmen, once the central figures in production, fell to minority status. Specialized craft workers and, later, factory and service workers were the expanding groups. The wage-earning population of greater Paris, thus, came to comprise four distinct categories (if we exclude domestic servants). The process of differentiation was equally pronounced in commerce. A fairly unified commercial sector, composed of merchants and their clerks, existed in the first third of the nineteenth century. The stage of an employee's career was then the primary determinant of his or her place in the office hierarchy. The growth of scale in commercial enterprises not only undermined solidarities between employees and employers but also established a demarcation between the superior white-collar personnel and the modest clerks.

Many working people never fully absorbed the shocks entailed in these changes nor acknowledged the permanence of the transformation. Nevertheless, they had to adapt and adjust to these initial disruptions of a maturing capitalistic society. During the Second Empire and up to the economic crisis of the mid-1880s, most groups worked out modes for resisting further changes and achieved accommodations with their employers. Such adaptation by necessity or choice may help explain why labor did not become the central issue during the Commune, as it had been in 1848. The nature of the settlements varied greatly from one group to another. Artisans who worked in the luxury branches of their trades were most secure in their settlement, for their well-being was intertwined with the enduring position of Paris as a center of great wealth and sophisticated consumers. As in 1848, these workers had demanded and received collective wage agreements, control over the work process, and courtesies on the job. Such benefits remained largely unchallenged until the very end of the century. Factories allowed enough compromise on work control and on the pace of innovation that laborers sought only wage gains when they protested in the 1870s and 1880s. Modest white-collar workers, enjoying an extensive and growing list of fringe benefits, accepted a laissez-faire social order during the early years of the Third Republic. They were also the beneficiaries of expanding employment opportunities at this time, a situation that made the status quo all the more palatable. Least secure in their accommodations with earlier structural changes were the craftsmen in "current" sectors of their trades. Protections against sweated conditions did exist but were fragile. Nonetheless, specialized workers displayed enough confidence in and affinity with their crafts to place their children in them as the Second Empire came to an end.

The specialization and bureaucratization that forced themselves upon the working people operated without great intensity upon most service workers. The personal relations with clients characteristic of artisanal production were being transferred to the service sector. To the extent that workers in transportation were proletarianized in the same manner that handicraftsmen were, they responded similarly, but the mass of laborers in retail trades remained idiosyncratic in their relative isolation from other sorts of wage-earners.

The structural realities and the compromises on which the adjustments to earlier economic change rested were called into question from the depressed 1880s to the dawn of the twentieth century. Then, the laboring people of Paris found themselves resisting the drift away from a work situation that never fully pleased them—for fear of still worse. Specialized craftsmen faced the most calamitous prospects as their fate became more separate and distinct from that of artisans. The mass-marketing of an ever greater range of commodities brought sweated conditions to an ever greater number of semi-artisans. Moreover, the weakening of the craft as an institution of social integration left specialized hand workers without the ability to launch protests that reflected the relative losses they suffered.

By the twentieth century, an element of embattlement characterized the elite craftsmen in the made-on-order sectors. The accelerating deterioration of apprenticeship and of artistic training was a sign that recruitment was more difficult. Intensified challenges to their autonomy at work reminded artisans of the fate they shared with other wage-earners. Many lived with a sense of impending adversity that was exaggerated but not altogether unfounded; large plants that devised new ways to produce commodities for the well-off were a major source of employment in the *banlieue*.

Laborers in factories, those "prisons," were highly self-recruiting by the new century. This may be a key to the factory workers' ability to adapt to an environment that other sorts of wage-earners emphatically rejected, and even to expand the scope of their lives within it. Managerial efforts to rationalize work procedures around the turn of the century seemed to fall most heavily below the level of the highly skilled and organized workmen. As factory labor became more routinized and as investment in capital mounted, the entrepreneur tried to curtail the liberties associated with piece rates. The affected groups reacted with noteworthy furor to the threats that were not truly fundamental to their situation at the workplace and often forced the employers to relent. In the longer run, though, management became convinced that still more strident steps were necessary in order to master the work force.

Many humble white-collar workers developed a sense of bitterness and victimization as the nineteenth century ended: Their earnings seemed inadequate to them; their opportunities, constrained; and their work pressures, fearsome. At this point, however, analogies with manual laborers break down. White-collar employees continued to define themselves in terms of their integral relation to management and evolved a strategy for protest on this basis. Furthermore, clerks were not primarily interested in demanding control over their work regime; they were eager to establish compensations off the job.

The confrontations that marked the first decade of the twentieth century were inconclusive for both working people and management. No new sort of *modus vivendi* emerged, or even appeared to be emerging at the workplace. As the case of the white-collar employees illustrates, though, work was not the only sphere in which adjustments could be made or compensations accepted.[2] In this study, we have considered the possibility of a working-class culture that was becoming significantly more privatized and centered about the home. Although signs of changes in this direction were not lacking, the shifts before 1914 were far from profound and thoroughgoing. For all the expanding wealth in this "age of material progress," manual laborers' experience of rising standards of living was undramatic and even insignificant in some respects. The development of "consumerism" in working-class ghettos was still a modest affair, which, in any case, barely reached the mass of wage-earners. As for the employees, though their earnings kept pace with those of workers, they did not experience—and certainly did not have the sense of experiencing—notable improvements in living standards.

A simple reading of the working-class press demonstrates the growing importance of a commercialized leisure that was divorced from work-related activities. White-collar workers most fully integrated such leisure into their lives. The factory labor force, benefiting from more predictable work schedules, displayed an undeniable enthusiasm for commercial spectacle. On the other hand, craftsmen did cling tenaciously and rather successfully to the sociable traditions of their trades, which survived even in industries that experienced continuous reorganization. Moreover, the quest for a richer life illustrated by the working-class passion for theater, cinema, and music hall did carry over into the workplace. There were few signs of wage-earners internalizing that proverbial "rule" of mature industrial society: to express discontents at work purely in terms of demands for monetary compensations.

The assumption that workers were developing the same domestic ethic as their social superiors by the end of the last century has informed much speculation on their private lives. Though we agree that family relations may have been at a crossroad, they probably did not take a fundamentally new path at this time. Rather, working-class households seemed to build on traditional solidarities in incorporating scientific advances and family planning into parental concerns. The bonds among family members resisted transformations until levels of security were a good deal higher than prewar material progress had made them. It is doubtful, then, that off-the-job life offered working people much opportunity for adjustment to economic maturation. In many cases, pressures at home exacerbated tensions that rapid change produced.

In the forty years before the Great War this capital of conspicuous consumption, audacious ideas, and sensual pleasures did not simply preside over a Europe in rapid transition from a preindustrial to a mature industrial society. It participated quite fully in the transition. Indeed, structural economic changes occurred in a rather clear-cut form in Paris and its periphery. This sort of change, as much as the position of Paris as the center of political life and intellectual movements, explains why its working people tended to be on the cutting edge of protest. They continued to offer leadership into the twentieth century as working people all over France had to reckon with industrial and bureaucratic maturation.

Abbreviations

A.N.	Archives nationales
A.D.S.	Archives départementales de la Seine et de la Ville de Paris
A.P.P.	Archives de la Préfecture de Police
A.M. Argenteuil	Archives municipales d'Argenteuil
A.M. Bezons	Archives municipales de Bezons
A.M. Ivry	Archives municipales d'Ivry-sur-Seine
A.M. Puteaux	Archives municipales de Puteaux
A.M. Saint-Denis	Archives municipales de Saint-Denis
A.M. Saint-Ouen	Archives municipales de Saint-Ouen
BHVP	Bibliothèque historique de la Ville de Paris

Notes

Preface

1. William Sewell, *Work and Revolution in France: The Language of Labor from the Old Regime to 1848* (Cambridge, 1980), pp. 153–154.
2. Christopher Johnson, *Utopian Communism in France: Cabet and the Icarians, 1839–1851* (Ithaca, N.Y., 1974); "Economic Change and Artisan Discontent: The Tailor's History, 1800–1848," in *Revolution and Reaction: 1848 and the Second French Republic*, ed. Roger Price (London, 1975), pp. 87–114.
3. Joan Scott, *The Glassworkers of Carmaux* (Cambridge, Mass., 1974); Eugen Weber, *Peasants into Frenchmen. The Modernization of Rural France, 1870–1914* (Stanford, 1976); Patrice Higonnet, *Pont-de-Montvert; Social Structure and Politics in a French Village, 1700–1914* (Cambridge, Mass., 1971).
4. Peter Stearns, *Lives of Labor: Work in a Maturing Industrial Society* (New York, 1975), p. 13.
5. Theresa McBride, *The Domestic Revolution. The Modernization of Household Service in England and France, 1820–1920* (London, 1976).
6. Henri Leyret, *En plein faubourg (moeurs ouvriers)* (Paris, 1895), p. 79.

Chapter I

1. Adeline Daumard et al., *Les Fortunes françaises au XIXᵉ siècle* (Paris, 1973), p. 192.
2. Adrien Dansette, *Naissance de la France moderne: Le Second Empire* (Paris, 1976), chaps. 1, 3, 4, 5, 8; Jeanne Gaillard, *Paris, la ville, 1852–1870* (Paris, 1977); Christopher Johnson, *Utopian Communism in France, 1839–1851* (Ithaca, N.Y., 1974), chap. 4.
3. Gaillard, *Paris*, pp. 455–482.
4. L.T.C. Rolt, *A Short History of Machine Tools* (Cambridge, Mass., 1965), p. 152.
5. Edouard Blanc, *La Ceinture rouge. Enquête sur la situation politique, morale et sociale de la banlieue de Paris* (Paris, 1927). Blanc notes the public indifference in regard to the *banlieue* until the Communist victories in the postwar elections. The purpose of his book was to inform the public about this unknown workers' world
6. M. Daumas, *L'Evolution de la géographie industrielle de Paris et sa proche banlieue au XIXᵉ siècle* (3 vols., Paris, 1976), II, 374, 517.
7. Statistique générale de la France, *Résultats statistiques du recensement général de la population effectué le 5 mars 1911* (2 vols., Paris, 1911), II, 6–8. I have excluded domestic servants from these and all the figures on active population in this chapter. Including domestics would have distorted the data because their numbers depended on the presence of bourgeois households.
8. Gérard Jacquemet, "Belleville au XIXᵉ siècle. Du faubourg à la ville" (Doctorat d'Etat, Université de Paris-IV, 1979), pp. 1087–1088.
9. See the fine article by Marilyn Boxer, "Women in Industrial Homework: The Flowermakers of Paris in the Belle Epoque," *French Historical Studies*, XII (1982), 401–423.

10. Georges Mény, *Le Travail à bon marché. Enquêtes sociales.* (Paris, 1907), p. 54. See also Charles Benoist, *Les Ouvrières de l'aiguille à Paris* (Paris, 1895).

11. A.D.S., D 1 M⁸ no. 2.

12. *De la situation légale des ouvriers bijoutiers travaillant dans leur domicile* (Paris, 1842).

13. A. Focillon, "Tailleur d'habits de Paris," *Les Ouvriers des deux mondes*, 1ᵉ série, II (1858), 147. The census of 1866 put the number of manufacturing enterprises at 57,000. That number had only grown to 62,000 at the time of the census of 1906.

14. A.P.P., B/a 1388, Dossier: Employés des magasins de nouveautés.

15. The census placed the number of *employés d'industrie* at 34,846 in 1866 and 36,126 in 1911.

16. On the female employees, see the fine study of Theresa McBride, "A Woman's World: Department Stores and the Evolution of Women's Employment, 1870–1920," *French Historical Studies*, X (1978), 664–683. Also, Claudie Lesselier, "Employées de grands magasins à Paris avant 1914," *Le Mouvement social*, no. 105 (1978), pp. 109–126; Francoise Parent-Lardeur, *Les Demoiselles de magasin* (Paris, 1970).

17. Chambre de commerce de Paris, *Statistique de l'industrie de Paris résultant de l'enquête faite par la Chambre de commerce pour les années 1847–1848* (Paris, 1851), pp. 40–41.

18. These figures exclude domestic servants from the active population.

19. Jean Bastié, *La Croissance de la banlieue parisienne* (Paris, 1964), pp. 137–160; Jean-Paul Brunet, "L'Industrialisation de la région de Saint-Denis," *Acta géographica*, XXIII (1970), 223–260.

20. Louis Chevalier, *La Formation de la population parisienne au XIXᵉ siècle* (Paris, 1950), pp. 132–139. The best sources on the industrial development of the suburbs are the monographs of each commune in the department of the Seine published around the turn of the century by the prefecture under the collective title, *Etats des communes*.

21. Denis Poulot, *Le Sublime. Enquête sociale* (Paris, 1887), p. 76.

22. Henri Sellier, *La Crise du logement et l'intervention publique en matière d'habitation populaire dans l'agglomération parisienne* (Paris, 1921), p. 19.

23. A.P.P., B/a 400, Enquête parlementaire sur la classe ouvrière (1872). These quarter-by-quarter police reports serve as a very good introduction to the economic geography of Paris.

24. Jacques Valdour, *De la Popinqu' à Ménilmuch'* (Paris, 1924), p. 37.

25. David Landes, *The Unbound Prometheus: Technological Change and Industrial Development in Western Europe from 1750 to the Present* (Cambridge, 1969), chaps. 3, 4, 5.

26. Valdour, *De la Popinqu'*, p. 16.

27. J.-P. Mazaroz, *Causes et conséquences de la grève du Faubourg Saint-Antoine d'octobre et novembre 1882* (Paris, 1882), p. 36.

28. Guillaume Janneau, *L'Apprentissage dans les métiers d'art* (Paris, 1914), p. 1.

29. Even before the Revolution of 1848, local industries in Toulouse suffered from the competition with cheaper Parisian goods. See Ronald Aminzade, *Class, Politics, and Early Industrial Capitalism: A Study of Mid-Nineteenth-Century Toulouse, France* (Albany, N.Y., 1981), p. 36.

30. While there is little written on most trades, contemporaries produced a number of significant studies on furniture making. Among them are Henri Fourdinois, *Etude économique et sociale sur ameublement* (Paris, 1894); Pierre Du Maroussem, "Le Système parisien du meuble et le 'sweating system,'" *Revue d'économie*

politique, VI (1892): 569–581; Charles Mayet, *La Crise industrielle: L'Ameublement* (Paris, 1883); Ministère du commerce. Office du travail, *Rapport sur l'apprentissage dans les industries de l'ameublement* (Paris, 1905). For a recent analysis of this industry, see Lee Shai Weissbach, "Artisanal Response to Artistic Decline: The Cabinetmakers of Paris in the Era of Industrialization," *Journal of Social History*, XVI (1982): 67–82.

    31.   Jacques Valdour, *Le Faubourg. Observations vécues* (Paris, 1925), pp. 67–227. Julien Turgan, "Mazaroz, fabrique d'ameublement en bois massif," in *Les Grandes Usines. Tableau de l'industrie française au XIXe siècle* (20 vols., Paris, 1860–1895), V, 182–196.

    32.   Fourdinois, *Etude économique*, pp. 8–12. See the advertisements for the Klein Furniture Palace in such journals as *L'Employé. Organe du syndicat des employés du commerce et de l'industrie* (1901–1912).

    33.   Office du travail, *Apprentissage dans l'ameublement*, pp. 155–158; A.P.P., B/a 1372, Dossier: Grèves des ébénistes, contains numerous police estimates on the size and composition of the furniture trades.

    34.   Pierre Du Maroussem, "Ebéniste parisien de haut luxe," *Les Ouvriers des deux mondes*, 2e série, IV (1895), 98–100. With the growth of a department-store clientele, *trôliers* took their products to the very doors of these stores. See, for example, the warning from the management of the Dufayel Department Store "not to confuse [its merchandise] with that of the numerous merchants grouped on the paths to the furniture showroom," in its catalogue *Journal illustré de grands magasins Dufayel*.

    35.   François Bassieux, *L'Industrie de la chaussure en France* (Paris, 1908). On tailors, see the historical account that union members wrote of their trade in A.P.P., B/a 1358, Dossier: Syndicat des tailleurs.

    36.   Ibid., B/a 1358, Dossier: Grève des bijoutiers.

    37.   Ibid., B/a 175, Dossier: Grève générale des selliers, report of 14 mai 1877; Ministère de l'instruction publique et des beaux-arts, *Commission d'enquête sur la situation des ouvriers et des industries d'art* (Paris, 1884), p. 107; L'Assemblée nationale, *Procès-verbal de la commission chargée de faire une enquête sur la situation des ouvriers de l'industrie et de l'agriculture en France et de présenter un premier rapport sur la crise industrielle à Paris* (Paris, 1884), pp. 183–185.

    38.   A.P.P., B/a 181, Dossier: Grève des gantiers (avril 1881).

    39.   Turgan, "Carrosserie Belvallelte," *Les Grandes Usines*, X, 49–80; "Carrosserie," ibid., XII, 151–153.

    40.   Louis Radiguer, *Maîtres imprimeurs et ouvriers typographes* (Paris, 1903), pp. 236–238; Ministère du commerce. Office du travail, *Rapport sur l'apprentissage dans l'imprimerie, 1899–1901* (Paris, 1902).

    41.   Joseph Barberet, *Le Travail en France. Monographies professionnelles* (7 vols., Paris, 1886–1890), II, 443.

    42.   Chambre de commerce de Paris, *Statistique de l'industrie de Paris résultant de l'enquête faite par la Chambre de commerce pour l'année 1860* (Paris, 1864), p. xxxiv. Office du travail, *Apprentissage dans l'imprimerie*, p. lxv. For the general state of apprenticeship in each trade at the turn of the century, see Conseil supérieur du travail, *Apprentissage. Rapport de M. Briat au nom de la commission permanente. Enquête et documents* (Paris, 1902).

    43.   Octave Gréard, *L'Enseignement primaire à Paris et dans le Département de la Seine de 1867 à 1877* (Paris, 1878), pp. 95–96, 154.

    44.   Délégation française du Ministère de l'instruction publique et des beaux-arts, *Deuxième congrès international de l'enseignement du dessin tenu à Berne du 2 au 6 août 1904* (Berne et Paris, 1904), p. 72.

    45.   Barberet, *Travail en France*, II, 233. For an appreciation of founding at

midcentury, see the comments of a master founder, A.D.S., V D⁶ 343 no. 1, Dossier: Joseph, dit Richard. For the beginning of the twentieth century, see Conseil supérieur du travail, *Apprentissage*, p. 259.

46. Rolt, *History of Machine Tools*, p. 121.

47. Poulot, *Le Sublime*, p. 150.

48. The proud claim was made by a union officer. See A.P.P., B/a 161, Dossier: Syndicat de mécaniciens, report of 6 novembre 1876.

49. Denis Poulot, *Méthode de l'enseignement manuel pour former un apprenti mécanicien* (Paris, 1889), pp. 1–5. Also, René Champly, *Comment on devient tourneur sur métaux* (Paris, 1914), p. 8.

50. Turgan, "Derosne et Cail," *Les Grandes Usines*, II, 49.

51. Mazaroz, *Causes et conséquences*, p. 78. For an attempt to explain the acculturation process among workers, see Barberet, *Travail en France*, III, 481.

52. A.D.S., V 4 E, Actes de mariage, 1869; D 1 M² no. 2.

53. "Définition des mots 'usine' et 'manufacture,' " *Bulletin de l'Inspection de travail*, VIII (1900), 786–790.

54. Etienne Riché, *La Situation des ouvriers dans l'industrie automobile* (Paris, 1909), p. 47. Michael Hanagan ("Urbanization, Worker Settlement Patterns, and Social Protest in Nineteenth-Century France," in *French Cities in the Nineteenth Century*, ed. John Merriman [New York, 1981], p. 218) makes the useful distinction between "artisans" and "skilled workers": The jobs of the latter were created by the subdivision of the artisan's work and by the use of supervisors to coordinate the new kind of labor. "Skilled workers," in this sense, were an important segment of the factory labor force.

55. Turgan, "Forges d'Ivry," *Les Grandes Usines*, XIV, 1–32.

56. See A.M. Ivry, Actes de mariage, 1870–1890.

57. Turgan, "Etablissements Alexis Godillot," *Les Grandes Usines*, XIII, 15–32.

58. For a guide to factories in Paris proper in the 1870s, see A.P.P., B/a 400.

59. Chevalier, *La Formation de la population*, pp. 130–139.

60. Turgan, "Orfèvrerie Christofle," *Les Grandes Usines*, I, 281–320.

61. A.P.P., B/a 1384, Dossier: Grèves des mégissiers (Combes).

62. Département de la Seine, *Etat des communes: Levallois-Perret* (Montévrain, 1903), pp. 115–132. Saint-Ouen had one piano manufacturer who produced 3,000 a year. This should be compared to the quality piano makers, like Alexandre in Ivry or Pleyel in Saint-Denis, who produced their instruments entirely and by hand in their plants. See Département de la Seine, *Etats des communes: Saint-Ouen* (Montévrain, 1902), pp. 103–111.

63. Jacques Néré, "La Crise industrielle de 1882 et le mouvement Boulangiste" (2 vols., Doctorat ès-Lettres, Université de Paris, 1959), II, 158–160.

64. The series of communal monographs published by the prefecture at the turn of the century provides figures on the sizes of factories. Unfortunately, they do not always furnish the name of each firm.

65. Turgan, "Usine Lorilleux à Puteaux," *Les Grandes Usines*, XIII, 6.

66. A.N., F²² 574, Industries de métaux ordinaires. Situation en 1910. Paris et banlieue.

67. Ibid. Delauny-Belleville employed 1,913 workers in 1911. According to Bastié, *La Croissance de la banlieue*, p. 148, the Compagnie générale des lampes incandescentes, in Ivry, employed 3,000 by 1914.

68. Patrick Fridenson, *Histoire des usines Renault, Vol. l: Naissance de la grande entreprise, 1898–1939* (Paris, 1972), pp. 83, 85.

69. A.D.S., D 1 M², Liste électorales, 1902.

70. Riché, *La Situation des ouvriers*, p. 47.

71. Riché (ibid., p. 49) claimed that a tenth of the mechanics in the automobile industry were toolmakers. See also, Alain Touraine, *L'Evolution du travail aux usines Renault* (Paris, 1955).

72. Michelle Perrot, *Les Ouvriers en grève. France, 1871–1890* (2 vols., Paris, 1974), I, 385.

73. See the description of semiskilled labor in Charles Benoist, "Le Travail dans la grande industrie. II. La Métallurgie," *La Revue des deux mondes*, XII (1902), 586–614, XV (1903), 637–661.

74. Turgan, "Derosne et Cail," *Les Grandes Usines*, II, 63.

75. Riché, *Les Ouvriers dans l'industrie automobile*, pp. 47–50.

76. Statistique générale, *Résultats du recensement 1911*, II, 6–23.

77. Statistique générale de la France, *Résultats statistiques du recensement générale de la population effectué le 4 mars 1906* (2 vols., Paris, 1909), II, 27.

78. Joan Scott and Louise Tilly (*Women, Work, and Family* [New York, 1980]) stress the long-term continuities in women's work.

79. Turgan, "Parfumerie Ed. Pinaud," *Les Grandes Usines*, XIV, 14; "Compagnie française du chocolat," ibid., p. 12.

80. A.D.S., D 1 M², Listes nominatives, 1911. These censuses provided the names of employers, so that it was possible to separate factory workers from other types of workers.

81. The census of 1911 placed the number of male common laborers at 33,558 and the number of female ones at 30,905.

82. A.M. Bezons, Actes de mariage, 1872–1881; liste nominative, 1881. I have described the process of industrialization in Bezons in my article, "The Formation of a Factory Proletariat: Rubber and Cable Workers in Bezons, France (1860–1914)," *Journal of Social History*, XV (1981), 163–186.

83. A.M. Bezons, Actes de mariage, 1901–1908; liste nominative, 1911.

84. A.M. Saint-Ouen, Actes de mariage, 1874–1876, 1902–1903.

85. Bastié, *La Croissance de la banlieue*, pp. 137–160.

86. A.M. Ivry, Actes de mariage, 1873–1876; Turgan, "Forges d'Ivry," *Les Grandes usines*, XIV, 1–32.

87. A.M. Ivry, Actes de mariage, 1901–1903.

88. Yves Lequin finds a similar continuity in industrial development for the region of Lyons. See his *Les Ouvriers de la région lyonnaise (1848–1914)* (2 vols., Lyons, 1977), I, 207–221. For other recent work on the origins of a proletariat, see the special issue of *Le Mouvement social*, no. 97 (1976) on "Naissance de la classe ouvrière."

89. A.D.S., D 1 M², Liste nominative, Ivry, 1911. The census of Ivry shows that well over half the children of day laborers had moved into semiskilled or even skilled positions.

90. This analysis is based on marriage records from Saint-Denis, Saint-Ouen, and Argenteuil.

91. Turgan, "Forges d'Ivry," *Les Grandes Usines*, XIV, 1–32.

92. Anatole Le Grandais, *Physiologie des employés de ministères* (Paris, 1862); J. Poisle Desgranges, *Voyage à mon bureau. Aller et retour* (Paris, 1861).

93. One occupational journal described insurance employees as "daddy's boys [*fils à papa*], rentiers, law students and failed poets." This would apply to some ministerial employees, too. See *L'Employé*, no. 84 (avril 1901), p. 5.

94. Auguste Besse, *L'Employé de commerce et d'industrie* (Lyons, 1901); A.-J.-M. Artaud, *La Question de l'employé en France* (Paris, 1909); L. O'Followell and H. Goudal, *L'Hygiène des employés de commerce et d'administration* (Paris, 1901).

95. Louis Montaru, *Réorganisation du service de l'Octroi. Amélioration du sort des employés* (Paris, 1871).

96. A.D.S., V 8 O[1] no. 149. See the clippings from the newspaper of the gas clerks' union, *L'Echo du gaz*.

97. See the description of the work of a stock boy for Félix Potin, A.P.P., B/a 1388, Dossier: Commis d'épicerie Potin. The police described the stock boys, sixteen to twenty years old, as "possessing a very incomplete education."

98. One of the railroad companies, with 23,000 employees nationally, received about 5,000 job applications a year. See W. Eddy, *L'Employé des chemins de fer, sa condition en France et en Angleterre* (Paris, 1883), pp. 10–11.

99. David Lockwood, *The Blackcoated Worker. A Study of Class Consciousness* (London, 1958); Rolf Dahrendorf, *Class and Class Conflict in Industrial Society* (Stanford, 1959), chaps. 2, 3.

100. Jacques Destray (ed.), *La Vie d'une famille ouvrière. Autobiographies* (Paris, 1971), p. 25.

101. A.M. Saint-Denis, Q, 3/11/3/2, letter of Beaucerf to Mayor of 12 novembre 1899.

102. Jacquemet, "Belleville au XIXe siècle," pp. 718–720.

103. Arno Mayer, "The Lower Middle Class as a Historical Problem," *Journal of Modern History*, XLVII (1975), 434.

104. Daumard, *Les Fortunes françaises*, pp. 188–193.

105. Françoise Raison-Jourde, *La Colonie auvergnate à Paris au XIXe siècle* (Paris, 1976), pp. 206–211.

106. Workers in the food-services industries lived with a sense of declining opportunities for independence. See Linda Young, "Mobilizing Food-, Restaurant, and Café Workers in Paris: A Case Study of Direct Action Syndicalism, 1900–1914" (Ph.D. diss., New York University, 1981), pp. 90, 95.

107. The mechanic cited is Poulot, *Le Sublime*, p. 270.

108. The friends of tramway workers residing in the Thirteenth and Eighteenth arrondissements broke down as follows: manufacturing workers—31.4 percent; service workers—23.2 percent; white-collar workers—11.3 percent; shopkeepers—27.4 percent; and others—6.7 percent.

Chapter II

1. Octave Du Mesnil and Charles Mangenot, *Enquête sur les logements, professions, salaires, et budgets (loyers inférieurs à 400 francs)* (Paris, 1899).

2. See Statistique générale de la France, *Salaires et coût de l'existence à diverses époques, jusqu'en 1910* (Paris, 1911), pp. 53, 102.

3. Du Mesnil and Mangenot, *Enquête sur les logements,* pp. 142–143.

4. Ministère du commerce, Office du travail, *Enquête sur le travail à domicile dans l'industrie de la chaussure* (Paris, 1914).

5. Ibid., p. 361.

6. Jacques Rougerie, "Remarques sur l'histoire des salaires à Paris au XIXe siècle," *Le Mouvement social*, no. 63 (1968), p. 89. The rise in wages after 1905 was tied to intensified inflation.

7. Jeanne Singer-Kérel, *Le Coût de la vie à Paris de 1840 à 1954* (Paris, 1954), pp. 92–103.

8. Joseph Barberet, *Le Travail en France. Monographies professionnelles* (7 vols., Paris, 1886–1890), III, 184. See the distribution of weekly earnings for one hatter during 1883.

9. A.P.P., B/a 1394, Dossier: Grève des tailleurs.

10. Barberet, *Le Travail en France*, III, 477.

11. A.D.S., V 8 O¹ no. 151, Dossier: Personnel ouvrier; A.P.P., B/a 180, Dossier: Grève des briquetiers.

12. A.P.P., B/a 400. These reports of the police commissioners are replete with comments about the workers' fears of winter and the employers' willingness to exploit these fears.

13. For some notion of the size of this core at various firms and in various industries during the economic crisis of the mid-1880s, see ibid., B/a 399.

14. Pierre Du Maroussem, "Ebéniste parisien de haut luxe," *Les Ouvriers des deux mondes*, 2ᵉ série, IV (1895), 76.

15. A.M. Argenteuil, 32 F.

16. A.M. Saint-Denis, F, 3/9/1/3/.

17. Rougerie, "Remarques sur l'histoire des salaires," pp. 89–94, 105–107; Singer-Kérel, *Le Coût de la vie*, pp. 100–102.

18. A.P.P., B/a 399.

19. A.M. Ivry, F-7, Mouvement de la population; D-47, fol., 192–193; A.M. Argenteuil, Délibérations municipales, session of 10 janvier 1883; A.M. Saint-Denis, F, 5/3/3/1/, Mouvement de la population.

20. Yves Lequin, *Les Ouvriers de la région lyonnaise (1848–1914)* (2 vols., Lyons, 1977), II, 78–80.

21. Guillaume Janneau, *L'Apprentissage dans les métiers d'art. Une enquête* (Paris, 1914), pp. 1–10, 149–151; Conseil supérieur du travail, *Apprentissage. Rapport de M. Briat au nom de la commission permanente* (Paris, 1902).

22. A.D.S., V 8 O¹ no. 151, Dossier: Personnel ouvrier. Yves Lequin believes that whatever improvement in employment conditions there was occurred primarily in the larger plants. See his "Les Citadins, les classes, et les luttes sociales," in *Histoire de la France urbaine. Tome IV: La Ville de l'âge industrielle* (Paris, 1983), p. 503.

23. Du Mesnil and Mangenot, *Enquête sur les logements*, pp. 142–143.

24. See the census of households in Saint-Denis classified by the age of the household head, A.M. Saint-Denis, F, 3/5/2/1.

25. Jean Marchal and Jacques Lecaillon, *La Répartition du revenu national* (2 vols., 1958), I, 351–358 for the long-term trend and on the "inevitable" closing of the gap between the best and the worst paid workers.

26. Rougerie, "Remarques sur l'histoire des salaires," p. 89 and table VI for the most important wage indexes. Note that the case of the navvies (*terrassiers*), with their rapidly rising wages at the turn of the century, was exceptional because of the construction of the metropolitan railroad.

27. A.M., Argenteuil, 29 F.

28. Chambre de commerce de Paris, *Statistique de l'industrie à Paris résultant de l'enquête faite par la Chambre de commerce pour les années 1847–48* (Paris, 1851), pp. 49–51; Chambre de commerce de Paris, *Statistique de l'industrie résultant de l'enquête faite par la Chambre de commerce pour l'année 1860* (Paris, 1864), pp. xxxvii-xxxviii; Ministère du commerce, Office du travail, *Salaires et durée du travail dans l'industrie française* (4 vols., Paris, 1893–97), I, 530–531. These studies put the average wage for men at 3.8 francs and for women at 1.63 francs in 1848; in 1860, 4.51 francs for men and 2.14 francs for women; in 1893, 6.2 francs for men and 3.15 francs for women.

29. The figure of 135,000 comes from the published census of 1906. Government investigations found that 62 percent of domestic flower makers earned less than 2.5 francs a day in the first decade of the twentieth century and that over 85 percent of *lingères* earned less than 26 centimes an hour. See Ministère du commerce, Office du travail, *Enquête sur le travail à domicile dans l'industrie de la fleur artificielle*

(Paris, 1913), p. 392; Office du travail, *Enquête sur le travail à domicile dans l'industrie de la lingerie* (5 vols., Paris 1907–1909), I, 742.

30. Conseil municipal de Paris, *Rapport sur le régime des égouts et sur les améliorations à réaliser* (Paris, 1914), pp. 167–168.

31. During the violent strike of 1888, the navvies demanded that the municipal council enforce the regulations it placed in public contracts, but the body refused to do so. According to Jacques Néré, the council abandoned its efforts to influence work conditions about that time. See his "La Crise industrielle de 1882 et le mouvement boulangiste" (2 vols., Doctorat ès-Lettres, Université de Paris, 1959), II, 406.

32. G.-M.-A. Cadoux, *Les salaires et les conditions du travail des ouvriers et employés des entreprises municipales de Paris* (The Hague, 1911).

33. The well-known indexes, such as those constructed by Rougerie, Singer-Kérel, and Simiand, are based on the wage agreements registered with the *Conseil de prud'hommes.*

34. A.P.P., B/a 169, B/a 174, B/a 179, B/a 1372, B/a 1358, B/a 1384, B/a 1438.

35. Ibid., B/a 1368, Dossier: Grève des cordonniers. On the mechanical production of shoes, see François Bassieux, *L'Industrie de la chaussure en France* (Paris, 1908), pp. 24–27.

36. Patrick O'Brien and Caglar Keyder, *Economic Growth in Britain and France, 1780–1914* (London, 1978), pp. 68–72.

37. Henri Sellier, *La Crise du logement et l'intervention publique en matière d'habitation dans l'agglomération parisienne* (Paris, 1921), p. 19.

38. Statistique générale de la France, *Salaires et coût de l'existence*, pp. 57–58.

39. On the new habits of consumption among workers, see Barberet, *Le Travail en France*, III, 301; IV, 1.

40. Rougerie, "Remarques sur l'histoire des salaires," pp. 94–97. Jeanne Gaillard (*Paris, la ville, 1852–1870* [Paris, 1975], pp. 233–245) disputes Rougerie's claims for a "revolution of consumption" under the Second Empire. These scholars are both correct. Gaillard compares levels of meat consumption in 1853 with those in 1869 and finds little change. Rougerie compares comsumption in the 1860s with that in 1830–1850 and finds a vast improvement. The point is that there was a steep rise in meat eating between 1848 and 1853.

41. Statistique de la France, *Salaires et coût de l'existence*, p. 52; Du Maroussem, "Ebéniste parisien"; Pierre Du Maroussem, "Charpentier indépendant de Paris," *Les Ouvriers des deux mondes*, 2ᵉ série, III (1892), 344–348; Jacques de Reviers, "Serrurier-forgeron de Paris," *Les Ouvriers des deux mondes*, 1ᵉ série, V (1885), 222–232.

42. Adolphe Morillon, *Rapport sur les consommations de Paris et la gestion des halles, marchés, et abattoirs* (Paris, 1885), pp. 16–17.

43. Feilbogen, "L'Alimentation populaire à Paris," *Revue d'économie politique,* XXVII (1913), 719–732.

44. Du Maroussem, "Ebéniste parisien," p. 66. On the frequentation of restaurants by workers, see Louis Landouzy and Henri L'abbé, *Enquête sur l'alimentation d'une centaine d'ouvriers et d'employés* (Paris, 1905).

45. The averages for Paris were: eggs—160 to 180 pieces, carpenter (1890)—40 pieces, cabinetmaker—62 pieces, carpenter (1889)—4 pieces. For fish: Paris—12 to 13 kilograms, ironsmith—3 kg., cabinetmaker—2.2 kg, carpenter (1890)—7.5 kg. For butter: Paris—7.7 kg, carpenter (1890)—2.2 kg, ironsmith—4.3 kg., carpenter (1889)—2.4 kg.

46. René Michaud, *J'avais vingt ans. Un jeune ouvrier au début du siècle* (Paris, 1967), pp. 19–23.

47. Jacques Caroux-Destray (ed.), *Un Couple ouvrier traditionnel* (Paris, 1974), p. 49.

48. A.M. Bezons, Délibérations du bureau de bienfaisance (session of juin 1912).

49. Statistique générale de la France, *Salaires et coût de l'existence*, pp. 58, 72.

50. A.M. Puteaux, Délibérations municipales, session of 11 mai 1913.

51. Département de la Seine, *Etat des communes: Clichy* (Montévrain, 1903), p. 99.

52. Singer-Kérel, *Le Coût de la vie*, pp. 183, 462–463.

53. Jacques Valdour, *De la Popinqu' à Ménilmuch'* (Paris, 1924), p. 52.

54. Alain Faure ("L'Epicerie parisienne au XIXᵉ siècle, ou la corporation éclatée," *Le Mouvement social*, no. 108 [1979], pp. 120–122) argues on the basis of the grocery trade that "grande commerce" did not penetrate into the worker's way of life. His argument does not hold so far as some aspects of large-scale commerce and some sectors of the working-classes were concerned.

55. A.-J.-M. Artaud, *La Question de l'employé en France* (Paris, 1909), pp. 24–30.

56. A.D.S., D 4 U¹, Actes de juridiction gracieuse, 1903. These figures represent the profile of debtors of the major department stores as well as of smaller dry goods, clothing, and furniture stores. Customers who owed money to neighborhood purveyors of foodstuffs are not included in these figures.

57. *L'Emancipation. Organe d'unité socialiste-révolutionnaire de la IIᵉ circonscription de Saint-Denis*, no. 110 (19 mars 1904).

58. *L'Humanité. Organe socialiste quotidien*, no. 246 (19 décembre 1904), p. 3.

59. Philippe Perrot, *Les Dessus et les dessous de la bourgeoisie. Une histoire du vêtement au XIXᵉ siècle* (Paris, 1981), p. 128.

60. Daniel Roche argues that these sorts of consumer habits can be found in the eighteenth century, but he does not specify how this might have come about. See his *Le Peuple de Paris. Essai sur la culture populaire au XVIIIᵉ siècle* (Paris, 1981), pp. 145, 167, 175–177, 186, 197.

61. Frédéric Le Play and A. Focillon, "Charpentier de Paris," *Les Ouvriers des deux mondes*, 1ᵉ série, I (1857), 27–68; Du Maroussem, "Charpentier indépendant de Paris," 325–368.

62. The following analysis has been inspired by the thesis of Alain Metton, "L'Appareil commercial de détail en banlieue parisienne" (Doctorat ès-Lettres, Université de Paris-I, 1978).

63. Bottin, *Annuaire du commerce Didot-Bottin, 1875* (Paris, 1875). On the reliability of the commercial almanacs, see Metton, "L'Appareil commercial," p. 455.

64. Metton, "L'Appareil commercial," p. 466. Metton argues that retail commerce "anticipates" purchasing power, so that early stages of population growth were accompanied by an "overstimulation" of commercial development. He uses the commune of Courbevoie as his case study.

65. Singer-Kérel, *Le Coût de la vie*, p. 225.

66. Maurice Halbwachs, *La Classe ouvrière et les niveaux de vie* (Paris, 1912), p. 444.

67. Docteur Stéphane Courgey, *Recherches et classement des anormaux. Enquête sur les enfants des écoles de la ville d'Ivry-sur-Seine* (Leipzig, 1908).

68. Donald Stewart McLaren, *Malnutrition and the Eye* (New York, 1963) explains the links between dietary and ophthalmic problems.

69. Gérard Jacquemet, "Belleville au XIXᵉ siècle. Du Faubourg à la ville" (Doctorat d'Etat, Université de Paris-IV, 1979), p. 892.

70. G. J. Ebrahim, "The Problem of Under-Nutrition," in *Nutrition and Disease*, ed. R. J. Jarrett (Baltimore, Md., 1979), pp. 63–73; L. Cheraskin et al., *Diet and Disease* (Emmaus, Pa., 1968).

71. James Lambert Mount, *The Food and Health of Western Man* (New York,

1975), pp. 62–86; Roy Acheson, "Effects of Nutrition and Disease on Human Growth," in *Human Growth*, ed. J. M. Tanner (New York, 1960).

72. L. Comby, "Alfortville. Commune en banlieue" (Doctorat de troisième cycle, Université de Paris, 1966), p. 50.

73. On conditions in the first half of the century, see Louis Chevalier, *Classes laborieuses et classes dangereuses à Paris pendant la première moitié du dix-neuvième siècle* (Paris, 1958).

74. Standish Meacham, *A Life Apart: The English Working Class, 1890–1914* (London, 1977), p. 27. On the housekeeping efforts of poor Parisians, see Du Mesnil and Mangenot, *Enquête sur les logements*, pp. 35–64.

75. Anne-Louise Shapiro, "Working-Class Housing and Public Health in Paris, 1850–1902" (Ph.D. diss., Brown University, 1980), chaps. 5–6; David Pinkney, *Napoleon III and the Rebuilding of Paris* (Princeton, 1958), chap. 5.

76. Francisque Sarcey, *Les Odeurs de Paris. Assainissement de la Seine* (Paris, 1882).

77. "De l'augmentation de la fréquence des principales maladies épidémiques à Paris pendant la période 1865–1885," in the special issue of the *Annuaire statistique de la ville de Paris* in the Bibliothèque administrative (Hôtel de ville de Paris).

78. George Rosen, "Acute Communicable Disease," in *The History and Conquest of Common Diseases*, ed. Walter Bett (Norman, Okla., 1954), pp. 3–70 and Rosen's *A History of Public Health* (New York, 1958), pp. 288–340.

79. Shapiro, "Working-Class Housing," pp. 208–314.

80. A.M. Saint-Ouen, Délibérations municipales, session of 13 mars 1905.

81. Ibid.

82. Jean-Pierre Goubert, "Eaux publiques et démographie historique dans la France urbaine du XIXᵉ siècle," *Annales de démographie historique*, 1975, pp. 115–121.

83. G. Bechmann, *Salubrité urbaine. Distribution d'eau. Assainissement* (Paris, 1888), pp. 61–131; 510–511; Léon Colin, *Paris, sa topographie, son hygiène, ses maladies* (Paris, 1885), pp. 53–88.

84. *Annuaire statistique de la ville de Paris*, volume on "Eaux" at the Bibliothèque administrative (Hôtel de ville de Paris).

85. Michaud, *J'avais vingt ans*, p. 19.

86. Bechmann, *Salubrité urbaine*, pp. 417–418. The municipality of Saint-Ouen paid 2.6 francs per resident, and Neuilly paid 6.4 francs.

87. A.M. Argenteuil, 71 I; Docteur Testelin, *Note sur la fièvre typhoïde et la diphtérie en rapport avec l'eau servant à l'alimentation dans la région d'Argenteuil* (Argenteuil, 1890), pp. 2–18; Colin, *Paris, son hygiène*, p. 53; Adrien Le Roy des Barres, *Exposé des titres et travaux scientifiques* (Saint-Denis, 1896), p. 14.

88. A.M. Saint-Ouen, Délibérations municipales, session of 29 avril 1902.

89. A.M. Saint-Denis, J, 5/2/1/7; Adrien Le Roy des Barres, *Le Choléra à Saint-Denis en 1892* (Paris, 1893), pp. 1–10; Docteur Stéphane Courgey, *Epidémiologie à Ivry-sur-Seine de 1877 à 1899* (Paris, 1901), pp. 4–29.

90. Comby, "Alfortville," p. 159.

91. A.M. Saint-Denis, F, 5/3/3/1.

92. A.M. Ivry, Liste électorale, 1893.

93. *Le Courrier socialiste. Organe des groupes et syndicats ouvriers de la circonscription*, no. 229 (28 juillet 1906).

94. Courgey, *Epidémiologie à Ivry*, pp. 73–91; Le Roy des Barres, *Le Choléra à Saint-Denis*, p. 7; Docteur Louis Dubousquet-Laborderie, *Exposé de la constitution médicale actuelle de la commune de Saint-Ouen-sur-Seine* (Paris, 1885), pp. 3–7.

95. Gérard Jacquemet, "Urbanisme parisien: La Bataille du tout-à-l'égout à la

fin du XIXe siècle," *Revue d'histoire moderne et contemporaine*, XXVI (1979), 505–548; Alfred Durand-Claye, *Assainissement de la Seine* (Paris, 1885).

96. Conseil municipal de Paris, *Rapport sur le régime des égouts*, pp. 261–269; Jacquemet, "Urbanisme parisien," pp. 541–542.

97. Conseil d'hygiène publique et de salubrité, *Rapport général à Monsieur le Préfect de Police sur les travaux des commissions d'hygiène des arrondissements du département de la Seine, 1904* (Paris, 1905), p. 110.

98. These figures derive from data presented in the communal monographs, *Etats des communes*, published by the prefecture at the turn of the century. The proportion of street surface served by sewer lines was 47.6 percent in Ivry, 53.4 percent in Puteaux, 37.1 percent in Issy-les-Moulineaux, and 33.3 percent in Saint-Ouen.

99. A.M. Argenteuil, 62 I¹, Dossier: Fosses d'aisance; Alexandre Tourteaux, *L'Assainissement de la ville de Levallois-Perret* (Levallois-Perret, 1901), pp. 3–11.

100. Gaillard, *Paris, la ville,* pp. 305–321.

101. Du Maroussem, "Charpentier indépendant," pp. 328–330.

102. See, for example, A.D.S., V bis 11 Q² no. 1. A doctor recommended that a sickly child, the son of a poor widow, receive roasted meat and Bordeaux wine each day for a month.

103. Docteur Paul Traverse, *Etude sur les dispensaires pour enfants malades à Paris* (Paris, 1899).

104. *Annuaire statistique de la ville de Paris*, special edition in the Bibliothèque administrative (Hôtel de ville), volume on "Réfuges de nuit, asiles, crèches, dispensaires."

105. Cruveilhier, "Ligue contre la mortalité infantile," *La Revue philanthropique*, XXXV (1914), 37–57. See also Raoul Peret, "Subvention aux oeuvres d'assistance maternelle," *La Revue philanthropique*, XXXV (1914), 75–106; Jacquemet, "Belleville au XIXe siècle," pp. 875–900. The social elite responsible for these efforts in one suburban town consisted of three manufacturers, a wholesale merchant, and a doctor. See *Société du dispensaire gratuit de Pantin-Aubervilliers pour les enfants malades indigents* (Pantin, 1898), p. 15.

106. A.M. Ivry, D-62, session of 12 mai 1892.

107. *Annuaire statistique de la ville de Paris*, special edition at the Bibliothèque administrative. In 1897, for example, 6,807 infants were seen at the dispensaries of the Nineteenth Arrondissement, and there were 3,806 births during that year.

108. A.M. Bezons, Etat civil. On the absence of dispensaries, see Délibérations municipales, session of 2 décembre 1907.

109. Etienne van de Walle and Samuel Preston, "Mortalité de l'enfance au XIXe siècle à Paris et dans le département de la Seine," *Population*, XXXIX (1974), 89–107.

110. Marcel Lecoq, *La Crise du logement populaire* (Paris, 1912), pp. 1–4.

111. Gérard Jacquemet, "Les Maladies populaires à Paris à la fin du XIXe siècle," in *L'Haleine des faubourgs*, vol. XXIX of *Recherches*, ed. Lion Murard and Patrick Zylberman (Fontenay-sous-Bois, 1977), 361; Docteur Elie Goubert, *Les Maladies des enfants à Paris* (Paris, 1891).

112. Paul Juillerat and A. Fillassier, "Dix années de mortalité parisienne chez les enfants de 0 à 14 ans," *La Revue philanthropique*, XXXV (1914), 147–164; Jacquemet, "Les Maladies populaires," pp. 350–352.

113. Pierre Guillaume, *La Population de Bordeaux au XIXe siècle; essai d'histoire sociale* (Paris, 1972), pp. 150–156; Selman Waksman, *The Conquest of Tuberculosis* (Berkeley, Calif., 1964), pp. 48–91; Ministère de l'intérieur, *Recueil des travaux de la commission permanente de préservation contre la tuberculose* (3 vols., Paris, 1905);

Docteur Louis Dubousquet-Laborderie and Léon Duschesne, *Contribution à l'étude de la pathogène et de la prophylaxie de la tuberculose* (Clermont, 1897).

114. Docteur H. Dehau and R. Leroux-Lebord, *La Lutte antituberculeuse en France* (Paris, 1906), pp. 96–108.

115. A.M. Saint-Denis, J, 3/8/5/2. For the effort to create an antitubercular dispensary in Ivry, see A.M. Ivry, D-79, fols. 20, 90.

116. According to Doctor Le Roy des Barres of Saint-Denis, the first disinfection service functioning in the *banlieue* was organized in 1887. See his *Exposé des titres*, p. 9.

117. A.M. Saint-Ouen, Délibérations municipales, session of 28 février 1891.

118. Ibid., Dossier: Hygiène et salubrité, 1864–1905, letter of veuve Bayle to Mayor of 18 juillet 1899.

119. Docteur L. O'Followell and H. Goudal, *Hygiène des employés de commerce et d'administration* (Paris, 1901), p. 9.

120. *Causes des décès par maladies épidémiques et contagieuses dans la commune de Saint-Ouen* (Paris, 1889), pp. 28–32.

121. *Epidémiologie à Ivry*, pp. 8–9.

122. A.M. Saint-Ouen, Délibérations municipales, session of 10 juillet 1908.

123. See Chapter V.

124. A.M. Saint-Ouen, Dossier: Elections municipales (1912).

125. A.M. Puteaux, Délibérations municipales, session of 13 décembre 1913.

126. A.M. Saint-Ouen, Délibérations municipales, session of 16 février 1914.

127. Jacques Léonard, *La Médecine entre les pouvoirs et les savoirs* (Paris, 1981), pp. 173–177.

128. *L'Employé. Organe du syndicat des employés du commerce et de l'industrie* no. 158 (5 juin 1907), p. 94; no. 159 (5 juillet 1907), p. 109.

129. Ibid., no. 119 (25 mars 1904), pp. 5–6.

130. Typists-stenographers generally earned 125 to 150 francs a month. The most skilled seamstresses earned 4 to 5 francs a day. See Charles Benoist, *Les Ouvrières de l'aiguille à Paris* (Paris, 1895), pp. 80–86.

131. Claudie Lesselier, "Employées de grands magasins à Paris avant 1914," *Le Mouvement social*, no. 105 (1978), p. 114.

132. Marchal and Lecaillon, *La Répartition du revenu national*, I, 399–400.

133. Michelle Perrot, "Les Classes populaires urbaines," in Jean Bouvier et al., *Histoire économique et sociale de la France, Tome IV: L'Ere industrielle et la société d'aujourd'hui* (Paris, 1979), p. 491; Marchal and Lecaillon, *La Répartition du revenu national*, I, 401–404.

134. Marchal and Lecaillon show that the incomes of office heads in state administrations rose faster than those of employees. See *La Répartition du revenu national*, I, 431.

135. The rising social significance of consumerism is an important and intriguing theme in Michael Miller, *The Bon Marché. Department Stores and Bourgeois Culture in France, 1869–1920* (Princeton, 1981).

136. Ibid., p. 83; *L'Employé*, no. 141 (25 janvier 1906), p. 2.

137. *L'Employé*, no. 119 (25 mars 1904), pp. 5–6; no. 180 (5 avril 1909), p. 50.

138. A.D.S., D 2 U^{10} no. 4–6 for the cases of 1910, which I have analyzed in Chapter III. This claim is based on a sample of 140 cases.

139. Jacquemet, "Belleville au XIXe siècle," p. 1090; Auguste Besse, *L'Employé de commerce et d'industrie* (Lyons, 1901), pp. 26–30.

140. A.D.S., V 8 O^1 no. 149, Dossier: Procès-verbal de l'audience du 16 décembre 1892.

141. *L'Employé*, no. 143 (5 janvier 1907), p. 8.

142. A.P.P., B/a 1404, Dossier: Grèves des ouvriers et employés des trams.

143. Marchal and Lecaillon, *La Répartition du revenu national*, pp. 399–400. *L'Employé* (no. 83 [5 mars 1901], p. 2) places the average salary of bank clerks at 2,000 francs in 1901.

144. Cadoux, *Les Salaires et les conditions du travail*, appendix III.

145. *Le Journal des employés. Organe officiel des associations syndicales d'employés de toutes catégories*, no. 5 (12–19 juin 1897), p. 1; *L'Employé*, no. 87 (juillet 1901), pp. 3–4.

146. Maurice Halbswachs, "Budgets de familles ouvrières et paysannes en France en 1907," *Bulletin de la Statistique de la France*, IV (1914–1915), 70.

147. A.P.P., B/a 901, Dossier: Usine Cail, report of 9 juin 1875; Ministère de l'Intérieur, *Enquête de la commission extra-parlementaire des associations ouvrières* (2 vols., Paris, 1893), II, 226.

148. A.D.S., V 4 E, Actes de naissance, 1869. These figures are based on an analysis of birth records, which stated the occupation of the mother.

149. Bottin, *Annuaire du commerce Didot-Bottin, 1900*, p. 2604 (rubric: "Vente à crédit").

150. A.D.S., V K^2 nos. 4–25.

151. Ibid., V 8 O^1 no. 163, Dossier: Assimilation du personnel.

152. Ibid., D R^1, Registers of Eighteenth Arrondissement, 1902–1903.

153. *L'Employé*, no. 94 (10 février 1902), p. 20. The mortality rate for persons in the age category twenty to thirty-nine was said to be 39.7 per thousand for cashiers and bookkeepers, 29.9 for construction workers, 32 for mechanics, and 34 for chemical workers.

154. Préfecture de la Seine, *Rapport sur les recherches effectuées au Bureau du casier sanitaire pendant l'année 1911 relative à la répartition de la tuberculose dans les maisons de Paris* (Paris, 1912), pp. 106–107; on postal workers, Ministère de l'intérieur, *Recueil des travaux de la commission permanente de préservation contre la tuberculose* (2 vols., Melun, 1909), II, 91.

155. *Journal des Employé*s, no. 6 (19–26 juin 1897), p. 2; *L'Employé*, no. 87 (juillet 1901), pp. 3–4.

156. L. Marcillon, *Trente ans de vie de grands magasins* (Nice, 1924), pp. 55–58.

157. A.D.S., V 8 O^1 no. 153, Dossier: Procès-verbal de l'audience donnée le 2 novembre 1892.

Chapter III

1. Peter Stearns, *Lives of Labor: Work in a Maturing Industrial Society* (New York, 1975), pp. 1–3.

2. Yves Lequin, *Les Ouvriers de la région lyonnaise (1848–1914)* (2 vols., Lyons, 1977), I, 221–253.

3. See the comments of union members on their trade, A.P.P., B/a 151, Dossier: Syndicat des tailleurs, reports of 14 mai 1878, 14 octobre 1878. See, too, Christopher Johnson, "Patterns of Proletarianization: Parisian Tailors and Lodève Woolen Workers," in *Consciousness and Class Experience in Nineteenth-Century Europe*, ed. John Merriman (New York, 1979), pp. 65–84.

4. Joseph Barberet, *Le Travail en France. Monographies professionnelles* (7 vols., Paris, 1886–1890), V, 108.

5. J. Bith, "Précis d'une monographie d'un monteur en bronze," *Les Ouvriers des deux mondes*, 1e série, V (1885), 255.

6. Just under a fifth of the sons of tailors and shoemakers became printers. They also went into the jewelry trade in substantial numbers.

7. Ministère du commerce, Office du travail, *Rapport sur l'apprentissage dans les industries de l'ameublement* (Paris, 1905), p. 310; Jacques Valdour, *De la Popinqu' à Ménilmuch'* (Paris, 1924), pp. 88–99.

8. The recruitment registers of the Second Empire list the occupations of both the father and son. Those of the twentieth century do not. One must undertake the tedious task of linking the recruitment registers with electoral lists for the latter period. The effort is complicated by the absence of many names from the electoral documents.

9. This, of course, is the theme of one of the most distinguished works in French labor history: Joan Scott, *The Glassworkers of Carmaux* (Cambridge, Mass., 1974).

10. David Montgomery, *Workers' Control in America: Studies in the History of Work, Technology, and Labor Struggles* (Cambridge, 1979).

11. Conseil supérieur du travail, *Apprentissage. Rapport de Monsieur Briat au nom de la commission permanente* (Paris, 1902), pp. 247–248, 263, 268, passim.

12. A.N., F^{22} 571, Dossier: Emploi du chalumeau chez les bijoutiers.

13. A.P.P., B/a 1372, Dossier: Grèves des ébénistes.

14. Jacques Valdour, *Le Faubourg. Observations vécues* (Paris, 1925), pp. 67–115.

15. Julien Turgan, *Les Grandes Usines. Tableau de l'industrie française au XIXe siècle* (20 vols, Paris, 1860–1895), X, 54; XIII, 151–152. *L'Industrie vélocipédique. Organe des fabricants, mécaniciens, etc.* (août-septembre 1891), pp. 198–199.

16. Turgan, "Manufacture de pianos Pleyel, Wolff et Cie," *Les Grandes Usines*, II, 200; "Manufacture de MM. Alexandre," IV, 150–154.

17. François Bassieux, *L'Industrie de la chaussure en France* (Paris, 1908), pp. 28–29. A.P.P., B/a 1368, Dossier: Grèves des cordonniers.

18. Jean Vial, *La Coutume chapelière. Histoire du mouvement ouvrier dans la chapellerie* (Paris, 1941); Turgan, "Fabrique de chapeaux de M. Berteil," *Les Grandes Usines*, XI, (n. p.).

19. Louis Cochrane, *Modern Industrial Progress* (Philadelphia, 1904), pp. 364–369.

20. Louis Radiguier, *Maîtres imprimeurs et ouvriers typographes* (Paris, 1903), p. 491.

21. A.N., F^{22} 571, Dossier: Salubrité dans les ateliers de composition typographique.

22. A.P.P., B/a 1389, Dossier: Maison Hanch (1897).

23. Barberet, *Le Travail en France*, III, 184–195. These pages also describe the hatters' practice of *ardoise*, by which workers divided pay equally among themselves in periods of distress.

24. See the statements of the various crafts in L'Assemblée nationale, *Procès-verbal de la commission chargée de faire une enquête sur la situation des ouvriers de l'industrie et de l'agriculture en France et de présenter un premier rapport sur la crise industrielle à Paris* (Paris, 1884).

25. For the origins of the *tarif*, see William Sewell, *Work and Revolution in France* (Cambridge, 1980), pp. 180–186.

26. Cabinetmakers, joiners, and some molders, for example, were paid by piece rates. These were set to achieve a certain daily wage if a worker produced at a "normal" pace. See Ministère de l'instruction publique et des beaux-arts, *Commission d'enquête sur la situation des ouvriers et des industries d'art* (Paris, 1884), p. 275. A significant number of *tarifs* for various trades are to be found in the strike records of the A.P.P.

27. Adelaide Blasquez (ed.), *Gaston Lucas, serrurier. Chronique de l'anti-héros* (Paris, 1976), p. 110.

28. Barberet, *Le Travail en France*, III, 361–364; Pierre du Maroussem, "Char-

pentier indépendant de Paris," *Les Ouvriers des deux mondes*, 2ᵉ série, III (1892), 325–368.

29. See the statement of Mazaroz on the furniture industry, *Causes et consé-quences de la grève du Faubourg Saint-Antoine (d'octobre et novembre 1882)* (Paris, 1882).

30. L'Assemblée nationale, *Commission chargée de faire une enquête*, p. 263; Ministère de l'instruction publique, *Commission sur la situation des ouvriers*, p. 307.

31. Blasquez, *Gaston Lucas*, p. 109.

32. On employers' distrust of vocational training, see Conseil supérieur du travail, *Apprentissage*.

33. Du Maroussem, "Charpentier indépendant"; A.P.P., B/a 1389, Dossier: Société Parisienne.

34. Ministère de l'instruction publique, *Commission sur la situation des ouvriers*, p. 61.

35. L'Assemblée nationale, *Commission chargée de faire une enquête*, pp. 217–219.

36. A.P.P., B/a 1387, Dossier: Maison Huchet. This incident occurred in 1905.

37. Ibid., B/a 1384, Dossier: Maison Grimar.

38. Jewelry makers did poor work on an order for the purpose of demonstrating to the boss that a particular foreman was incapable of directing them. See ibid., B/a 1358, Dossier: Maison Collet.

39. Ibid., B/a 168–182. See Chapter V for an analysis of these strikes.

40. Ministère du commerce, Office du travail, *Statistique des grèves et des recours à la conciliation et à l'arbitrage* for 1893–1913 (20 vols., Paris, 1894–1915).

41. A.P.P., B/a 1358, Dossier: Osselin.

42. Blasquez, *Gaston Lucas*, pp. 108–116.

43. Guillaume Janneau, *L'Apprentissage dans les métiers d'art* (Paris, 1914). This book was predicated on the existence of a crisis in the luxury trades. It contains the testimonies of many experts explaining the roots of the crisis.

44. BHVP, série 119, Dossier: Apprentissage (article: "La Crise des métiers").

45. Janneau, *L'Apprentissage*, pp. 151–152.

46. A.P.P., B/a 1383, Dossier: Maison Duclos, report of 29 mars 1899.

47. Arthur Fraysse, *Le Marchandage dans l'industrie du bâtiment* (Paris, 1911).

48. A.P.P., B/a 1387, Dossier: Maison Rodez.

49. A.P.P., B/a 1372 on the cabinetmakers; Chambre de commerce de Paris, *Statistique de l'industrie à Paris résultant de l'enquête faite par la Chambre de Commerce pour les années 1847–48* (Paris, 1851), pp. 129–132 for bronze workers.

50. Ministère du commerce, Office du travail, *Salaires et durée du travail dans l'industrie française (grande et moyenne industrie)* (4 vols., Paris, 1893), I, 531.

51. Albert Aftalion, *Le Développement de la fabrique et le travail à domicile dans les industries de l'habillement* (Paris, 1906), pp. 24–131.

52. For a detailed description of the Dressoir and Prémartin shoe factory, the largest of its kind in France, see *L'Industrie progressive* (20 novembre 1901), pp. 1–2.

53. Ministère du commerce, Office du travail, *Rapport sur l'apprentissage dans l'imprimerie, 1899–1901* (Paris, 1902), p. xciii; Radiguier, *Maîtres imprimeurs*, pp. 453–468. In 1884 female typographers composed 2.4 percent of the trade; in 1902 they composed 21.4 percent.

54. A.P.P., B/a 1368, Dossier: Plé.

55. Ibid., Dossier: Coruble.

56. J.-M. Lahy, "Recherches sur les conditions du travail des ouvriers typo-graphes composant à la machine dite linotype," *Bulletin de l'Inspection du travail*, XVIII (1910), 93; Radiguier, *Maîtres imprimeurs*, pp. 478–484.

57. Chambre de commerce de Paris, *Statistique de l'industrie pour les années 1847–48*, pp. 659–660, 669.

58. Ministère de l'instruction publique, *Commission d'enquête*, p. 50.

59. On the effects of prefabricated parts in carpentry, see Barberet, *Le Travail en France*, III, p. 355–381; Marcelin-René Bonnet, *Petite histoire de la charpenterie et d'une charpente* (Paris, 1960), pp. 24–28.

60. Georges Mény, *Le Travail à bon marché. Enquête sociale* (Paris, 1907); René Descoust, *Marchandage et sweating système* (Paris, 1918).

61. A.P.P., B/a 181, Dossier: Maison Rhein, Barrière.

62. See the strikes by metal polishers to raise piece rates for the "small hands": ibid., B/a 1389, Dossiers: Maison Julie, Maison Avriller.

63. Ministère de l'instruction publique, *Commission d'enquête*, p. 52.

64. Pierre Du Maroussem, "Ebéniste parisien de haut luxe," *Les Ouvriers des deux mondes*, 2ᵉ série, IV (1895), 71. This committed revolutionary set himself up as a jobber with a small sum inherited from his parents.

65. A.P.P., B/a 180, Dossier: Grève des passementiers.

66. L'Assemblée nationale, *Commission chargée de faire une enquête*, pp. 223–226.

67. A.P.P., B/a 170, Dossier: Ouvriers vanniers; B/a 1384, Dossier: Maison Chouipe; B/a 1387, Dossier: Legris-Picard.

68. Ibid., B/a 1389, Dossier: Maison Berlaud.

69. Ibid., B/a 1384, Dossier: Maisons de Gentilly.

70. Ibid., B/a 1424, Dossier: Syndicat de gantiers, report of 22 novembre 1877.

71. BHVP, série 119, Dossier: Apprentissage.

72. Adeline Daumard et al., *Les Fortunes françaises au XIXᵉ siècle* (Paris, 1973), p. 200.

73. A.P.P., B/a 1422, Dossier: Chambre syndicale de l'ébénisterie et du meuble sculpté.

74. A.N., F¹² 4663, Dossier: Grèves et coalitions.

75. Charles Mayet, *La Crise industrielle: L'Ameublement* (Paris, 1883).

76. A.P.P., B/a 399, "Rapport sur les émigrations d'ouvriers ébénistes allemands."

77. Michael Miller, *The Bon Marché. Bourgeois Culture and the Department Store, 1896–1920* (Princeton, 1981), p. 50. Bon Marché began to sell integrated room sets by the 1880s. See also, Henri Fourdinois, *Etude économique et sociale sur ameublement* (Paris, 1894); Ministère du commerce, Office du travail, *Rapport sur l'apprentissage dans les industries de l'ameublement* (Paris, 1905), p. 150.

78. A.P.P., B/a 1372, Dossier: Ebénistes en commodes toilettes.

79. *Journal illustré de grands magasins Dufayel*, no. 1 (15 mai 1892).

80. A.P.P., B/a 1372, Dossiers: Ebénistes en vide-poches; Ebénistes en toilette anglaise.

81. Valdour, *Le Faubourg*, pp. 3–19.

82. Ministère de l'instruction publique, *Commission d'enquête*, pp. 110–111.

83. A.P.P., B/a 1438, Dossier: Syndicat des selliers, report of 8 septembre 1883.

84. Ministère du commerce, Office du travail, *Enquête sur le travail à domicile dans l'industrie de la chaussure* (Paris, 1914), p. 369.

85. A.P.P., B/a 1384, Dossier: Grèves des mégissiers.

86. Descoust, *Marchandage et sweating système*.

87. On female workers, see Paul Leroy-Beaulieu, *Le Travail des femmes au XIXᵉ siècle* (Paris, 1873); special issue of *Le Mouvement social*, no. 105 (1978) on "Travaux de femmes dans la France au XIXᵉ siècle;" Marilyn Boxer, "Women in Industrial Homework: The Flowermakers of Paris in the Belle Epoque," *French*

Historical Studies, XII (1982), 401–423; Joan Scott and Louise Tilly, *Women, Work, and Family* (New York, 1978).

88. On that work culture, see Jeanne Bouvier, *Mes Mémoires, ou 59 années d'activité industrielle, sociale, et intellectuelle d'une ouvrière* (Poitiers, 1936), pp. 55–74.

89. Département de la Seine, *Etats des communes: Montrouge* (Montévrain, 1905), p. 121.

90. Aftalion, *Le Développement de la fabrique*, p. 160; Michelle Perrot, "De la nourrice à l'employée," *Le Mouvement social*, no. 105 (1978), pp. 3–10; Robyn Dasey, "Women's Work and the Family: Women Garment Workers in Berlin and Hamburg before the First World War," in *The German Family*, ed. Richard Evans and W. R. Lee (London, 1981), p. 234.

91. A.P.P., B/a 1368, Dossier: Maison Coruble.

92. Patrick O'Brien and Caglar Keyder, *Economic Growth in Britain and France, 1780–1914* (London, 1978), pp. 191–193.

93. Gérard Jacquemet found that only 32 percent of the graduates of one apprenticeship school were exercising the trade that they had learned twenty years earlier. See his "Belleville au XIXᵉ siècle. Du Faubourg à la ville" (Doctorat d'Etat, Université de Paris-IV, 1979), p. 1115.

94. E. P. Thompson, "Time, Work-Discipline, and Industrial Capitalism," *Past and Present*, no. 38 (1967), pp. 56–97.

95. A.D.S., V 8 O¹ no. 90, Dossier: Renseignements sur le personnel du service des cokes.

96. L.T.C. Rolt, *A Short History of Machine Tools* (Cambridge, Mass., 1965); U.S. Department of Commerce and Labor, *Machine-Tool Trade in Germany, France, Switzerland, Italy, and the United Kingdom* (Washington, 1909). pp. 97–138; André Garanger, *Petite histoire d'une grande industrie* (Paris, n.d.).

97. L. Descroix, "Matériel et outillage mécanique de la fonderie," *La Technique moderne*, VI (1913), 261–267, 339–342, 380–386; H. J. Fryth and Henry Collins, *The Foundry Worker. A Trade Union History* (Manchester, 1959), pp. 44–85.

98. A. About, "Travail d'usine," *Revue de métallurgie*, X (1913), 1147–1175.

99. Ibid.

100. Charles Benoist, *L'Organisation du travail* (2 vols., Paris, 1905), I, 354–368. Compare this glassworks with the one depicted by Joan Scott in *Glassworkers of Carmaux*, chap. 4.

101. U.S. Department of Commerce, *Machine-Tool Trade*, pp. 113, 117.

102. About, "Travail d'usine," p. 1154.

103. U.S. Department of Labor, *Machine-Tool Trade*, pp. 99–103.

104. Michelle Perrot, "Les Classes populaires urbaines," in Jean Bouvier et al., *Histoire économique et sociale de la France, Tome IV: l'Ere industrielle et la société d'aujourd'hui* (Paris, 1979), p. 482.

105. Rolt, *Machine Tools*, p. 169.

106. U.S. Department of Labor, *Machine-Tool Trade*, p. 141.

107. Georges Friedmann, *Industrial Society. The Emergence of the Human Problems of Automation* (New York, 1964), pp. 195–197.

108. A.P.P., B/a 161, Dossier: Syndicat des mécaniciens, report of 24 avril 1881. A recent study of the engineering industry in England also finds relatively small declines in demands for skilled workers between 1870 and 1914. See Charles More, *Skill and the English Working Class, 1870–1914* (New York, 1980), pp. 184–188.

109. A.P.P., B/a 175, Dossier: Forges de La Villette.

110. A.D.S., V 8 O¹ no. 151, Dossier: Grève des chauffeurs.

111. Pierre-Jean Bardou et al., *The Automobile Revolution*, trans. James Laux (Chapel Hill, N.C., 1982), pp. 62–63; Patrick Fridenson, "Une Industrie nouvelle:

L'Automobile en France jusqu'en 1914," *Revue d'histoire moderne et contemporaine*, XIX (1972), 557–578; Michèle Flageolet-Lardenois, "Une Firme pionnière: Panhard et Levassor jusqu'en 1918," *Le Mouvement social*, no. 81 (1972), p. 36.

112. Etienne Riché, *La Situation des ouvriers dans l'industrie automobile* (Paris, 1909).

113. I have borrowed this concept from Jack Russell, "The Coming of the Line: The Ford Highland Park Plant, 1910–1914," *Radical America,* XII (1978), 28–45. See also Stephen Meyer, *The Five Dollar Day. Labor Management and Social Control in the Ford Motor Company, 1908–1921* (Albany, N.Y., 1981), pp. 10–44.

114. U.S. Department of Commerce, *Machine-Tool Trade*, p. 120, 127.

115. Aimée Moutet, "Les Origines du système Taylor en France. Le Point de vue patronal (1907–1914)," *Le Mouvement social*, no. 93 (1975), p. 24.

116. A.M. Puteaux, I 1. 128. III.

117. Meyer, *Five Dollar Day*, pp. 9–36 and chap. 2.

118. Montgomery, *Workers' Control in America*, p. 10.

119. My principal sources for factory management are the reports of police informers inside the factories, A.P.P., B/a 899 (Saint-Denis, 1871–1886); B/a 901 (Usine Cail); B/a 914 (Saint-Denis); B/a 916 (Puteaux, 1871–1899); B/a 1575 (Saint-Ouen).

120. For an enlightening discussion of inside contracting, see Dan Clawson, *Bureaucracy and the Labor Process. The Transformation of U.S. Industry* (New York, 1980), chap. 3.

121. See *L'Humanité. Journal quotidien socialiste*, no. 347 (30 mars 1905), p. 2; no. 348 (31 mars 1905), p. 2 for agreements on the abolition of internal subcontracting in the machine-building industries.

122. A.P.P., B/a 901, report of 3 août 1873. According to the police report on the Cail plant, "Almost all the workers, properly speaking, are on piece rates, so that they can work ten, twelve, or fourteen hours, provided that their jobs are finished at the established time." See, too, Turgan, *Les Grandes Usines*, XIV on the Forges d'Ivry.

123. A.P.P., B/a 1384, Dossier: Mors, report of 17 décembre 1902.

124. Ibid., B/a 169, Dossier: Raffinerie du sucre.

125. Jacques Valdour, *Ateliers et taudis de la banlieue de Paris* (Paris, 1923), p. 13.

126. A.P.P., B/a 1383, Dossier: Barriquand et Marre, report of 21 mai 1899.

127. See the suggestive remarks of Robert Linhart, *The Assembly Line*, trans. Margaret Crosland (Amherst, Mass., 1981), p. 48.

128. Paul Devinat, *L'Organisation scientifique du travail en Europe* (Geneva, 1927), pp. 22–24; Moutet, "Les Origines du système Taylor," pp. 15–49; Emile Pouget, *L'Organisation du surmenage* (Paris, 1914); F. Beaufils, "L'Introduction du système Taylor en France (1900–1913)," (Mémoire de matrise, Université de Paris-I, 1970). One author writes of a "crisis of confidence" in piece rates in the 1890s. See Bernard Mottez, *Systèmes de salaires et politiques patronales* (Paris, 1966), p. 123.

129. A.P.P., B/a 1389, Dossiers: Cathala, Junger, Castor.

130. Ibid., B/a 169, Dossier: Cail; B/a 178, Dossier: Cail.

131. Ibid., B/a 1387, Dossier: Grève générale, report of 21 février 1905; B/a 1389, Dossier: Dion-Bouton.

132. Ibid., Dossier: Kessler et Billard, report of 21 mai 1893; B/a 1387, Dossier: Cothias. On the proud spirit of the molders in the small shops of the Marais, see Valdour, *De la Popinq'*, pp. 86–109.

133. A.N., F¹² 4663.

134. See Chapter V.

135. A.P.P., B/a 1384, Dossier: Cohendet.

136. Emile Cheysson, *Le Cruesot. Condition matérielle, intellectuelle, et morale de la population* (Paris, 1869); Patrick Zylberman and Lion Murard, *Le Travailleur infatigable. Villes-usines, habitat et intimités au XIXe siècle*, vol. XXV of *Recherches* (Fontenay-sous-Bois, 1976). On England, see Patrick Joyce, *Work, Society and Politics. The Culture of the Factory in Late Victorian England* (London, 1980).

137. A.P.P., B/a 400, report on Clichy.

138. Among the firms that did provide some housing for workers were the Say Sugar Refinery, Alexandre Pianos, and Dupont Printing Company.

139. A.M. Bezons, Délibérations municipales (see the sessions of the 1880s); on the deplorable condition of the housing stock in Bezons at the opening of the rubber plant, see Délibérations de la commission de salubrité.

140. A.D.S., D M², Liste nominative, Puteaux, 1911. The figures are based on a sample of 200 households.

141. Ibid., Liste nominative, Ivry, 1911; A.M. Argenteuil, 11 F, Liste nominative, 1911.

142. *Le Travail. Organe socialiste et syndical des travailleurs du canton d'Argenteuil*, no. 20 (1 mai 1905).

143. A.P.P., B/a 400. The police commissioner of each quarter or commune reported on the mutual aid societies of his district.

144. Ibid., B/a 1384, Dossier: Chouipe, report of 27 février 1892.

145. See the policy of the Parisian Gas Company, A.D.S., V 8 0¹ no. 162, Dossier: Affaires individuelles.

146. A.M. Puteaux, I 1. 128. III.

147. On the Renault experiment, see Georges de Ram, "Quelques notes sur un essai d'application du système Taylor dans un grand atelier de mécanique français," *Revue de métallurgie*, VI (1909), 929–933.

148. A.P.P., B/a 181, Dossier: Pivert.

149. A.D.S., V bis 19 Q⁶ no. 13, fol. 235.

150. *L'Echo d'Argenteuil. Journal Radical-Socialiste du canton*, no. 319 (2 juin 1901).

151. *Le Courrier socialiste. Organe des groupes et syndicats ouvriers de la circonscription*, no. 143 (3 décembre 1904), no. 216 (28 avril 1906), no. 268 (23 novembre 1907); *L'Emancipation. Organe d'unité socialiste-révolutionnaire de la IIe circonscription de Saint-Denis*, no. 574 (1 février 1913); no. 590 (24 mai 1913).

152. Friedmann, *Industrial Society*, pp. 108–120.

153. A.D.S., V bis 19 Q⁶ nos. 10–28. The Nineteenth Arrondissement was chosen for analysis solely because the accident records for that district were among the few to have survived.

154. On the legal ramifications, see Charles Puech, *De l'Application de la loi sur les accidents du travail* (Paris, 1903); L. Mirman, *Les Accidents du travail. Guide pratique de l'ouvrier* (Reims, 1903); A. Dillon, *Histoire et statistique des accidents du travail* (Chatou, 1911).

155. This observation was also true on a national level. See the national figures, Ministère du travail, *Receuil de documents sur les accidents du travail. Numéro 40. Statistique des accidents du travail* (Paris, 1910), p. 13.

156. A.D.S., V bis 3 Q⁶ no. 10, fol. 81.

157. U.S. Department of Commerce, *Machine-Tool Trade*, p. 135.

158. A.P.P., B/a 399 (*pièce* 102).

159. Lenard Berlanstein, "The Formation of a Factory Labor Force: Rubber and Cable Workers in Bezons, France (1860–1914)," *Journal of Social History*, XV (1981), 167.

160. A.D.S., V 8 O¹ no. 162, report of 15 février 1903; no. 163, Dossier: Personnel ouvrier.

161. Françoise Raison-Jourde, *La Colonie auvergnate à Paris au XIXe siècle* (Paris, 1976), pp. 121–212.

162. On the relative comforts of construction workers, see Barberet, *Le Travail en France*, III, 298–299.

163. *L'Employé. Organe du syndicat des employés du commerce et de l'industrie*, no. 94 (février 1902), p. 20.

164. A.P.P., B/a 1357, Dossier: Garçons bouchers, report of 27 juin 1891; B/a 1404, Dossier: Ouvriers des tramways; BHVP, série 119, Dossier: Repos hebdomadaire.

165. Turgan, *Les Grandes Usines*, "Etablissements Duval," XIV, n.p.

166. The waitresses at Duval struck just before the Exposition for a twelve-hour day and over the fee they had to pay the employer. See A.P.P., B/a 180, Dossier: Filles de salle de restaurant.

167. BHVP, série 119, Dossier: Repos hebdomadaire.

168. Ministère du commerce, Office du travail, *Le Placement des employés, ouvriers, et domestiques en France. Son histoire—son état actuel* (Paris, 1893); BHVP, série 119, Dossier: Placement.

169. Nicholas Papayanis, "Depression and Crisis in the 'Corporation' of Paris Coachman," paper presented to the Society for French Historical Studies, New York, 1982.

170. A.P.P., B/a 1359, Dossier: Grève des charretiers-camionneurs.

171. Ibid., Dossier: Maison Benoix; B/a 1404.

172. Workers of the metropolitan railroads complained of the unjustified firings by inspectors; the management claimed to fire "only" two workers a month for drunkenness or indiscipline. See ibid., B/a 894, report of 5 mars 1907.

173. A.D.S., V 8 O¹ no. 164, Livre du personnel. Walter Licht makes a similar point about the intractability of American trainmen in *Working for the Railroad. The Organization of Work in the Nineteenth Century* (Princeton, N.J., 1983), pp. 79–134.

174. Auguste Besse, *L'Employé de commerce et de l'industrie* (Lyons, 1901); see the numerous articles that sounded a nostalgic note in *Le Journal des employés. Organe officiel des associations syndicales d'employés de toutes catégories*.

175. Blasquez, *Gaston Lucas*, pp. 112–116.

176. A.D.S., D 2 U¹⁰ nos. 4–6. The analysis that follows is based on a one-in-ten sample of the cases.

177. *L'Employé*, no. 119 (25 mars 1904), pp. 5–6; no. 183 (5 juillet 1909), p. 105.

178. Ibid., no. 118 (5 avril 1909), p. 50.

179. Managers subscribed to newspaper clipping services partly to learn about such potential scandals.

180. A.D.S., V 8 O¹ no. 149.

181. A. Demonceaux, *Le Choix d'une carrière commerciale, industrielle, ou financière* (Paris, 1904).

182. A.D.S., V 8 O¹ no. 162.

183. Susan Porter Benson, "The Clerking Sisterhood. Rationalization and the Work Culture of Saleswomen," *Radical America*, XII (1978), 41–55.

184. There were reportedly 4,500 employed by *bazars* and 5,000 by credit stores. See A.-J.-M. Artaud, *La Question de l'employé en France* (Paris, 1909), pp. 32–33; A.P.P., B/a 1388, Dossier: Courtiers d'abonnement.

185. Chambre de commerce de Paris, *Statistique de l'industrie à Paris résultant*

de l'enquête faite par la Chambre de commerce pour l'année 1860 (Paris, 1864), pp. 1047–1054.

186. A.D.S., V 8 O[1] no. 163, Dossier: Personnel fixe.

187. Susan Bachrach, "The Feminization of the French Postal Service, 1750–1914" (Ph.D. diss., University of Wisconsin-Madison, 1981), p. 131.

188. Miller, *Bon Marché*, pp. 112–121.

189. *L'Humanité. Journal socialiste quotidien*, no. 431 (22 juin 1905), p. 2.

190. G.-M.-A. Cadoux, *Les Salaires et les conditions du travail des ouvriers et employés des entreprises municipales de Paris* (The Hague, 1911), p. 38.

191. See Chapter V.

192. A.D.S., V 8 O[1] no. 149, Dossier: Syndicat des employés.

193. Ibid., Dossier: Revendications du personnel. Department stores considered the meals and lodgings—and the paternalistic protection—they gave to saleswomen as important fringe benefits.

194. Ibid., D 2 U[10] no. 4, case of 10 février 1910; A.P.P., B/a 1388, Dossier: Commis d'épicerie Potin; *L'Employé*, no. 81 (5 janvier 1901), p. 4.

195. *L'Emancipation*, no. 17 (5 juillet 1902). The management of the Crédit Lyonnais did not set fixed hours for its employees; instead, it declared that "all their time belongs to us." See Jean Bouvier, *Le Crédit lyonnais de 1863 à 1882* (2 vols., Paris, 1961), I, 361.

196. Artaud, *La Question de l'employé*, p. 16.

197. A.D.S., V 8 0[1] no. 90, Dossier: Renseigements...sur le service de la comptabilité des abonnés.

198. One clerk at Bon Marché took great pride in his ability to do calculations at an amazing speed, but he admitted that most of his peers lived in terror of the threats and reproaches that were the results of making errors. See L. Marcillon, *Trente Ans de vie de grands magasins* (Nice, 1924), pp. 18, 109.

199. The timing of such managerial efforts is very difficult to discern at this point for lack of evidence. More studies of large commercial enterprises are needed before there will be a clear picture of this aspect of the employee's work.

200. Perrot, "Les Classes populaires," pp. 461–462.

201. A.D.S., V 8 O[1] no. 153, Dossier: Rapport à M. les administrateurs....

202. Ibid., no. 149, report of 10 février 1906.

203. *L'Employé*, no. 148 (5 janvier 1907), p. 8. See the numerous requests for supplementary clerical work in this newspaper.

204. Marcillon, *Trente Ans*, pp. 18, 109; Artaud, *La Question de l'employé*, p. 13.

205. Miller, *Bon Marché*, p. 83.

206. A.D.S., D 2 U[10] no. 6, case of 19 septembre 1910.

207. Ibid., V 8 O[1] no. 153, Dossier: Contrôleurs de compteurs.

208. Ibid., no. 149, Dossier: Revendications du personnel.

209. Ibid., V K[2], Employés de la Préfecture de Paris. Many employees were reproached, but not fired, for improper dress. See the case of Emile Dalleux (carton no. 25), who was not fired even when he was drunk at work.

210. Anatole Le Grandais, *Physiologie des employés de ministères* (Paris, 1862), p. 181.

211. A.P.P., B/a 152, Dossier: Chambre syndicale des employés du commerce et de l'industrie; *Le Journal des employés*, no. 42 (1–15 février 1900), p. 2; A.D.S., V 8 0[1] no. 149, Dossier: Syndicat des employés.

212. Victor Miret, *Essai sur la sociologie à propos de la protestation des employés des postes, des telegraphes, et des chemins de fer* (Paris, 1881), p. 9.

213. A.D.S., V 8 O[1] no. 149, Dossier: Revendications du personnel.

214. *Le Journal des employés*, no. 10 (17 juillet 1897), p. 1; *L'Employé*, no. 218 (5 janvier 1912), p. 4.

215. A.P.P., B/a 1424, report of 29 septembre 1893.

216. Marcillon, *Trente Ans*, p. 55.

217. A.D.S., V 8 O¹ no. 90, Dossier: Création des divisions.

218. J. Poisle Desgrages, *Voyage à mon bureau. Aller et retour* (Paris, 1861), p. 99; Marcillon, *Trente Ans*, pp. 31–34.

219. A.D.S., V 8 O¹ no. 90.

220. Ibid., no. 163, Dossier: Personnel, report of 29 juillet 1907.

221. Ibid., no. 162, Dossier: Affaire l'Hôte, report of 30 mai 1893. Relations in department stores were not polite either; see Marcillon, *Trente Ans*, p. 109.

222. BHVP, série, 119, Dossier: Bourse du travail.

223. Marcillon, *Trente Ans*, p. 140.

224. See the collection of letters sent to the director of the Parisian Gas Company, A.D.S., V 8 0¹ no. 162, Dossier: Affaires individuelles.

225. Ibid., no. 90, Dossier: Directions et instructions générales; Bachrach, "Feminization of the Postal Service," p. 168.

226. A.P.P., B/a 894, report of 29 janvier 1901; Miret, *Essai sur la sociologie*, p. 4.

227. Bachrach, "Feminization of the Postal Service," chap. 5. Women had been clerks in rural postal offices and telegraph operators for some time.

228. Statistique générale de la France, *Résultats statistiques du recensement général de la population effectué le 5 mars 1911* (2 vols., Paris, 1911), II, 7. There were 19,123 male employees and 496 female clerks. Note that some of the male "employees" had, in effect, manual jobs.

229. A.D.S., V 8 O¹ no. 730, Procès-verbal du Conseil d'administration, fol. 46.

230. Miller, *Bon Marché*, p. 193; Artaud, *La Question de l'employé*, pp. 11, 27.

231. On the resentment of female clerks by the males, see Marcillon, *Trente Ans*, pp. 109, 129.

232. Guy Thuillier, *La Vie quotidienne dans les ministères au XIXᵉ siècle* (Paris, 1976), pp. 195–197.

233. On the adding machine and other technological innovations in the office, see Louis Couffignal, *Les Machines à calculer* (Paris, 1933).

234. *L'Employé*, no. 180 (5 avril 1909), p. 50.

Chapter IV

1. Michael Marrus, "Social Drinking in the *Belle Epoque*," *Journal of Social History*, VII (1974), 115–141; Peter Stearns, *Lives of Labor: Work in a Maturing Industrial Society* (New York, 1975), chaps. 7, 8, 10.

2. Ministère du commerce, Office du travail, *Salaires et durée du travail dans l'industrie française* (4 vols., Paris 1893–1897), I.

3. See the survey of work hours made by the municipality of Puteaux, A.M. Puteaux, F VII. 55.

4. L'Assemblée nationale, *Procès-verbal de la commission chargée de faire une enquête sur la situation des ouvriers de l'industrie et de l'agriculture en France et de présenter un premier rapport sur la crise industrielle à Paris* (Paris, 1884), pp. 183, 384.

5. A.P.P., B/a 1389, Dossier: Berlaud, report of 29 mars 1898; Dossier: Poccard, report of 17 septembre 1898; Joseph Barbaret, *Le Travail en France. Monographies professionnelles* (7 vols., Paris, 1886–1890,), II, 448.

6. Charles Benoist, *Les Ouvrières de l'aiguille à Paris* (Paris, 1895), p. 27.

7. E. P. Thompson, "Time, Work-Discipline and Industrial Capitalism," *Past and Present*, no. 38 (1967), pp. 56–97.

8. The analysis that follows is based on the reports of police and informers inside factories: A.P.P., B/a 1575; B/a 901; B/a 899; B/a 916.

9. Ibid., B/a 901, reports of 10 juillet 1872, 3 avril 1875, 5 juin 1878; B/a 1575, reports of 8 août 1873, 26 octobre 1877, 1 novembre 1876.

10. Ibid., B/a 1575, report of 1 novembre 1877.

11. Ibid., B/a 901, reports of 17 mai 1874, 3 août 1873, 28 décembre 1876.

12. Ibid., B/a 1575, report of 1 novembre 1877.

13. Ibid., B/a 901, reports of 3 août 1873, 28 octobre 1874, 9 août 1878.

14. Ibid., B/a 916, reports of 11 and 18 novembre 1876, 11 mars 1876.

15. Ibid., reports of 20 décembre 1875 and 29 janvier 1876.

16. Ibid., report of 8 janvier 1876.

17. Pierre Lelièvre, *Les Ateliers de Paris* (Paris, 1866), pp. 24, 46; Michelle Perrot, *Les Ouvriers en grève. France, 1871–1890* (2 vols., Paris, 1974), I, 225–229.

18. Denis Poulot, *Le Sublime. Question sociale* (Paris, 1887), p. 73; A.P.P., B/a 1383, Dossier: Maison Elwel (1898).

19. Ibid., B/a 400, reports of commissioners of Pantin and Saint-Denis; B/a 169, Dossier: Cail, report of 1 avril 1881. Carpenters claimed not to take Monday off because it would have prevented others in construction from working. See Barberet, *Le Travail en France*, III, 356.

20. Docteur Louis Dubosquet-Laborderie, *Causes des décès par maladies épidémiques et contagieuses dans la commune de Saint-Ouen* (Paris, 1889), p. 4.

21. A.M., Puteaux, R II. 181, Casino de Puteaux.

22. Alphonse Loyau, "La Semaine anglaise en France dans l'industrie mécanique de la Seine," *La Vie ouvrière. Revue syndicale bi-mensuelle*, IV (1912), 369–385. See the stimulating article by Douglas Reid, "The Decline of Saint-Monday, 1766–1876," *Past and Present*, no. 71 (1976), pp. 76–101.

23. Pierre Lhande, *Le Christ dans la banlieue. Enquête sur la vie religieuse dans les milieux ouvriers de la banlieue de Paris* (Paris, 1927), p. 12.

24. See A.M. Bezons, Délibérations municipales, session of 12 avril 1885. The aldermen of Bezons were revolted by the ugliness and by the industrial stench of Saint-Denis.

25. See *Le Courrier socialiste. Organe des groupes et syndicats ouvriers de la circonscription*, no. 58 (2 mai 1903) and no. 268 (23 novembre 1907). A dance on May Day 1903 lasted until six o'clock in the morning; another ball in November 1907 lasted until 4 a.m.

26. A.M. Saint-Denis, J, 3/8/5/2. On Parisian practices at dance halls, see André Warnod, *Les Bals de Paris* (Paris, 1922) and Victor Rozier, *Les Bals publics à Paris* (Paris, 1855).

27. A.M. Saint-Denis, J, 3/5/5/4.

28. This is not to say that Saint-Denis had been devoid of theatrical presentations. Traveling companies had long put on plays in makeshift theaters.

29. Département de la Seine, *Etats des communes: Boulogne-sur-Seine* (Montévrain, 1905), pp. 57–58.

30. A.M. Puteaux, R II. 281.

31. Pierre Hénon, *Levallois. Histoire d'une banlieue* (Brussels, 1981), p. 115.

32. A.M. Saint-Denis, R, 3/9/6/4.

33. Ibid., J, 3/8/4/1.

34. The programs of the Casino were reported almost weekly in *L'Emancipation. Organe d'unité socialiste-révolutionnaire de la IIe circonscription de Saint-Denis.*

35. Edward Tannenbaum, *1900: The Generation before the Great War* (Garden

City, N.Y., 1976), pp. 198–201; Gunther Barth, *City People: The Rise of Modern City Culture in Nineteenth-Century America* (New York, 1980), pp. 210–220.

36. Robert Isherwood, "Entertainment in the Parisian Fairs in the Eighteenth Century," *Journal of Modern History*, LIII (1981), 24–28.

37. A.M. Saint-Denis, J, 3/8/4/1; *L'Emancipation*, no. 462 (5 novembre 1910).

38. Ibid., no. 245 (20 octobre 1906); no. 462 (5 novembre 1910).

39. Ibid., no. 424 (26 février 1910).

40. Joffre Dumazedier, *Toward a Society of Leisure*, trans. Stewart McClure (New York, 1967).

41. *L'Emancipation*, no. 63 (23 mai 1903).

42. Ibid., no. 248 (10 novembre 1906). The Casino of Puteaux also presented "realistic theater" in 1906. Parents were warned not to take their children to these presentations. See A.M. Puteaux, R II. 281.

43. *L'Emancipation*, no. 258 (19 janvier 1907).

44. See Gaston Montéhaus, *Recueil des chansons humanitaires* (Paris, 1910).

45. *L'Emancipation*, no. 213 (10 mars 1906); no. 214 (17 mars 1906); 258 (19 janvier 1907); no. 271 (20 avril 1907), no. 445 (9 juillet 1910). In addition, the Municipal Theater showed the film *Capital et Travail* in July 1910.

46. A.M. Saint-Denis, J, 3/5/5/4.

47. René Michaud, *J'avais vingt ans. Un jeune ouvrier au début du siècle* (Paris, 1967), pp. 53–55.

48. *L'Emancipation*, no. 460 (22 octobre 1910). On the social deprivation of La Plaine, see Docteur Adrien Le Roy des Barres, *Rapport sur les maladies épidémiques et les maladies virulentes observées dans l'arrondissement de Saint-Denis* (Paris, 1894), pp. 17–20.

49. A.M. Saint-Denis, J, 3/5/5/4. I was surprised to find that requests to authorize boxing matches were rare. Why this was the case is not clear.

50. *L'Emancipation*, no. 313 (8 février 1908); no. 427 (19 mars 1910).

51. Jacques Valdour, *Ateliers et taudis de la banlieue de Paris* (Paris, 1923), pp. 75–80 describes the crowds of working-class families at the cinema on weekends.

52. A.M. Ivry, D-57, fol. 111.

53. *L'Emancipation*, no. 467 (10 décembre 1910).

54. A.M. Puteaux, I 145. I. For a brief overview of sports in France, see Richard Holt, "Introduction des sports anglais et la disparition du 'Gentleman Athlete'," in *Aimez-vous les Stades? Les Origines des politiques sportives en France, 1870–1930*, vol. XLIII of *Recherches*, ed. Alain Ehrenberg (Fontenay-sous-Bois, 1980), pp. 253–271. Holt has recently published a more detailed treatment of the subject, *Sport and Society in Modern France* (Hamden, Conn., 1981).

55. A.M. Ivry, D-83, fol. 143.

56. A.D.S., D R[1], Recrutement militaire, registers of Puteaux and Pantin, 1903. The cost of a bicycle declined from 1,655 man-hours of work in 1893 to 357 in 1913 (Val de Marne, Service éducatif des Archives départementales, *Sports et société, 1870–1914* [Créteil, 1979], p. 9), but was still far beyond the means of most laborers. It is possible that some mechanics were able to build bicycles for themselves.

57. *Le Courrier socialiste*, no. 341 (19 février 1910).

58. See *L'Emancipation*, no. 215 (24 mars 1910); no. 469 (24 décembre 1910). The editors applauded the Casino for satisfying "the lovers of gaiety who are so numerous in Saint-Denis."

59. *L'Emancipation*, no. 98 (26 décembre 1903).

60. The recently elected socialist municipality of Saint-Denis made football matches part of the annual local festival. The rubric "Sports" became nearly an entire column long in the socialist newspaper by 1913.

61. *L'Emancipation*, no. 468 (17 décembre 1910). The social segregation at

performances may have resulted from, or have been intensified by, the class differences in behavior at theaters. Working-class rowdiness and vocal participation in the show may have alienated middle-class spectators, who had different standards of decorum. See Roy Rosenzweig, *Eight Hours for What We Will. Workers and Leisure in an Industrial City, 1870–1920* (Cambridge, 1983), p. 199.

62. See the rare membership lists of sporting groups in A.M. Argenteuil, 32 R⁴.

63. For a fascinating study of leisure institutions and their wider significance, see Lewis Erenberg, *Steppin' Out. New York Nightlife and the Transformation of American Culture* (Westport, Conn., 1981).

64. Alain Faure, *Paris Carême-prenant. Du Carnaval à Paris au XIXᵉ siècle* (Paris, 1979).

65. Henri Leyret, *En plein faubourg (moeurs ouvrières)* (Paris, 1895), pp. 99–101.

66. Barberet, *Le Travail en France*, IV, 189–190.

67. Michaud, *J'avais vingt ans*, p. 83.

68. Ibid., pp. 82–85. For the preservation of craft sociability among copper molders beyond World War I, see Jacques Valdour, *De la Popinqu' à Ménilmuch'* (Paris, 1924), pp. 96–106.

69. Jeffry Kaplow, "La Fin de la Saint-Lundi. Etude sur le Paris ouvrier au XIXᵉ siècle," *Le Temps libre*, II (1981), 117; Faure, *Paris Carême-prenant*, p. 17.

70. Pierre Du Maroussem, "Ebéniste parisien de haut luxe," *Les Ouvriers des deux mondes*, 2ᵉ série, IV (1895), 69–70.

71. Jean-Paul Brunet, "Une Banlieue ouvrière. Saint-Denis (1890–1939)" (Doctorat d'Etat, Université de Paris-IV, 1978), p. 48.

72. Gérard Jacquemet, "Belleville au XIXᵉ siècle. Du Faubourg à la ville" (Doctorat d'Etat, Université de Paris-IV, 1979), p. 1251.

73. Norma Evenson, *Paris: A Century of Change, 1878–1978* (New Haven, 1979), pp. 257–260; Faure, *Paris Carême-prenant*, pp. 37–83.

74. See the enlightening description of daily existence in a seamstress's workshop in Jeanne Bouvier, *Mes Mémoires, ou 59 années d'activité industrielle, sociale, et intellectuelle d'une ouvrière* (Poitiers, 1936), pp. 46–74.

75. A.P.P, B/a 400, report of quartier Belleville.

76. Ibid., report of quartier Porte Saint-Denis.

77. Barberet, *Le Travail en France*, II, 447; Poulot, *Le Sublime*, p. 51; A. Focillon, "Tailleur d'habits de Paris," *Les Ouvriers des deux mondes*, 1ᵉ série, II (1858), 163–164.

78. Natalis Rondot, *Histoire et statistique des théâtres de Paris* (Paris, 1852), p. 9.

79. Bouvier, *Mes mémoires*, p. 55; Leyret, *En plein faubourg*, p. 97.

80. See Suzanna Barrows, "After the Commune: Alcoholism, Temperance, and Literature in the Early Third Republic," in *Consciousness and Class Experience in Nineteenth-Century Europe*, ed. John Merriman (New York, 1979), pp. 205–218; Marrus, "Social Drinking," pp. 115–141.

81. *Le Travail. Organe socialiste et syndicale des travailleurs du canton d'Argenteuil*, no. 16 (1 janvier 1905).

82. See, for example, E. Vandervelde, *L'Alcoolisme et les conditions de travail chez l'ouvrier* (Paris, 1900). Coming from employers, the observation that the best-paid workers drank the most might have been just a self-interested argument against higher wages. The fact that supporters of working-class movements made this observation renders it creditable.

83. Michael Marrus, "L'Alcoolisme social à la Belle Epoque," in *L'Haleine des faubourgs. Ville, habitat, et santé au XIXᵉ siècle*, vol. XXIX of *Recherches*, ed. Lion Murard and Patrick Zylberman (Fontenay-sous-Bois, 1977), 285–314. The culture

of the café is now under investigation by Professor Suzanna Barrows, and her study should shed new light on the increase in alcoholic consumption. For a comparative perspective, see James Roberts, "Drink and Industrial Work Discipline in Nineteenth-Century Germany," *Journal of Social History*, XV (1981), 25–38.

84. Leyret, *En plein faubourg*, pp. 40–59.

85. See Stearns, *Lives of Labor*, chaps. 7–8. We agree with Stearns that craft workers were slow to form new leisurely expectations, but he may have underestimated the importance of commercialized recreation for factory workers.

86. See the budgets of Parisian workers presented in *Les Ouvriers des deux mondes*, 2ᵉ série, I-V (1893–1899).

87. Nicolas Fanjung, "Précis d'une monographie du serrurier-poseur de persiennes en fer de Paris," *Les Ouvriers des deux mondes*, 2ᵉ série, V (1899), p. 359; Adelaïde Blasquez (ed.), *Gaston Lucas, serrurier. Chronique de l'anti-héros* (Paris, 1976), pp. 120–122.

88. Loyau, "La Semaine anglaise," p. 382.

89. H.-F. Hébert and E. Delbet, "Tisseur en châles de la fabrique urbaine collective de Paris," *Les Ouvriers des deux mondes*, 1ᵉ série, I (1857), 302.

90. See the annual reports of the Administration générale de l'assistance publique de Paris, *Rapport à Monsieur le Préfet de la Seine sur le Service des enfants moralement abandonnés* (Montévrain, 1881–1890); in particular, see the report of 1886, p. 9.

91. Lawrence Stone, *The Family, Sex, and Marriage in England, 1500–1800* (New York, 1977), pp. 470–480.

92. Administration générale de l'assistance publique de Paris, *Rapport . . . sur le Service, 1887*, pp. 3–6.

93. For an excellent anthropological study of family life—and a warning against the dangers of measuring the quality of family relations from surface manifestations of disorganization—see Thomas Belmonte, *The Broken Fountain* (New York, 1979). Also, Carol Stack, *All Our Kin: Strategies for Survival in a Black Community* (New York, 1974). These and other recent social-science works on poor families point to the need to explore how the members, themselves, understood familial relations.

94. Stone, *Family, Sex, and Marriage*; Philippe Ariès, *Centuries of Childhood*, trans. Robert Baldick (New York, 1962), pp. 365–415; Maurice Crubellier, *L'Enfance et la jeunesse dans la société française, 1800–1950* (Paris, 1979), p. 38; Michelle Perrot, "Eloge de la ménagère dans le discours des ouvriers français au XIXᵉ siècle," *Romantisme*, no. 13 (1976), pp. 105–121.

95. Alain Corbin, *Les Filles de noce. Misère sexuelle et prostitution aux XIXᵉ et XXᵉ siècles* (Paris, 1978), pp. 278–285.

96. Stearns, *Lives of Labor*, chap. 8

97. Joan Scott and Louise Tilly, *Women, Work, and Family* (New York, 1979), chap. 8; Robert Wheaton, "Recent Trends in the Historical Study of the French Family," in *Family and Sexuality in French History*, ed. Robert Wheaton and Tamara Hareven (Philadelphia, 1980), pp. 3–26; Michael Anderson, *Family Structure in Nineteenth-Century Lancashire* (Cambridge, 1971), chaps. 5, 6, 9, 10.

98. *L'Enseignement primaire à Paris et dans le département de la Seine de 1867 à 1877* (Paris, 1878), pp. 156–157.

99. Michaud, *J'avais vingt ans*, pp. 9–30.

100. Jacques Caroux-Destray (ed.), *Un Couple ouvrier traditionnel* (Paris, 1974), pp. 48–54.

101. Octave De Mesnil and Charles Mangenot, *Enquête sur les logements, professions, salaires, et budgets* (Paris, 1899), pp. 89–90.

102. Octave Du Mesnil, *Fragment d'une enquête dans le quartier des Gobelins* (Paris, 1895), p. 3.

103. The papers of the Orphanage are in the A.D.S., series V bis Q and V D⁶. For precise citations and a discussion of the orphans, see my article, "Growing Up as Workers in Nineteenth-Century Paris: The Case of the Orphans of the Prince Imperial," *French Historical Studies*, XI (1980), 551–576.

104. The discussion of the role of the mother owes much to Belmonte, *Broken Fountain*, chaps. 6–7.

105. J. Bith interviewed a bronze assembler who claimed to visit the grave of his mother every few months. See "Précis d'une monographie d'un monteur en bronze," *Les Ouvriers des deux mondes*, 1ᵉ série, V (1885), p. 249.

106. Caroux-Destray, *Un Couple ouvrier*, pp. 43–46.

107. Bith, "Précis d'une monographie," p. 253.

108. A.D.S., V D⁶ 21; V D⁶ 1925, no. 4; V D⁶ 1796, no. 4; V D⁶ 1415, no. 1.

109. A bronze worker told a social investigator that he had always regretted his father's "coldness." See Bith, "Précis d'une monographie," p. 255. The son of a day laborer noted that "it was mama who took care of us; one did not see papa." See Caroux-Destray, *Un Couple ouvrier*, pp. 46–47.

110. Caroux-Destray, *Un Couple ouvrier*, pp. 43–71; Blasquez, *Gaston Lucas*, pp. 119–126.

111. Berlanstein, "Growing Up in Paris," p. 555.

112. Philippe Ariès (*Histoire des populations françaises et de leurs attitudes devant la vie depuis le XVIIIᵉ siècle* [Paris, 1971], p. 193) describes the immigrant workers from the Nord as "peu évolués" —having children without concern for their futures and living from day to day.

113. Gréard, *L'Enseigment primaire*, pp. 133–137.

114. A.M. Saint-Denis, R, 3/11/7/4; R, 3/11/7/6. These figures are merely illustrative since children may have worked in other communes. It is worth noting, however, that Saint-Denis did contain industries that traditionally employed a child-labor force: glassmaking and cloth printing.

115. Leyret, *En plein faubourg*, p. 118.

116. Etienne van de Walle and Samuel Preston, "Mortalité de l'enfance au XIXᵉ siècle à Paris and dans le département de la Seine," *Population*, XXIX (1974): 89–107.

117. Francis Ronsin, *La Grève des ventres. Propagande néo-malthusienne et la baisse de la natalité française* (Paris, 1980), p. 63; Etienne van de Walle, "France," in *European Demographic and Economic Growth*, ed. W. R. Lee (London, 1979), p. 128.

118. Statistique générale de la France, *Statistique des familles en 1906* (Paris, 1912), p. 149.

119. On the social diversification of these quarters, see Conseil d'hygiène publique et de salubrité, *Rapport général à M. le Préfet de police sur les travaux des commissions d'hygiène des arrondissements du département de la Seine, 1893*, (Paris, 1894), p. 97; *1895* (Paris, 1896), pp. 99–100.

120. See Chapter II.

121. John Knodel (*The Decline of Fertility in Germany, 1871–1939* [Princeton, N.J., 1974], pp. 254–257) finds that the drop in fertility in Germany more than compensated for the decline in infant mortality; a new target family size had evolved. I lack the statistical sophistication to test for such changes among the residents of greater Paris.

122. For a general prespective on youth, see John Gillis, *Youth and History: Tradition and Change in European Age Relations, 1770–Present* (New York, 1974); Joseph Kett, *Rites of Passage: Adolescence in America, 1790 to the Present* (New York, 1977). Note that I am using the term "adolescent" merely to describe an age

category; I do not wish to imply that the youths under discussion had a particular set of cultural characteristics.

123. Belmonte, *Broken Fountain*, pp. 96–100; Hyman Rodman, *Lower-Class Families: The Culture of Poverty in Negro Trinidad* (New York, 1971).

124. A.D.S., V D⁶ 475, no. 2, report of août 1857.

125. Arlette Farge, *Vivre dans la rue au XVIIIᵉ siècle* (Paris, 1979).

126. Berlanstein, "Growing Up in Paris," pp. 560–561.

127. Michaud, *J'avais vingt ans*, pp. 29–32.

128. A.D.S., V D⁶ 2677 no. 1; V D⁶ 1925 no. 4; V D⁶ 1415 no. 2; V D⁶ 189 no. 4; V D⁶ 486 no.2.

129. A.M. Ivry, Liste nominative, 1876; A.D.S., D 2 M⁸ no. 115, Liste nominative, 1911.

130. Michaud, *J'avais vingt ans*, pp. 54–55.

131. Benoist, *Les Ouvrières de l'aiguille*, pp. 107–115; Bouvier, *Mes Mémoires*, p. 60.

132. *Le Travail*, no. 7 (1 décembre 1901); no. 8 (1 janvier 1902); no. 9. (1 février 1902).

133. A.P.P., B/a 899, report of 14 avril 1885.

134. Ibid., B/a 1575, report of 5 décembre 1880.

135. See ibid., D B 282, press clippings; Docteur Lejeune, *Faut-il fouetter les Apaches?* (Paris, 1910); Jacquemet, "Belleville au XIXᵉ siècle," pp. 1272–1275. Gordon Wright (*Between the Guillotine and Liberty* [New York, 1983], p. 171) relates the public outcry about the Apaches to a press campaign against the legislation to abolish capital punishment. There may be some truth to this connection, but socialist journalists supported the bill and were still obsessed with the problem of youth gangs.

136. *L'Emancipation*, no. 276 (23 mars 1907); no. 290 (31 août 1907); no. 426 (12 mars 1910).

137. *L'Humanité. Journal socialiste quotidien*, no. 16 (3 mai 1904), p. 1; no. 131 (26 août 1904), p. 1; no. 352 (4 avril 1905), p. 3.

138. A.P.P., DB 282, press clippings; *L'Emancipation*, no. 426 (12 mars 1910).

139. *L'Humanité*, no. 352 (4 avril 1905), p. 3.

140. A.M. Puteaux, Délibérations municipales, session of 13 décembre 1912.

141. A.M. Saint-Ouen, Délibérations municipales, session of 4 avril 1909.

142. *Le Travail*, no. 19 (1 novembre 1902) reported that workers and employers collaborated to circumvent the Millerand Law, which restricted the labor of youths in factories.

143. One memoir of an employee that I have been able to uncover is L. Marcillon, *Trente Ans de vie de grands magasins* (Nice, 1924). The author was raised in the provinces by an aunt who was a lodging-house keeper, so its relevance is somewhat limited.

144. A.D.S., V 4 E, Actes de mariage, 1869.

145. Ibid., D 2 M⁸ no. 7.

146. Statistique générale de la France, *Salaires et coût de l'existence à diverses époques, jusqu'en 1910* (Paris, 1911), pp. 451–464. Eighteen percent of employees' households had four or more members; 33.2 percent of workers' households did.

147. A.D.S., D R¹, Recrutement militaire, XIIIᵉ and XVIIIᵉ Arrondissements, 1868–1969.

148. I am extending the concept of the "family wage economy," which has been borrowed from Scott and Tilly, *Women, Work, and Family*, chap. 6.

149. *Le Journal des employés de chemins de fer*, no. 66 (5 avril 1884), p. 1.

150. Julien Turgan, *Les Grandes Usines de France. Tableau de l'industrie française au XIXᵉ siècle* (20 vols., Paris, 1860–1895), I, 318–319.

151. Adeline Daumard et al. *Les Fortunes françaises au XIXᵉ siècle* (Paris, 1973), p. 200.

152. A.P.P., B/a 152, Dossier: Chambre syndicale des employés de commerce (see the brochure, "Améliorations professionnelles," p. 15).

153. A.D.S., D R¹, Recrutement militaire, 1902–1903.

154. *L'Employé. Organe du syndicat des employés du commerce et de l'industrie*, no. 135 (25 juillet 1905), p. 102.

155. A.D.S., V 4 E, Actes de mariage, XVIIIᵉ Arrondissement, 1869.

156. Ibid., V K². Of the fifty dossiers examined, 7 contained references to drinking problems.

157. Françoise Raison-Jourde, *La Colonie auvergnate à Paris au XIXᵉ siècle* (Paris, 1976), pp. 320–322.

158. *L'Humanité*, no. 305 (16 février 1905), p. 1.

159. See Chapter II.

160. A.D.S., D 4 U¹, Justice de paix, actes de juridiction gracieuse, 1903.

161. A.D.S., V K². Eleven of fifty employees whose dossiers I examined had liens on their salaries. It is no wonder that employees began to demand legislation to give them the same protections from their creditors that wage-earners had.

162. A.D.S., V 8 O¹ no. 163, Dossier: Peines disciplinaires

163. The tension between the declining psychic rewards of work and the acceptance of rewards off the job is a major theme of Stearns, *Lives of Labor*.

Chapter V

1. Joan Scott, *The Glassworkers of Carmaux* (Cambridge, Mass., 1974); Rolande Trempé, *Les Mineurs de Carmaux* (2 vols., Paris, 1971). See also the special issue of *Le Mouvement social*, no. 97 (1976) on "Naissance de la classe ouvrière."

2. The following, brief discussion of working-class politics before the Commune is based on William Sewell, *Work and Revolution in France* (Cambridge, 1980); Ronald Aminzade, *Class, Politics and Early Industrial Capitalism* (Albany, N.Y., 1981); Bernard Moss, *The Origins of the French Labor Movement* (Berkeley, 1976); Alain Faure, "Mouvements populaires et mouvement ouvrier à Paris," *Le Mouvement social*, no. 88 (1974), 51–92.; William Sewell, "La Confraternité des prolétaires: Conscience de classe sous la monarchie de Juillet," *Annales: Economie, société, civilisation*, XXXVI (1981), 650–671; Christopher Johnson, *Utopian Communism in France, 1839–1851* (Ithaca, N.Y., 1974).

3. Sewell, *Work and Revolution*, chap. 11; Peter Amann, *Revolution and Mass Democracy: The Paris Club Movement of 1848* (Princeton, 1975); Roger Price, *The French Second Republic: A Social History* (London, 1972).

4. Sewell, *Work and Revolution*, p. 259.

5. Stewart Edwards, *The Paris Commune, 1871* (London, 1971), pp. 187–276; Michel Winock and Jean-Pierre Azéma, *Les Communards* (Paris, 1971).

6. Moss, *Origins of Labor Movement*, pp. 56–62. The Communards were willing to compensate the owners for the confiscations.

7. Louis Giard, "Les Elections à Paris sous la Troisième République" (Doctorat de IIIᵉ cycle, Université de Dakar, 1966–1968), p. 39.

8. A.P.P., B/a 151, Dossier: Syndicat des tailleurs, report of 15 avril 1878.

9. Ibid., B/a 161, Dossier: Syndicat des mécaniciens, report of 25 avril 1880.

10. Jacques Néré points out that Radicals had "the mentality of the primacy of politics." See his "La Crise industrielle de 1882 et le mouvement Boulangiste" (Doctorat ès-Lettres, 2 vols., Université de Paris, 1959), II, 35.

11. On the varieties of socialism, see Georges Lefranc, *Le Mouvement socialiste sous la Troisième République (1875–1940)* (Paris, 1963); David Stafford, *From Anarchism to Reformism: A Study of the Political Activities of Paul Brousse, 1870–90* (Toronto, 1971); Patrick Hutton, *The Cult of the Revolutionary Tradition: The Blanquists in French Politics, 1864–1893* (Berkeley, 1981).

12. Giard, "Les Elections à Paris," pp. 88–90.

13. Joseph Barberet, *Le Travail en France. Monographies professionnelles* (7 vols., 1886–1890), II, 449.

14. Ibid., III, 422–428.

15. Néré, "Crise de 1882," II, 546.

16. A.D.S., D 2 M² no. 23, Elections législatives.

17. Néré. "Crise de 1882," II, p. 209. The Radicals received 138,609 votes in 1884 and 138,802 in 1887.

18. Ibid., pp. 362–422.

19. Frederic Seager, *The Boulanger Affair* (Ithaca, N.Y., 1969); Patrick Hutton, "Popular Boulangism and the Advent of Mass Politics in France, 1886–90," *Journal of Contemporary History,* XI (1976), 85–106.

20. Jean-Jacques Feichter, *Le Socialisme français: De l'Affaire Dreyfus à la Grande Guerre* (Geneva, 1965), p. 10.

21. Giard, "Les Elections à Paris," p. 103. The figure of seventeen includes five Socialist-Revisionists, who had been involved with the Boulangist movement.

22. Ibid., p. 106.

23. Hutton, "Popular Boulangism," argues that the Socialist parties learned about mass-party tactics from the Boulanger movement.

24. Stewart Edwards (*Paris Commune*, p. 207) summarizes the standard view: "The workers in these large-scale industries had not yet formed their own working-class traditions of organizations and combat, particularly so as most of these workers in the factories in the suburbs of Paris were first-generation immigrants from the provinces." See, too, Jeanne Gaillard, "Les Usines Cail et les ouvriers métallurgistes de Grenelle," *Le Mouvement social,* nos. 33–34 (1961), pp. 35–53. An excellent comparative study of craftsmen and factory workers is Michael Hanagan, *The Logic of Solidarity* (Urbana, Ill., 1980).

25. A.P.P., B/a 899, Dossier: Saint-Denis, 1871–1886; B/a 901, Dossier: Usine Cail; B/a 914, Dossier: Saint-Denis; B/a 916, Dossier: Puteaux, 1871–1899; B/a 1575, Dossier: Saint-Ouen.

26. Ibid., B/a 899, report of 10 septembre 1873.

27. Ibid., B/a 901, report of 7 mars 1872.

28. Ibid., B/a 899, reports of 30 juillet 1874 and 10 août 1874.

29. Ibid., reports of 24 février 1874, 23 novembre 1875, 4 octobre 1879; B/a 916, report of 2 décembre 1875; B/a 1575, reports of 26 novembre 1874, 25 mai 1876, 28 juin 1877.

30. Ibid., B/a 1575, reports of 2 mars 1873, 21 mars 1874, 26 avril 1877.

31. Ibid., B/a 899, reports of 6 janvier 1872, 1 mars 1873; B/a 1575, reports of 17 janvier 1878, 3 février 1875.

32. Ibid., B/a 899, reports of 14 février 1874, 7 avril 1874; B/a 1575, report of 5 décembre 1880.

33. Ibid., B/a 916, reports of 2 décembre 1875, 4 décembre 1875, 3 novembre 1876.

34. A Parisian shoemaker won applause from his comrades when he proclaimed at a union meeting that he "did not like to associate with bosses, except when he was forced to do so." He expressed the desire to do violence to a *patron* every time he saw one. See ibid., B/a 1421, Dossier: Fédération de la cordonnerie de la Seine, report of 27 septembre 1882. See also the comments of a foreman locksmith, Adelaide

Blasquez (ed.), *Gaston Lucas, serrurier. Chronique de l'anti-héros* (Paris, 1976), pp. 110–112.

35. A.P.P., B/a 916, reports of 7 octobre 1874, 2 décembre 1875.

36. Ibid., B/a 1575, reports of 24 février 1876, 4 janvier 1877, 8 janvier, 22 mars 1877.

37. Ibid., B/a 916, reports of 22 septembre 1876 and 4 décembre 1875.

38. Ibid., B/a 899, reports of 13 and 17 décembre 1875.

39. Ibid., B/a 1575, report of 9 décembre 1877; B/a 899, report of 16 avril 1877.

40. Ibid., B/a 899, report of 18 juin 1877.

41. Ibid.

42. Claude Willard, "Contribution au portrait du militant guesdiste dans les dix dernières années du XIXᵉ siècle," *Le Mouvement social*, nos. 33–34 (1960–1961), pp. 55–66.

43. A.D.S., 2 M² no. 23. In Saint-Denis, Roche received 3,019 votes to 2,140 for Gaulier; in Saint-Ouen, 1,012 to 818. The results of the elections in the communes in the Arrondissement of Sceaux (southern portion of the *banlieue*) have been lost.

44. In Clichy, Roche received 1,120 votes to 1,343 for Gaulier; in Levallois-Perret, the vote was 1,270 to 1,809.

45. A.M. Saint-Ouen, Dossier: Elections. Abstentions in this election, however, reached over 50 percent.

46. The Socialists no longer represented Puteaux or Suresnes in the Chamber of Deputies after 1893.

47. A.P.P., B/a 1575, press clippings from *Le Matin* (7 novembre 1892).

48. A.M. Saint-Ouen, Délibérations municipales, sessions of 15 janvier 1887, 12 février 1887, 13 août 1887, 2 août 1888, 15 septembre 1888, 22 septembre 1888, 11 janvier 1890, 17 novembre 1894.

49. Ibid., sessions of 13 mars 1886, 13 octobre 1891, 1 octobre 1892.

50. A.P.P., B/a 1575, press clippings; A.M. Saint-Ouen, Dossier: Délibérations municipales, sessions of 3 and 10 septembre 1877.

51. The Radical municipal council of 1904 consisted of eleven white-collar workers, five businessmen, five retail merchants, a property-owner, and two workers.

52. A.M., Saint-Ouen, Délibérations municipales, session of 8 août 1905.

53. A.P.P., B/a 1575, reports of 28 avril 1889, 10 mars 1890, 30 août 1891.

54. A.M. Saint-Ouen, Dossier: Elections.

55. Jean-Paul Brunet, *Saint-Denis. La Ville rouge, 1890–1939* (Paris, 1980), pp. 34–76.

56. A.M. Ivry, D-70, fol. 195.

57. Ibid., D-79, fol., 190.

58. A.M. Puteaux, Délibérations municipales, session of 19 mai 1912.

59. For good examples of these types, see Pierre Du Maroussem, "Ebéniste parisien de haut luxe," *Les Ouvriers des deux mondes*, 2ᵉ série, IV (1895), 53–100; and his "Charpentier indépendant de Paris," ibid., III (1892), 325–368.

60. Gérard Jacquemet, "Belleville au XIXᵉ siècle. Du Faubourg à la ville" (Doctorat d'Etat, Université de Paris-IV, 1979), p. 1,312.

61. Ibid., p. 707.

62. Peter Stearns, *Revolutionary Syndicalism and French Labor* (New Brunswick, N.J., 1971); Frederick Ridley, *Revolutionary Syndicalism in France* (Cambridge, 1970).

63. Jacques Caroux-Destray (ed.), *Un Couple ouvrier traditionnel* (Paris, 1974), pp. 46–47.

64. One observer reported seeing many Breton women wearing their distinctive caps in Ivry well after World War I. See Pierre Lhande, *Le Christ dans la banlieue*.

Enquête sur la vie religieuse dans les milieux ouvriers de la banlieue de Paris (Paris, 1927), p. 79.

65. *L'Emancipation. Organe d'unité socialiste-révolutionnaire de la IIe circonscription de Saint-Denis*, no. 42 (27 décembre 1902).

66. Françoise Raison-Jourde, *La Colonie auvergnate à Paris au XIXe siècle* (Paris, 1976); Lenard Berlanstein, "The Formation of a Factory Proletariat: Rubber and Cable Workers in Bezons, France (1860–1914)," *Journal of Social History*, XV (1981), 163–186.

67. Alphonse Loyau, "La Semaine anglaise en France dans l'industrie mécanique de la Seine," *La Vie ouvrière. Revue syndicale bi-mensuelle*, IV (1912), 379.

68. A.P.P., B/a 894, report of 30 mars 1902.

69. According to police reports and union deliberations, the company union had 1,200 members whereas the independent group had only 300.

70. D. R. Watson, "The Nationalist Movement in Paris, 1900–1906," in *The Right in France*, ed. David Shapiro (Carbondale, Ill., 1969), p. 65.

71. See Chapter I.

72. Département de la Seine, *Etat des communes: Alfortville* (Montévrain, 1901), p. 10; L. Comby, "Alfortville. Commune de banlieue" (Doctorat de IIIe cycle, Université de Paris, 1966), p. 257; A.D.S., D 1 M² no. 803, liste électorale, 1902.

73. Henri Leyret, *En plein faubourg (moeurs ouvrières)* (Paris, 1895), pp. 85, 144–147.

74. René Michaud, *J'avais vingt ans. Un Jeune Ouvrier au début du siècle* (Paris, 1967), pp. 13–14.

75. On the other hand, workers were enraged by the indifference that bosses often displayed to their fate. See Leyret, *En plein faubourg*, p. 153.

76. *Le Travail. Organe socialiste et syndicale des travailleurs du canton d'Argenteuil*, no. 10 (1 juillet 1904). There was a total of 2,850 workers' votes here.

77. Francine Amaury, *Histoire du plus grand quotidien de la IIIe République: Le Petit Parisien, 1876–1944* (2 vols., 1972); Edward Tannenbaum, *1900: The Generation before the Great War* (Garden City, N.Y., 1976), pp. 228–232.

78. *Le Travail*, no. 14 (1 novembre 1904).

79. Leyret, *En plein faubourg*, p. 79.

80. For an insightful analysis of ideology and the working classes, see Yves Lequin, "Classe ouvrière et idéologie dans la région lyonnaise à la fin du XIXe siècle," *Le Mouvement social*, no. 69 (1969), pp. 3–20.

81. Moss, *Origins of Labor Movement*, emphasizes the enduring significance of trade organizations as the basis of working-class conceptions of emancipation.

82. Michelle Perrot, "Le Militant face à la grève dans la mine et la métallurgie au XIXe siècle," *Le Mouvement social*, no. 99 (1977), p. 77.

83. A.P.P., B/a 400, report of Saint-Denis.

84. A. Moutet, "Le Mouvement ouvrier à Paris du lendemain de la Commune au premier congrès syndical en 1876," *Le Mouvement social*, no. 58 (1967), pp. 3–39.

85. Madeleine Rebérioux, "Le Socialisme français de 1871 à 1914," in *Histoire générale du socialisme*, ed. Jacques Droz (4 vols., Paris, 1974), II, 139. On the national level, however, this period did not stand out as one of rising social demands. See Edward Shorter and Charles Tilly, *Strikes in France, 1830–1968* (Cambridge, 1974), chap. 5.

86. Before the publication of official strike statistics, one must rely on the rich records of the prefecture, A.P.P., B/a 168–182. That these records were more or less complete is confirmed by comparing them with a second list of strikes, A.N., F¹² 4663, Grèves et coalitions, 1880–1889.

87. A.P.P., B/a 177, Dossier: Ouvriers galochiers (juillet 1878).

88. Ibid., Dossier: Mécaniciens.

89. Michelle Perrot, *Les Ouvriers en grève. France, 1871–1890* (2 vols., Paris, 1974), II, 412–413, 424–426.

90. A.P.P., B/a 168, Dossier: Menuisiers de meuble sculpté.

91. Ibid., B/a 175, Dossier: Selliers de l'équipement militaire.

92. Ibid., B/a 172, Dossier: Ouvriers de la raffinerie du sucre.

93. For the basic data on strikes, I have used the information published in Ministère du commerce. Office du travail, *Statistique des grèves et des recours à la conciliation et à l'arbitrage, 1898–1902* (Paris, 1899–1903).

94. For the short-term economic fluctuations, see Jacques Rougerie, "Remarques sur l'histoire des salaires à Paris au XIXᵉ siècle," *Le Mouvement social*, no. 63 (1968), pp. 106–107.

95. One of the premier students of nineteenth-century workers, Michelle Perrot, raises, but does not develop, the theme of a crisis of factory discipline in her contribution to Jean Bouvier et al., *Histoire économique et sociale de la France, Tome IV: L'Ere industrielle et la société d'aujourd'hui* (Paris, 1979), p. 481.

96. According to *L'Emancipation*, no. 46 (24 janvier 1903), the director of the Jettings and Jonas plant in Saint-Denis carried a revolver in his vest pocket.

97. See Chapter III.

98. A.P.P., B/a 400, report of La Gare.

99. Ibid, B/a 182, Dossier: Usine Malétra.

100. Ibid., B/a 175, Dossier: Forges d'Alfortville.

101. Shorter and Tilly, *Strikes in France*, p. 120; Patrick Fridenson, "Les Premiers ouvriers français de l'automobile (1890–1914)," *Sociologie du travail*, XXI (1979), 318–319.

102. A.P.P., B/a 1383, Dossier: Compagnie Anglo-Française d'automobiles.

103. Ibid., B/a 1383, Dossier: Dion-Bouton, reports of 30 septembre 1899, 2 octobre 1899, and various press clippings.

104. Ibid., Dossier: Clément.

105. Ibid., Dossier: Gardner-Serpollet.

106. Ibid., Dossier: Dion-Bouton.

107. Ibid., B/a 1384, Dossier: Darracq.

108. Ibid., Dossier: Mors.

109. Ibid., Dossier: Richard.

110. Ibid., Dossier: La Minerve.

111. Ibid., report of 8 mars 1904.

112. Ibid., Dossiers: Corré (1905), Gardner-Serpollet, Clément (1905), Roche (1905), Mors (1906).

113. Office du travail, *Statistique des grèves, 1898*, p. 83.

114. A.P.P., B/a 1389, Dossier: Compagnie générale du cycle.

115. Ibid., B/a 1383, Dossier: Charles.

116. Ibid., Dossiers: Gouin, Bariquand et Marre.

117. Office du travail, *Statistique des grèves, 1901*. These workers have been described by Maire-Hélène Zylberberg-Hacquard, "Les Ouvrières d'Etat (tabac et allumettes) dans les dernières années du XIXᵉ siècle," *Le Mouvement social*, no. 105 (1978), pp. 87–107.

118. A.P.P., B/a 400, reports of quartier des Halles, Clichy.

119. Ibid., B/a 895, Dossier: Dupont.

120. Ibid., B/a 1368, Dossiers: Hattat, Coruble.

121. *Le Travail*, no. 14 (1 juin 1902); no. 17 (1 février 1905); no. 50 (5 février 1910).

122. A.M. Argenteuil, 30 F; *Le Travail*, no. 46 (5 octobre 1909). At the Industrial Embossing Company in Saint-Denis, workers struck because the foreman was never

polite to them. Moreover, he was a Belgian. See *L'Emancipation*, no. 66 (13 juin 1903).

123. A.P.P., B/a 1384, Dossier: Maison Corre, report of 11 avril 1905.

124. Ibid., B/a 1384, Dossier: Roche.

125. Ibid., Dossier: Gardner-Serpollet (1905).

126. Ibid., Dossier: Mors (1906), report of 11 avril 1906.

127. Ibid., Dossier: Mors (1903), report of 2 février 1903.

128. Ibid., B/a 895, Dossier: Dupont, report of 11 mars 1903; B/a 1367, Dossier: Hattat, report of 3 juin 1902.

129. Ibid., B/a 1383, Dossier: Dion-Bouton, report of 5 octobre 1899. Workers believed that an antirepublican bond was one reason why Dion would not fire Pivot.

130. For the role of union organizers, see ibid., Dossier: Panhard-Levassor, report of 6 juillet 1899.

131. The coming of the Exposition inspired an attempted general strike in the building trades and among railroad workers. See Office du travail, *Statistique des grèves, 1898*, pp. 252–271.

132. François Crouzet ("French Economic Growth in the Nineteenth Century Reconsidered," *History*, LIX [1974], p. 171) notes the "remarkable" productivity gains between 1896 and 1913; U.S. Department of Commerce and Labor, *Machine-Tool Trade in Germany, France, Switzerland, Italy, and the United Kingdom* (Washington, D.C., 1909), pp. 97–161.

133. A.P.P., B/a 1384, Dossiers: Darracq (1905), Corré, Renault.

134. Ibid., Dossier: Richard.

135. Ibid., Dossier: Panhard-Levassor.

136. Ibid., B/a 901, reports of 16 mai 1872, 28 décembre 1876, 17 janvier 1877; B/a 1575, report of 22 février 1877.

137. Ibid., B/a 1384, Dossier: Panhard-Levassor.

138. Ibid., Dossier: Clément (1905).

139. Ibid., Dossier: Charles, report of 8 décembre 1899.

140. Ibid., Dossier: Gouin.

141. Ibid., Dossier: Dion-Bouton.

142. Ibid., B/a 895, Dossier: Dupont, report of 11 novembre 1903. The well-paid *conducteurs* did not assume a leading role in the strike.

143. Ibid., B/a 1389, Dossier: Compagnie générale du cycle. On the advanced features of the plant, see *L'Industrie vélocipédique. Organe des fabricants, mécaniciens, etc.* (janvier 1891), pp. 7–8.

144. Ibid., Dossiers: Dion-Bouton, Clément.

145. Jacques Valdour, *Ateliers et taudis de la banlieue de Paris* (Paris, 1923), p. 108.

146. For the failure of worker-control struggles to have a political impact in one Canadian city, see Bryan Palmer, *A Culture of Conflict. Skilled Workers and Industrial Capitalism in Hamilton, Ontario, 1860–1914* (Montreal, 1979), p. 243.

147. A.M. Puteaux, K. II. 179.

148. On unionization, see Christian Gras, "La Fédération des Métaux en 1913–1914 et l'évolution du syndicalisme révolutionnaire français," *Le Mouvement social*, no. 77 (1971), p. 96.

149. Perrot in Bouvier, *Histoire économique et sociale*, pp. 478–479; Aimée Moutet, "Les Origines du système de Taylor en France. Le Point de vue patronal (1907–1914)," *Le Mouvement social*, no. 93 (1975), 15–49; Gary Cross, "Redefining Workers' Control: Rationalization, Labor Time, and Union Politics in France, 1900–1928," in *Work, Community, and Power: The Experience of Labor in Europe and America, 1900–1925*, ed. James Cronin and Carmen Sarianni (Philadelphia, 1983), pp. 147–150; Maurice Lévy-Leboyer, "Innovation and Business Strategies in Nine-

teenth- and Twentieth-Century France," in *Enterprise and Entrepreneurs in Nineteenth- and Twentieth-Century France*, ed. Edward Carter, Robert Forster, and Joseph Moody (Baltimore, 1976), pp. 116–117. Lévy-Leboyer makes the Renault incident the core of his discussion of prewar managerial innovation.

150. Office du travail, *Statistique des grèves, 1902*, p. 147.

151. A.P.P., B/a 1372, Dossier: Maison Nelson.

152. Office du travail, *Statistique des grèves, 1897*, p. 23.

153. Ibid., *1910*, p. 307.

154. Arthur Fraysse, *Le Marchandage dans l'industrie du bâtiment* (Paris, 1911), p. 146.

155. Strikes against internal subcontracting were especially vigorous at the Pleyel Piano Company in Saint-Denis. See *L'Emancipation*, no. 465 (26 novembre 1910) and no. 467 (10 décembre 1910).

156. A.P.P., B/a 1389, Dossiers: Cathala, Kessler et Billard, Romanetz, Junger, Kastor, and others.

157. Ibid., B/a 1359, Dossier: Charpentiers en fer; Office du travail, *Statistique des grèves, 1910*, pp. 212–220. There was also a sizable effort by copper molders to supress piece rates in 1904–1905.

158. Ibid, B/a 1387, Dossiers: Huchet, Débard (report of 31 mai 1904), Robert; B/a 1389, Dossiers: Cathala, Romanetz.

159. See Chapter IV.

160. Maurice Dommanget, *Histoire du premier mai* (Paris, 1972), p. 236.

161. A.P.P., B/a 1384, Dossier: Grève générale des mécaniciens (1906); *L'Humanité. Journal socialiste quotidien*, no. 753 (10 mai 1906), p. 3 places the number of mechanics on strike at 28,000. Confusion results from the fact that several thousand workers were locked out by their employers. See also no. 746 (3 mai 1906), p. 2; no. 749 (6 mai 1906), p. 1, and other issues in May 1906.

162. A.P.P., B/a 1384, Dossier: Grève générale, report of 10 mai 1906.

163. *L'Humanité*, no. 747 (4 mai 1906), p. 2.

164. A.P.P., B/a 1372, Dossier: Grève générale; B/a 1358, Dossier: Grève générale.

165. Ibid., report of 2 juin 1906. Among tailors, however, only the skilled *pompiers* participated. See B/a 1394, Dossier: Grève générale, report of 14 mai 1906.

166. Ibid., report of 7 mai 1906. For a description of mechanized furniture production, see Jacques Valdour, *Le Faubourg. Observations vécues* (Paris, 1925), pp. 3–19.

167. Ibid., B/a 1384, Dossier: Grève générale des mécaniciens; B/a 1372, Dossier: Grève générale. Also, BHVP, série 119, Dossier: Heures du travail, for brochures concerning the demands of the building workers.

168. *L'Humanité*, no. 746 (3 mai 1906), p. 2; Loyau, "La Semaine anglaise."

169. A.P.P., B/a 1372, Dossier: Grève générale; B/a 1358, Dossier: Grève générale des imprimeurs.

170. Etienne Riché, *La situation des ouvriers dans l'industrie automobile* (Paris, 1909), p. 51; Loyau, "La Semaine anglaise," pp. 373–374.

171. *L'Humanité*, no. 748 (10 juin 1906), p. 1; A.P.P., B/a 1372, report of 12 juillet 1906.

172. Office du travail, *Statistique des grèves, 1907*, pp. 192–238.

173. Ibid., *1910*, pp. 232–244.

174. A.P.P., B/a 1404.

175. Léon de Seilhac, *Les Grèves de l'année (1909–1910)* (Paris, 1911), pp. 211–226; François Caron, *Histoire de l'exploitation d'un grand réseau. La Compagnie du chemin de fer du Nord, 1846–1937* (Paris, 1973), pp. 361–362, 589; Margot Stein, "The Meaning of Skill: The Case of the French Engine Drivers, 1837–1917," *Politics*

and Society, VIII (1979), 399–427. The classification of this strike is all the more difficult in that railroad workers were not "classic" service workers; as Stein points out, they often had the same training and background as mechanics.

176. Office du travail, *Statistique des grèves, 1907*, pp. 48–49.

177. A.P.P., B/a 1357.

178. Ministère du commerce, Office du travail, *Enquête sur le placement des employés, ouvriers, et domestiques à Paris* (Paris, 1909).

179. *L'Humanité*, nos. 747–750 (4–7 mai 1906). The peaks of protest for commercial workers came in 1903 and 1907. See Linda Bishop Young, "Mobilizing Food-, Restaurant, and Café Workers in Paris: A Case Study of Direct Action Syndicalism, 1900–1914" (Ph.D. diss., New York University, 1981), pp. 103–141.

180. *L'Emancipation*, no. 30 (4 octobre 1902).

181. Ibid., no. 13 (7 juin 1902).

182. Barberet, *Le Travail en France*, IV, 454. "It is true. Most of us display a childish scorn in regard to manual workers," proclaimed the organ of one Socialist union. See *Le Journal des employés. Organe officiel des associations syndicales d'employés de toutes catégories*, no. 42 (1–15 février 1900), p. 3.

183. A.P.P., B/a 901, reports of 25 avril 1874 and 8 novembre 1876. The animosity persisted even though workers and clerks shared grievances about overtime pay. See the reports of 17 mai and 20 décembre 1876.

184. Ibid., B/a 1372, Dossier: Maison Eymonaud.

185. Ibid., B/a 1383, Dossier: Gardner-Serpollet.

186. Ibid., B/a 1422, Dossier: Union fraternelle des employés, report of 12 avril 1885.

187. A.D.S., V 8 O¹ no. 149, letter from union to director of 14 mars 1894.

188. Ibid., V 8 O¹ no. 153, Dossier: Ateliers et magasins du service extérieur.

189. I have drawn upon the large collection of letters to the director of the Parisian Gas Company. Ibid., V 8 O¹ no. 150.

190. Philip Nord, "Le Mouvement des petits commerçants et la politique en France de 1888 à 1914," *Le Mouvement social*, no. 114 (1981), pp. 35–55.

191. See Chapter III.

192. A.P.P., B/a 152. Dossier: Chambre syndicale des employés, reports of 8 août 1880, 2 octobre 1880, 8 janvier 1881. For a survey of unionizing activity among clerks, see Artaud, *La Question de l'employé en France* (Paris, 1909), pp. 123–146.

193. Auguste Besse, *L'Employé de commerce et d'industrie* (Lyons, 1901), p. 35.

194. A.D.S., D 3 M² no. 7.

195. Ibid.

196. A.P.P., B/a 152, Dossier: Chambre syndicale des employés, report of 17 avril 1907.

197. A.D.S., D 3 M² no. 7.

198. Nord, "Le Mouvement des petits commerçants."

199. A.P.P., B/a 1523, report of 12 octobre 1907.

200. These figures are derived from the registers of municipal deliberations in each commune.

201. A.M. Ivry, K-27.

202. Ibid., K-137. Coutant received 54 percent of the vote in Ivry-Centre, 54.4 percent in Petit-Ivry, and 60 percent in Ivry-Port.

203. Madeleine Rebérioux, *La République radicale? 1898–1914* (Paris, 1975), p. 14.

204. *Le Journal des employés de chemins de fer*, no. 1 (6 janvier 1883), p. 1; no. 13 (31 mars 1883), p. 1; no. 19 (12 mai 1883), p. 1. *L'Avenir des employés de chemins de fer*, no. 117 (22 avril 1893), p. 1.

205. L. Marcillon, *Trente Ans de vie de grands magasins* (Nice, 1924), pp. 55–60. See also, L. O'Followell and H. Goudal, *Hygiène des employés de commerce et d'administration* (Paris, 1901).

206. *Le Journal des employés*, no. 38 (3 avril 1899), p. 1.

207. Artaud, *La Question de l'employé*, p. 191.

208. A.D.S., V 8 0¹ no. 149, clipping from *L'Echo du Gaz*.

209. Jeanne Gaillard, *Paris, la ville , 1852–1970* (Paris, 1977). pp. 550–553.

210. *L'Emancipation*, no. 13 (7 juin 1902) and no. 14 (14 juin 1902). There was also violence over the issue of Sunday closings.

211. A.P.P., B/a 152, report of 12 octobre 1907.

212. Ibid.

213. Ibid., B/a 152, report of 12 janvier 1906.

214. *L'Emancipation*, no. 408 (6 novembre 1909).

215. A.P.P., B/a 152, report of 13 juin 1906 for the attempt at the Bazar de l'Hôtel de ville; B/a 1424, report of 2 juin 1901 for the Parisian Gas Company.

216. Ibid., B/a 894, report of 5 mars 1907.

217. M. Launay, "Le Syndicat des employés du commerce et de l'industrie de 1887 à 1914," *Le Mouvement social*, no. 68 (1969), p. 49.

218. A.P.P., B/a 882, Dossier: Bazar de l'Hôtel de Ville.

219. The police reports present a very confusing picture of the particpation of the personnel from the store, so I have not been able to draw firm conclusions about this aspect of the strike.

220. A.P.P., B/a 1390–1392. My notions of the stike have been refined by consulting the excellent dissertation by Susan Bachrach, "The Feminization of the French Postal Service, 1750–1914" (Ph.D. diss., University of Wisconsin-Madison, 1981), chap. 7.

221. A.P.P., B/a 1383, Dossier: Dufayel.

222. Ibid., Dossier: Employés des maisons de nouveautés.

223. Ibid., Dossier: Les Galeries Lafayette.

224. *L'Humanité*, no. 854 (16 octobre 1907), p. 2.

225. For the case of the Parisian Gas Company, see A.P.P., B/a 1424, report of 5 juin 1903 and A.D.S., V 8 0¹, no. 159, Dossier: Grève de 1899.

226. A.P.P., B/a 1424. See the proceedings of the union meetings.

Chapter VI

1. The phrase is taken from Edward R. Tannenbaum, *1900. The Generation before the Great War* (Garden City, N.Y., 1976), chap. 1. Tannenbaum treats a theme that is echoed in such distinguished works as Joan Scott, *The Glassworkers of Carmaux* (Cambridge, Mass., 1974) and Eugen Weber, *Peasants into Frenchmen: The Modernization of Rural France, 1870–1914* (Stanford, 1976).

2. Gary Cross argues that leaders of organized labor (in the CGT) came to accept scientific management by the end of the war as the inevitable future for labor, and these leaders directed the rank and file to seek compensations in higher wages and more leisure. Cross does not believe that the mass of workers shared their new outlook, however. See his article, "Redefining Workers' Control: Rationalization, Labor Time, and Union Politics in France, 1900–1928," in *Work, Community, and Power*, ed. James Cronin and Carmen Sirianni (Philadelphia, 1983), pp. 143–172.

Bibliography

I. Primary Sources

A. *Manuscripts*

1. *Archives nationales*
   F^{12} 2337–2338, L'Industrie à Paris en 1848.
   F^{12} 4663, Grèves et coalitions.
   F^{17} 10263–10267, Inspection des écoles, Paris et banlieue.
   F^{22} 237, Grèves, Paris et banlieue (1907).
   F^{22} 504, Conditions de travail, Magasins de commerce (1889–1915).
   F^{22} 527, Lutte contre la tuberculose (1900–1920).
   F^{22} 571, Rapports sur divers industries.
   F^{22} 574, Industries des métaux ordinaires.

2. *Archives départementales de la Seine et de la Ville de Paris*
   D 1 M^2, Listes électorales.
   D 1 M^8, Listes nominatives.
   D 1 M^8 no. 2, Résultats du recensement de 1886.
   D 1 M^8 no. 6, Résultats du recensement de 1891.
   D 2 M^2, Elections législatives.
   D 3 M^2, Elections législatives.
   D R^1, Recrutement militaire (1866–1907).
   D 11 U^1, Justice de paix, VIe Arrondissement.
   D 4 U^1, Justice de paix, I^e Arrondissement.
   D 2 U^{10}, Conseil de prud'hommes, Commerce (1910).
   V D^6 128, 129, 218, 342, 343, 363, 364, 475, 563, 678, 1490, 1790, 2107, 2359, 2543, Fonds de l'Orphelinat du Prince Impérial.
   V D^6 647, Pétition des ouvriers ébénistes.
   V D^6 734–735, Bureau de placement, 1890–1903.
   V D^6 2030–2031, Ecoles primaires, XIe Arrondissement.
   V D^6 2082, Rapport sur l'insalubrité. Cité Doré.
   V D^6 2112, Statistiques des industries et des salaires (XVe Arrondissement).
   V D^6 1246, Comité de patronage des apprentis.
   V D^6 1506, Enfants dans l'industrie (VIIe Arrondissement).
   V D^6 21, 189, 486, 619, 1261, 1415, 1796, 1925, 2677, Bourses des apprentis municipaux.
   V 4 E, Etat civil (to 1869).
   V F^2 19, Enquête sur l'industrie textile.
   V K^2, cartons 2–25, Personnel de la Préfecture (dossiers).
   V 8 0^1, Fonds de la Compagnie Parisienne de l'éclairage et du chauffage par le gaz.
   V bis Q^2, Fonds de l'Orphelinat du Prince Impérial.

V bis 3 Q⁶, Accidents du travail (IIIᵉ Arrondissement).
V bis 19 Q⁶ Accidents du travail (XIXᵉ Arrondissement).

3. *Archives de la Préfecture de Police*
    B/a 122, Banquet des maires socialistes.
    B/a 152–153, Syndicats.
    B/a 167–184, Grèves (classified by trade).
    B/a 199–201, Socialisme en France.
    B/a 213, Elections de 1902.
    B/a 214, Elections de 1906.
    B/a 237, Elections de 1906 (Arrondissement de Saint-Denis).
    B/a 486, Enquête sur les loyers à Paris.
    B/a 882, Bazar de l'Hôtel de Ville.
    B/a 890, Compagnie Parisienne du Gaz.
    B/a 894, Syndicat des ouvriers et employés du Métropolitain.
    B/a 895, Grève des ouvriers lithographes.
    B/a 901, Usine Cail.
    B/a 914, Ville de Saint-Denis, 1887–1909.
    B/a 916, Puteaux, 1871–1899.
    B/a 1351–1420, Grèves (classified by industry).
    B/a 1421–1438, Syndicats (classified by industry).
    B/a 1477, Socialisme à Ivry, Gentilly.
    B/a 1575, Saint-Ouen, 1871–1894.
    DB 282, Les Apaches.

4. *Archives municipales d'Argenteuil*
    D, Délibérations municipales, 1880–1914.
    E, Etat civil, 1871–1914.
    1 F³, Mouvement de la population, 1871–1914.
    6 F, Statistiques industrielles.
    20 F², Loyers; crise du logement.
    25 F¹, Repos hebdomadaire.
    27 F³, Syndicat des ouvriers du bâtiment.
    27 F¹³, Syndicat des métallurgistes.
    29 F, Chômage.
    30 F, Grèves.
    31 F, Apprentissage.
    11 I, Cinéma, jeux.
    37 I, Grèves et manifestations.
    61 I, Bains publics.
    62 I¹, Fosses d'aisance; vidanges.
    65 I³, Dossiers des principales usines.
    71 I, Service de la désinfection.
    2 K⁶, Elections municipales.
    10 O, Eaux.
    8 O¹, Egouts.
    27 Q, Habitations à bon marché.
    36 Q, Accidents du travail.

39 Q, Assistance aux vieillards.
32 R, Sociétés sportives.

5. *Archives municipales de Bezons* (documents unclassified)
   Commission de salubrité, 1865–1890.
   Délibérations du bureau de bienfaisance, 1860–1914.
   Délibérations municipales, 1865–1914.
   Etat civil, 1860–1914.
   Maîtrise cadastrale.
   Recensements, 1886, 1901, 1911.
   Registres des impôts.

6. *Archives municipales d'Ivry-sur-Seine*
   D 47–87, Délibérations municipales, 1884–1912.
   E, Etat civil, 1866–1914.
   F-7, -14, Mouvement de la population, 1871–1906.
   F-18, Recensements, 1876–1911.
   I-95, Débits de boisson, 1894–1898.
   K-27, Election législative, 1893.
   K-137, Election législative, 1898.
   K-160, Liste électorale, 1900.

7. *Archives municipales de Puteaux*
   D, I. 10., Délibérations municipales, 1882–1914.
   F, I. 36., Recensement.
   F, VII. 5., Enquête sur les conditions du travail; Chambres
     syndicales.
   I, 1. 118., Débits de boisson.
   I, 127^1, Enterrement.
   I, V. 162., Etablissements insalubres.
   I, I. 128. III., Secours de chômage.
   I, III. 149., Justice de paix.
   I, 145. I., Associations; réunions révolutionnaires.
   K, I. 174., Elections législatives.
   K, II. 179., Employés d'octroi.
   R, II. 281., Casino de Puteaux.

8. *Archives municipales de Saint-Denis* (temporary classifica-
   tion)
   E, Etat civil, 1860–1910.
   F, 3/4/3/2, Statistiques industrielles.
   F, 3/5/2/1, Chômage.
   F, 3/5/3/1, Recensements, 1886–1911.
   F, 3/9/1/1, Statistiques diverses; statistique sur le logement.
   F, 3/9/1/3, Mouvement de la population, 1871–1906; plaintes
     sur le manque d'eau; chômage dans les usines de caout-
     chouc, 1896.
   F, 4/6/2/4, Travail des enfants.
   J, 3/4/3/5, Registre des associations de Saint-Denis.

J, 3/5/5/3, Réunions publiques, 1880–1892; hygiène: enquêtes et correspondance.

J, 3/5/5/4, Demandes d'autorisation de spectacles, 1900–1905.

J, 3/8/5/2, Demandes d'autorisation de bals et de concerts, 1884–1898; dispensaire anti-tuberculaire; sociétés sportives.

J, 3/8/5/3, Fêtes diverses, 1881–1912.

J, 3/8/5/4, Logements insalubres.

J, 3/8/6/1, Fêtes.

J, 3/11/3/3, Rapports sur les inondations.

J, 3/11/4/2, Protection des enfants en bas âge.

J, 5/2/1/7, Concerts, 1907–1912; bains publics; prévention des épidémies.

Q, 3/8/1/3, Stérilisation du lait.

Q, 3/11/3/2, Commission de secours, 1878–1914; secours aux indigents; dispensaire anti-tuberculaire, 1903–1938.

Q, 3/11/3/3, Retraite ouvrière, 1911.

Q, 3/11/4/3, Secours aux chômeurs; soupes populaires.

Q, 3/11/5/4, Assistance aux chômeurs.

Q, 3/11/6/2, Service médicale de nuit.

R, 3/8/4/1, Théâtre, 1830–1901.

R, 3/8/4/4, Bibliothèque municipale.

R, 3/9/6/4, Ecoles primaires: Fréquentations, 1900–1906; Théâtre de Saint-Denis; cantine scolaire.

R, 3/11/7/4, Commission scolaire: Mesures disciplinaires; sociétés sportives.

R, 3/11/7/6, Ecole de demi-temps pour les enfants dans les manufactures.

9.   *Archives municipales de Saint-Ouen* (unclassfied)
Délibérations municipales, 1876–1914.
Elections cantonales.
Elections législatives.
Elections municipales, 1876–1914.
Etat civil, 1860–1910.
Hospice et assistance.
Hygiène et salubrité, 1864–1905.
Mouvement de la population.
Statistiques industrielles.

10.   *Mairie du XXe Arrondissement*
Actes de mariage, 1902–1903.

11.   *Mairie du XVIIIe Arrondissement*
Actes de mariage, 1902–1904.

B.   Printed Sources

1.   *Newspaper-Clipping Collections*
Bibliothèque historique de la ville de Paris:
Série 80, Economie, domestique, ménage.
Série 119, Condition des ouvriers.

2. Newspapers
    La Banlieue socialiste. Organe des groupes du Parti ouvrier socialiste révolutionnaire. 1896–1900.
    Le Courrier socialiste. Organe des groupes et syndicats ouvriers de la circonscription Asnière-Gennevilliers-Saint-Ouen-Epinay-Ile-Saint-Denis. 1903–1913.
    L'Echo d'Argenteuil. Journal Radical-Socialiste du canton. 1901–1912.
    L'Emancipation. Organe d'unité socialiste-révolutionnaire de la IIe circonscription de Saint-Denis. 1902–1913.
    L'Employé. Organe du syndicat des employés du commerce et de l'industrie. 1901–1914.
    L'Extra-Muro. Journal de la banlieue. 1830–1891.
    L'Humanité. Journal socialiste quotidien. 1904–1914.
    L'Industrie progressive. 1898–1903.
    L'Industrie vélocipédique. Organe des fabricants, mécaniciens, etc. 1891–1894.
    Le Journal des Employés. Organe officiel des associations syndicales d'employés de toutes catégories. 1897–1900.
    Le Journal des employés de chemins de fer. 1883–1885.
    Le Journal illustré des grands magasins Dufayel. 1892.
    Le Réveil social. Organe du parti socialiste de l'arrondissement de Sceaux. 1903–1904.
    Le Socialiste de Levallois-Clichy. Organe des revendications prolétariennes. 1905–1906.
    Le Travail. Organe socialiste et syndicale des travailleurs du canton d'Argenteuil. 1901–1912.

3. Official Publications and Reports
    Administration générale de l'assistance publique de Paris. *Rapport à Monsieur le Préfet de la Seine sur le Service des enfants moralement abandonnés, 1880–1889.* 10 vols. Montévrain, 1881–1990.
    L'Amélioration du logement ouvrier. Enquête sur le logement des familles nombreuses à Paris. Paris, 1912.
    L'Assemblée nationale. *Procès-verbal de la Commission chargée de faire une enquête sur la situation des ouvriers de l'industrie et de l'agriculture en France et de présenter un premier rapport sur la crise industrielle à Paris.* Paris, 1884.
    Chambre de commerce de Paris. *Statistique de l'industrie à Paris résultant de l'enquête faite par la Chambre de commerce pour les années 1847–48.* Paris, 1851.
    ————. *Statistique de l'industrie à Paris résultant de l'enquête faite par la Chambre de commerce pour l'année 1860.* Paris, 1864.
    Conseil d'hygiène publique et de salubrité. *Rapport général à Monsieur le Préfet de Police sur les travaux des commissions d'hygiène des arrondissements du département de la Seine, 1878–1904.* 25 vols. Paris, 1880–1905.

Conseil municipal de Paris. *Rapport sur le régime des égouts et sur les améliorations à réaliser*. Paris, 1914.

Conseil supérieur du travail. *Apprentissage. Rapport de Monsieur Briat au nom de la commission permanente. Documents et enquête*. Paris, 1902.

De la situation légale des ouvriers bijoutiers travaillant dans leur domicile. Paris, 1842.

Délégation française du ministère de l'instruction publique et des beaux-arts. *Deuxième congrès international de l'enseignement du dessin tenu à Berne du mardi 2 au samedi 6 août 1904*. Paris and Berne, 1904.

Département de la Seine. *Etats des communes. Notices historiques et renseignements administratifs*. Montévrain, 1900–1905.

Gréard, Octave. *L'Enseignement primaire à Paris et dans le département de la Seine de 1867 à 1877*. Paris, 1878.

Loyau, Alphonse. "La Semaine anglaise en France dans l'industrie mécanique de la Seine." *La Vie ouvrière. Revue syndicale bi-mensuelle*, IV (1912), 369–385.

Ministère de l'instruction publique et des beaux-arts. *Commission d'enquête sur la situation des ouvriers et des industries d'art*. Paris, 1884.

Ministère de l'intérieur. *Enquête de la Commission extra-parlementaire des associations ouvrières*. 2 vols. Paris, 1883.

————. *Recueil des travaux de la Commission permanente de préservation contre la tuberculose*. 3 vols. Paris, 1905.

————. *Recueil des travaux de la Commission permanente de préservation contre la tuberculose*. 2 vols. Melun, 1909.

Ministère du commerce. Office du travail. *Les Associations professionnelles ouvrières* 4 vols. Paris, 1894–1904.

————. *Les Bureaux municipaux de placement à Paris en 1909*. Paris, 1910.

————. *Enquête sur le placement des employés, ouvriers, et domestiques à Paris*. Paris, 1909.

————. *Enquête sur le travail à domicile dans l'industrie de la chaussure*. Paris, 1914.

————. *Enquête sur le travail à domicile dans l'industrie de la fleur artificielle*. Paris, 1913.

————. *Enquête sur le travail à domicile dans l'industrie de la lingerie*. 5 vols. Paris, 1907–1911.

————. *L'Industrie du chiffon à Paris*. Paris, 1903.

————. *Note de l'Office du travail sur le marchandage*. Paris, 1898.

————. *La Petite Industrie (salaires et durée du travail)*. 2 vols. Paris, 1893–1896.

————. *Le Placement des employés, ouvriers, et domestiques en France. Son histoire—son état actuel*. Paris, 1893.

————. *Rapport sur l'apprentissage dans l'imprimerie, 1899–1901.* Paris, 1902.

————. *Rapport sur l'apprentissage dans l'industrie de l'horlogerie.* Paris, 1911.

————. *Rapport sur l'apprentissage dans les industries de l'ameublement.* Paris, 1905.

————. *Recueil de documents sur les accidents du travail. Numéro 40. Statistique des accidents du travail.* Paris, 1910.

————. *Répartition des salaires du personnel ouvrier dans les manufactures d'état et les compagnies de chemin de fer.* Paris, 1896.

————. *Salaires et durée du travail dans l'industrie française (grande et moyenne industrie).* 4 vols. Paris, 1893–1897.

————. *Seconde enquête sur le placement des employés, des ouvriers, et des domestiques.* Paris, 1901.

————. *Statistique des grèves et des recours à la conciliation et à l'arbitrage, 1893–1914.* 21 vols. Paris, 1894–1915.

Ministère du travail et de la prévoyance sociale. *Sociétés de secours mutuels du département de la Seine.* Melun, 1907.

Pradinaud, François, and Lucien Devillers. *Délégation ouvrière de Saint-Denis à l'Exposition internationale et coloniale de Lyon.* Saint-Denis, 1896.

Préfecture de la Seine. *Annuaire statistique de la ville de Paris.* 32 vols. Paris, 1882–1914.

————. *Rapport sur les recherches effectuées au bureau du casier sanitaire pendant l'année 1911 relative à la répartition de la tuberculose dans les maisons de Paris.* Paris, 1912.

Rapport des délégués de la bijouterie à l'Exposition universelle de Paris. Paris, 1879.

Rapport des délégués de l'industrie des cuirs et peaux du département de la Seine. Paris, 1867.

Rapport des délégués ouvriers dans l'orfèvrerie à l'Exposition universelle de Paris. Paris, 1879.

Société du dispensaire gratuit de Pantin-Aubervilliers pour les enfants malades indigents. Pantin, 1989.

Statistique générale de la France. *Résultats généraux du dénombrement de 1866.* Strasbourg, 1869.

————. *Résultats statistiques du recensement général de la population effectué le 4 mars 1906.* 2 vols. Paris, 1909.

————. *Résultats statistiques du recensement général de la population effectué le 5 mars 1911.* 2 vols. Paris, 1911.

————. *Salaires et coût de l'existence à diverses époques, jusqu'en 1910.* Paris, 1911.

————. *Statistique des familles en 1906.* Paris, 1912.

U.S. Department of Commerce and Labor. *Machine-Tool Trade in Germany, France, Switzerland, Italy, and the United Kingdom.* Washington, 1909.

Ville de Saint-Ouen. *Association philotechnique pour l'instruction gratuite des adultes. Compte rendu.* Paris, 1886.

4. *Social Surveys, Memoirs, Social Commentaries, First-Hand Accounts*

About, A. "Travail d'usine." *Revue de métallurgie*, X (1913), 1147–1175.

Avalle, E. "Porteur d'eau de Paris." *Les Ouvriers des deux mondes*, 1ᵉ série, II (1858), 321–362.

Badier, A.-F. "Compositeur-typographe de Paris." *Les Ouvriers des deux mondes*, 1ᵉ série, IV (1862), 241–281.

Barbaud, Roger. *Manuel des candidats du surnumérariat des postes et télégraphes.* Paris, 1888.

Barberet, Jospeh. *Le Travail en France. Monographies professionnelles.* 7 vols. Paris, 1886–1890.

Benoist, Charles. *L'Organisation du travail.* 2 vols. Paris, 1905.

————. "Le Travail dans la grande industrie. II. La Métallurgie." *Revue des deux mondes*, XII (1902), 586–614; XV (1903), 637–661.

Blasquez, Adelaide (ed.). *Gaston Lucas, serrurier. Chronique de l'anti-héros.* Paris, 1976.

Bonnet, René. *A l'Ecole de la vie.* Paris, 1945.

————. *Petite histoire de la charpenterie et d'une charpente.* Paris, 1960.

Bottin. *Annuaire du commerce Didot-Bottin.* 36 vols. Paris, 1875–1911.

Bouvier, Jeanne. *Mes Mémoires, ou 59 années d'activité industrielle, sociale, et intellectuelle d'une ouvrière.* Poitiers, 1936.

Champly, René. *Comment on devient tourneur sur métaux.* Paris, 1913.

Clayton, Louisa. *The Story of Miss de Broen's Mission at Belleville, Paris.* 4th ed. London, 1886.

Courgey, Docteur Stéphane. *Recherches et classement des anormaux. Enquête sur les enfants des écoles de la ville d'Ivry-sur-Seine.* Leipzig, 1908.

Courteille, M., and J. Gautier. "Manoeuvre à famille nombreuse de Paris." *Les Ouvriers des deux mondes*, 1ᵉ série, III (1861), 373–412.

Destray-Caroux, Jacques (ed.). *Un Couple ouvrier traditionnel.* Paris, 1974.

————. *La Vie d'une famille ouvrière. Autobiographies.* Paris, 1971.

Doublet, Victor. *Petit Dictionnaire des professions; ou Guide des familles pour les diriger dans le choix d'un état pour leurs enfants.* Paris, 1860.

Du Maroussem, Pierre. "Charpentier indépendant de Paris." *Les Ouvriers des deux mondes*, 2ᵉ série, III (1892), 325–368.

――――――. "Ebéniste parisien de haut luxe." *Les Ouvriers des deux mondes*, 2ᵉ série, IV (1895), 53–100.

――――――. "Ouvrière en cartonnage d'une fabrique collective de jouets parisiens." *Les Ouvriers des deux mondes*, 2ᵉ série, V (1899), 173–224.

Dumay, Jean-Baptiste. *Mémoire d'un militant ouvrier du Creusot (1841–1901)*. Grenoble, 1976.

Du Mesnil, Octave. *Fragment d'une enquête dans le quartier des Gobelins*. Paris, 1895.

――――――, and Charles Mangenot. *Enquête sur les logements, professions, salaires, et budgets (loyers inférieurs à 400 francs)*. Paris, 1899.

Fanjung, Nicolas. "Précis d'une monographie du serrurier poseur de persiennes en fer de Paris." *Les Ouvriers des deux mondes*, 2ᵉ série, V (1899), 347–364.

――――――. "Serrurier-forgeron du quartier Picpus à Paris." *Les Ouvriers des deux mondes*, 2ᵉ série, V (1899), 317–346.

Focillon, Adolphe-Jean. "Tailleur d'habits de Paris." *Les Ouvriers des deux mondes*, 1ᵉ série, II (1858), 445–492.

Guérin, Urbain. "Ouvrier cordonnier de Malakoff." *Les Ouvriers des deux mondes*, 1ᵉ série, V (1885), 145–200.

Guixou-Pagès, J. *Chez les gars de la Villette*. Paris, 1901.

Hevert, H.-F., and E. Delbert. "Tisseur en châles de la fabrique urbaine collective de Paris." *Les Ouvriers des deux mondes*, 1ᵉ série, I (1857), 299–372.

Historique de la grève du bronze en 1867. Paris. 1867.

Janneau, Guillaume. *L'Apprentissage dans les métiers d'art. Une enquête*. Paris, 1914.

Landouzy, Louis, Henri Labbé, and Marcel Labbé. *Enquête sur l'alimentation d'une centaine d'ouvriers et employés parisiens*. Paris, 1905.

Le Grandais, Anatole. *Physiologie des employés de ministères*. Paris, 1862.

Leneveux, Henri. *Manuel d'apprentissage. Guide pour le choix d'un état industriel*. Paris, 1855.

Lhande, Pierre. *Le Christ dans la banlieue. Enquête sur la vie religieuse dans les milieux ouvriers de la banlieue de Paris*. Paris, 1927.

Le Play, Frédéric, and Adolphe Focillon. "Charpentier de Paris." *Les Ouvriers des deux mondes*, 1ᵉ série, I (1857), 27–68.

Leyret, Henri. *En plein faubourg (moeurs ouvrières)*. Paris, 1895.

Linhart, Robert. *The Assembly Line.* Trans. Margaret Crosland. Amherst, Mass., 1981.

Marcillon, L. *Trente Ans de vie de grands magasins.* Nice, 1924.

Mauclair, Camille. "Le Nouveau Paris du peuple." *Revue bleue,* LXXVII (1906), 79–83.

Mazaroz, Jean-Paul. *Causes et conséquences de la grève du Faubourg Saint-Antoine (d'octobre et novembre 1882).* Paris, 1882.

Michaud, René. *J'avais vingt ans. Un Jeune Ouvrier au début du siècle.* Paris, 1967.

Montaru, Louis. *Réorganisation du service de l'octroi. Amélioration du sort des employés.* Paris, 1871.

Montéhus, Gaston. *Recueil des chansons humanitaires.* Paris, 1910.

Mothé, Daniel. *Militant chez Renault.* Paris, 1965.

Paris-Employé. Annuaire des employés de Paris et banlieue. Paris, 1912.

Poisle-Desgranges, Joseph. *Voyage à mon bureau. Aller et retour.* Paris, 1861.

Poulot, Denis. *Méthode d'enseignement manuel pour former un apprenti mécanicien.* Paris, 1889.

————. *Le Sublime. Question sociale* 3rd. ed. Paris, 1887.

————, and Hippolyte Fontaine. *Etudes pratiques sur les machines-outils servant aux constructions mécaniques.* Paris, 1871.

Reviers, Jacques de. "Serrurier-forgeron de Paris." *Les Ouvriers des deux mondes,* 1ᵉ série, V (1885), 201–259.

Spretson, N. E. *A Practical Treatise on Casting and Founding Including Descriptions of the Modern Machinery Employed in the Art.* London, 1878.

Turgan, Julien. *Les Grandes Usines. Tableau de l'industrie française au XIXᵉ siècle.* 20 vols. Paris, 1860–1895.

Valdour, Jacques. *Ateliers et taudis de la banlieue de Paris.* Paris, 1923.

————. *De la Popinqu' à Ménilmuch'.* Paris, 1924.

————. *Le Faubourg. Observations vécues.* Paris, 1925.

II. Secondary Works

A. *Works on the Paris Region*

Agulhon, Maurice. "L'Opinion politique dans une commune de banlieue sous la Troisième République." *Etudes sur la banlieue de Paris.* Ed. Pierre George. Paris, 1950.

Amann, Peter. *Revolution and Mass Democracy: The Paris Club Movement of 1848.* Princeton, 1975.

Azéma, Jean-Pierre, and Michel Winock. *Les Communards*. Paris, 1971.

Barberet, Jospeh. *Le Mouvement ouvrier à Paris de 1870 à 1874*. Paris, 1874.

Bastié, Jean. *La Croissance de la banlieue parisienne*. Paris, 1964.

Bechmann, Georges. *Salubrité urbaine. Distribution d'eau. Assainissement*. Paris, 1888.

Benoist, Charles. *Les Ouvrières de l'aiguille à Paris*. Paris, 1895.

Berlanstein, Lenard "The Formation of a Factory Labor Force: Rubber and Cable Workers in Bezons, France (1860–1914)." *Journal of Social History*, XV (1981), 163–186.

————. "Growing Up as Workers in Nineteenth-Century Paris: The Case of the Orphans of the Prince Imperial." *French Historical Studies*, XI (1980), 551–576.

————. "Illegitimacy, Concubinage, and Proletarianization in a French Town, 1760–1914." *Journal of Family History*, V (1980), 360–374.

————. "Vagrants, Beggars, and Thieves: Delinquent Boys in Mid-Nineteenth Century Paris." *Journal of Social History*, XII (1979), 531–552.

Berthaud, Docteur Paul. *Fumée et poussière de Paris, spécialement dans le Neuvième Arrondissement*. Clermont, 1899.

Bertillon, Jacques. *De la Fréquence de la fièvre typhoïde à Paris pendant la période 1865–82*. Paris, 1883.

————. *Essai de statistique comparée du surpeuplement des habitations à Paris et dans les grandes capitales européennes*. Paris, 1894.

Blanc, Edouard. *La Ceinture Rouge. Enquête sur la situation politique, morale, et sociale de la banlieue de Paris*. Paris, 1927.

Bonneff, Louis, and Maurice Bonneff. *La Vie tragique des travailleurs. Enquête sur la condition économique et morale des ouvriers*. Paris, 1908.

Boxer, Marilyn. "Women in Industrial Homework: The Flowermakers of Paris in the Belle Epoque." *French Historical Studies*, XII (1982), 401–423.

Brennan, Thomas. "Cabarets and Laboring-Class Communities in Eighteenth-Century Paris." Ph.D. diss., Johns Hopkins University, 1981.

Brunet, Jean-Paul. "Une Banlieue ouvrière: Saint-Denis (1890–1939)." Doctorat d'Etat, Université de Paris-IV, 1978.

————. "L'Industrialisation de la région de Saint-Denis." *Acta géographica*, XXIII (1970), 223–260.

————. *Saint-Denis, la ville rouge. Socialisme et communisme en banlieue ouvrière, 1890–1939*. Paris, 1980.

Cadoux. G.-M.-A. *Les Salaires et les conditions du travail des ouvriers et employés des entreprises municipales de Paris*. The Hague, 1911.

Chatelain, Abel. "La Vie des migrants maçons limousins dans le

Ve Arrondissement de Paris au début de XXe siècle." *Etudes de la région parisienne*, XLIII (1969), 32–45.

Chevalier, Louis. *Classes laborieuses et classes dangereuses à Paris pendant la première moitié du XIXe siècle*. Paris, 1958.

————. *La Formation de la population parisienne au XIXe siècle*. Paris, 1950.

————. *Montmartre du crime et du plaisir*. Paris, 1980.

————. *Les Parisiens*. Paris, 1967.

Colin, Léon. *Paris, sa topographie, son hygiène, ses maladies*. Paris, 1885.

Comby, Louis. "Alfortville. Commune de banlieue." Doctorat de IIIe cycle, Université de Paris, 1966.

Constantin, Marc. *Histoire des cafés-concerts et des cafés de Paris*. Paris, 1872.

Courgey, Stéphane. *Epidémiologie à Ivry-sur-Seine de 1877 à 1899*. Paris, 1901.

Cruveilher. "Ligue contre la mortalité infantile." *La Revue philanthropique*, XXXV (1914), 37–57.

Dalotel, Alain, Alain Faure and Claude Friermuth. *Aux Origines de la Commune: Le Mouvement des réunions publiques à Paris, 1868–1870*. Paris, 1980.

Daumard, Adeline. *Maisons de Paris et propriétaires parisiens au XIXe siècle, 1809–1880*. Paris, 1965.

————. "Quelques remarques sur le logement des Parisiens au XIXe siècle." *Annales de démographie historique*, 1975, 49–64.

Daumas, Maurice. *L'Evolution de la géographie industrielle de Paris et sa proche banlieue au XIXe siècle*. 3 vols. Paris, 1976.

Delvau, Alfred. *Dictionnaire de la langue verte. Argots parisiens comparés*. Paris, 1866.

Dewinck. *Paris depuis un demi-siècle au point de vue industriel et commercial*. Paris, 1874.

Dubousquet-Laborderie, Docteur Louis. *Causes des décès par maladies épidémiques et contagieuses dans la commune de Saint-Ouen*. Paris, 1889.

————. *Exposé de la constitution médicale actuelle de la commune de Saint-Ouen-sur-Seine*. Paris, 1885.

————, and Léon Duchesne. *Contribution à l'étude de la pathogène et de la prophylaxie de la tuberculose*. Clermont, 1897.

Du Maroussem, Pierre. "Le Système parisien de l'industrie du meuble et le 'sweating system.'" *Revue d'économie politique*, VI (1892), 569–581.

Durand-Claye, Alfred. *Assainissement de la Seine*. Paris, 1885.

Edwards, Stewart. *The Paris Commune, 1871*. London, 1971.

Evenson, Norma. *Paris: A Century of Change, 1878–1978*. New Haven, Conn., 1979.

Farge, Arlette. *Vivre dans la rue à Paris au XVIIIe siècle*. Paris, 1979.

Faure, Alain. "L'Epicerie parisienne au XIXe siècle, ou la corporation éclatée." *Le Mouvement social*, no. 108 (1979), 113–130.

————. "Mouvements populaires et mouvement ouvrier à Paris." *Le Mouvement social*, no. 88 (1974), 51–92.

————. *Paris Carême-prenant. Du Carnaval à Paris au XIXe siècle*. Paris, 1978.

Feilbogen. "L'Alimentation populaire à Paris." *Revue d'économie politique*, XXVII (1913). 719–732.

Flageolet-Lardenois, Michèle. "Une Firme pionnière: Panhard et Levassor jusqu'en 1918." *Le Mouvement social*, no. 81 (1972), pp. 27–49.

Fourdinois, Henri. *Etude économique et sociale sur l'ameublement*. Paris, 1894.

Fourgerousse, A. *Patrons et ouvriers de Paris*. Paris, 1880.

Frey, Michel. "Du Mariage et du concubinage dans les classes populaires à Paris (1846–1847)." *Annales: Economie, société, civilisation*, XXXIII (1978), 803–829.

Fridenson, Patrick. *Histoire des usines Renault, Vol. 1: Naissance de la grande entreprise, 1898–1939*. Paris, 1972.

————. "Une Industrie nouvelle: L'Automobile en France jusqu'en 1914." *Revue d'histoire moderne et contemporaine*, XIX (1972), 557–578.

————. . "Les Premiers ouvriers français de l'automobile (1890–1914)." *Sociologie du travail*, XXI (1979), 297–325.

Gaillard, Jeanne. *Paris, la ville, 1852–1870*. Paris, 1975.

————. . "Les Usines Cail et les ouvriers métallurgistes de Grenelle." *Le Mouvement social*, nos. 33–34 (1960–1961), 35–53.

Gastinel, Adrien. *Les Egouts de Paris. Etude d'hygiène urbaine*. Paris, 1894.

Giard, Louis. "Les Elections à Paris sous la Troisième République." Doctorat de IIIe cycle de sociologie, Université de Dakar, 1966–1968.

Goubert, Docteur Elie. *Les Maladies des enfants à Paris. Rapport de la mortalité avec la morbidité*. Paris, 1891.

Hénon, Pierre. *Levallois. Histoire d'une banlieue*. Brussels, 1981.

————. "Processus d'urbanisation de la banlieue ouest." Doctorat de IIIe cycle, Université de Paris-VIII, 1979.

Isherwood, Robert. "Entertainment in the Parisian Fairs in the Eighteenth Century." *Journal of Modern History*, LII (1981), 24–48.

Jacquemet, Gérard. "Belleville au XIXe siècle. Du Faubourg à la ville." Doctorat d'Etat, Université de Paris-IV, 1979.

————. "Belleville ouvrière à la Belle Epoque." *Le Mouvement social*, no. 118 (1982), 61–77.

————. "Urbanisme parisien: La Bataille du tout-à-l'égout à la fin du XIXe siècle." *Revue d'histoire moderne et contemporaine*, XXVI (1979), 505–548.

Johnson, Christopher. "Economic Change and Artisan Discontent: The Tailor's History, 1800–1848." *Revolution and Reaction: 1848 and the Second French Republic*. Ed. Roger Price. London, 1975.

Juillerat, Paul, and Alfred Fillassier. "Dix Années de mortalité parisienne chez les enfants de 0 à 14 ans." *La Revue philanthropique*, XXXV (1914), 147–164.

Kaplow, Jeffry. "La Fin de la Saint-Lundi. Etude sur le Paris ouvrier au XIXᵉ siècle." *Le Temps libre*, II (1981), 107–118.

Lagneau, Gustave. *Rapport sur les maladies épidémiques observées en 1890 dans le département de la Seine*. Paris, 1891.

Landouzy, Louis. "La Mortalité parisienne par tuberculose il y a vingt ans." *Congrès international de la tuberculose*, vol. II (Paris, 1906), 696–706.

Lavedan, Pierre. *Histoire de l'urbanisme à Paris*. Paris, 1975.

Lecoq, Marcel. *La Crise du logement populaire*. Paris, 1912.

Lejeune, Docteur. *Faut-il fouetter les Apaches?* Paris, 1910.

Lelièvre, Pierre. *Les Ateliers de Paris*. Paris, 1866.

Leroux, Charles, and W. Grunberg. "Enquête sur la descendance de 442 familles ouvrières tuberculeuses." *Revue de médecine*, XXXII (1912), 900–941.

Le Roy des Barres, Docteur Adrien. *Le Choléra à Saint-Denis en 1892*. Paris, 1893.

————. *Exposé des titres et travaux scientifiques*. Saint-Denis, 1896.

————. *Rapport sur les maladies épidémiques et les maladies virulentes observées dans l'arrondissement de Saint-Denis*. Paris, 1894.

Lesselier, Claudie. "Employées de grands magasins à Paris avant 1914." *Le Mouvement social*, no. 105 (1978), 109–126.

McBride, Theresa. "A Woman's World: Department Stores and the Evolution of Women's Employment, 1870–1920." *French Historical Studies*, X (1978), 664–683.

March, Lucien. "Familles parisiennes en 1901." *Journal de la Société de statistique de Paris*, XLV (1904), 21–33.

Mayet, Charles. *La Crise industrielle: L'Ameublement*. Paris, 1883.

Metton, Alain. "L'Appareil commercial de détail en banlieue parisienne." Doctorat ès-Lettres, Université de Paris-I, 1978.

Meyer, Odile. "La Croissance de la commune de Puteaux entre 1880 et 1914." Diplôme de maîtrise, Université de Paris-X, 1975–1976.

Miller, Michael. *The Bon Marché. Bourgeois Culture and the Department Store, 1896–1920*. Princeton, N.J., 1981.

Mollat, Michel (ed.). *Histoire de l'Ile-de-France et de Paris*. Toulouse, 1971.

Morillon, Adolphe. *Rapport sur les consommations de Paris et la gestion des halles, marchés, et abattoirs. Année 1884*. Paris, 1885.

Moss, Bernard. *The Origins of the French Labor Movement, 1830–1914. The Socialism of Skilled Workers*. Berkeley, Calif., 1976.

Moutet, Aimée. "Le Mouvement ouvrier à Paris du lendemain de la Commune au premier congrès syndical en 1876." *Le Mouvement social*, no. 58 (1967), 3–39.

Nord, Philip. "Le Mouvement des petits commerçants et la politique en France de 1888 à 1914." *Le Mouvement social*, no. 114 (1981), 35–55.

Papayanis, Nicolas. "Depression and Crisis in the 'Corporation' of Paris Coachmen." Paper presented to the Society for French Historical Studies, New York City, March 1982.

Le Peuplement intensif de la banlieue parisienne. Paris, 1900.

Pinkney, David. *Napoleon III and the Rebuilding of Paris*. Princeton, N.J., 1958.

Perret, Raoul. "Subvention aux oeuvres d'assistance maternelle." *La Revue philanthropique*, XXXV (1914), 75–106.

Raison-Jourde, Françoise. *La Colonie auvergnate à Paris au XIXe siècle*. Paris, 1976.

Roche, Daniel. *Le Peuple de Paris. Essai sur la culture populaire au XVIIIe siècle*. Paris, 1981.

Rondot, Natalis. *Histoire et statistique des théâtres de Paris*. Paris, 1852.

Riché, Etienne. *La Situation des ouvriers dans l'industrie automobile*. Paris, 1909.

Rives, Docteur. *Etude des causes d'insalubrité spéciales au quartier de la Maison-Blanche*. Paris, 1887.

Rougerie, Jacques. "Composition d'une population insurgée." *Le Mouvement social*, no. 48 (1964), 31–48.

————. "Remarques sur l'histoire des salaires à Paris au XIXe siècle." *Le Mouvement social*, no. 63 (1968), 71–108.

Rozier, Victor. *Les Bals publics à Paris*. Paris, 1855.

Rudoff, Raymond. *The Belle Epoque: Paris in the Nineties*. New York, 1972.

Saint-Albin, Albert de. *Les Sports à Paris*. Paris, 1889.

Sarcey, Francisque. *Les Odeurs de Paris. Assainissement de la Seine*. Paris, 1882.

Seidman, Michael. "The Birth of the Weekend and the Revolt against Work: The Workers of the Parisian Region during the Popular Front (1936–38)." *French Historical Studies*, XII (1981), 249–276.

Sellier, Henri. *La Crise du logement et l'intervention publique en matière d'habitation populaire dans l'agglomération parisienne*. Paris, 1921.

Shapiro, Anne-Louise. "Working-Class Housing and Public Health in Paris, 1850–1902." Ph.D. diss., Brown University, 1980.

Singer-Kérel, Jeanne. *Le Coût de la vie à Paris de 1840 à 1954*. Paris, 1954.

Sordes, René. *Histoire de Suresnes*. Suresnes, 1965.

Stein, Margot. "The Meaning of Skill: The Case of the French

Engine Drivers, 1837–1917." *Politics and Society*, VIII (1979), 399–427.

Testelin, Docteur. *Note sur la fièvre typhoïde et la diphtérie en rapport avec l'eau servant à l'alimentation dans la région d'Argenteuil.* Argenteuil, 1890.

Touraine, Alain. *L'Evolution du travail ouvrier aux usines Renault.* Paris, 1955.

Tourteaux, Alexandre. *L'Assainissement de la ville de Levallois-Perret.* Levallois-Perret, 1901.

Tranchant, Marius. *L'Habitation du parisien en banlieue.* Paris, 1908.

Traverse, Paul. *Etude sur les dispensaires pour enfants malades à Paris.* Paris, 1899.

Val de Marne. Service éducatif des Archives départementales. *Sports et société, 1870–1914.* Créteil, 1979.

Van de Walle, Etienne, and Samuel Preston. "Mortalité de l'enfance au XIXe siècle à Paris et dans le département de la Seine." *Population*, XXIX (1974), 89–107.

Vanier, Henriette. *La Mode et ses métiers, 1830–1870.* Paris, 1960.

Warnod, André. *Les Bals de Paris.* Paris, 1922.

Watson, David R. "The Nationalist Movement in Paris, 1900–1906." *The Right in France, 1890–1919.* Ed. David Shapiro. Carbondale, Ill., 1962.

Weber, William. "Artisans in Concert Life in Mid-Nineteenth-Century London and Paris." *Journal of Contemporary History*, XIII (1978), 253–268.

Weissbach, Lee Shai. "Artisanal Response to Artistic Decline: The Cabinetmakers of Paris in the Era of Industrialization." *Journal of Social History*, XVI (1982), 67–82.

Young, Linda Bishop. "Mobilizing Food-, Restaurant, and Café Workers in Paris: A Case Study of Direct Action Syndicalism, 1900–14." Ph.D. diss., New York University, 1981.

Zylberberg-Hocquand, Marie-Hélène. "Les Ouvriers d'Etat (tabac et allumettes) dans les dernières années du XIXe siècle." *Le Mouvement social*, no. 105 (1978), 87–107.

B. *General Works on France and on Areas Other Than Paris*

Accampo, Elinor. "Entre la classe sociale et la cité; identité et intrégration chez les ouvriers de Saint-Chamond, 1815–1880." *Le Mouvement social*, no. 118 (1982), 39–59.

Ackerman, Evelyn. *Village on the Seine. Tradition and Change in Bonnières, 1815–1914.* Ithaca, N.Y., 1978.

Aftalion, Albert. *Le Développement de la fabrique et le travail à domicile dans les industries de l'habillement.* Paris, 1906.

Agulhon, Maurice, Françoise Choay, Maurice Crubellier, Yves Lequin, and Marcel Roncayolo. *Histoire de la France urbaine. Tome IV: La Ville de l'âge industrielle.* Paris, 1983.

Amaury, Francine. *Histoire du plus grand quotidien de la IIIe République: Le Petit Parisien, 1876–1944.* 2 vols. Paris, 1972.

Aminzade, Ronald. *Class, Politics, and Early Industrial Captialism. A Study of Mid-Nineteenth-Century Toulouse, France.* Albany, N.Y., 1981.

Anderson, Robert D. *France, 1870–1914. Politics and Society.* London, 1977.

Ariès, Philippe. *Centuries of Childhood. A Social History of Family Life.* Trans. Robert Baldick. New York, 1962.

————. *Histoire des populations françaises et de leurs attitudes devant la vie depuis le XVIIIe siècle.* Paris, 1971.

Artaud, A.-J.-M. *La Question de l'employé en France.* Paris, 1909.

Bachrach, Susan. "The Feminization of the French Postal Service, 1750–1914." Ph.D. diss., University of Wisconsin-Madison, 1981.

Bardou, Jean-Pierre, Jean-Jacques Chanaron, Patrick Fridenson, and James Laux. *The Automobile Revolution.* Trans. James Laux. Chapel Hill, N.C., 1982.

Bassieux, François. *L'Industrie de la chaussure en France.* Paris, 1908.

Beaufils, François. "L'Introduction du système Taylor en France (1900–13)." Mémoire de maîtrise, Université de Paris-I, 1970.

Besse, Auguste. *L'Employé de commerce et d'industrie.* Lyons, 1901.

Bez, Marcel. *Etude sur la tannerie et les industries travaillant les peaux brutes en France.* Toulouse, 1923.

Bonneff, Léon, and Maurice Bonneff. *La Classe ouvrière.* Paris, 1911.

Bouvier, Jean. *Le Crédit lyonnais de 1863 à 1882.* 2 vols. Paris, 1961.

————, André Armengaud, Pierre Barral, François Caron, Adeline Daumard, René Girault, Christian Gras, Michelle Perrot, and Claude Willard. *Histoire économique et sociale de la France. Tome IV: L'Ere industrielle et la société d'aujourd'hui.* Paris, 1979.

Bouvier, Jeanne. *Histoire des dames employées dans les Postes, Télégraphes, et Téléphones.* Paris, 1930.

Cadoux, Gaston-M.-A. *Les Conditions du travail et les salaires des agents de la Compagnie française du chemin de fer du Nord.* The Hague, 1911.

Caron, François. *Histoire de l'exploitation d'un grand réseau. La Compagnie du chemin de fer du Nord, 1846–1937.* Paris, 1973.

Carter, Edward, Robert Forster, and Joseph Moody (eds.). *Enterprise and Entrepreneurs in Nineteenth- and Twentieth-Century France.* Baltimore, 1976.

Cheysson, Emile. *Le Creusot. Condition matérielle, intellectuelle, et morale de la population.* Paris, 1869.

Corbin, Alain. *Les Filles de noces. Misère sexuelle et prostitution aux XIXe et XXe siècles.* Paris, 1978.

Côte, Léon. *L'Industrie gantière et l'ouvrier gantier à Grenoble.* Paris, 1903.

Couffignal, Louis. *Les Machines à calculer. Leurs principes. Leur évolution.* Paris, 1933.

Crouzet, François. "French Economic Growth in the Nineteenth Century Reconsidered." *History*, LIX (1974), 167–179.

Crubellier, Maurice. *L'Enfance et la jeunesse dans la société française, 1800–1950.* Paris, 1979.

Daumard, Adeline, Félix Codaccioni, Georges Dupeux, Jacqueline Herpin, Jacques Godechot, and Jean Sentou. *Les Fortunes françaises au XIXe siècle.* Paris, 1973.

Dehau, Docteur Henri, and René Ledroux-Lebard. *La Lutte antituberculeuse en France.* Paris, 1906.

Delon, Pierre. *Les Employés. Un Siècle de lutte.* Paris, 1969.

Demonceaux, A. *Le Choix d'une carrière commerciale, industrielle, ou financière.* Paris, 1904.

Descoust, René. *Marchandage et sweating system.* Paris, 1918.

Descroix, L. "Matériel et outillage mécanique de la fonderie." *La Mécanique moderne*, VI (1913), 261–267; 339–342, 380–388.

Dillon, P. *Histoire et statistique des accidents du travail.* Chatou, 1911.

Dommanget, Maurice. *Histoire du premier mai.* Paris, 1972.

Drancourt, M. "Etude sur les conditions d'hygiène des ouvriers dans les fabriques d'accumulateurs électriques." *Bulletin de l'Inspection du travail*, X (1902), 303–325.

Droz, Jacques (ed.). *Histoire générale du socialisme.* 4 vols. Paris, 1974.

Eddy, W. *L'Employé des chemins de fer, sa condition en France et en Angleterre.* Paris, 1883.

Ehrenberg, Alain (ed.). *Aimez-vous les stades? Les Origines des politiques sportives en France, 1870–1930.* Vol. XLIII of *Recherches.* Fontenay-sous-Bois, 1980.

Elwitt, Sanford. *The Making of the Third Republic. Class and Politics in France, 1868–1884.* Baton Rouge, 1975.

Feichter, Jean-Jacques. *Le Socialisme français: De l'Affaire Dreyfus à la Grande Guerre.* Geneva, 1965.

Flandrin, Jean-Louis. *Families in Former Times: Kinship, Household, and Sexuality.* Trans. Richard Southern. Cambridge, 1979.

Flonneau, Jean-Marie. "Crise de vie chère et mouvement syndical (1910–1914)." *Le Mouvement social*, no. 72 (1970), 49–81.

Fraysse, Arthur. *Le Marchandage dans l'industrie du bâtiment.* Paris, 1911.

Frémont, Charles. *L'Evolution de la fonderie de cuivre d'après les documents du temps.* Paris, 1903.

————, and Fernand Huillier. *Etude sur la production des machines-outils façonnant les métaux.* Paris, 1899.

Friedmann, Georges. *Industrial Society. The Emergence of the Human Problems of Automation.* New York, 1964.

Garanger, André. *Petite histoire d'une grande industrie.* Paris, n.d.

Gemahling, Paul. *Travailleurs au rabais.* Paris, 1910.

Goubert, Jean-Pierre. "Eaux publiques et démographie historique dans la France urbaine du XIXᵉ siècle." *Annales de démographie historique,* 1975, 115–121.

Gras, Christian. "La Fédération des métaux en 1913–1914 et l'évolution du syndicalisme révolutionnaire français." *Le Mouvement social,* no. 77 (1971), 85–111.

————. "L'Ouvrier mouleur à travers le journal de sa fédération: *La Fonderie* (1900–1909)." *Le Mouvement social,* no. 53 (1965), 51–68.

Guillaume, Pierre. *La Population de Bordeaux au XIXᵉ siècle; essai d'histoire sociale.* Paris, 1972.

Halbwachs, Maurice. "Budgets de familles ouvrières et paysannes en France, en 1907." *Bulletin de la Statistique générale de la France,* IV (1914–1915), 47–83.

————. *La Classe ouvrière et les niveaux de vie.* Paris, 1912.

Hanagan, Michael. *The Logic of Solidarity: Artisans and Industrial Workers in Three French Towns, 1871–1914.* Urbana, Ill., 1980.

Hayward, J.E.S. "The Official Social Philosophy of the French Third Republic: Léon Bourgeois and Solidarism." *International Review of Social History,* VI (1961), 19–48.

Higonnet, Patrice. *Pont-de-Montvert. Social Structure and Politics in a French Village, 1700–1914.* Cambridge, Mass., 1971.

Holt, Richard. *Sport and Society in Modern France.* Hamden, Conn., 1981.

Hutton, Patrick. *The Cult of the Revolutionary Tradition: The Blanquists in French Politics, 1864–1893.* Berkeley, Calif., 1981.

————. "Popular Boulangism and the Advent of Mass Politics in France, 1886–90." *Journal of Contemporary History,* XI (1976), 85–106.

————. "The Role of the Blanquist Party in Left-Wing Politics in France, 1879–90." *Journal of Modern History,* XLVI (1974), 277–295.

Imbert, Henri. *L'Alcoolisme chronique dans ses rapports avec les professions.* Paris, 1897.

Johnson, Christopher. *Utopian Communism in France: Cabet and the Icarians, 1839–1851.* Ithaca, N.Y., 1974.

Kelso, Maxwell. "The Inception of the Modern French Labor Movement (1871–79)." *Journal of Modern History,* VIII (1936), 173–193.

Laboulaye, Charles. *Dictionnaire des arts et manufactures.* 4 vols. Paris, 1881.

Lahy, Jean-Maurice. "Recherches sur les conditions du travail des ouvriers typographes composant à la machine dite linotype." *Bulletin de l'Inspection du travail,* XVIII (1910), 45–103.

L'Angle-Beaumanoir, Raoul de. *La Traite des blancs au XIXᵉ siècle. La Situation des employés de chemins de fer en 1883*. Paris, 1883.

Launay, Michel. "Le Syndicat des employés du commerce et de l'industrie de 1887 à 1914." *Le Mouvement social*, no. 68 (1969), 35–56.

Laux, James. *In First Gear: The French Automobile Industry to 1914*. Liverpool, 1976.

Lefranc, Georges. *Le Syndicalisme en France*. Paris, 1973.

Léonard, Jacques. *La Médecine entre les pouvoirs et les savoirs*. Paris, 1981.

Lequin, Yves. "Classe ouvrière et idéologie dans la région lyonnaise à la fin du XIXe siècle." *Le Mouvement social*, no. 69 (1969), 3–20.

―――――. *Les Ouvriers de la région lyonnaise (1848–1914)*. 2 vols. Lyons, 1977.

L'Huillier, Fernard. *La Lutte ouvrière à la fin du Second Empire*. Paris, 1957.

Louis, Paul. *Histoire du mouvement syndical en France*. 2 vols. Paris, 1947.

McBride, Theresa. *The Domestic Revolution. The Modernization of Household Service in England and France, 1820–1920*. London, 1976.

Maitron, Jean (ed.). *Dictionnaire biographique du mouvement ouvrier français*. 15 vols. Paris, 1973.

Marchal, Jean, and Jacques Lecaillon. *La Répartition du revenu national*. 2 vols. Paris, 1958.

Marrus, Michael. "Social Drinking in the *Belle Epoque*." *Journal of Social History*, VII (1974), 115–141.

Martial, René. *L'Ouvrier. Son Hygiène, son atelier, son habitation*. Paris, 1908.

Melluci, Alberto. "Action patronale, pouvoir, organisation. Règlements d'usine et contrôle de la main-d'oeuvre au XIXe siècle." *Le Mouvement social*, no. 97 (1976), 139–159.

Mény, Georges. *Le Travail à bon marché. Enquêtes sociales*. Paris, 1907.

Merriman, John (ed.). *Consciousness and Class Experience in Nineteenth-Century Europe*. New York, 1980.

―――――(ed.). *French Cities in the Nineteenth Century*. New York, 1981.

Miret, Victor. *Essai sur la sociologie à propos de la protestation des employés des postes, télégraphes, et chemins de fer* Paris, 1888.

Mirman, Léon. *Les Accidents du travail. Guide de l'ouvrier*. Reims, 1903.

Mottez, Bernard. *Systèmes de salaires et politiques patronales*. Paris, 1966.

Moutet, Aimée. "Les Origines du système de Taylor en France.

Le point de vue patronal (1907–1914)." *Le Mouvement social*, no. 93 (1975), 15–49.

Néré, Jacques. "La Crise industrielle de 1882 et le mouvement Boulangiste." Doctorat ès-Lettres, Université de Paris, 1959.

Office du travail. "Définition des mots 'usine' et 'manufacture.'" *Bulletin de l'Inspection du travail*, VIII (1900), 786–790.

O'Followell, Ludovic, and Hippolyte Goudal. *Hygiène des employés de commerce et d'administration*. Paris, 1901.

Papayanis, Nicolas. "Merrheim and the Strike of Hennebout." *International Review of Social History*, XVI (1971), 159–183.

Parent-Larduer. Françoise. *Les Demoiselles de magasin*. Paris, 1970.

Pelloutier, Fernand, and Maurice Pelloutier. *La Vie ouvrière en France*. Paris, 1900.

Perrot, Michelle. "De la nourrice à l'employée . . . . Travaux de femmes dans la France du XIXᵉ siècle." *Le Mouvement social*, no. 105 (1978), 3–10.

————. "L'Eloge de la ménagère dans le discours des ouvriers français au XIXᵉ siècle." *Romantisme*, no. 13 (1976), 105–121.

————. "Grèves, grévistes et conjonctures. Vieux problème, travaux neufs." *Le Mouvement social*, no. 63 (1968), 109–124.

————. "Le Militant face à la grève dans la mine et la métallurgie au XIXᵉ siècle." *Le Mouvement social*, no. 99 (1977), 77–95.

————. *Les Ouvriers en grève. France, 1871–1890*. 2 vols. Paris, 1974.

Perrot, Philippe. *Les Dessus et les dessous de la bourgeoisie. Une Histoire du vêtement au XIXᵉ siècle*. Paris, 1981.

Phillips, Roderick. *Family Breakdown in Late Eighteenth-Century France. Divorce in Rouen, 1792–1803*. Oxford, 1980.

Puech, Charles. *De l'application de la loi sur les accidents du travail*. Paris, 1903.

Radiguer, Louis. *Maîtres imprimeurs et ouvriers typographes*. Paris, 1903.

Rebérioux, Madeleine. *La République radicale? 1898–1914*. Paris, 1975.

Reybaud, Louis. *Rapport sur la condition morale, intellectuelle, et matérielle des ouvriers qui vivent de l'industrie du fer. Fourchambault et Commentry*. Paris, 1868.

Ridley, Frederick. *Revolutionary Syndicalism in France*. Cambridge, 1970.

Ronsin, Francis. *La Grève des ventres. Propagande néo-malthusienne et la baisse de la natalité française*. Paris, 1980.

Scott, Joan. *The Glassworkers of Carmaux*. Cambridge, Mass., 1974.

————, and Louise Tilly. *Women, Work, and Family*. New York, 1979.

Seager, Frederic. *The Boulanger Affair*. Ithaca, N.Y., 1969.

Seilhac, Léon de. *Les Grèves de l'année (1909–1910)*. Paris, 1911.

Sewell, William. "La Confraternité des prolétaires. Conscience de classe sous la monarchie de Juillet." *Annales: Economie, société, civilisation,* XXXVI (1981), 650–671.

—————. *Work and Revolution in France. The Language of Labor from the Old Regime to 1848.* Cambridge, 1980.

Shattuck, Roger. *The Banquet Years: The Origins of the Avant Garde in France, 1885 to World War I.* New York, 1968.

Stafford, David. *From Anarchism to Reformism: A Study of the Political Activities of Paul Brousse, 1870–1890.* Toronto, 1971.

Stearns, Peter. "Patterns of Strike Activity during the July Monarchy." *American Historical Review,* LXX (1965), 371–394.

—————. *Revolutionary Syndicalism and French Labor.* New Brunswick, N.J., 1971.

Sussman, George. *Selling Mother's Milk: The Wet Nursing Business in France, 1815–1914.* Urbana, Ill., 1982.

Thuillier, Guy. *La Vie quotidienne dans les ministères au XIXe siècle.* Paris, 1976.

Tilly, Charles, and Edward Shorter. *Strikes in France, 1830–1968.* Cambridge, 1974.

Van de Walle, Etienne. "France." *European Demographic and Economic Growth.* Ed. W. R. Lee. London, 1979.

Vial, Jean. *La Coutume chapelière. Histoire du mouvement ouvrier dans la chapellerie.* Paris, 1941.

—————. *L'Industrialisation de la sidérurgie française, 1814–1864.* Paris, 1967.

—————. "L'Ouvrier métallurgiste français." *Droit social,* XIII (1950), 58–68.

Weber, Eugen. "Gymnastics and Sports in Fin-de-Siècle France. Opium of the Classes?" *American Historical Review,* LXXVI (1971), 70–98.

—————. *Peasants into Frenchmen. The Modernization of Rural France, 1870–1914.* Stanford, Calif., 1976.

Wheaton, Robert, and Tamara Hareven (eds.). *Family and Sexuality in French History.* Philadelphia, 1980.

Willard, Claude. "Contribution au portrait du militant guesdiste dans les dix dernières années du XIXe siècle." *Le Mouvement social,* nos. 33–34 (1960–1961), 55–66.

—————. *Le Mouvement socialiste en France. Les Guesdistes.* Paris, 1965.

Williams, Rosalind. *Dream Worlds: Mass Consumerism in Late Nineteenth-Century France.* Berkeley, Calif., 1982.

Wright, Gordon. *Between the Guillotine and Liberty.* New York, 1983.

Zylberberg-Hocquard, Marie-Hélène. *Femmes et féminisme dans le mouvement ouvrier français.* Paris, 1981.

Zylberman, Patrick, and Lion Murard. *Le Petit travailleur infatigable. Villes-usines, habitat, et intimités au XIXe siècle.* Vol. XXV of *Recherches.* Fontenay-sous-Bois, 1976.

_____(eds.). *L'Haleine des faubourgs. Ville, habitat, et santé au XIXe siècle*. Vol. XXIX of *Recherches*. Fontenay-sous-Bois, 1977.

C. **Works of Cross-Cultural Interest**

Anderson, Michael. *Approaches to the History of the Western Family, 1500–1914*. London, 1980.
_____. *Family Structure in Nineteenth-Century Lancashire*. Cambridge, 1971.
Acheson, Roy. "Effects of Nutrition and Disease on Human Growth." *Human Growth*. Ed. J. M. Tanner. New York, 1960.
Barth, Gunther. *City People: The Rise of Modern City Culture in Nineteenth-Century America*. New York, 1980.
Benson, Susan Porter. "The Clerking Sisterhood. Rationalization and the Work Culture of Saleswomen." *Radical America*, XII (1978), 41–55.
Belmonte, Thomas. *The Broken Fountain*. New York, 1979.
Bendix, Reinhard. *Work and Authority in Industry. Ideologies of Management in the Course of Industrialization*. Berkeley, Calif., 1974.
Bette, Walter. *The History and Conquest of Common Diseases*. Norman, Okla., 1954.
Cheraskin, Emanuel, J. W. Clark, and W. R. Ringsdorf. *Diet and Disease*. Emmaus, Pa., 1968.
Cochrane, Charles. *Modern Industrial Progress*. Philadelphia, 1904.
Clawson, Dan. *Bureaucracy and the Labor Process. The Transformation of U.S. Industry, 1860–1920*. New York, 1980.
Crew, David. *Town in the Ruhr. A Social History of Bochum, 1860–1914*. New York, 1979.
Cronin, James, and Carmen Sirianni (eds.). *Work, Community, and Power: The Experience of Labor in Europe and America, 1900–1925*. Philadelphia, 1983.
Dahrendorf, Rolf. *Class and Class Conflict in Industrial Society*. Stanford, Calif., 1959.
Davis, Margery. "Women's Place Is at the Typewriter: The Feminization of the Clerical Labor Force." *Radical America*, VIII (1974), 1–24.
Dawley, Alan. *Class and Community: The Industrial Revolution in Lynn*. Cambridge, Mass., 1976.
Degler, Carl. *At Odds: Women and the Family in America from the Revolution to the Present*. New York, 1980.
Devinat, Paul. *L'Organisation scientifique du travail en Europe*. Geneva, 1927.
Dubos, René, and Jean Dubos. *The White Plague: Tuberculosis, Man, and Society*. Boston, 1952.
Ebrahim, G. J. "The Problem of Under-Nutrition." *Nutrition and Disease*. Ed. R. J. Jarrett. Baltimore, Md., 1979.
Erenberg, Lewis. *Steppin' Out. New York Nightlife and the Trans-

formation of American Culture, 1890–1930. Westport, Conn., 1981.

Evans, Richard (ed.). *The German Working Class, 1880–1933. The Politics of Everyday Life.* London, 1982.

————, and W. R. Lee (eds.). *The German Family. Essays on the Social History of the Family in Nineteenth- and Twentieth-Century Germany.* London, 1981.

Fyrth, H. J., and Henry Collins. *The Foundry Worker. A Trade Union History.* Manchester, 1959.

Geary, Dick. *European Labor Protest, 1848–1939.* London, 1981.

Gillis, John. *Youth and History: Tradition and Change in European Age Relations, 1770–Present.* New York, 1974.

Gitelman, Howard. *Workingmen of Waltham. Mobility in American Urban Development.* Baltimore, Md., 1974.

Groh, Dieter. "Intensification of Work and Industrial Conflict in Germany, 1896–1914." *Politics and Society,* VIII (1979), 349–397.

Hareven, Tamara. *Family Time and Industrial Time. The Relationship between the Family and Work in a New England Industrial Community.* Cambridge, 1982.

Hartwell, Ronald Maxwell. "The Tertiary Sector in the English Economy during the Industrial Revolution." *L'Industrialisation en Europe au XIXe siècle.* Ed. Pierre Léon. Paris, 1972.

Hirsch, Susan. *Roots of the American Working Class. The Industrialization the the Crafts in Newark, 1840–1860.* Philadelphia, 1978.

Hobsbawm, Eric, and Joan Scott. "Political Shoemakers." *Past and Present,* no. 89 (1980), 86–114.

Kett, Joseph. *Rites of Passage: Adolescence in America, 1790 to the Present.* New York, 1977.

Kocka, Jrgen. *Unternehmerverwaltung und Angestellenshaft.* Stuttgart, 1969.

Knodel. John. *The Decline of Fertility in Germany, 1871–1939.* Princeton, N.J., 1974.

Landes, David. *The Unbound Prometheus. Technological Change and Industrial Development in Western Europe from 1750 to the Present.* Cambridge, 1969.

Lee, W. Robert. (ed.). *European Demographic and Economic Growth.* London, 1979.

Licht, Walter. *Working for the Railroad. The Organization of Work in the Nineteenth Century.* Princeton, N.J., 1983.

Lockwood, David. *The Blackcoated Worker. A Study of Class Consciousness.* London, 1958.

McKay, John. *Tramways and Trolleys: The Rise of Urban Mass Transport in Europe.* Princeton, N.J., 1976.

McLaren, Donald. *Malnutrition and the Eye.* New York, 1963.

Manocha, Sohan. *Malnutrition and Retarded Human Development.* Springfield, Ill., 1972.

Mayer, Arno. "The Lower Middle Class as a Historical Problem." *Journal of Modern History*, XLVII (1975), 409–436.

Meacham, Standish. *A Life Apart: The English Working Class, 1890–1914.* London, 1977.

Meyer, Stephen. *The Five Dollar Day. Labor Management and Social Control in the Ford Motor Company, 1908–1921.* Albany, N.Y., 1981

Montgomery, David. *Workers' Control in America: Studies in the History of Work, Technology, and Labor Struggles.* Cambridge, 1979.

———— "Workers' Control of Machine Production in the Nineteenth Century." *Labor History*, XVII (1976), 485–509.

More, Charles. *Skill and the English Working Class, 1870–1914.* New York, 1980.

Mount, James Lambert. *The Food and Health of Western Man.* New York, 1975.

Musson, Albert Edward. "Class Struggle and the Labor Aristocracy, 1830–60." *Social History*, III (1976), 335–356.

Nelson, Daniel. *Managers and Workers: The Origins of the New Factory System.* Madison, Wis., 1975.

O'Brien, Patrick, and Caglar Keyder. *Economic Growth in Britain and France, 1780–1914.* London, 1978.

Palmer, Bryan. *A Culture in Conflict. Skilled Workers and Industrial Capitalism in Hamilton, Ontario, 1860–1914.* Montreal, 1979.

Pollard, Sidney, and Paul Robertson. *The British Shipbuilding Industry, 1870–1914.* Cambridge, Mass., 1979.

Reid, Douglas. "The Decline of Saint-Monday, 1766–1876." *Past and Present*, no. 71 (1976), 76–101.

Roberts, James. "Drink and Industrial Work Discipline in Nineteenth-Century Germany." *Journal of Social History*, XV (1981), 25–38.

Rodman, Hyman. *Lower-Class Families: The Culture of Poverty in Negro Trinidad.* New York, 1971.

Rogers, Daniel. *The Work Ethic in Industrial America, 1850–1920.* Chicago, 1974.

Rolt, L. T. C. *A Short History of Machine Tools.* Cambridge, Mass., 1965.

Rosen, George. *A History of Public Health.* New York, 1958.

Rosenberg, Charles. *The Cholera Years. The United States in 1832, 1849, and 1866.* Chicago, 1962.

Rosenzweig, Roy. *Eight Hours for What We Will. Workers and Leisure in an Industrial City, 1870–1920.* Cambridge, 1983.

Sandiford, Keith. "The Victorians at Play. Problems in Historiographical Methodology." *Journal of Social History*, XV (1981), 271–288.

Schomerus, Heilwig. *Die Arbeiter der Maschinenfabrik Esslingen.* Stuttgart, 1977.

Stack, Carol. *All Our Kin. Strategies for Survival in a Black Community.* New York, 1974.

Stearns, Peter. *Lives of Labor: Work in a Maturing Industrial Society.* New York, 1975.

Stone, Lawrence. *The Family, Sex, and Marriage in England, 1500–1800.* New York, 1977.

Tannenbaum, Edward. *1900: The Generation before the Great War.* Garden City, N.Y., 1976.

Thompson, Edward Palmer. "Time, Work-Discipline, and Industrial Capitalism." *Past and Present*, no. 38 (1967), 56–97.

Vetterli, Rudolf. *Industriearbeit, Arbeiterbewusstein, und Gewerkschaftliche Organisation: Dargestellt am Beispiel de Georg Fischer AG (1890–1930).* Gottingen, 1978.

Waksman, Selman. *The Conquest of Tuberculosis.* Berkeley, Calif., 1964.

Walkowitz, Daniel. *Worker City, Company Town. Iron- and Cotton-Worker Protest in Troy and Cohoes, N.Y.* Urbana, Ill., 1978.

Walvin, James. *Leisure and Society, 1830–1950.* London, 1978.

Woodbury, Robert. *History of the Lathe to 1850. A Study in the Growth of a Technological Element of an Industrial Economy.* Cambridge, Mass., 1961.

Wrigley, Chris (ed.). *A History of British Industrial Relations, 1875–1914.* Amherst, Mass., 1982.

Index